# Blue Jacket

# Blue Jacket

*Warrior of the Shawnees*

JOHN SUGDEN

University of Nebraska Press

Lincoln & London

©2000

by John Sugden

All rights reserved

Manufactured in the United States of America

⊗

Library of Congress

Cataloging-in-Publication Data

Sugden, John, 1947–

Blue jacket : warrior of the Shawnees / John Sugden.

   p.   cm. — (American Indian lives)

Includes bibliographical references and index.

ISBN 0–8032–4288–3 (cl: alk. paper)

1. Blue Jacket, b. ca. 1752.   2. Shawnee Indians — Kings
and rulers — Biography.   3. Shawnee Indians — Wars.

I. Title.   II. Series.

E99.S35 B537   2000

979'.004973'0092 — dc21

[B]   00–022192

*This one is for the*

*Newberry Fellowship*

*Year of 1989 and*

*the staff and friends*

*who made it special.*

# Contents

## Illustrations

# Preface

In the late eighteenth century there was an invasion of what is now Ohio.

The Revolutionary War was over. But the needy government of the new republic wanted land to survey and sell in lots for money, land to populate and to turn into new states of the Union. The Northwest Ordinance of 1787 boldly proclaimed the determination of the United States to govern the vast and rich regions north of the Ohio River. Individual states, such as Connecticut and Virginia, also coveted lands between the Ohio and Lake Erie so that they could reward their revolutionary veterans, and speculators were eager to traffic in lands — to purchase them in bulk from Congress and sell them to settlers for profit. Even before the arrival of the hardy pioneers who build permanent farms in what is now Ohio, white "squatters" were spilling in, hewing clearings in the thick woods, building log cabins, and hunting and raising corn for a while before moving on.

The impetus for the invasion came from population growth in the eastern states and a belief that a freer and more prosperous life might be had in the West. In the 1780s thousands of settlers flatboated down the Ohio River. The population of Kentucky multiplied sixfold in as many years. Over the Ohio, Marietta was established in 1788, Cincinnati in 1790, and three years later twenty-four hundred settlers were living on the Symmes grant between the Great and Little Miami Rivers. Stout wooden forts were raised at strategic points to defend the influx, and they were garrisoned by the first standing army ever to be established by the United States.

For this was no peaceful occupation of an empty land. It was an invasion under arms, and there was a long and bloody war.

Those who defended the Ohio country were a diverse fraternity. Canadian traders, both British and French, whose livelihoods depended on the wilderness fur trade, fought shoulder to shoulder beside painted and scalplocked Indian warriors, who loved this land and lived on it. Most of those Indians remembered that the British had acknowledged the Ohio to be the boundary between ceded and unceded land at the treaty of Fort Stanwix in 1768, and they recognized no treaty that had been concluded since. They were ready to fight for the Ohio line, and hovering behind them were British redcoats, dispensing provisions and ammunition from their forts at Niagara, Detroit, and Mackinac. The British were unwilling to participate in the conflict themselves but clung to the last vestiges of their power south of the Great Lakes.

The war was one of the most ferocious in the entire history of Indian relations with the United States, and both sides were driven to unprecedented efforts. The Indians understood that only intertribal unity and cooperation could supply the manpower to resist the invasion, and they strove to overcome deep-seated differences and autonomies to maintain a powerful confederacy. On their part, the Americans began with cavalier dismissals of Indian rights to the land, but as their armies went down beneath blasts of musketry and flashing tomahawks, they agreed that they would have to purchase it from all the tribes of the hostile confederacy. And recognizing the shortcomings of their militia system, they were forced to confront constitutional prejudices and bring into being a substantial trained regular army.

Ultimately, of course, the superior material resources of the United States, and the avalanche of numbers, told. Even when the Indians were winning the field battles, they were steadily retreating before a line of forts that shafted into their country.

The victors not only seized the land. They wrote the histories, and while the white pioneers and such figures as Anthony Wayne, whose army finally defeated the Indians, became familiar to new generations of Americans, those who defended Ohio so desperately received far less attention. The most determined of those defenders had been the Shawnees. Other tribes, including Wyandots, Delawares, Miamis, Ottawas, Potawatomis, and Ojibwes, had been significant members of the Indian confederacy, but it was the Shawnees — with small numbers of Cherokees, Mingoes, and Delawares who lived among them — who were its heart. They were the ones whose homes stood in the direct path of the invasion, and it was they, more than any others, who took the organization of the confederacy from the Iroquois in 1789. Some historians have appreciated the importance of the Shawnees, and Randolph C. Downes, Reginald Horsman, A. F. C. Wallace, Helen Hornbeck Tanner, Colin Calloway, Gregory Dowd, and Richard White, among others, have touched on it in valuable accounts of other subjects. But no one has hitherto explored their contribution in full.

The names of the Shawnee leaders who shaped the intertribal confederacy, such men as Captain Johnny, Red Pole, Snake, and Blackbeard, are barely known, even to scholars. The most significant of them all, Blue Jacket, the warrior and diplomat who is the subject of this book, has been clouded by mythology. Most writers have portrayed him as a subsidiary, even a discredited, figure, and some even stripped him of his racial identity and denied that he was an Indian at all. He was, they said, a white man, captured and raised by the Shawnees.

The chief's contemporaries knew better. Even after his final defeat in the battle of Fallen Timbers, Blue Jacket commanded more influence than any other leader of the confederacy. Buckongahelas of the Delawares, Egushaway of the Ottawas, and Little Turtle of the Miamis, great warriors all, sometimes resented Blue Jacket's pretensions but still followed his lead, and American and British officials competed for his support. That the head warrior of the Shawnees still held such sway at the end of a decade of continual fighting is clear evidence that after being tested and retested in circumstances of unusual difficulty he measured up.

This book is the first biography of Blue Jacket. As a leader he has been unworthily forgotten. Imagine, for a moment, that he had been a white American, a statesman who had worked to unite fractious states or parties at a time of national peril; a soldier who had led the armies of the United States into battle against superior invading forces and twice overthrown them; and a memory that inspired leaders among a younger generation. It is inconceivable that his name would not have been commemorated, in literature if not in stone. Yet Blue Jacket was not even deemed worthy of an entry in the old *Dictionary of American Biography*, a measure of how lightly American Indian history has often been regarded and of how little it has been explored. Such a figure, a primary player in the history of Ohio and the Old Northwest, and the struggle of the Shawnee people under his leadership, deserved a better fate. It seemed to me that it was a story Americans might want to know. That is why I wrote this book.

The idea occurred to me way back in 1982, but it gained momentum six years later, when I met one of the most respected authorities on the Indian history of the Great Lakes region, Helen Hornbeck Tanner. I discovered that she, too, had thought of such a task. Since then many another generous and informed person has thrown a shoulder to the wheel and helped haul the project from the ruts I met along the way. In the acknowledgments I have recorded their names with gratitude. They not only helped me understand a world long gone but made my journey a richly rewarding and memorable experience.

# Acknowledgments

I cannot remember when I first heard of Blue Jacket, but it was Robert Breckinridge McAfee, the assiduous Kentucky historian of the War of 1812, who first made me think seriously about him. Writing eight years after the chief's death, McAfee opined that the Indian confederacy of Tecumseh had been the brainchild of Blue Jacket. The older chief "did not live to execute his schemes," said McAfee, but found "an able and persevering coadjutor" in Tecumseh. McAfee's brief notice of Blue Jacket was erroneous in many respects, not the least in its failure to recognize that political pan-Indianism had a much richer history, but it was one of the first to acknowledge that Blue Jacket was a figure of significance.

I soon found that McAfee was right about one thing. Many of the ideas and strategies associated with Tecumseh and the Prophet had an earlier advocate in Blue Jacket, and the old Shawnee war chief had been one of the brothers' most important advisers. I began to collect references to Blue Jacket, and as I turned over the records, a conviction grew in me that the Shawnee warrior had been greatly misjudged by historians. He had generally been portrayed as the inferior of Little Turtle and sometimes something of a blunderer. Once the contemporary sources were given their just preeminence over later, less reliable, materials, however, he began to emerge not only as the most noted leader of the northwestern confederacy of the 1790s but also as a formidable pan-Indian warrior and diplomat. It was a story, I thought, that was worth salvaging, for itself and for the light it shed on Shawnee history, the defense of Ohio in the late eighteenth century, and Tecumseh.

During my research, I came across others who had fortuitously stumbled on the same quest. In 1988 I met Helen Hornbeck Tanner, then a research associate of the Newberry Library in Chicago and the editor of *The Atlas of Great Lakes Indian History*, deservedly one of the standard contributions to the Indian history of the Old Northwest. Helen had been an expert witness before the Indian Claims Commission, and from her study of the treaty of Greenville and the Lakes region generally, she had read some of the same documents I had found and reached some of the same conclusions. It was she who first urged me to write this book, and at every difficulty and moment of self-doubt, she was there, always supportive, always strong. Without Helen's unstinting enthusiasm at every stage of the project I doubt that the book would ever have been finished.

I had never believed the story that Blue Jacket was actually Marmaduke van Sweringen, captured when young and raised by the Indians, but the issue generated furious debate in Ohio in recent decades. If nothing else, it raised the profile of Blue Jacket and stimulated descendants of the families concerned to investigate the matter.

Among them were Louise Franklin Johnson of Round Rock, Texas, and a distant cousin, Chris H. Bailey of New Hartford, Connecticut. They were connected to the Sweringens, and they joined local historian Robert Van Trees of Fairborn, Ohio, in a search for the real Blue Jacket. From 1993 Louise also took time from her studies and her love of Texas frontier history to correspond with me about the chief. Simultaneously, two cousins, Norma Gore Luallen of Alexandria, Louisiana, and Marylen Mackenzie Williams of Tulsa, Oklahoma, descendants of Blue Jacket through his son George, were working on a family history. Letters between Louise, Norma, Marylen, and me crisscrossed the Atlantic for a while and fed me valuable pieces of information. These women, I discovered, were genealogists of the first order, who wanted no truck with mythology. They worked hard among local sources, unearthing church registers, land deeds, census records, and other scattered data. I am grateful to all of them and regret that Norma never lived to see this book. She died in February 1998. She had worked on Blue Jacket almost daily, and I understand that her papers are to be deposited at the Alexandria Historical and Genealogical Library, where she had once been employed.

Sadly, this book also came too late for Dan L. Thrapp of Tucson, Arizona, one of its warmest enthusiasts. Dan was an acknowledged authority on Apaches, rather than Shawnees, but he loved almost everything to do with the old frontier. We corresponded from 1990, when he was winding up the final volume of his encyclopedia of frontier figures and I was an associate editor for *American National Biography*, trying hard to increase the representation of Indians in that monument to America's past. Until his untimely death in April 1994, Dan stood ever ready to share informed opinions, information, and contacts, and I miss him terribly. He testified to our friendship in his last book, and now it is my turn, in this book he so wanted to read.

I am grateful to the following institutions for access to or permission to quote from manuscript collections: the American Philosophical Society, Philadelphia; the British Library, London, England; The Burton Historical Collection of the Detroit Public Library; the National Archives of Canada, Ottawa; the Chicago Historical Society; the University of Chicago Library; the Cincinnati Historical Society; the William L. Clements Library of the University of Michigan, Ann Arbor; the Filson Club, Louisville; the Indiana State Library, Indianapolis; the Library of Congress, Washington DC.; the Eli Lilly Library, Bloomington, Indiana; the Massachusetts Historical Society, Boston; Millsaps College, Jackson, Mississippi; the National Archives, Washington DC.; the Ohio Historical Society, Columbus; the Historical Society of Pennsylvania, Philadelphia; the Public Record Office, Kew, England; and the State Historical Society of Wisconsin, Madison.

Once again I have an opportunity to acknowledge those wonderful people at the Indiana Historical Society in Indianapolis. Doug E. Clanin never failed to emerge from his exacting work as editor of the Harrison Papers to respond to my inquiries with outstanding efficiency, and the enthusiasm of the late Bob M. Taylor Jr. of the Education Department, who died suddenly as this book was going to press, was a major inspiration. I must also thank Carolyn Autry, Teresa Baer, Tom Mason, Margaret Bierlein, Annabelle J. Jackson, Glenn L. McMullen, and Paul Brockman, who, among others, made my visits to the society so rewarding. It is my hope that the Indiana Historical Society's new building will eventually provide a home for all my papers dealing with the Shawnees, Tecumseh, and Blue Jacket.

Among individuals who generously helped locate materials or shared their opinions or information with me, I must mention Rodney Staab of

Kansas City, Kansas; Barry L. Chad of the Carnegie Library of Pittsburgh; Clay Skinner, who showed me his work on early pan-Indianism when we met in Chicago; John C. Fredriksen; Christopher S. Peebles of Indiana University, Bloomington; Alvin M. Josephy Jr. for taking time from his own demanding projects to help mine; James Alexander Thom, one of the country's finest historical novelists, and his wife, Dark Rain, who is working on a Shawnee biography of her own; Jacqueline A. Matte of Birmingham, Alabama, and Don Rankin of the same place, himself a Shawnee; Dr. Gerlinde Sabathy-Judd of London, Ontario, for her material from the Moravian archives; Gaylord Carlyle Hinshaw, another Blue Jacket descendant; Hjordis Halvorson of the Newberry Library, Chicago; Guy St. Denis of London, Ontario; Michael Friedrichs of Augsburg, Germany; Colin G. Calloway of Dartmouth College; Jennifer A. Harrison of Indianapolis; and Kathleen Moore and Stewart Platts of Arnside, Cumbria, England. The Ford Foundation enabled me to benefit from the incomparable resources of the Newberry Library, Chicago, and the British Academy of London funded research trips to Ohio and Kentucky. The maps in this book were drawn by Malcolm Ward.

Some obligations know no bounds, and in this respect I particularly thank Professor Cecil King and Dr. Catherine Littlejohn of Saskatoon, Canada, whose friendship always surpasses the most generous interpretation of duty; my brother Philip for his endless wisdom; and my partner, Terri, who has bravely borne the burden of my obsession with the old Shawnees for many, many years.

# Blue Jacket

# Introduction

On 15 February 1877 the *Ohio State Journal* published a strange story. It told how a white man had become a war chief of the Shawnee Indians and led the tribe into battle against his own people. The story, written by a newspaperman named Thomas Jefferson Larsh, concerned the adventures of one Marmaduke van Sweringen. Sweringen, Larsh said, had been captured by Shawnees during the Revolutionary War, when he was "about seventeen years of age" and "a stout, healthy, well-developed, athletic youth" to boot.

According to Larsh, the Shawnees were extraordinarily amenable the day they captured Marmaduke and his younger brother. They even bargained with the boys and agreed to let the younger one go if Marmaduke consented to be their prisoner. And so Marmaduke joined the Shawnees, learned their ways, and grew to manhood among them. He married a Shawnee woman "and reared several children," all but one of them daughters. His adopted people named him Blue Jacket on account of a "blue linsey blouse or 'hunting shirt'" he wore at the time of his capture. So styled, he rose to prominence, becoming a chief by the age of twenty-five and enjoying a most distinguished career.

It was at this point that history took root, for though Marmaduke van Sweringen was unknown to Ohio readers, Blue Jacket assuredly was not. The Shawnee war chief was a notable figure in the annals of the Old Northwest and had participated in some of the most severe defeats Indians had ever inflicted upon United States armies. Now, in his remarkable tale, Larsh was telling everyone that Blue Jacket had not been an Indian at all.

On the face of it, the story was not entirely unconvincing. Larsh said that his own grandmother Sarah was the sister of Marmaduke van Sweringen. He went further and claimed that the descendants of Blue Jacket acknowledged the truth of his statements themselves. Larsh apparently had an acquaintanceship and correspondence with Charles Blue-Jacket, a grandson of the famous warrior, who was "an exact facsimile of the Van Sweringens." In truth, no one knew much about Larsh. He may have counted the Larsh family of fur traders among his forebears, and he undoubtedly admired Indians greatly, having named his three sons for famous leaders — Black Hawk, White Cloud, and Blue Jacket.

With little attempt at verification, several writers aired Larsh's tale about Blue Jacket in the following years. William Albert Galloway's *Old Chillicothe* (1934), a work of local history, and John Bennett's *Blue Jacket, War Chief of the Shawnees* (1943) conferred some respectability on the legend by uncritically reproducing it. And Allan W. Eckert took it one step further, embroidering the yarn with new fictions in a series of influential novels: *The Frontiersmen* (1967), *Blue Jacket, War Chief of the Shawnees* (1969), and *A Sorrow in Our Heart* (1992). Since 1981 hundreds of thousands of visitors to Xenia, Ohio, have happily sat through annual performances of W. L. Mundella's dramatic pageant *Blue Jacket, White Shawnee War Chief.* Of course, historical accuracy is not a necessary condition of public entertainment, and there is no reason why Mundella's fanciful version of Blue Jacket's life should not continue to please in the same way that the largely invented saga of Robin Hood has enthralled generations of the young and young-at-heart on both sides of the Atlantic. If nothing else, the production has increased interest in an Indian leader who has suffered undue neglect.

Those who prefer history to folklore are also entitled to satisfaction, however, and, fortunately, they, too, have had their champions. A number of local historians, bravely brandishing the banner of truth, have chipped away some of the grosser constructions of the mythmakers.[1] Experienced historians had always doubted the story. Helen Hornbeck Tanner, Reginald Horsman, Paul Stevens, and Dan Thrapp successively attacked it. Historical instances of white captives achieving positions of influence among the Indians were known. The Wyandot leader Adam Brown was one example. But stories, such as Larsh's, that emerge long after all genuine witnesses have been gathered to their fathers, always invite suspicion.[2]

The skepticism of professional historians was fully justified. Contemporary documents leave no doubt that Larsh's story was made out of whole cloth. Marmaduke van Sweringen really existed; but the story that he was captured by Indians lacks confirmation, and there is no doubt that he was not the same man as the Shawnee chief Blue Jacket. According to a family Bible, Marmaduke was born in 1763, and Larsh had him captured during the Revolution, when he was about seventeen years old. Unfortunately, Blue Jacket belonged to an older generation. He was born in the early 1740s and made his debut in historical documents as a leading man among the Shawnees in 1773 — before the Revolutionary War had begun.[3]

Blue Jacket was undoubtedly an Indian. Not one of the chief's contemporaries, not Indians, Indian agents, traders, army officers, not even white captives themselves, ever referred to him as anything but an Indian. Had he been a white boy, captured in his teens, he would have known English. Blue Jacket mixed much with the whites, especially French traders, and appeared "to be a good deal civilized," but he had to be attended by interpreters during discussions with Americans or the British.[4]

The evidence of Blue Jacket's children is also pretty conclusive. The chief married a white woman, a former captive named Margaret Moore, and she bore him two surviving children, Joseph and Nancy. Both were acknowledged by whites and Shawnees who knew them to be half-bloods. Thus when the Shawnees collected their treaty annuities at Fort Wayne, Indiana Territory, on 2 October 1810, they granted each of the Moore children small tracts of their land. Joseph was then described as a "half breed of their tribe" and Nancy as "a half blood of their said tribe." Three years later a white official with the Ohio Shawnees similarly referred to Joseph as "a half Indian." And years afterward one who remembered mother and daughter recalled the contrast they made: Margaret, a white, and Nancy's "decidedly Indian features."[5]

Larsh's story was mythology, surfacing long after the deaths of those who had known Blue Jacket and who could have told the truth. His grandson Charles Blue-Jacket seems to have accepted the myth, but he had never seen his grandfather, who had died a decade before Charles was born. Even Charles's father had died when the boy was only fourteen. One reason why some of the Blue Jacket descendants found the story believable was that white blood undeniably flowed through their veins. But that came from Chief Blue Jacket's wives, one Margaret Moore, a white captive, and the other a woman of mixed Shawnee and French parentage.

But Larsh was by no means the first person to bury Blue Jacket beneath a layer of mythology, and the older strata have been even more impenetrable.

Indeed, even today Blue Jacket's important role as a warrior and diplomat is almost universally underappreciated, largely because of persistent misstatements about one of his rivals, a Miami war chief named Little Turtle. The legend of Little Turtle depicted him as a Miami Napoleon, who masterminded a series of victories over the Americans. Blue Jacket was in every way his inferior. Only when Blue Jacket ousted Little Turtle from his position as supreme war chief of the intertribal Indian forces did disaster overtake their arms. Some historians went further still and insisted that it was Little Turtle's people, the Miamis, who were the political as well as the military leaders of the pan-tribal confederacy that defended the Old Northwest between 1790 and 1795. Some were so little acquainted with the original sources that they spoke of "the Miami confederacy."[6]

Just as Larsh's story passed unchallenged by many writers, so the Miami myth remained untroubled by serious research. In fact it, too, was at variance with the bulk of the historical documentation. That material, brought together from widely scattered sources, paints a different picture than the one found in conventional textbooks.

Those who had lived through the northwestern struggle would have been astonished to see the Shawnees reduced to the status of secondary actors. In 1808, for example, the lieutenant governor of Upper Canada sought advice from the Indian agents who had worked with the tribes more than a decade before on how to cultivate Indian favor. He learned that it was the Shawnees who had "heretofore preserved a decided superiority in the general councils of the western [Indian] confederacy" and possessed "a commanding influence in all their measures." So, too, the United States Indian agent Thomas Forsyth, who worked on the upper Mississippi a short time later, stated that "by consent of the confederacy the Shawanoe nation were formerly the leading nation. That is to say, the Shawanoes had the direction of the wars that the parties might be engaged in, the power of convening the allies, etc." Jacques Lasselle, who spent a lifetime trading with the Miamis and Shawnees, simply referred to the latter as "a nation without whom the others could do nothing."[7]

Such statements are validated by the detailed history of the Indian war of the 1790s. The Shawnees were responsible for reviving the Indian confederacy in 1789, after it had temporarily collapsed. It was principally their diplomats who recruited for the confederacy, journeying great distances, north, west, and south, to urge Indians to stand together against those they called the Big Knives. The Shawnees hosted the intertribal congresses that thrashed out policy and generally set the political agenda, and Shawnee war chiefs were in the forefront of the great military expeditions. Of course, Shawnee leaders worked to achieve a consensus among their allies, but it was their homelands that were immediately threatened by the American invasion, and it was they who formed the soul of the Indian opposition.

During those troubled times, Blue Jacket was the principal war chief of the Shawnees, and his importance has been seriously undervalued by the Miami myth. There is no reason to debunk Little Turtle. That he was a brave, skilled, and respected war chief is beyond question. But his admirers have credited him with being a commander in chief, a position neither he nor anyone else possessed, and they eagerly put him into events whether or not there was evidence for his participation. In fact, an intertribal council of war leaders did the military planning, and it was Blue Jacket, not Little Turtle, who cut the largest single figure in the contemporary testimony. As one American officer wrote in his diary, Blue Jacket was "said to be the greatest warrior among all the tribes," and both allies and enemies singled him out. They called him "the famous" or "the celebrated" Blue Jacket, or even "General Blue Jacket."[8]

Blue Jacket owed his standing to his war record, his position as the senior military leader of the Shawnees, his dual role as warrior and diplomat, and his personal influence with key groups of Indians and whites. As this book will show, his prestige enabled him to become the main Indian architect of the treaty of Greenville in 1795, a role that has scarcely appeared in published histories of the conflict.

Little Turtle seems to have developed a jealousy toward Blue Jacket, and in 1796 Maj. Gen. Anthony Wayne had trouble fitting them both in an Indian delegation he was sending to the president. He wrote that the party included "the famous Shawanoe chief, Blue Jacket, who, it is said, had the chief command of the Indian army on the 4th of November 1791 against Genl. St. Clair. The Little Turtle, a Miamia chief, who also claims that honor, and who is his rival for fame and power — and said to be daily gaining ground with the Wabash Indians — refuses or declines to proceed in company with Blue Jacket."[9]

Although Blue Jacket emerges the stronger of the two from the historical records of the 1780s and 1790s, it was Little Turtle's interpretation of events that posterity embraced. Blue Jacket slipped into retirement in the succeeding years, while the star of the younger man rose. Little Turtle became a major force in the early days of Indiana Territory, and his white son-in-law William Wells served as United States Indian agent at Fort Wayne. Wells had been captured by Miamis in 1784, when he was about fourteen years old, and remained with the Indians until 1792. He was a courageous, informed, and energetic man but was also dishonest, vocal, and self-seeking. As agent he collaborated with Little Turtle, and in 1803 Governor William Henry Harrison complained that "when Wells speaks of the Miami Nation being of this or that opinion he must be understood as meaning no more than the Turtle and himself."[10]

The Little Turtle myth was substantially grounded on the testimony of the chief himself and his son-in-law. However questionable, it passed through influential writers such as Constantin Volney into secondary literature and orthodoxy. Over the years the kernel of truth it contained was exaggerated. The Miamis, who had relatively few warriors at the heart of the confederacy and far fewer than either the Shawnees, Delawares, Wyandots, or Ottawas, became paramount, and Little Turtle was transformed into the military genius of the Indian wars.[11]

In disregarding these and other legends and returning to original sources, we rediscover one of the most prominent American Indians and the momentous and brutal struggle of the Shawnee people to protect their Ohio homelands and ultimately their way of life. It is a story populated by a little-known cast of characters, plucked from obscure records and events sometimes only slightly more famous, but it is an important slice of American history nonetheless, for the Indians of those regions, the new republic, and British North America.

But to appreciate Blue Jacket and his associates, it is first necessary to visit their world, the world inhabited by the durable, adaptable, and free-spirited Shawnee Indians who made their homes in the Ohio Valley in the middle of the eighteenth century.

# I

# Blue Jacket's People

They called themselves the "saanwanwa."[1] The term has no meaning in modern Shawnee, but similar words in related (Algonquian) languages signify "southerners," and the tribe may have derived its name from an early location on the southern flank of the Algonquian range. If nothing else, the Shawnees were great and hardy wanderers.

Like all peoples, Shawnees accounted for their existence in stories that were reworked over time, according to changing circumstances and the inclinations of individual narrators. In Blue Jacket's day Shawnee creation myths may also have absorbed Christian ideas, gathered fragmentarily from contacts with white traders or filtered through other Indians more influenced by European missionaries. These traditions also suggested a southern connection. A flood, they said, had once destroyed the world and its original people. Only an old woman was spared, drawn from the waters clinging to the tail of a panther, according to one version. Her grief moved the creator, Waashaa Monetoo, the Great and Good Spirit, to fashion a new world. He produced an island, stocked with game and resting on the back of a turtle, and beside a river at its center he placed the first of his new human beings, the Mekoche Shawnees. This river, which the Indians remembered as the Shawnee River, was somewhere in the south and perhaps recalled the Savannah River in South Carolina, near which many Shawnees lived in the late seventeenth century.[2]

The Shawnee "tribe" was really a loose confederation of villages linked by a common language and culture, ties of kinship, and a rudimentary notion of unity. Each village belonged to one or more of the five groups into which the Shawnees were divided: Mekoche, Chillicothe, Pekowi, Kispoko, and Hathawekela. Sometimes a town was formed by Shawnees of several divisions, but commonly it was established by one, from which it took its name. Shawnee history was sprinkled with towns named Pekowi, Chillicothe, and Mackachack (Mekoche).

Shawnees inherited their division from their fathers and proudly carried the affiliation through life. Linguistic evidence shows that these divisions must have splintered from a parent stock, but in Blue Jacket's time Shawnees believed some of them to have been separate creations. The Mekoches claimed seniority, for they had been the first people made by the Great Spirit after the flood. They boasted that this conferred upon them the prerogative of directing the affairs not only of other Shawnees but also of other tribes:

> The Great Spirit who made the four quarters of the world placed us in the middle of it to hold it steady. . . . The Great Spirit ordered that everything upon and under the earth should obey us. . . . He put his heart into our tribe [Mekoche division] and made it the chief of all the [Shawnee] tribes, and king over the other [Indian] nations. We then went three times to Heaven, where we were taught the king's song and sang it down to earth. The Great Spirit gave us tobacco also to send to the four winds. He gave us also corn and game. The Great Spirit having done all this for us, we think we have a right to look upon ourselves as the head tribe of all nations.[3]

For their part, the Chillicothes, and perhaps the Hathawekelas, preserved a tradition of having first joined the Mekoches after making a journey across the sea. The Pekowis and Kispokos seem to have been regarded as junior divisions of the nation. The Mekoches said the first Pekowi had sprung as a child from the ashes of a fire Waashaa Monetoo had kindled for the Mekoches and had been adopted and raised by the senior division. Another story maintained that he was formed from the backbone of an elk slain by the Chillicothes. The Mekoches arrogantly referred to the Pekowis as their "younger brothers," in need of advice and guidance.

Despite the pretensions of the Mekoches, all the divisions claimed the privilege of exercising one function or another on behalf of the tribe. The Pekowis, for example, appear to have claimed the office of head war chief. Such monopolies, however, had been weakened by the historic fragmentation of the tribe. During the mid-seventeenth century it had been located in the valleys of the Ohio and Cumberland Rivers, but shortly afterward marauding Iroquois warriors from what is now New York came in search of beaver pelts and prisoners and scattered the Shawnees. Some settled the Illinois and others the Savannah and elsewhere, but by the time Blue Jacket was born in the early 1740s most had regrouped in present-day Ohio, Pennsylvania, and Alabama. Many Shawnees dreamed of reunifying the nation, but at no time in Blue Jacket's lifetime was the ambition fulfilled.[4]

Authority of any kind was limited among the Shawnees, for they were a liberal and egalitarian people who generally reserved the right to make decisions to individuals. The chiefs had no standing forces and few means of coercion at their disposal, and they relied on argument and example to carry their points. Internal law and order, for instance, relied less on the chiefs than on a variety of deterrents, including the strength of public opinion and the right of relatives of victims to seek compensation or revenge for grievances. On unusual occasions, when the community at large was in danger of becoming embroiled in some dispute, chiefs might intervene, perhaps to persuade offenders to expiate their crimes by making reparations, but generally they did not participate in what were considered to be private affairs.

Each village, which is often to say each division, had its councillors, who deliberated in the public council house, and both civil and war chiefs, female as well as male. The leading civil chief had usually inherited his office from his father, and he presided over the town or division in peacetime. Unlike the woman war chief, whose role was largely ceremonial, the female peace chief was a considerable force in the village. She supervised the work of the women, such as planting and cooking, represented their views, and impressed the virtues of moderation upon the war chiefs. Most significant of all the civil chiefs, however, was the head Mekoche civil chief. By reason of his division's claim to superiority, he convened such tribal councils as extraordinary circumstances demanded and was effectively the tribal civil chief. Sometimes whites referred to him as a "king," but in truth the title was entirely inappropriate to his powers and condition. David Jones, a missionary who visited one such tribal head chief, Kishshinottisthee (Hardman), in 1773, found him "neither distinguished in apparel or house, that being one of the least in town, being about fourteen feet by twelve."[5]

War chiefs such as Blue Jacket achieved their positions by merit, by their proven courage, skill, and fortune in numerous forays against enemies, but they, too, were usually dependent on the support of their councils and the willingness of the warriors to accept their judgment and leadership. In the field the problems of managing and controlling war parties of excited young men relatively unamenable to discipline were never far away. The war chiefs were, nevertheless, greatly admired, and warfare was a major path by which warriors secured prestige and influence. During periods of prolonged conflict they even assumed the premier responsibility for the community's affairs and sat in front of the civil chiefs in the council house.[6]

The Shawnees were never numerically strong, even by Indian standards. In Blue Jacket's time their total population probably did not exceed twenty-five hundred, and that was divided among geographical locations that were sometimes great distances apart. Yet for all that the Shawnees enjoyed enormous respect among both Indian and Euro-American peoples, in part because of their ferocity as warriors but also for their prestige as intertribal diplomats. The Shawnees had been regularly uprooted and displaced. Bands of them lived at different times with the southern Creeks and Cherokees, the northern Mingoes and Delawares, and the Indians of Illinois, establishing far-flung ties of kinship through intermarriage. These constant peregrinations also resulted in an efficient command of intertribal trade jargons and protocol, an exceptional knowledge of distant trails and waterways, and a broad perspective of the Indian predicament. Those Shawnees who colonized western Pennsylvania and reoccupied the Ohio Valley in the eighteenth century, the group to which Blue Jacket belonged, found themselves fitted by experience, skills, and a useful geographical position between the northern and southern Indians to turn deft hands to intertribal diplomacy.

Shawnees also advertised their mythological claim to have been the firstborn of the Indian nations. Waashaa Monetoo had once loved them above all others, they sometimes said, and given them a piece of his heart, and all other tribes had descended from them. Such pretensions were not always admitted by Indian neighbors, but some seniority was accorded the tribe in public discourse. In intertribal councils the Shawnees deferred to the powerful Iroquoian peoples, including the Wyandots, and styled them "elder brothers" or "uncles," while they addressed the Delawares as "grandfathers." But the many other Indian nations were described by the Shawnees as "younger brothers."[7]

The Indian world was typically a world of small villages and decentralized and democratic political systems and one of narrow horizons and local concerns, but among those who moved in wider circles, none were more accomplished or more universally known than the restless Shawnees.

∗    ∗    ∗

The focus of every Shawnee community was the village, even though it was fully occupied only in the spring and summer. The Indians regathered to the village after the winter to renew friendships, raise crops, talk, share the major ceremonies, and play games. In September the inhabitants dispersed to family winter camps scattered about the range and hunted until the following spring.

The summer village might contain a dozen family houses or as many as a hundred or more and was erected on high ground, above a river or stream where the rich bottomlands could be turned into cornfields. Those Blue Jacket knew possessed a variety of houses, of which perhaps the commonest was still the traditional bark-sided dwelling built around a rectangular floor plan. The frame consisted of stalwart upright posts forked at the top to support cross-timbers, and at one end an entrance would be covered by a blanket. One such house, owned by Chief Kakinathucca in 1788, was about twenty feet long and fourteen feet wide. These homes had no chimneys, and smoke from the fires kindled in the center of the only room escaped through a hole in the roof. But log houses with chimneys also existed as early as the 1760s, reflecting increased contact with Europeans. Interiors also displayed variety. Some, such as Blue Jacket's, were festooned with the spoils of successful hunting, raiding, and trading, and others were entirely prosaic. A few had European furniture, but there was still a dependence on crude beds, seats, and tables fashioned from platforms made of bound reeds or sticks or of poles thrust into the ground to support cross-sticks. Skins served as coverings.

Each town was dominated by the huge council house, sometimes more than one hundred feet long, and used for public meetings and ceremonies. Three parallel rows of vertical posts supplied the frame, the center row greater in height to form the summit of a pitched roof. The rafters were cross-beams, and the roof and walls were planked. Doorways were allowed at each end of the building, and inside logs placed against the walls provided seats while the centers were free for fires.

Women were the mainstays of the village. They tapped the maples for sugar in the spring and gathered wild fruits and salt. They used simple hand tools to raise maize, beans, pumpkins, and tobacco in the open fields. They maintained homes and fires, made clothes and implements, and supervised children. They pounded and kneaded the corn, boiling or roasting it or baking it in hot ashes, and prepared meat or fish brought in by their men. Visitors noticed that European trade was enriching both diet and cooking. David Jones breakfasted on chocolate as well as buffalo and beaver tail while among the Shawnees, and Kakinathucca's wife began her day with portions of deer and turkey, seasoned with dry herbs and fried in a pan with bears' oil. She washed it down with green tea boiled in a copper kettle and served from a teapot in cups and saucers of yellow ware. [8]

The small winter camps to which most Shawnees resorted after the harvest were merely temporary shelters. They usually housed one or a few family units, each in a dome-shaped lodge made of skins covering a frame of poles, and from them the men issued to hunt and trap throughout the cold season. Successful hunting was essential to the Shawnees, not only because it supplied meat and other commodities but also because the peltries were exchanged for the European goods upon which the Indians were becoming increasingly dependent. Native technologies were not always supplanted by the invasion of these sophisticated European manufactures. Even in his prime Blue Jacket would have known deer hoof combs and pails and cups made from gourds, and bows and arrows were still being used by Shawnees almost a century later. Nonetheless, European goods were flooding into Shawnee villages — guns, powder and lead, flints, knives, axes, tools, kettles, containers, baubles, paint, beads, and cloth.[9]

By Blue Jacket's time the European influence had been of long standing. Horses, introduced by the newcomers, and some manufactures had reached the Shawnees even before they made extensive contacts with the colonists. They came through other Indians — middlemen, who lived closer to the white settlements. During the seventeenth and eighteenth centuries the tribe had trafficked directly with the Spaniards, French, and English, and from his earliest days in the Ohio Valley young Blue Jacket became accustomed to seeing Pennsylvania traders coming across the Allegheny Mountains with packloads of merchandise to barter for deerskins, beaver pelts, and other furs in the Indian towns. They often married Shawnee women, accepting the obligations that went with kinship, fathered mixed-bloods, and kept permanent homes in the villages.

In 1773 Jones found them in almost every Shawnee settlement on the Scioto: Moses Henry at Chillicothe, Alexander McKee at Crooked Nose's Town, John Irwine at Blue Jacket's Town, and Richard Butler at the Kispoko village.

Perhaps the most obvious evidence of this trade was to be seen in the appearance of the Shawnees. They still dressed in a time-honored aboriginal style. Men often wore the scalplock along the crown, particularly in wartime, and they tattooed and painted themselves. Their noses were pierced to accept rings and their ears punctured or split to carry ornaments. But from head to foot both sexes reflected the European trade. Leggings, breechcloths, skirts, mantles, and turbans were no longer made from animal skins but of imported cloths, linen, woolens, and cotton calicos. European shirts of linen and cotton had replaced the traditional deerskin tops, and glass beads and ribbons were being used for decoration instead of quills, bones, shells, and wood. Shawnee men and women garbed themselves in trade silver — bracelets, armbands, brooches, gorgets, and necklaces — and they carried implements and tools they had bought from whites. Muskets, knives, tomahawks, and pipes were all part of the merchant's display.

The fur trade unquestionably enriched the material culture of the Shawnees, and it slotted neatly into their existing economy, depending as it did on the winter hunt. Yet it carried penalties, some almost imperceptible in their growth, others sudden and ferocious. It sharpened the acquisitive instincts of what was still a relatively egalitarian people, gnawing at their economic communism and ethic of sharing. Goods were still readily dispensed as gifts, most of the harvests went into public storehouses, and whatever food a family possessed was at the disposal of others. "Nothing is too costly or too good to be set before a friend," wrote one observer. "What one has is freely set before another, and in this way all they have is soon entirely consumed."[10] But the fur trade was encouraging a new kind of Shawnee, an individualist who accumulated property in the style of the whites and whose home reflected a fatter living. As yet these modern Shawnees were few, but Blue Jacket would become their exemplar.

Materialism had other consequences too. It made the Shawnees increasingly reliant on white traders, who supplied the desired manufactures, and it undermined self-sufficiency and independence. Politically, while the French, Spanish, British, and later people from the United States were still competing for empires in America, the Shawnees could avoid a dependence on any one uncertain ally, but as soon as European power receded, the Indians began to lose their freedom of action. In addition, the demand for trade goods encouraged the Indians to degrade their environment by overhunting. This problem was compounded by the advance of white settlements from the east. Homesteads denuded the habitat for wildlife, and most of the white settlers supplemented their farming by hunting. As early as 1752 Shawnees blamed the scarcity of game in Pennsylvania for their recent migration to the richer hunting grounds of the Ohio Valley.[11]

More immediately, by fraternizing with whites, Shawnees imported into their villages two commodities that threatened to tear them apart; strong liquor and new diseases against which their bodies had developed few biological defenses. Shawnees acknowledged that "strong drink was made for white men, as they know how to use it, but it makes Indians crazy," and sometimes they took precautions before indulging in drinking bouts. Weapons might be removed or some warriors detailed to remain sober to police any disorder. But drunkenness and violence were not the only symptoms of the liquor trade. Imprudent Indians squandered their possessions to buy spirits, and frequently the returns of rigorous winter hunts, needed to pay for trade good⌐, were exhausted on liquor. In 1729 a Shawnee delegation had to abandon a visit to the governor of Pennsylvania because they had sold their provisions for rum. Attempts to curb this damaging traffic were never successful, although Pennsylvania prohibited the trade in 1722, and chiefs periodically declared they would break open any kegs brought into the nation. Too many Indians simply found it irresistible, and there were always traders, Indians as well as whites, who were willing to profit by satisfying the demand.[12]

Disease was a weightier matter still, especially smallpox, which ravaged villages wholesale, leaving gaping wounds in tightly knit interdependent communities such as those of the Shawnees. Even before Blue Jacket's time the tribe may have been severely weakened by European diseases. Shawnees remembered there had once been a sixth division, the "Shauwonoa," and that the number of tribal clans or totems had fallen from about thirty-four to a dozen. These reductions were probably the work of disease, warfare, and dispersal, and the remnants of those groups were absorbed into those that were vigorous and surviving.[13]

The onset of a serious epidemic and its apparent invulnerability to all the sacred powers the Indian doctors could command also raised powerful doubts about the tribe's spiritual standing. For Shawnees believed that everything on earth was controlled by deities or spirits. Success and well-being testified that the spirits were looking upon them with favor, whereas disasters such as virulent pestilences indicated that the spirits had been offended and the tribe was being punished. Guilt-ridden introspection, a search for the sources of offense, and reforms were commonly the result.

No Shawnee could afford to ignore the wishes of the spirits, for this was an intensely religious people.

When Shawnees died and were buried, their souls traveled westward to the edge of the world, where the sea touched the sky. There they found a path to another realm, above the roof of the world. It was the home of a benign white-haired ancient who exercised ultimate power on earth: Waashaa Monetoo, the Great and Good Spirit. He was assisted, Shawnees believed, by Waupoathee and her grandson. She it was who had persuaded Waashaa Monetoo to restock the earth after the flood, and she was visible to humans as the moon.

Young Shawnees were taught that the Great Spirit had once favored their tribe above all others. He had given them part of his heart and a bundle of sacred objects that could be used to summon supernatural advice and assistance in moments of difficulty. Since then, Shawnees supposed, they must have fallen from grace because their tribe had become so fragmented. But the tribal sacred bundle was still there, attended by appointed custodians, who consulted it as a source of influence and wisdom. Daniel Boone evidently saw it among the Chillicothes in 1778 and thought it "a kind of ark, deemed among their sacred things." More than fifty years later another observer described it as a large gourd with the bones of a deer affixed to its neck.[14]

Waashaa Monetoo and the grandmother were the supreme Shawnee deities, but other wondrous beings also shaped the world, including the sun, the star people, the four winds, the great bird that created thunder and lightning, and Earth Mother, who determined the fruitfulness of the soil. And innumerable minor spirits existed, in places and all living things, all of them capable of furthering the business of life if they were courted and pleased or of inflicting harm if they took offense. Indeed, individual Shawnees possessed their own personal guardian spirits, identified in adolescence during vision quests in which the youths fasted and meditated. These tutelar spirits, commonly conceived to be animals, made themselves known through dreams, hallucinations, or some revelatory event. Shawnee people kept the identities of their particular guardian spirits secret, but they carried fetishes of them in private sacred bundles and appealed to them for help and protection.[15]

The Shawnees also recognized spirits that were constitutionally evil, among them Motshee Monetoo, the Bad Spirit, who had the power to possess living organisms, and the great horned water monsters. It is possible that Motshee Monetoo had been belatedly incorporated into Shawnee mythology as an echo of the Christian devil and that the serpents were older embodiments of evil. Whatever their origin, Shawnees believed that medicine made from the remains of such water monsters had been preserved. Witches, who could be men or women, harbored this medicine in their personal sacred bundles and used it to invoke supernatural powers for malicious purposes. The baleful influence of witches was almost universally admitted by the Shawnees. It was entirely logical to suppose that if holy men and doctors could solicit sacred power in aid of the community, perhaps to bring good fortune or cure sickness, and if everyone could apply for assistance to guardian spirits, then wickedly disposed persons might require evil spirits to help them cause illness and death.

All Shawnees agreed that the goodwill of the deities was necessary for success and tranquility, and they invested a great deal of time conciliating and communicating with the spirit world. Dreams were interpreted as messages from the spirits, while gifts, prayers, thanksgivings, and the manipulation of fetishes conveyed wishes in the other direction. Tobacco was a common offering, especially placed on a fire so that the smoke could carry it to Heaven. Indians who were conspicuously successful, in whatever field, were said to possess unusual spiritual favor, and for this reason there was no clear differentiation between fortunate chiefs and warriors and religious leaders. All were supplicants for sacred power, with greater or lesser success. Thus an interviewer speaking to George Ash, who spent many years among the Shawnees, concluded that "Blue Jacket appears to have been a priest as well as a warrior."[16]

At some times of the year the benedictions of the spirits were particularly important, and the Shawnees based their major ceremonies around them. Each spring, about May, thanks were given for the winter hunt and blessings entreated for the newly sown crops, and in the latter part of August the maturation of the harvest was celebrated in a similar festival, which featured a feast of the green corn. These auspicious occasions occupied several days and nights and were not monopolized by religious solemnity. In addition to worship, the Shawnees indulged themselves in dances, sports, and gift-giving, and sometimes the festivals ended in a state of general inebriation. Nevertheless, their spiritual purpose was fundamental.[17]

Shawnee ceremonialism was designed to focus sacred power where it was needed, but the tribe's reverence for the deities was demonstrated no less strongly in its reactions to unusual misfortunes or strange natural events. Such occurrences were often received with dismay, contrition, and penitence, for they betokened the wrath of the spirits. In 1805 epidemic diseases propelled a Shawnee medicine man named Lalawéthika, a brother of Tecumseh, into his career as a famous prophet. He insisted that Waashaa Monetoo was chastising the Indians for drunkenness, witchcraft, violence, and their neglect of ancient ceremonies and practices and convinced his band that confession and reform were essential. Less well known is the response of some Missouri bands of Shawnees in 1812, when the New Madrid earthquakes shook much of the Mississippi Valley. According to a contemporary account, "an almost obsolete Indian rite" was revived "to avert the divine displeasure." A general hunt provided deer for sacrifice, and while the animals were suspended for three days with their heads toward "the heavens" the Shawnee warriors fasted and prayed. Abstaining from sleeping with their women, they spent each night "lying on the back upon fresh deer skins, turning their thoughts exclusively upon the happy prospect of immediate protection, that they may conceive dreams to that effect, the only vehicle of intercourse between them and the Great Spirit." At the close of the three days the Indians were said to have narrated their dreams, consumed the deer, and contented themselves that, once more, they enjoyed the patronage of Waashaa Monetoo.[18]

\*　\*　\*

Kinship was also important to Shawnees. Rearing and education, welfare, food and shelter, protection, and ultimately burial all rested primarily on kinfolk.

Kinship was regulated through a dozen or so patrilineal and exogamous clans. Every Shawnee inherited membership in one of the clans from his or her father and kept it through life. The clans were named for an animal, such as a snake or a hawk, and cut across all the divisions of the tribe. Thus while a Pekowi was as free to marry another Pekowi as a member of any of the other Shawnee divisions, a panther clan member was not permitted to marry another panther but selected a partner from the other clans. Clan affiliation was taken seriously, and there was a friendly rivalry among the clans. An Indian visiting another Shawnee town would find ready hospitality among fellow clan members, and the clan, as well as the immediate family, revenged atrocities visited on its people.[19]

Because children promised their parents security in their old age, they were immensely valued, and during periods of warfare young captives were eagerly adopted by families who had few or no offspring. The assimilation of such children, including white and a few black youngsters, was often complete, and records contain the names of several whites who, captured as boys, resisted eventual repatriation: men such as Richard Sparks, Joseph Jackson, George Ash, Stephen Ruddell, and Peter Waggoner. Truthfully did one who knew the Shawnees observe:

> It is an easy thing to make an Indian out of a white person, but very difficult to civilize or Christianize an Indian. I have known a number of whites who had been taken prisoners by the Indians when young, and without exception they formed such attachments that after being with them some time, they could not be induced to return to their own people. There was a woman among the Shawnees, supposed to be near a hundred years of age, who was taken prisoner when young in eastern Pennsylvania. Some years after their friends, through the agency of traders, endeavoured to induce her to return, but in vain. She became, if possible, more a squaw in her habits and appearance than any female in the nation.[20]

Many attempts were made to compel the Shawnees to surrender whites living in their towns, but the Indians resisted them tenaciously. A civil chief, Lawoughgua, once returned some white prisoners with the plea: "We have taken as much care of these prisoners as if they were our own flesh and blood. They are now become unacquainted with your customs and manners, and therefore, Fathers, we request you will use them tenderly and kindly, which will be a means of inducing them to live contentedly with you."[21]

Sometimes adults other than parents gave lessons to children, perhaps in hieroglyphics, public speaking, or oral traditions, but most of the care and preparation of the young took place within the family. Parents placed their infants in cradleboards, especially designed to strengthen little limbs and backs, and in time they shouldered the burdens of education. They supervised the vision quests of budding adolescents and played important roles in traditional marriages. It was the parents of intending young couples who exchanged wedding gifts and organized the ceremonies and they, too, who often determined the choice of appropriate partners. Such choices were important. Even among the relatively egalitarian Shawnees, marriages were a way of harnessing other influential families to the obligations that went with kinship. Shawnees were frequently polygamous, and although marriages were fragile and separations commonplace, a Shawnee warrior might connect himself to several important families during his lifetime.[22]

Justice was another responsibility that lay primarily in the hands of kinsmen. Shawnees recognized the right to retaliate for injuries done. In cases of murder it was believed that the soul of the victim could make its journey to the afterworld only if satisfaction had been secured by the relatives. One of the filial obligations of the Shawnee warrior was, therefore, his readiness to defend his family and perhaps his clan from insult and injury.

Although an instrument of justice, the law of reprisal could embroil the Shawnees in serious difficulties. If an injury had been done by members of a different tribe, for example, expeditions of private revenge might easily incite counter reprisals and fledge into full-blown intertribal feuds. Or they could regenerate conflicts about to subside. On such occasions Shawnee chiefs might intervene and attempt to negotiate a settlement, but the history of the tribe was punctuated by intertribal altercations, most of them short but some festering and fiercely fought.

War, in fact, was part of the Shawnee war of life.

\*   \*   \*

Above all the Shawnees were known as warriors and wanderers. Even the Iroquois, who defeated the Shawnees in the seventeenth century, warned the French about their ferocity.

Revenge was only one reason why Shawnees occasionally went to war. Sometimes they fought to defend territory or to support allies, and the war trail was one means by which young men obtained plunder, prestige, and authority. During wars with the whites the flow of captured goods into Shawnee villages was often considerable and a lucrative substitute for the previous spoils of peaceful trade.

Whatever the purpose of war, it was a serious business, for in a society in which every warrior was also a hunter, lives could not be squandered lightly. True, captives adopted by the Shawnees offset military losses, but the tribe could not afford to sustain severe casualties. The successful war chief was skilled in the surprise tactics necessary to inflict maximum damage upon opponents at the least cost to his own party. Casualties could also be reduced by appealing to the spirits for help and guidance. Augurers were employed to divine the prospects of success, and purification rituals attended the departure and return of war parties, including fasting and the imbibing of root substances that were supposed to infuse or defuse energy. On the war trail warriors carried fetishes that could be turned to account at the critical moment by summoning the assistance of tribal or individual guardian spirits.[23]

Each expedition was preceded by war dances, accompanied by drums, rattles, and songs, and successful warriors also performed upon their return. The differences between these dances are not clear, but all seem to have involved young men stripping and painting their bodies and forming a circle around a war post; a period in which the music and dancing were suspended to allow each warrior in turn to strike the post with his tomahawk and recount his military exploits; and general dancing and whooping. The dances advertised glories won, exhorted the men to action, and induced the appropriate psychological mood.[24]

Shawnees were formidable warriors, and frequently they were also ruthless. Eighteenth-century white prisoners of the tribe circulated fearful stories of women and children being butchered indiscriminately; of scalps ripped off victims, dried, and stretched on hoops as trophies; of babies dashed against trees; and of bound prisoners being tormented with burning brands and red-hot hatchets. The return of victorious war parties to their towns was graphically pictured in captivity narratives: the warriors sending messengers ahead to alert the villagers, while they prepared themselves for entry by painting their bodies. The marking of the captives: red on the faces of those to be spared, black for death. The noisy return, with warriors whooping and firing guns and capering behind a war pole held aloft, decorated with fresh scalps. The prisoners being chaperoned forward, forced to sing and shake rattles. The lines of jeering men, women, and children waiting to receive them, ready to beat them with sticks as they passed. And the council house, where the fates of those captives who had not yet been assigned to anyone were decided.

There was much truth in these pictures, although horrific tales made good copy and demand prudent evaluation. But we must beware of generalizing too hastily. In fact, the fate of prisoners was by no means easy to predict. Some were killed outright, often by a blow of a tomahawk, and others were slain elsewhere, but many were also very well treated. Much depended on whether the Indians had losses to avenge; whether there were practical reasons for killing prisoners, perhaps the lack of sufficient guards or the danger of a hot pursuit; and on the disposition of the individual captor. Warriors were usually considered to be the owners of property or prisoners they had personally taken in an attack, and once an Indian had successfully claimed a captive as his own, he was free to slay, sell, or spare him as he wished. The treatment of prisoners, consequently, varied greatly.

Many Shawnees, such as Blue Jacket and Tecumseh, were extremely generous to prisoners. Thomas Ridoubt, taken in 1788, found his captor a "friend . . . who never once forfeited the appellation." Daniel Boone, captured ten years before in Kentucky, was adopted by a Shawnee family. He "had a great share in the affection of my new parents, brothers, sisters and friends," while the Shawnee chief Blackfish "took great notice of me, and treated me with profound respect and entire friendship." But Mrs. Kinnan had little good to say about her Shawnee captors and was eventually purchased from them by a Delaware woman, while Margaret Erskine also had her problems. At one time a warrior who had adopted her as a daughter resolved to kill her, and she was saved by another Indian who purchased her life with a gun. Even so, Margaret judged the Shawnees fairly and in later years "repeatedly asserted that in the four years of her captivity she was never offered any indignity or insult from an Indian, their chastity being a strong feature of their character."[25]

The stereotype of the savage, oblivious to the innumerable shades of human circumstance and temperament, was no more applicable to the Shawnees than to Indians far less famed for military prowess.

No less than others in their unsafe world did they value peace, and they celebrated it with elaborate rituals, including feather dancing, in which performers with the tail feathers of eagles in one hand and rattles in the other bowed or stretched their bodies to the beat of a drum. The best account of this ceremony was given in 1786 and described how the head civil chief, thumping a drum and singing a peace song, led two hundred Shawnees to the council house to confirm peace negotiations with the Americans. Two warriors, armed with pipes decorated with wampum and eagle feathers, led dancers in "truly fantastic" and "elegant" movements. At their destination the head chief and his dancers continued to perform while the Indians filed into the council house, the women entering by its eastern doorway, the men by the western entrance. Once inside, the Shawnee men divided, the chiefs seating themselves to the left and the warriors to the right. In this ceremony the women, headed by the senior female civil chief, brought up the tail of the procession.[26]

The recognized champion of peace in Shawnee villages was the female civil chief, who appealed to the war chiefs for moderation, citing the sufferings of mothers in bringing life into the world and deploring unnecessary bloodshed. Surprisingly often Shawnees did avoid confrontations, sometimes most strikingly by migrating. This may have been a reason why the tribe was often considered to be culturally conservative. Rather than remaining in uncomfortable situations, whether they were the result of conflict, the proximity of irksome neighbors, or the poor hunting, Shawnees were prone to removing, finding new homes where they could follow their own inclinations unmolested.

Tenacious in battle the Shawnees may have been, but they were not a consistently aggressive people. Nor did they generally conform to the popular image of the austere stoic, always averse to public displays of emotion and braving the vicissitudes of life with dour fortitude. Danger, uncertainty, and hardship were never far from the Shawnees. Even in the Ohio Valley, with its fertile soils and abundant game, an exceptionally wet summer or a hard winter could ravage a simple economy, and for more than twenty of the years between 1750 and 1795 the tribe was on a wartime footing. But for all that, the Shawnee existence was widely tempered with good humor and frivolity.

The missionary Jones, for example, found the Shawnees "the most cheerful and merry people ever I saw." Chief Kakinathucca would seem to have been so, for he sang as soon as he rose in the morning and chattered cheerfully the livelong day. Tecumseh generously kept his followers supplied with jokes, and Charles Johnston recalled how the grave demeanor of his Shawnee captors could easily dissolve into hilarity. He recorded a form of cards played by adults, in which the victor had the privilege of tweaking the nose of the loser. The loser, on his part, was supposed to endure the forfeit by remaining expressionless, under pain of additional penalties. "At every fillip," mused Johnston, "the bystanders would burst into a peal of laughter."[27]

During the warmer seasons, when each Shawnee community regathered in its permanent village, life was particularly susceptible to lighter moments. Infants spun wooden tops, boys stalked and ambushed each other in mock warfare, men smoked, and adults of both sexes diced or engaged in occasional team games. One game involved scoring by rolling balls into bunkers, and another was a form of soccer that pitted teams of women against teams of men. The female contenders had the privilege of managing the ball with their hands as well as their feet and were often the victors. Some gift-giving ceremonies, such as those at the green corn festival or those honoring a deceased person, also included sports. A smooth or greased stick was thrown for the younger Indians to retrieve. They chased each other, snatching the stick when they could, and whoever returned it received a reward. Shawnees were also brought together by dancing and singing. Some of it, certainly, was turned to such auspicious purposes as prayer or mourning, but much of it served the interests of amusement and fraternity. The number and nature of Shawnee dances changed over time, but by 1860 one who visited the tribe was able to itemize twenty-one of them.[28]

And the Shawnees were great storytellers. A few of their stories preserved memories of actual historical events. One, in which a quarrel between the Shawnees and Delawares developed after two children began fighting over a grasshopper, may have recalled the migration of Shawnees from the Wyoming Valley of Pennsylvania to the Ohio. Other stories were creation myths, designed to account for the existence of tribes, divisions, or clans or perhaps to explain aspects of the natural world, such as the white hawk ("Alark Oakwaa, the Star Woman"), the markings of the blue jay ("Meskwaunkwaatar, the Red Head"), or the wood duck ("Autthoakaukau, A Story"). Many, however, were adventure stories, filling long firelit winter evenings with rambling episodic tales, tales steeped in the communion between man, nature, and the spirit world and replete with such miraculous events as the transformation of humans into animals or vice versa. Typically, they described the travels of a hero — perhaps a man seeking a wife — and his encounters with malevolent forces such as man-eating giants, magicians, and such marvelous beings as the Winter Men, who froze people with their very breath. Often the hero, or heroine, was abetted by spirits, both great (the sun in "Motshee Linnee, the Bad Man") and small (a dog familiar in "Pukeelauwau, Thrown Away") and reflected the importance Shawnees placed on the interplay between the natural and spiritual worlds.[29]

Shawnees needed their sense of humor, their moments of levity, and their resilience in what were, for them, extremely trying times. Not the least problem was finding a home. After Iroquois war parties flushed the Shawnees from the Ohio in the seventeenth century, they had scattered in many directions, searching for suitable places to build their villages. Their astounding peregrinations became notorious. To many the Shawnees seemed incurably footloose, constantly uprooting to start anew somewhere else, often far afield, where fresh terrains had to be learned and relationships with strangers forged.

Most of the Shawnees Blue Jacket knew had experienced these migrations. They spoke of the Illinois prairies, the mighty Mississippi, the salt waters lapping on the Gulf coast, the river valleys that coursed through the Alleghanies and the piedmont, and many another area that had promised, too often fleetingly, a homeland. They remembered the slow processions, the warriors in the lead and the women with the baggage behind, marching over Indian trails and across fords. Occasionally Shawnees lashed logs together with vines to make rafts, stretched buffalo hides over frames to create sizable boats, or pushed dugout canoes along with poles, but usually they went overland, navigating if needs be by the sun, the north star, and their firm grasp of woodland lore. The tribe hardly ever traveled as a complete unit. Different villages or divisions decamped at will, and parts of the tribe were forever splintering, regrouping, and splintering again.[30]

Reunification was a constant, but entirely elusive, dream in the days of Blue Jacket. To bring those scattered bands together again, to increase the strength of the tribe and, consequently, its standing was more than a desirable fancy for some Shawnees. It was a search for redemption. For if the tribe could consolidate, if it could call in its scattered bands and regroup, it would have proven itself worthy of the pride and protection of the Great Spirit. Again Waashaa Monetoo would smile upon the people who had once been closest to his heart. Again they would prosper.

Toward the middle of the eighteenth century Shawnees who had settled in western Pennsylvania began moving to the upper Ohio and in time to consider whether the broken pieces of their tribe might be reassembled there. The Ohio, which the Shawnees knew as the "Mspeleaweesepe," the Big Turkey River, seemed the ideal place. Many remembered that this country had once been their own and believed that they were reclaiming old ground. One was an aged headman named Paxinosa. When he left Pennsylvania in 1758, he said that he was tired of living close to the British settlements and was taking his family back to the Ohio, "where he was born."[31]

# 2

# Beginnings

When Blue Jacket was born about 1743 the Shawnee re-colonization of the Ohio was already in full swing.

Those Shawnees who lived in and about Pennsylvania in the early eighteenth century, on the Susquehanna, the Allegheny, and elsewhere, had soon wearied of their new habitations. At that time the Indians enjoyed almost exclusive use of the fertile lands west of the Appalachians, although a handful of small and widely scattered French posts clung precariously to the skirts of the western Great Lakes and to the Maumee, Wabash, and Mississippi Rivers. From the east, though, British settlements were pressing vigorously against the Appalachian mountain barrier, and the game in Pennsylvania was becoming harder to find. The eastern Shawnees were also irritated by the interference they suffered from the lordly Iroquois Confederacy of New York, which was allied to the British. They found the lure of the western country, where trade goods could be had from the French as well as the British and where the land was more bountiful, undeniable. From the 1730s bands of Shawnees ventured down the twisting Ohio. They built new towns such as Logstown (Ambridge, Pennsylvania) and Lower Shawnee Town at the mouth of the Scioto. By the 1750s the tribe had extensive settlements on the upper Ohio, principally on the Muskingum River, with the Delawares, and along the Scioto River.

It was a lush country, green, coursed by innumerable streams, and alive with wildlife. It was a land of plenty. Here, the Shawnees believed, was a good place to regather the nation, to restore it to its former importance, and perhaps to recapture the benefices of Waashaa Monetoo. It was an ambition doomed never to be realized, but for almost a century a thousand or so Shawnees made their homes on the Ohio and its tributaries, in this ancient birthright of their people.[1]

Blue Jacket was one of them.

We know almost nothing of his early life and are left to conjecture about even the most basic facts, his birthdate, for example. When he was first mentioned in records at the beginning of 1773, he was already an important war chief and was so prominent in his own village that it was known to whites as Blue Jacket's Town. Such a status suggests that he was unlikely to have been under thirty. In 1778, however, he was described by Henry Hamilton as a "young" chief. An age of about thirty-five for 1778 would reasonably fit both pieces of evidence. Together with a description of Blue Jacket as "an old man" in 1807 and remarks the chief is said to have made at that time, the sources would indicate a birthdate about 1743. By then his people were establishing themselves on the Ohio.[2]

Equally, little survives about the chief's parentage or original family. We know Blue Jacket had a sister and that he was a relation, as well as a close ally, of another famous Shawnee chief, the orator and civil leader Musquaconocah, or Red Pole. On three occasions one or other of these noted men specifically referred to the other as his "brother," in ways that implied a blood connection. The word "brother" served the Shawnees in several ways. It could be applied to parallel cousins, for example, but in this instance it seems to have meant that Blue Jacket and Red Pole were half-brothers, sharing the same mother.

There are two reasons for making this assumption. In 1795 Red Pole mentioned that his "aged father" was still alive, whereas there are no suggestions that either parent of Blue Jacket survived so long. Much more significantly, Blue Jacket probably belonged to the Pekowi division of the tribe, and Red Pole did not. He was a Mekoche and duly laid claim to the privileges of the Mekoches. Since Shawnees inherited divisions from their fathers, it follows that Blue Jacket's mother had two husbands, a Pekowi, by whom she had Blue Jacket, and a Mekoche, who gave her the younger son. Whatever the origin, a very important consequence flowed from the relationship between Blue Jacket and Red Pole. The former became the tribe's senior war chief, but during times of peace the Shawnees were directed by their civil chiefs, and the senior civil chieftainship was a prerogative of the Mekoche division. But if Blue

Jacket was debarred from being head civil chief, Red Pole was not. In short, between them the brothers were able to contend for the two key positions in the Shawnee nation.[3]

Shawnee children received names in infancy but were at liberty to change them later in life. So it was with Blue Jacket. Originally, he was known as Se-pet-te-ke-na-the, the Big Rabbit, a name he used as late as 1776. In another year or so, however, he adopted the name Waweya-piersenwaw, which evidently signified "a whirlpool." Yet throughout his career the chief was colloquially known as Blue Jacket. No explanation for the use of that name has come down,.[4]

Some authors have described Blue Jacket as a Mekoche, but such was not the case. Indeed, at his peak Blue Jacket had running disputes with the Mekoches. He once complained that a Maumee trader named Knaggs had falsely claimed a small pony belonging to Blue Jacket, while the Mekoches were after his wampum. "The wampum he received was not for the Mequijake [Mekoche] chiefs," he said, "but for his own purpose." A major bone of contention was the right of the Mekoches to manage the affairs of the tribe in peacetime. They resented the war chief Blue Jacket's long period of supremacy during the extended warfare of the 1790s. In 1795, when Blue Jacket boasted of holding a British commission, three Mekoche chiefs raised a jealous outcry over the matter. They charged "the English . . . for having made any chiefs among them, especially the younger brothers; if any were made, they say it ought to have been some of them." And they coupled their complaint with an account of the origins of the Mekoches and the Pekowis, which established that the "younger brothers" had merely grown from the ashes of a Mekoche fire. This attack on Blue Jacket would seem to identify him satisfactorily as a Pekowi.[5]

As for the Shawnee clan, which Blue Jacket also inherited from his father, that was betrayed by his name, for Shawnees generally bestowed personal names indicating the clans to which infants belonged. Big Rabbit speaks for itself. Blue Jacket belonged to the rabbit clan and in turn passed it to his own children.[6]

Blue Jacket grew to manhood in a bloody period that offered sharp lessons in war and politics — allies and enemies, for example. The new homeland claimed by the Shawnees was debatable territory. It was shared with other Indians, and, far worse, it became a theater for the imperial ambitions of France and Britain. In the 1740s and 1750s the French considered the Ohio country essential to the political and economic security of New France in Canada and employed Indian allies from among the Great Lakes tribes to help them gain control over it. And in the eastern English-speaking colonies no less greedy gazes were fixed upon the lands on the Ohio. Population growth, inefficient land use, the flight from poverty, colonial policies, and a multiplicity of personal motives fed land hunger in the British colonies, and many looked to the West for profits from hunting, Indian trade, and real estate. The British rested their claims to the Ohio Valley on the spurious grounds that it had been conquered by their "subjects," the Iroquois, and placed under the king's protection. The Iroquois Confederacy certainly supported this argument. They contended that Indians who used the Ohio, such as the Shawnees and Delawares, did so merely by their sufferance because they had conquered it in the previous century.

Blue Jacket quickly learned that his people, with their immediate neighbors (the Delawares and an Iroquois splinter group known as the Mingoes) were shifting uneasily between major power blocks hungry for the ground they stood on. To the northeast and east were the British colonies and their allies the Six Nations of the Iroquois Confederacy. The Iroquois were exploiting their political and trade connections with the British to strengthen their influence among the western tribes. To the north and northwest were the French and their Indian supporters, such as the Ottawas. Sandwiched between such powerful forces, the Ohio Indians felt underpowered. The Shawnees and Delawares began to strengthen their tribal organizations, and about 1747 they joined the Mingoes in a loose confederacy of their own, with its focus, or "council fire," at Logstown.

Intertribal unity was not a normal state among the Indians, but the Ohio Confederacy was by no means unique. True, the aboriginal world was generally a world of small villages with narrow horizons and concerns and of local rivalries between tribes, bands, towns, clans, or individuals. It was also a world in which common action was difficult to organize, riven as it was by diverse languages, ancient and deep-rooted animosities, and weak decentralized systems of government. Yet for all that, powerful threats were easily understood, and groups of Indians had occasionally combined to meet them.

To create an armed force of sufficient size, even if its purpose was merely to compel a strong adversary to negotiate, intertribal cooperation was essential. Alone, or in small groups, Indian communities were inevitably vulnerable. During this period the Indians were confronted by escalating and unprecedented pressures, primarily from the whites, and an increasingly sophisticated tradition of pan-Indianism developed. Simple alliances fledged into confederacies, in which central "council fires" attempted to concert policy on a regular basis. Blue Jacket himself was to become a major contributor to the tradition, but it had a much older history.

In the previous century the fear of Iroquois war parties had drawn various Algonquian groups together on the Great Lakes and the Illinois River. Allied with the French, they had even managed to repulse the Iroquois and force them to terms. Feeling insecure in turn, the Iroquois Confederacy, a union of five and later six tribes, tried to restore its damaged prestige through diplomacy and early in the eighteenth century strove to create alliances with the Ohio Valley tribes. Iroquois interference played a part in prompting the Ohio Indians to establish their intertribal council fire at Logstown. Thus potential enemies saw unity as a means of improving security and status in threatening times.[7]

Certainly, that unity was primitive. Such confederacies as developed were weak, with little central power or means to ensure the compliance of the disparate members. They were easily fractured and usually temporary, and the wider and more ambitious the organization, the more susceptible it was to breakdown, as the Ohio Confederacy was to learn. In the 1740s, when the French seemed to be the greater threat and British trade more satisfying, the Shawnees tried to broaden the Ohio Confederacy into a large-scale anti-French coalition, but without much success. They were encouraged by Wyandots and Piankeshaws, who defected from the French sphere of influence, but efforts to recruit allies among Indians of the South, such as the Creeks, made little headway.[8]

Nevertheless, even in Blue Jacket's childhood, Shawnees were using their knowledge of overland trails and waterways, their experience of intertribal diplomacy, and their kinship links both north and south to support their hold on the Ohio, and they had a new confidence. In 1750 an Ohio chief boasted that the Indians there had "become a great body, and desire to be taken notice of as such."[9]

Intertribal politics, as frustrating as they were necessary, surrounded the young Blue Jacket. So did war. He was too young to participate in the great struggle the French and British waged for the Ohio country between 1754 and 1760. At first, the Ohio Indians wavered uncertainly. Some, including their main spokesman, the Mingo Tanaghrisson, favored throwing in with the British, but others hesitated to be caught on what they feared would be the losing side. Neutrality was broken after the

French and Lakes Indians cut Gen. Edward Braddock's army to shreds in 1755. Awed by French power, most of the former Ohio confederates now turned upon the British, ravaging the frontiers of Virginia and Pennsylvania. Not until 1758, when a new army of redcoats captured the French Fort Duquesne at the forks of the Monongahela, did the belligerent Shawnees, Delawares, and Mingoes step aside to allow the French to be expelled from the Ohio for good.

Blue Jacket was still a youth when the French and Indian War ended. He was still learning to hunt, track, and fight and trying to identify the guardian spirits that would guide him through life. But he was probably old enough to realize that although the French and British were necessary suppliers of trade goods, neither was to be depended on. The French were beaten and gone, but a chain of forts they had built from the forks of the Monongahela to Lake Erie remained. The British were more intent on occupying than dismantling them, and once the French had been defeated and the usefulness of the Indians to the British declined, the king's servants began to implement a new frontier policy. Abandoning the old forms of backwoods diplomacy, the British commander-in-chief in North America cut the issue of goodwill presents and supplies to the Indians. Old Indian allies of the French mourned the passing of a regime they believed to have been more liberal and paternalistic, and rumors spread that the British were trying to weaken the tribes so as to destroy them. Among other Indian grievances, including indications that their lands were at risk, were smallpox epidemics. They convinced some tribesmen, particularly among the Delawares, that the Creator was punishing them for allowing their forests and cultures to be contaminated by the redcoats.

In 1763 the pot boiled over. Many of the Indians between the Ohio and the Great Lakes rose against the British, and the Shawnees joined in, scourging the borders once again. Small wooden forts, sheltering skeleton garrisons of British soldiers and sprinkled strategically across a vast wilderness, fell before a general Indian assault, and hundreds of settlers were killed, carried off, or driven from their homes. The Indians soon ran out of ammunition and trade goods, but the war alerted the British to the importance of forming a coherent western policy and justified the Royal Proclamation of 1763 by which George III prohibited white settlement west of the Appalachians.[10]

Blue Jacket almost certainly earned his place as a warrior in the fierce raids of 1763 and 1764, but although he spent a lifetime fighting British and American settlers and soldiers, at no time did he resent the whites as such. In fact, he regularly fraternized with them and was always open to learning from their successes. Neither of the two wives he took was of full Indian blood.

One, probably the first, was a white woman. Margaret Moore was said to have been the younger of two daughters of a homesteader, John Moore. Both girls were captured in Virginia during the war between the French and the British, sometime between 1755 and 1758. About nine at the time of her capture, Margaret was raised in the Indian towns and eventually became a wife of Blue Jacket. They had a son, who remained with the Indians and was remembered as Joseph Moore. Margaret was pregnant with another child when Blue Jacket allowed her to visit her family in Virginia. She seems to have enjoyed a good relationship with her husband but was persuaded to remain in Virginia rather than return to the Shawnees. It was in Virginia that Nancy Moore was born.

Blue Jacket did not see his daughter until both she and her mother returned to Ohio about 1804, after the Indian wars had ended. Margaret lived in the white settlements, which by then had displaced most of the native towns, and Nancy was already married to a Virginian, one James Stewart. Nevertheless, Nancy was accepted by both her father and the Shawnees and spent much of her remaining years with them. The two women — wife and daughter of Blue Jacket — were a marked contrast, according to one who knew them. The former retained her good looks, whereas Nancy's decidedly Indian features were severely marked by smallpox. Still, people remembered Nancy as a "a nice woman" who "appeared neat and tidy, as much so as other women. She talked good English, and must have been good-looking when young."[11]

Blue Jacket's other wife was the progeny of a French-Canadian trader, Jacques Dupéront Baby. Such traders often took Indian wives during their sojourns in the native villages, establishing important kinship ties with Indian families, and Blue Jacket may have been connected to more than one of them. Both Alexander McKee, known to the Shawnees as Wapemassawa, and Matthew Elliott traded in the Shawnee towns on the Scioto in the 1770s and married Indian women. It has been said that Blue Jacket was related to them. If so, benefits would have flowed in both directions because Blue Jacket became a powerful chief and McKee and Elliott rose to head Britain's Indian affairs in the West. By mixing with them, Blue Jacket was able to broaden his understanding of the Indian predicament; if he was their kinsman he would probably have been in an even better position to manipulate them for his own and the tribal good.[12]

Jacques Dupéront Baby was born in Montreal and was trading with the Logstown Shawnees before the French and Indian War, counteracting British influence where he could in the interests of New France. In due course he fathered a Shawnee daughter, who was raised with her mother's people. Baby's usefulness among the Indians was such that although he had been with the French forces during the war, the British retained his services afterward. He earned the respect of his new masters, who referred to him as "a French gentleman of undisputable loyalty." In addition, he was well connected, and in 1760 he married Susanne Réaume, of a noted mercantile family.[13]

Baby's métis daughter understood French but spoke only Shawnee. She kept in touch with her father, and when Blue Jacket took her for a wife he created important ties with the traders operating out of Montreal and Detroit. The marriage gave Blue Jacket at least four children. Jim Blue-Jacket, the oldest, was thought by his nephew to have been born about 1765, but an American officer described him in 1786 as "a boy about eighteen years of age," which implies a birthdate about 1768. The younger children were Mary Louise, Sally, and George Blue-Jacket, born respectively about 1775, 1778, and 1781.[14]

Blue Jacket's family was substantial, but he kept it well provided for and his domestic relationships attracted no untoward comment. The family flourished, and today the many and diverse descendants are proud of their mixed Indian and white heritage.

*　　*　　*

When the contemporary record takes up Blue Jacket in January 1773, he was a man of standing and about thirty years of age. A missionary named David Jones was then exploring the prospects for evangelism beyond the Royal Proclamation Line established ten years before. Jones inspected five Shawnee towns on the west bank of the Scioto. Upstream of three of them — Chillicothe, Crooked Nose's Town, and Pekowi — he found "a small town, situated W.N.W. of Pickaweeke [Pekowi] about three miles. By the English it is called Blue Jacket's town, an Indian of that name residing there." Jones described it as "situated [on the] east [bank] of Deer Creek, and north of a large plain. This creek is clear and beautiful, appearing useful for mills and healthful for the inhabitants. The buildings here are logs, their number about twelve. This is a peaceable town, and in it lives Kishshinottisthee, who is called a king, and is one of the head men of this nation. The English of his name is Hardman."[15]

Hardman was not a king but the principal civil chief of the Ohio Shawnees and therefore a member of the Mekoche division. His main residence was further east, at Wakatomica on the Muskingum, but he obviously maintained a cabin on the Scioto, where most of the Shawnees were settled. Hardman's choice of Blue Jacket's Town for his home may reflect close and long-standing relationships with the Pekowi war chief and his associates.[16]

As a war chief, Blue Jacket owed his advancement to merit rather than birth, but his connections with British and French-Canadian traders seem to have stimulated his appetite for business, and he became the most entrepreneurial Indian in the Shawnee nation. But whether war chief or trader, he cut a magnificent figure in his prime. Our only descriptions of him are brief and come from the 1790s or later, but they are worth quoting here, as we form our picture of the man. Whites found him "a brave, masculine figure of a man," or "lofty and masculine," but noticed his propensity to swagger in extravagant dress. Joseph Wade, who remembered him passing through Adams County, Ohio, and making a hunting camp on Brush Creek, recalled "a fine-looking Indian."[17]

But the most detailed portrait was given by Oliver M. Spencer, who was captured by the Indians in 1792, when he was eleven years old. His memory of a visit to Blue Jacket's home captures the flavor of the chief and his family:

> This chief was the most noble in appearance of any Indian I ever saw. His person, about six feet high, was finely proportioned, stout [strong], and muscular; his eyes large, bright and piercing; his forehead high and broad; his nose aquiline; his mouth rather wide, and his countenance open and intelligent, expressive of firmness and decision. He was considered one of the most brave and accomplished of the Indian chiefs, second only to Little Turtle and Buck-on-ge-ha-la. . . .
>
> On this day, receiving a visit from The Snake . . . and Simon Girty, he was dressed in a scarlet frock coat, richly laced with gold, and confined around his waist with a party-colored sash, and in red leggings and moccasins ornamented in the highest style of Indian fashion. On his shoulders he wore a pair of gold epaulets, and on his arms broad silver bracelets, while from his neck hung a massive silver gorget and a large medallion of His Majesty, George III.

Around his lodge were hung rifles, war clubs, bows and arrows, and other implements of war; while the skins of deer, bear, panther and otter, the spoils of the chase, furnished pouches for tobacco, or mats for seats and beds. His wife [Baby's daughter] was a remarkably fine looking woman. His daughters [Mary and Sally], much fairer than the generality of Indian women, were quite handsome, and his two sons [Jim and George], about eighteen and twenty years old, educated by the British, were very intelligent.[18]

Although written long after the event and incorporating information and ideas inappropriate to 1792, Spencer's narrative faithfully reflects the chief's dash, success, and ability. It also contains indications, particularly in its reference to education, of Blue Jacket's willingness to mix with and benefit from the society of white associates. He was no simple woodsman but a sophisticated Indian leader, proud of his Shawnee heritage but eager to profit from his wider contacts.

In that way, Blue Jacket was firmly planted in what historians have recently called the "middle ground," the world of overlapping cultures, where Indians and whites met, adapted, and exchanged to create shared ways of life and understandings, a world that helped bridge the cultures and draw them closer together.

Trade was a keystone of that cultural bridge, and the traders, with their Indian wives and métis children, were its most significant builders. Although the basic pattern of Shawnee life remained stubbornly resistant to change, all Shawnees were being influenced by the whites, to a greater or lesser extent. Some were conservative, but others displayed considerable cultural melding, changing their bark-sided houses for log cabins and even raising stock to supplement their hunting and horticulture. A tiny number of the more entrepreneurial Shawnees may have been influenced by missionaries. One Indian woman, the Grenadier Squaw, a sister of Cornstalk, who had a herd of nearly fifty cattle in the 1770s, was one of the few Shawnees to have a relationship with the Moravians. Most in the van of change were close to the traders, however, and Blue Jacket was the prime example.

He needed knowledge of those two overlapping worlds, the Indian and the white, in the challenges he met through life. In 1773, when Jones visited his town, the Proclamation Line, which was supposed to pin the British colonists behind the Appalachian Mountains, was leaking like a sieve. The West was on the brink of an invasion. Less than forty years later, in 1810, almost a million white settlers would occupy the states of Kentucky, Tennessee, and Ohio and the territories of Michigan, Indiana, and Illinois, an area that had lately been the preserve of few more than fifty thousand Indians.

With that invasion and its concurrent dispossession of the tribes, the future of Blue Jacket and the Shawnees changed forever.

# 3

# Defending the Dark and Bloody Ground

The Iroquois remembered its famous grasslands and called it "Kentake," but unquestionably the Shawnees knew it better.[1]

The land south of the Ohio was prolific and varied. Watered by numerous rivers and springs, it sported rich, undulating timberland, giant trees, grassy "barrens," and what Kentucky's first historian, John Filson, called "fine cane." It had all the game an Indian could want, big and small: bears, turkeys, and herds of buffalo and deer. There were no longer any permanent Indian villages in the region, although the Shawnees had until recently maintained an important town on the Kentucky River, Eskippakithiki, or Blue Lick Place. But Shawnees and Cherokees prized the rich valleys and hills as a hunting ground. During the colder seasons they built hunting camps in its sheltered places and crisscrossed it with their trails. So regularly did the industrious Shawnees cross the Ohio into Kentucky that they sometimes kept ferries by the river, large boats made of buffalo hides stretched over frames, capable of transporting twenty people.[2]

To such people as the Shawnees, who depended as much on hunting as horticulture and gathering, Kentucky was of tremendous importance.

It was a magnet for others too, particularly the inhabitants of the British colonies in the East. Even the Royal Proclamation of 1763, by which George III had prohibited white settlement west of the crest of the Appalachians, manifestly failed to halt the penetration of what was declared to be, for the time being, Indian country. Intrepid hunters, clad like Indians in long hunting shirts and leggings, led packhorses into the interior in search of pelts. Some were also reconnoitering for land speculators in North Carolina and Virginia, men who lusted for cheap Indian land which they could profitably sell to eager settlers. The long hunters John Finley and Daniel Boone, for example, acted for Richard Henderson and his associates in North Carolina. And the settlers were themselves pouring over the Proclamation Line, particularly the needy Scots-Irish and German peoples moving southwest from the Monongahela.[3]

For the whites Kentucky was a land yet to be won, but the powerful Iroquois Confederacy already claimed it. There was little substance to their pretension. It was true that the Iroquois had once cleared the Erie Indians from south of Lake Erie and dislodged the Shawnees from the Ohio in the seventeenth century, but they had made little use of those territories, and their wars had not been waged for land. Blue Jacket and the Shawnees were not disposed to take the Iroquois claims seriously, but others found them extremely convenient — particularly British expansionists eager to alienate Indian title to the land.

Britain insisted that the Crown, not mere Indians, held sovereignty over the West. The tribes had usufruct, or rights to the use of the soil, and these would have to be liquidated before lands could be opened to white settlement. To facilitate that process, insofar as the Ohio Valley was concerned, certain British parties happily invested those rights of usufruct in the Iroquois, who were believed to be ready to sell. One such party was Sir William Johnson, the northern superintendent of Indian affairs. Encouraged by Pennsylvania merchants hungry for land to offset the losses they had suffered during the uprising of 1763 and by the interests of speculators and settlers alike, Johnson swept the Ohio Indians aside in his hurry to recognize the Iroquois claims. As he wrote the Earl of Hillsborough, secretary of state for the colonies, "The north side of the [Ohio] river which they [the Shawnees] still occupy is more than they have any title to, having been often moved from place to place by the Six Nations [of Iroquois], and never having [had] any right of soil there."[4]

In October and November 1768 Johnson assembled the Iroquois, with whom he had great influence, at Fort Stanwix, and tore up the Proclamation Line of 1763. For £10,000 the Iroquois ceded claims to western Pennsylvania and Kentucky and created a new boundary that ran from the head of the Mohawk River in New York and down the Ohio from Fort Pitt as far as the mouth of the Tennessee River. In a single deal between Johnson and his Iroquois friends, Shawnee and Cherokee claims to Kentucky were obliterated. The Cherokees would get some compensation from three separate treaties concluded between 1768 and 1775, but no one bothered to consult the Shawnees. Many years later, when the Shawnees were struggling to defend their land north of the Ohio from American encroachments, the tribe would recognize the Stanwix line as the only acceptable boundary. They would surrender Kentucky, albeit regretfully, in an effort to protect their ground in what is now Ohio. But in 1768 that resignation was still far off.

The king's ministers also understood the impudence with which the Shawnee rights in Kentucky had been swept away by Johnson's treaty. Hillsborough, for one, lamented the "fatal" folly of using the disputed pretensions of one group of Indians to dispossess another. But little was done to control the rapacity of the colonial governments, and the treaties unlocked a floodgate. In the spring of 1769, when the new purchase was opened for sale, the land office was besieged with applications. Within four months more than a million acres had been sold.

There was much to disturb the Shawnees during these years. The exchange of deerskins for European goods was a source of constant dissension. Most Indians were anxious to achieve greater access to those goods, but most also worried about the deleterious effects of the rum trade, which brought violence and poverty into the native villages. Some Shawnees on the Muskingum, influenced by a Delaware prophet, Scattameck, contended that all the influences of the whites, including their manufactures, should be avoided as abominations to the Great Spirit. And all Shawnees were disturbed by the thefts and occasional murders visited by both sides on the frontier. But between 1768 and 1783 the issue that primarily forged the relationships between the Shawnees and the whites was the land. It was bound to create conflict.

As Chief Dragging Canoe warned Richard Henderson at the treaty of Sycamore Shoals in 1775, when the Cherokees ceded most of their claims to Kentucky, the whites had bought a fair land, but a "dark cloud" hung over the country. "It was the bloody ground, and would be dark and difficult to settle."5

*   *   *

Blue Jacket was close to thirty when the treaty of Fort Stanwix was signed. He would soon be the recognized leader in one of the Scioto towns and was perhaps already so. Certainly he was important enough to have played a significant role in the events that followed and was likely a principal confidant of Hardman, the tribal head civil chief who shared Blue Jacket's village. Hardman was no agitator, but he was a voluble advocate of Shawnee rights. He spoke up for them at Fort Pitt, before Johnson's treaty, and he stopped the Moravian missionary David Zeisberger in his tracks in 1773. When Zeisberger attempted to carry his mission to the Shawnees, Hardman halted him with a tirade against the whites, accompanied by an accusing finger. It is inconceivable that Blue Jacket did not imbibe some of Hardman's spirit.[6]

Although we have no direct evidence of Blue Jacket's role, he was probably party to the difficult diplomacy that embroiled the tribe in the years after the treaty of Fort Stanwix. On the one hand, the chiefs urged restraint on their young warriors, eager to stop the increasing flow of surveyors and hunters into Kentucky; and on the other, they cast around for allies and prepared for a conflict many thought to be inevitable.

Although some tribesmen talked of sending a deputation to England to make a direct appeal to the king — he who still called himself their benign father — few Shawnees considered the idea viable. So they readied themselves for war. They abandoned the most vulnerable of their settlements, such as Logstown. They stored guns, powder, and ball. And they sent emissaries in all directions. Their messengers went to the southern Creeks, Cherokees, and Chickasaws and to the northern Wyandots, Ottawas, Potawatomis, and Ojibwes. They went west to the Miamis, Weas, Piankeshaws, Mascoutens, and Kickapoos of the Wabash and the Illinois and even northeast to the Iroquois, whom they still disparaged as mere minions of the whites. Everywhere they urged Indians to unite, "to be all of one mind and of one color," and to put aside ancient quarrels. They tried to broker peace between old enemies, such as the Cherokees and the Wabash Indians, and the Choctaws and the Creeks, and between 1770 and 1774 the Shawnees hosted four intertribal congresses at the Scioto towns. They drew attention to the colonial advance and lobbied for a consensus.[7]

All came to nought. When he learned of the Shawnee activity, Sir William Johnson employed the Iroquois as counteragents. He had them visit the tribes telling them to close their ears to the Shawnees. Across the frontier Indians were also too dependent on the British trade system, too indifferent to any but immediate and local threats, and too riven by intra- and intertribal animosities to unite behind the Shawnees. Their one enthusiastic ally was Agaustarax (Mud Eater), a formidable anti-British

Seneca chief from Chenussio on the Genesee River (New York), but he had little sway with his fellow Iroquois and died in the summer of 1769. Even the other Ohio Indians spurned the Shawnees. The Delawares understood their plight but wanted nothing to do with a war, while the Mingoes, who did eventually fight, refused to turn out for the crucial battle. When the showdown finally came, Blue Jacket and the other Shawnees stood alone against their Virginian opponents, massively inferior in numbers, provisions, and firepower.

Events moved to a head in 1774. John Murray, Earl of Dunmore, the new governor of Virginia, spearheaded expansion. To outpace the rival colony of Pennsylvania, he seized Fort Pitt, abandoned by the Crown, and declared Kentucky to be a new county of Virginia. In December 1773 he authorized the owners of military warrants, that is of lands granted by the Crown in return for service, to claim their tracts, and within months surveyors from Virginia were scattered about the Ohio and the Kentucky basin.

Early in 1774 Dunmore's representative at Pittsburgh, Dr. John Connolly, was ready to clear the Shawnees out of the way. He had mustered an aggressive militia, and when he heard of the murder of a trader by a Cherokee he whipped the borderers into a fighting mood. The Shawnees, he said, were "ill disposed" to the whites and ready for war. Soon inflamed backcountrymen were descending the Ohio, ready to butcher any Indian they could find. In April two Shawnees and a Delaware were murdered on the river, and on the thirtieth a party of Mingoes were massacred at the mouth of Yellow Creek (Wellsville, Ohio). They included the mother, cousin, and sister of a Mingo leader named John Logan, who had previously been friendly to the whites. He was devastated by the blow and more than a year later, after he had retaliated, could not describe it without tears. "I appeal to any white man to say if ever he entered Logan's cabin hungry, and he gave him not meat, if ever he came cold or naked, and he clothed him not," the chief complained. Now he was alone in the world. "There runs not a drop of my blood in the veins of any human creature. . . . Who is there to mourn for Logan? Not one!"[8]

The war could no longer be stopped, as both sides took to arms. After the Shawnee custom, Hardman transferred his powers to the head warrior, Cornstalk, and the war chiefs, including Blue Jacket, took command of the nation. Some, including Cornstalk, knew that the Shawnees were not ready. They had certainly been considering war these past few years, but frantic diplomacy had not given them any important allies, and now they faced a three-pronged invasion of their country. In August 1774 one force destroyed their towns on the Muskingum, with the year's corn harvest, and then in the fall two mighty columns advanced on the Scioto. One, led by Col. Andrew Lewis, marched from western Virginia, while the other came down the Ohio from Fort Pitt, headed by Dunmore himself. Together they numbered twenty-three hundred men.

To oppose them Cornstalk, Blue Jacket, Black Snake, Puckeshinwau, and other Shawnee war chiefs had a mere three hundred or so Shawnees and a scattering of Mingoes, Delawares, and Wyandots. Yet they made a bold decision. Their only prospect of victory lay in defeating the oncoming armies piecemeal, preventing them from combining. Thus it was that one cold October day the flower of the Shawnee nation silently filed along forest trails on a mission of acute desperation. This was no small-scale foray, in which the chances of success were high, but something far more ambitious, unusual, and risky. Cornstalk and Blue Jacket were going to meet Lewis's column as it lumbered down the Kanawha toward the Ohio.

\*     \*     \*

That Blue Jacket participated in the battle of Point Pleasant, as it came to be called, was remembered by both Indians and whites, but no contemporary reference to his role survives. Many years later Shawnees told John Johnston, who served them as Indian agent, that Blue Jacket participated in the attack; and indeed, since this was a tribal effort, which demanded a full turnout of warriors, that is what we would have expected.[9]

John J. Jacob was the first to publish about Blue Jacket's participation in 1826. Jacob was not in the battle himself and was only seventeen when it was fought. He was then employed by Michael Cresap, who was a notable participant, and later he married Cresap's widow and inherited many of his papers. It was possibly from Cresap that Jacob learned that during the battle "the two Indian captains," Cornstalk and Blue Jacket, "performed prodigies of valor."

Unfortunately, the stories that grew up about Blue Jacket's role in the battle must be accounted as legendary. In 1840 the son of the commander of the Virginians at Point Pleasant wrote, "I do not know of any of the chiefs besides the Cornstalk but the Blue Jacket, a Shawnee chief, who was known to be at the governor's [Dunmore's] camp on the 9th of October, and in the battle on the 10th." This surprising statement had Blue Jacket shuttling from Dunmore's army on the Hocking several miles up the Ohio to the battlefield at the mouth of the Kanawha. But it cannot be regarded as accurate. It was part of a silly idea, prevalent in 1840, that Dunmore had been collaborating with the Shawnees *against* the colonists. In fact, there were no Shawnees in Dunmore's camp on 9 October.

Six years after Lewis junior offered his tidbit, Samuel Murphey, who as a sixteen-year-old boy had served in Dunmore's army, came up with a different tale. He said he had information from a white man who had fought with the Indians that memorable day on the Kanawha. The Indians pressed their attack bravely, he said, but Blue Jacket had to kill one cowardly warrior and Cornstalk whipped another to keep them at their task. This story, too, fails to withstand scrutiny. It was probably a distorted version of a story published thirteen years earlier, in which John Stuart claimed he had been "informed" that Cornstalk killed an Indian who had retreated too quickly. But it is unlikely to be true. The Shawnees did not have an authoritarian command structure, but they did believe in the right of relatives to avenge injuries done their kinfolk. Neither Blue Jacket nor Cornstalk could have slain a warrior without opening themselves to retaliation from his relatives. No, the only judicious conclusion is that while Blue Jacket was almost certainly one of the leaders at Point Pleasant and fought vigorously, nothing is known about his specific actions.[10]

These commentators were right about one thing, though. The Indians threw themselves upon Lewis's army with unusual fury. Their scouts had shadowed the ungainly column of soldiers, pack animals, and herded livestock and watched it descend the Elk and the Kanawha. Even before Lewis set up his camp in the upper fork formed by the junction of the Kanawha and Ohio Rivers on 6 October, some of his men had been wounded in occasional sniping. Moving up the north bank of the Ohio toward Lewis, the Shawnee army was bent on what was at best a desperate venture. The warriors must have made exceptional appeals to the spirits for aid. Holy men accompanied the expedition, but every warrior had his own guardian spirit and was praying to it for protection. As a measure of the importance the Indians placed on the campaign, a holy man was appointed to carry a sacred medicine bundle into the battle on a pole, like a standard.[11]

Cornstalk, Blue Jacket, and their men slunk silently up the north bank of the Ohio, passing the mouth of the Kanawha and Lewis's camp on the other side. Above the Virginian camp they crossed the river on

9 October, using seventy or so rafts made of logs or poles bound with vines. A few Indians remained on the north bank to prevent their enemies from escaping across the river, but Cornstalk and Blue Jacket slid back downstream with the main force, toward Lewis's army. They made their evening camp only a few miles away and planned to strike at first light.

This was the first of Blue Jacket's great battles, and it presaged the tactics of his greatest victory, the defeat of Arthur St. Clair's army in 1791. On both occasions the Indian villages were threatened by advancing superior armies. On both the Indians opted to stop them with an offensive, rather than to wait behind an entrenched position. On both the warriors stormed the enemy camp at daylight. That fall of 1774 Cornstalk and Blue Jacket hoped to keep the Virginian armies divided, but if they failed they could still make a stand on the Scioto or evacuate their towns, where the harvests had been gathered, and retreat westward into the forests.

While it was still dark, on the night of 9-10 October, the Indians prepared themselves. Their bodies were painted, and most had plucked the hair from their heads, leaving only scalplocks along the crown. Some rounded up a few cattle that had strayed from the Virginian camp. Before sunrise the Indian army was on the move again, creeping stealthily toward its target.

But it was difficult to control so many warriors, and firing began prematurely. Just before dawn an advance party of Indians came upon two soldiers out hunting. They shot one of them down, but the other bolted back to the Virginian camp, where a drum was soon beating the men from their tents and to arms. Lewis soon had three hundred men formed into two equal columns, one under his brother. Col. Charles Lewis, and the other led by William Fleming. He sent them upstream, toward the Indians, but less than a mile away Cornstalk, Blue Jacket, and the others were waiting for them. Squatting behind cover, and almost invisible to the Virginians, they waited until the two caterpillars came within range and then delivered a heavy, disciplined fire into their fronts. The Virginians crumbled before the horrifying screams of the attackers and the storm of bullets. Charles Lewis was hit as he stood in the open, bravely encouraging his flagging men. He returned to the base camp on foot, fatally wounded. As he left he told his men, "I am wounded, but go you on and be brave!"

As for Fleming, he had an arm shattered by two musket balls and another shot through the lungs, and he fell grievously incapacitated. Thrown into confusion, the Virginians fell back to the cover of some trees and then retreated toward their main force. Flushed with success, the Shawnees and their allies swarmed from their positions in pursuit.

The Virginians fell back about a quarter of a mile, but then some two hundred reinforcements stiffened their ranks and tilted the balance of numbers against the Indians. Now the warriors were forced back, but slowly and in orderly fashion, as they fired from tree to tree and punished the whites for every rash advance. Eventually, the Indians occupied thick timber and fallen trees on a small ridge that passed between the Ohio and the Kanawha and formed a front about a mile long. There they stood off the Virginian attack.

It was a furious struggle. A colonial officer on the scene shortly afterward admitted: "From what I can gather here I cannot describe the bravery of the enemy in the battle. It exceeded every man's expectations. . . . Their chiefs ran continually along the [Indian] line, exhorting the men to 'lie close' and 'shoot well,' 'fight and be strong.'" From across the Ohio those Indians who had remained to prevent the Virginians from escaping that way shouted encouragement to their colleagues, urging them to "drive the white dogs in!" And the warriors of Cornstalk and Blue Jacket did their utmost to do so. Despite the mounting superiority of the Virginian numbers and their greater firepower, the Indians made desperate assaults on the white line. According to one witness, they "disputed the ground with the greatest obstinacy, often running up to the very muzzles of our guns."[12]

By noon both sides had decided that they were too weak to expect victory, and the firing began to subside. The cries of wounded men and the dozens of dead testified to the valor of both parties. Unable to disperse Lewis's army, however, Cornstalk had no choice but to withdraw. While some warriors entertained the enemy with a light fire, the Indian dead were thrown into the Ohio to prevent them from falling into enemy hands, and some had their scalps removed to deprive the Virginians of trophies. The wounded were carried off. The Shawnee rear guard enjoyed themselves deriding the colonists with their own oaths. Some called upon the Virginians to come on, calling them "sons of bitches" and scorning their fifes and whistles. They ridiculed the treaty of Fort Stanwix and boasted that they would bring more than a thousand extra warriors into the attack.

The Shawnee shouting was mere bravado, but the Virginians were no more willing to continue the battle. The ferocity of the Shawnee attack had shaken them. "Never did Indians stick closer to it, nor behave bolder," marveled the wounded Colonel Fleming. Seventy whites had been killed or fatally wounded and another seventy injured. The Indian loss was unknown, but it was heavier than the twenty or so scalps the Virginians collected indicated. Around sunset the Shawnees finally withdrew, recrossing the Ohio during the night and falling back to their villages on the Scioto. They had nothing of which to be ashamed. They had attacked a force more than twice their own strength and fought it to a standstill. But the battle was still a strategic defeat for the Shawnees, for without a clear-cut victory they could not halt the invasion of their country or rally other tribes to their sides. Those bitter conclusions had to be faced in heated discussions on the Scioto. According to one who spoke to Cornstalk some years later, the chief struck his tomahawk into the center post of the council house and said, "I'll go and make peace." Matthew Elliott, the white trader who was married to a Shawnee, carried a flag of truce to Lord Dunmore calling for terms.[13]

The result was a humiliating meeting at Camp Charlotte (Hocking County). Four hostages, one of them Cornstalk's son Cutemwha, the Wolf, were surrendered to guarantee the good behavior of the tribe, and the Indians agreed to restore any property and prisoners taken from the whites and to accept such trade regulations as the British might impose. In his official report Dunmore also inferred that the Shawnee spokesmen accepted the loss of Kentucky, for they agreed "they should not hunt on our side the Ohio, nor molest any boats passing thereupon."[14]

It seemed that Blue Jacket and his people had lost their war.

\*   \*   \*

Within months speculators pounced on the spoils. The summer of 1775 saw surveyors for the Ohio Company of Virginia claiming two hundred thousand acres on the forks of the Licking River and Elkhorn Creek in Kentucky. Even earlier Richard Henderson's Transylvania Company of North Carolina had been at work. Violating the Crown's policy of restricting private land purchases from the Indians, Henderson extinguished Cherokee claims to most of Kentucky at the treaty of Sycamore Shoals in March 1775. In its wake his axemen, led by Daniel Boone, hewed the Wilderness Road into the new lands. Romantic writers have depicted the pioneers as courageous agents of manifest destiny, and in a sense they were. Settlements appeared — McClellan's Station, Harrodsburg, Boonesborough, St. Asaph's, and Boiling Spring. In the middle of 1775 probably three hundred whites were living in Kentucky.

To strengthen their victory, the Virginians also constructed new forts on the Ohio, including Fort Randolph at Point Pleasant.

Unfortunately, the Shawnees had a different understanding of the agreement at Camp Charlotte, one that significantly failed to acknowledge the loss of their lands south of the Ohio. And they saw nothing laudable about the settlers entering Kentucky. To the Shawnees these newcomers were destroyers of the land.

They said so in a protest sent to their "English and Virginia brothers" in June 1775. It protested the cutting of "our timber," the killing of "our deer," and "the destroying of our trees" and complained that the whites "are coming in the middle of us like crazy people, and want to shove us off our land entirely." They hoped the colonists "will not come further on our land, but let us live in friendship as long as we live." Two months later Hardman repeated the point to James Wood, a Virginia official. His charge that the whites were "settling in great numbers in the midst of their [Shawnee] hunting grounds" is clear testimony that the Shawnees viewed the peace of Camp Charlotte through very different eyes than Lord Dunmore.[15]

The truth was that the Shawnees were fiercely divided, with the Pekowi and Chillicothe divisions deeply distrustful of Mekoche attempts to appease the Virginians. Cornstalk and the Mekoches, who had spoken to Dunmore at Camp Charlotte, were accused of being "wedded" to the Big Knives, as the Indians colorfully described the Virginians. The summer of 1775 found the Pekowis, Blue Jacket's own division, even threatening to join the still disaffected Mingoes in attacks upon "any new settlements whenever they can."[16]

Although divided about how to deal with the crisis, no Shawnees, not even the more pacific Mekoches, were reconciled to losing Kentucky. As an Iroquois leader remarked within a year of the battle at Point Pleasant, Cornstalk looked upon the Iroquois and Delawares as "dogs or servants of the white people" for their failure to support his tribe. "And the Sh[awnee] people said they still loved the land and would not part with it."[17]

For many of those Shawnees, including Blue Jacket, the war was not yet over.

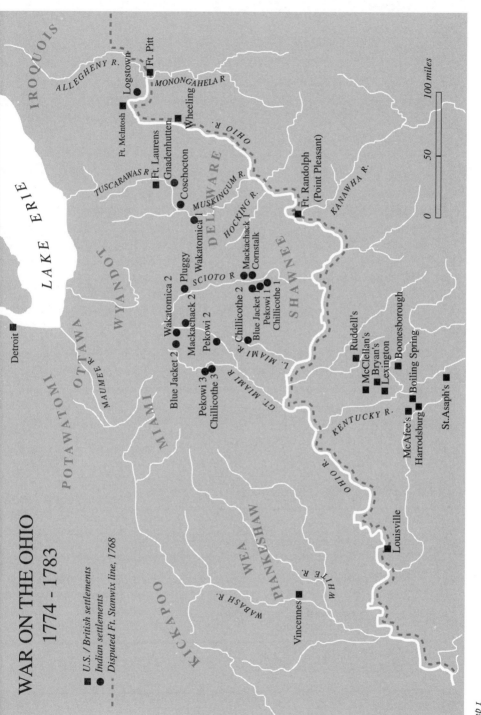

# WAR ON THE OHIO
# 1774 - 1783

■ U.S. / British settlements
● Indian settlements
- - - Disputed Ft. Stanwix line, 1768

IROQUOIS

ALLEGHENY R.

Ft. Pitt
Logstown
MONONGAHELA R.

Ft. McIntosh

Wheeling

Ft. Laurens
Gnadenhutten
Coschocton
TUSCARAWAS R.

LAKE ERIE

Detroit

WYANDOT

OTTAWA

POTAWATOMI

MAUMEE R.

MIAMI

DELAWARE

MUSKINGUM R.

Wakatomica 1

HOCKING R.

OHIO R.

Ft. Randolph
(Point Pleasant)

KANAWHA R.

Pluggy
Wakatomica 2
SCIOTO R.
Mackachack 1
Cornstalk

SHAWNEE

Blue Jacket 2
Mackachack 2
Pekowi 2

Chillicothe 2
Blue Jacket 1
Pekowi 1
Chillicothe 1

Pekowi 3
Chillicothe 3

L. MIAMI R.

GT. MIAMI R.

Ruddell's
McClellan's
Bryan's
Lexington
Boonesborough
Boiling Spring

McAfee's
Harrodsburg
St.Asaph's

KENTUCKY R.

OHIO R.

Louisville

WEA

PIANKESHAW

KICKAPOO

WABASH R.

WHITE R.

Vincennes

100 miles

50

0

Map 1

# 4

## The Second War for Kentucky

On 2 July 1775 a trail-weary party of Indians marched into the Delaware missionary village of Gnadenhütten, on the Tuscarawas River in present-day Tuscarawas County, Ohio. They were Shawnees, some of the most important in the nation. Blue Jacket was among them, along with Cornstalk and his brothers, Nimwha and Silver Heels, and the Pekowi war chief known as Aquitsica or Wryneck. The visitors spent six days about the place, carefully examining the neat cabins, talking to the Moravian missionaries, and even venturing upriver to see the neighboring mission, Schoenbrunn. Cornstalk claimed that the Moravians had befriended him the year before, but the Shawnees were not making a simple social call. They were on an important embassy to Pittsburgh. The Virginians, or Big Knives as they called them, still held Shawnee hostages, and Blue Jacket and his companions needed to preserve the precarious peace and secure their freedom.

Possibly the preliminary call on the Moravians was designed to gather information and to reassure the travelers that they would be safe putting themselves in the hands of the Virginians. If so, it was successful. Certainly Blue Jacket and his friends showed no alarm when they reached Pittsburgh on 16 July. They were immediately given presents. Alexander McKee, the trader, issued them tobacco, lead, powder, vermilion paint, ruffled shirts, pork, flour — and two gallons of rum. The Shawnees were drunk for two days.[1]

Drunkenness was a bane of Shawnee villages. There were abstemious

Indians, but Blue Jacket was not one of them, and on one occasion overindulgence landed him in a difficult position. During a drinking bout on the Maumee River about 1794 Blue Jacket got into a fracas with an Indian with whom he had had differences for twenty-two years. Blue Jacket killed his opponent. Once he had sobered up, the chief was mortified and went to the British commandant of a nearby post, Fort Miamis. He knew the dead man's relatives would demand satisfaction, possibly his life. Blue Jacket explained that the was willing to pay the ultimate forfeit if necessary, but it was usual to offer horses, trinkets, and weapons in expiation of such offenses, and the chief wanted the British to intercede for him. Evidently it worked, for nothing more was recorded of the dispute.[2]

Fortunately, no such violence marred the Pittsburgh revel. On 18 July the Indians convened to hear James Wood, a commissioner employed by Virginia, assure them that the two hostages still in their hands were safe and would be released at a forthcoming council in the fall. The Shawnees remained anxious for their incarcerated kinsmen but appeared eager to keep the peace.

At Pittsburgh Blue Jacket and his fellows learned more about a new crisis that was looming — the American Revolution. Although the Shawnees understood little about its causes, they knew that the colonists, or Big Knives, were squabbling with the Crown and that both sides would appeal to the Indians. Fort Pitt, in fact, was to be the focus of the new republic's attempts to pacify the western Indians, and, at least initially, to keep them neutral, out of British hands, and away from the vulnerable frontiers. Both the Virginia Assembly and the Continental Congress appointed commissioners, and both were soon attempting to bring the Indians to peace conferences at Pittsburgh.

British officers at posts such as Niagara, Oswego, Detroit, and Michilimackinac were also sensible of the need to curry Indian favor. In a war their thin garrisons would need the thousands of Indian warriors in the interior, and Crown officials could point out that it was the colonies, rather than the king, who had been most interested in seizing Indian land in the years since the Royal Proclamation of 1763.[3]

There was much for Blue Jacket, Hardman, Cornstalk, and the other Shawnee leaders to consider, but first there were those hostages to release and a need for immediate security.

In September and October 1775 Cornstalk and a small group of Shawnees were among the substantial gathering of Indians at Pittsburgh, where they were addressed by both the Virginia and federal commissioners. Blue Jacket does not appear to have been a member of this delegation, probably because of wild rumors then circulating among the Indian villages that the Big Knives had invited the Shawnees to Pittsburgh for the purpose of stripping their villages of men and leaving them exposed to attack. Finally, Cornstalk had gone forward with a small entourage, but most of the warriors, probably including Blue Jacket, remained behind.

After some argument in Pittsburgh, Cornstalk freed the hostages and committed the Shawnees to peace and neutrality. He was pressed to deliver prisoners kept by the Indians and promised to do his best. It was as far as he could go. Shawnee custom gave him no right to commandeer prisoners, who were regarded as the property of the individual captor and not of the tribe, and Cornstalk's influence was already declining among the more militant Pekowi, Chillicothe, and Kispoko divisions.

The Indians were firmly reminded that the lands south of the Ohio had been purchased, but no one labored the point. Whatever Cornstalk might have said, his fellow tribesmen on the Scioto had their own ideas, and Hardman for one had insisted less than two months before that he still regarded the region of the Kentucky River as a tribal hunting ground.[4]

A flimsy peace settled over the Shawnee country in 1776. Traders, licensed in Pittsburgh, again led their packhorses to the Scioto, offering matchcoats, shirts, paint, saddles, bridles, traps, knives, lace, and ribbons, although apparently not much in the way of ammunition and guns. Cornstalk tried hard to honor his pledges to return prisoners and property and to alert the Americans of possible dangers. But the resentments unleashed by the seizure of Kentucky and the war of 1774 had not been extinguished, and Blue Jacket and his people were confronting difficult decisions about whether to remain on the Scioto or seek safer homes and about whether to remain at peace or go to war.

*    *    *

Most of the Mekoches, including leaders such as Hardman, Cornstalk, Nimwha, Kekewepelethy (also known as Great Hawk and Captain Johnny), and White Fish, and a few Pekowis such as Wryneck, favored peace.

But most of the nation doubted that course. Many called for a military onslaught against the new settlements in Kentucky. During 1775 and 1776 they had considerable encouragement from the Mingoes of the Oleantangy River (Ohio), from occasional Wyandots from the Sandusky and the Detroit Rivers, and from Canadian Iroquois who brought news of American defeats on the St. Lawrence. But it was the British who gave the strategy credibility. Surely, some Shawnees thought, British arms, supplies, and aid could help them clear Kentucky of the Big Knives. Historians have often described the Indians as pawns of the British, but in this case the exploitation was reciprocal. These Shawnees planned to use the redcoats to fight their war.

In 1776 the British commandant at Detroit, Lieutenant Governor Henry Hamilton, had no authority to turn Indians against the American frontiers. He could supply them, urge the tribes to unite for mutual defense, and rally them to his assistance if he was attacked. Hamilton envisaged recruiting on a wide scale, but his greatest recourse was to the Indians closest to Detroit: the Mingoes; the Lakes peoples — the Wyandots of the Sandusky and Detroit Rivers; the Ottawas, Potawatomis, and Ojibwes of the Detroit region; and ultimately the Shawnees on the Ohio. Not until 1777, however, was he instructed to incite these formidable warriors against Virginia, Pennsylvania, and Kentucky. In London Lord George Germain, the colonial secretary, hoped that such attacks would divert enemy attention and resources from strategically more important theaters in the east.

Gradually, the peace and war factions of the Shawnees pulled apart, but as late as the autumn of 1776 a veneer of unity existed. In October a large delegation of Shawnees, almost a hundred in number, visited American officials in Pittsburgh. The party was led by Cornstalk, who had his mother, brother (Nimwha), sister (Cawechile), and son (Allanawissica) with him, as well as Blue Jacket, Captain Johnny, a mulatto interpreter named Caesar, and others. As before, they dropped in on Gnadenhütten before proceeding to Pittsburgh to join five hundred other Indians in a peace conference with the United States Indian agent George Morgan. When Blue Jacket and the other Shawnees joined the discussions on 1 November they saw Delawares under White Eyes, Killbuck, Buckongahelas, and Pipe, and Iroquois led by White Mingo and Flying Crows, but no Wyandots, Mingoes, or western Indians. In short, this was the rump that would try to maintain peace with the American forces.

Cornstalk stove hard for peace. He indicted the Mingoes as mischief-makers and urged the Iroquois Confederacy of New York to recall them from the Ohio region. And he even delivered a message to Morgan on 7 November. It was a plea to the Continental Congress for justice. Cornstalk pointed out that the Shawnees had never sold Kentucky and needed the area to hunt, and he indicated that he could not prevent his people from going to war unless the issue was addressed. "This is what sits heavy [on our] hearts," he explained, " . . . and it is impossible [for us to] work as we ought to do whilst we are thus oppressed [of our] right."[5]

Yet that winter of 1776–77 saw a chasm open between the Shawnee factions. They decided to break up the concentration on the Scioto and split. Hardman, Cornstalk, and Wryneck would take most of the Mekoches and a few Pekowis to the Delaware capital of Coshocton on the Tuscarawas River to create a neutral block, huddling together for self-defense. The more belligerent Shawnees would look for their security further west, in the more inaccessible regions of Ohio, along the valleys of the Little and Great Miami.

Up to the autumn of 1776 Blue Jacket had stood beside Cornstalk and Hardman and had accompanied the moderates on their journeys east, to Gnadenhütten and Pittsburgh. But now he changed his mind. He threw in with the war party, dismantled his town on the Scioto, and headed some seventy miles to the northwest to build a new home.

⁕    ⁕    ⁕

It was apparently in 1777 that Blue Jacket established his new town near the headwaters of the Mad River, at the site of present Bellefontaine, in Logan County, Ohio. A black woman, Rachel Reno, later claimed to have been born at Blue Jacket's village, about 1780. Close by other Shawnee militants were erecting fresh towns: eastward, on the upper Mad, Wakatomica, and strung along the stream below it "Mackachack" (a Mekoche town), Wapakoneta, and Pekowi and Kispoko Towns. The greatest of these towns, however, was Chillicothe, situated on the Little Miami, south of Pekowi, and it was from here that Blackfish, the war chief of the Chillicothe division, led the first important Shawnee raids into Kentucky in 1777.[6]

If Blue Jacket ever doubted the wisdom of their removal and the geographical and political distance they had put between themselves and the Americans, his misgivings were probably diminished by an event that occurred the following November. As far as Blue Jacket and the belligerent Shawnees were concerned, nothing more graphically illustrated the dangers of treating with the Big Knives. Cornstalk had gone into Fort Randolph at Point Pleasant. His motives were entirely pacific, since he was even then preparing to join the neutral Delawares at Coshocton, but the fort's commandant thought that he could guarantee the good behavior of all the Shawnees by seizing hostages. No matter that Cornstalk and his party had consistently protected the peace and suffered increasing isolation among their own people. The chief and some of his entourage were detained.

Some weeks later, when a militiaman was slain by Indians outside the fort, an inflamed mob stormed into the garrison toward the cabin where the Shawnee hostages were held. As they spilled into the doorway, Cornstalk rose calmly to his feet to face them and died in a volley of musket fire. His son Allanawissica and two other Shawnees were shot, battered, or cut to death. The murders had few immediate consequences. Blue Jacket, Blackfish, and the other militant Shawnees had already broken with Cornstalk and had begun to raid across the Ohio, while the dead chief's own following, amounting to some twenty families, resisted the temptation to join the war party. In February 1778 they settled with the Delawares, as their lost leader had intended. Yet the murder of Cornstalk was still a monumental blunder on the part of the Americans. It hardened hostile attitudes and cost them the ablest ally they had among the Shawnee people.[7]

The exact reasons why Blue Jacket split from Hardman, Cornstalk, and Wryneck and their Mekoches and Pekowis are unknown, but the memory endured for many years. Alexander McKee, who became an Indian agent for the British in 1778, chided the Mekoches with it as late as 1795. When the Mekoches then reproached McKee for the attentions paid Blue Jacket by the British, McKee reminded them how the Shawnee war chief had been "forward in promoting the King's interest in the late war" and merited respect "as a soldier." He added, "I am sure the Maguitchees [Mekoches] cannot have forgot the periods wherein he [Blue Jacket] has distinguished himself, though some of them might probably have been prior to their joining the King, their Father [in 1781], for I believe the Maguitchees were the last of the Shawanoe who joined him."[8]

Blue Jacket may simply have found the settlement of Kentucky too much to stomach, but probably he was no less influenced by his connections with white traders who were in British service. Chief among these was Blue Jacket's father-in-law, Jacques Dupéront Baby. In June 1777 Henry Hamilton made him a captain at Detroit and appointed him interpreter to the Shawnees and Delawares. It was clearly intended that Baby would encourage those tribes to join the British and inconceivable that he did not call on Blue Jacket to that end. Baby continued to prosper. He owned land on both sides of the Detroit River and two years before his death in 1789 would become lieutenant colonel of the Detroit militia. Through him Blue Jacket undoubtedly met other important traders, including Charles Réaume, another member of Hamilton's Indian service, who was related to Baby by marriage.[9]

The consequences of these connections were clear to all of Blue Jacket's people. For one thing, they saw him adopt the acquisitive lifestyle of the whites and turn his hand to farming and trading. Glimpses of these activities are furnished by white prisoners captured during the Revolutionary War and taken to the Shawnee towns. Mrs. Honn was carried off in 1780. Looking back many years later, she considered herself fortunate indeed to have been taken into the family of Blue Jacket himself, for he was a kind man who treated her well. The chief was raising cattle at the time, and Mrs. Honn kept the cows and made butter for the chief's family. Another prisoner who affectionately remembered Blue Jacket was Margaret Paulee, captured in 1779 and adopted by a Shawnee chief called Wabekahkahto, or White Bark. She was then twenty-six years old and supplied the place of a daughter, receiving the name Yellow Gold. Released in 1784, Margaret later provided two versions of her reminiscences. "There was an Indian chief named Blue Jacket," said one, "who had married a half French woman of Detroit, they living in what was considered great style, having curtained beds and silver spoons." In the other version Margaret recalled of Blue Jacket, "I was fond of visiting this house; they always seemed kind and desirous of giving me tea &c. He had his Negro slaves." Cattle, four-posters, silver cutlery, and black slaves. These pictures, more redolent of an urbane country gentleman than a stereotypical Indian war chief, illustrate the unusual ground that Blue Jacket occupied, ground between the white and native peoples.[10]

Shawnees also saw Blue Jacket taking pains to give his children a command of that dual world. George Blue-Jacket was born about 1781 and educated at Detroit, through the instrumentality of his French grandfather. His fluency in Shawnee and English would make him useful to both races in the years to come, and some Shakers, who benefited from his services, left a portrait of him in 1807. "George is 26 years old," they wrote, "a likely, sensible man, [who] has a wife and two children, and carries on farming at Detroit, where he got his learning. He was a long time interpreter with the Presbyterian missionaries among the Indian tribes. He treated us with great kindness." The son, like his father, understood the importance of being familiar with both red and white on a difficult frontier.[11]

Clearly Blue Jacket mixed much with the Detroit traders and imbibed many of their ideas and prejudices, for good or ill. There seems little doubt that their influence directed him toward the British and that he considered an alliance with the redcoats to be entirely compatible with the Shawnee ambition to defend their lands from the Big Knives. Blue Jacket was soon fighting beside his new British allies.

In 1777, when Shawnee war parties made their first serious attempts to clear Kentucky, their new villages on the rivers of the Great and Little Miami effectively formed a British front line. From them issued the Shawnee and Mingo warriors who scourged the Virginia frontier or crossed the Ohio into Kentucky, and through them also came Indians from the Great Lakes and British partisans, who used the towns as forward bases. When the Kentuckians struck back, however, it was almost always at the Shawnees.

In those first years the war went badly for Blue Jacket and his comrades. Blackfish invaded Kentucky twice in 1778, capturing Daniel Boone and twenty-seven men on the Licking in February but unsuccessfully besieging Boonesborough the following September. In the next year Blackfish himself was mortally wounded when the Big Knives retaliated and partially burned Chillicothe.[12]

One problem was manpower. The Shawnees could seldom muster sufficient numbers, for either defense or offense. While the Lakes Indians close to Detroit were within the British fold, Indians further afield stood aloof. Apart from the Mingoes, the only allies the Shawnees had among the Ohio Indians in those first years were a breakaway band of Delawares under Wyondochella and Buckongahelas. In 1778 this band left the Walhonding to form a town three miles north of Blue Jacket's. They were certainly important allies. In three years Buckongahelas increased his following to 240 warriors, gaining recruits as the neutral faction of Delawares crumbled. And Buckongahelas formed a close partnership with Blue Jacket. Indeed, in the years ahead it was the prestige, strength, and support of Buckongahelas that lent Blue Jacket much of his power.[13]

Buckongahelas notwithstanding, allies were few and far between. In the fall of 1778 the Shawnees made an unsuccessful appeal to the southern Creeks, and then Alexander McKee arrived on the Great Miami recruiting for a British expedition that promised to rally the Wabash tribes. Henry Hamilton had assembled a force of Lakes Indians and whites, including a detachment of the Eighth (King's) Regiment of Foot from Detroit, and was leading it up the Maumee. He meant to seize the French settlements of Vincennes on the Wabash and Kaskaskia and Cahokia on the Illinois, all of which had been recently occupied by the Americans, and restore them to British discipline. In the process Hamilton intended bringing the Indians of those regions into the British alliance. By the end of October he had already reached the headwaters of the Wabash and persuaded some of the local Miamis to join him.[14]

Most of the Shawnees were out hunting when McKee arrived with his presents and ammunition, but Blue Jacket seized the opportunity to contribute. McKee left the Shawnee town of Wakatomica for the Maumee on 26 October. When he arrived at the British camp at the head of the Wabash on 4 November, Blue Jacket was with him, along with White Fish and a young warrior named Janithaa. The two chiefs took command of a small Shawnee contingent accompanying Hamilton's expedition.[15]

Journeying downstream with four hundred whites and Indians gave Blue Jacket his first experience of campaigning under British supervision. He must have noted Hamilton's efforts to prevent the Indians from slipping ahead and squandering the chances of surprising the enemy and watched the soldiers exercising their six-pounder or small arms or laboring in freezing water to shift bateaux and pirogues. He probably also heard the Miami chief Le Gris call for toleration of the alien customs and practices of the heterogeneous elements that composed the force, and he met other important leaders, such as the Miami, Pacanne, and the Ottawa, Egushaway. Egushaway was another figure with whom Blue Jacket was destined to work closely. His influence was great among all the Three Fire tribes — the Potawatomis, Ojibwes, and his own Ottawas, who spoke a common language — and it had even reached the Wabash Indians during a diplomatic mission to Vincennes the previous year. To his facility for tact and management, Egushaway added a solid reputation as a fighting man. Only recently he had headed a party of Detroit Indians who had supported a British invasion of New York and bloodied an army of American militia at Oriskany in 1777.[16]

On 7 December, as the army approached Vincennes, Blue Jacket and the Shawnees asked Hamilton for permission to move ahead to secure a prisoner for information. The lieutenant governor agreed, but some of the other Indians jealously protested at Blue Jacket being thus privileged. Hamilton countermanded the order the next day, but the Shawnee war chief was too eager to undertake his mission to let the matter rest. He waited for another opportune moment.

Hamilton was trying to prevent the Indian warriors from wasting ammunition by firing from the boats at wild turkeys flapping across the river. On the ninth one such shot struck White Fish, blinding him in one eye. The old Shawnee was philosophical about his misfortune, declaring simply that he regretted that he had not sustained the injury in battle. But the upshot was a conference at Hamilton's tent the following day. Le Gris threw his authority behind British pleas for the conservation of ammunition and the preservation of order. He bluntly complained that White Fish would not have been wounded if simple precautions had been taken. After Hamilton had also spoken, Blue Jacket, "the young Shawanese chief," as Hamilton called him, replied for his people. He thanked Le Gris for "his friendly condolence" but again slipped in his plan to reconnoiter Vincennes. According to Hamilton, the chief "spoke on the necessity of sending parties ahead, and gave good reasons why the Shawnees should be employed on that service." Hamilton was impressed and privately urged Blue Jacket's plan upon Egushaway, although he tactfully suggested that the advance should be composed of warriors of different nations. Blue Jacket's arguments had nevertheless gone home, for it was acknowledged that the Shawnees and Kickapoos were the fittest to enter Vincennes. Groups of these Indians were often seen on the streets of the town bartering pelts.

As it happened, the move proved unnecessary. On 5 December a party of men from Fort Sackville, at Vincennes, fell into British-Indian hands, and using their information Hamilton closed in on the garrison on the sixteenth. An advance consisting of British, Indians, and a six-pounder sealed the fort from the riverside, and when Hamilton brought up his main force the next day he found the American commander, Capt. Leonard Helm, in a critical position. His French volunteers had fled at the approach of the British, and he had hardly any defenders left. Once Hamilton promised that prisoners would be treated humanely, Helm surrendered.

Indians acknowledged plunder and prisoners to belong to the in-dividual captor and were impatient of restraints. Frightened his allies would run amok, Hamilton placed sentries on the gate to prevent excited warriors from entering the fort. But it was futile. Oblivious to protests from Indian agents and chiefs, eager tribesmen clambered through two gunports and pushed aside the redcoat guards. The British watched helplessly while the Indians scampered about shouting and looting. Some got through the windows of Helm's house. Blue Jacket sought out Helm himself and, placing a hand on his shoulder, declared that since the American commandant could not defend himself he was Blue Jacket's prisoner. Helm could have done much worse because Blue Jacket was a responsible and inherently kind man, but at this point a mixed Ottawa-Miami named Kissingua also put a hand on Helm's head to make a rival claim. The Indians had to convene a council to arbitrate the matter. Blue Jacket magnanimously surrendered his claim, announcing that henceforth Kissingua should be regarded as the captor of Helm, and he alone should be entitled to sell the prisoner to the British for wampum. Despite considerable disorder, Helm and his soldiers avoided injury, and the Indians were eventually even induced to return some of the goods they had confiscated from the fort.

Vincennes had not been a difficult conquest. Fort Sackville mounted only two guns, and although triangular projections on each side enabled defenders to cover all the walls, it contained only one substantial building. There was no barracks, well, or locks to the gate. Moreover, it was too late in the season to advance on Kaskaskia, and Hamilton busied himself returning the local French to the allegiance of the king and repairing the fort. Nevertheless, the victory had redeemed British arms and raised British prestige among the Indians of the Wabash. It was important to carry the good news eastward, to the villages of the Shawnees and Mingoes, as well as to reconnoiter up the Ohio toward enemy positions in Kentucky. It is significant that Blue Jacket, along with the Indian agent Matthew Elliott, was asked to lead the party charged with those duties.

They set out before the end of the year but ran into difficulties. Near the falls of the Ohio, between the Wabash and the Great Miami, the Americans had built Fort Nelson. Blue Jacket's scouts found so many Kentuckians in the area that his party doubted it could cut its way through to the Shawnee villages. Afraid to continue, they decided to scuttle back to Vincennes. Blue Jacket himself refused to hear of it and completed the journey alone, leaving Elliott to return with the fainthearted. They covered their pusillanimity with a thin story that Blue Jacket had personally directed them to go no further than the falls of the Ohio.[17]

Blue Jacket had proven himself a dependable and enterprising leader on his first campaign with the British, but if he hoped the expedition would strengthen intertribal support for the Shawnees and encourage more Indians to join the war, he was to be disappointed. The Big Knives quickly recouped their position, not only recapturing Vincennes in 1779 but also scooping Hamilton himself into the bag. Word was also spreading that the Americans were gaining European allies, first France and then Spain, awakening memories of the "French Father" for whom some of the Indians had fought twenty or so years before. And close to the Shawnees, a new surge of colonists flooded into Kentucky, partly stimulated by a land law in Virginia. New clearings were being hewn out of the forest and stations erected, some, such as Ruddell's on the south fork of the Licking and those built near Fort Nelson at the falls, close enough to the Ohio to act as springboards for attacks on the Shawnee towns. It was clear that two years of Indian raids had neither dislodged the existing settlements nor stemmed the ambitions of land-hungry emigrants. In 1780 an army of Kentuckians crossed the Ohio and destroyed Chillicothe on the Little Miami and Pekowi and Kispoko Town on the Mad River.

In these circumstances, the Shawnees found that even their existing allies were faltering. Some of the Wyandots continued raiding, but most refused to muster for the British, and some even sent representatives to Pittsburgh to confer with the Americans. The Ottawas, Potawatomis, and Ojibwes of the Detroit region spurned British invitations to attack Fort Laurens on the Tuscarawas River in 1779, and only the Mingoes turned out. Blue Jacket and his fellow Shawnees were not only no nearer their objectives but more isolated than they had been since their defeat at the hands of Dunmore in 1774.[18]

Nor surprisingly, despair set in. Early in 1779 one group of Shawnees under Yellow Hawk and Black Stump abandoned the Ohio. The next year they were reported "on the Cherokee [Tennessee] River between the Cherokee and Chickasaw settlements," but their ultimate destination was the Creek country, in what is now Alabama. Some Shawnee towns were still to be found there.[19]

Neither the Mekoche rump under Hardman, Cornstalk's old following, huddling on the Tuscarawas, trusted by no one, nor the fiery Shawnee warriors of the Miami valleys were finding the paths they had chosen anything but stony.

✳    ✳    ✳

Toward the end of 1779 the outlook for Blue Jacket's embattled people began to improve.

On 5 October spirits rose when the Shawnees and their Indian allies captured an American military convoy on the Ohio, below the mouth of the Little Miami. Some of the Spanish provisions, ammunition, and specie that it was ferrying from the Mississippi to Virginia found its way into the needy Shawnee towns. Much more important, Shawnee appeals for more British assistance in the field, especially to defend their villages, seemed to have been heard. Maj. Arent Schuyler De Peyster, who assumed responsibility for Britain's effort in the West after the capture of Hamilton, got permission to raise some rangers to act with the Indians, and in December and January their commander, William Caldwell, toured the Shawnee towns. Caldwell found the tribe indulging in its usual pan-tribal diplomacy. Two parties of Cherokees were being entertained at Wakatomica, and Wryneck, who had abandoned the neutral Shawnees and rejoined Blue Jacket, said the Wabash tribes had promised to help the Shawnees in the summer. But with the Kentucky settlements creeping ever closer, increasing the dangers to the Shawnee towns, it was more British commitment that the chiefs required.

And they got it. Not only did the Shawnees get pledges of support from Indians on the Great Lakes and the Wabash and Illinois Rivers, but De Peyster declared that as soon as the ice cleared from the rivers he would throw a detachment of soldiers and two fieldpieces against the Kentuckians.[20]

The truth was that the pendulum was swinging against the Americans. On the Ohio the Shawnee strategy of getting the British to help break up the Kentucky settlements was beginning to work, while on the New York frontier, where four of the Iroquois tribes supported the British, the Indians struck back hard in retaliation for a powerful American invasion of their country in 1779. Despite the support of France and Spain, the Americans also manifestly lacked impetus in the West. Bedeviled with credit, supply, and manpower problems, they could not provide their Indian friends with sufficient goods; they evacuated their advanced posts at Fort Laurens and Vincennes; and they aborted their plans to attack Detroit. Regaining the initiative, in 1780 and 1781 the British formed the greatest pan-tribal combination yet seen. The Miamis and Kickapoos of the Wabash and the Potawatomis of the St. Joseph (Michigan) began to participate in the alliance, while in the south Cherokees, Chickasaws, Choctaws, and Creeks also supported the redcoats. Even the "neutral" Shawnees and Delawares, convinced the United States could not protect them, went over to the British in 1781. Once again the Ohio Shawnees were reunited in their battle for Kentucky.[21]

Spring 1780 saw McKee at Pekowi, dispensing supplies and recruiting for the new offensive over the Ohio. About 26 May his party was joined at the forks of the Miami by the Detroit contingent: Capt. Henry Bird, a detachment of whites, and about one hundred local Indians, with a six- and a three-pounder. Other reinforcements dribbled in slowly, until by the middle of June Bird had nearly seven hundred warriors on the Ohio. Most of the Shawnees were there, and Blue Jacket was one of their chiefs.[22]

McKee wanted to strike at Fort Nelson, near the falls of the Ohio, before it could be reinforced, but the Shawnees objected to going so far down the Ohio, leaving their villages exposed to counterthrusts from the Kentuckians on the Licking. They insisted on dealing with those stations first. Bird grumbled at the "ridiculous" delays on the part of the Indians but went along, and in the last week of June the army arrived at Capt. Isaac Ruddell's fort on the south fork of the Licking.

In truth, the Indians contributed little to the victory. Before daylight about two hundred warriors sealed off the station, but surprise was thrown away by a few hasty Indians who fired on a grass-cutting party from the fort. There was a general exchange of fire until noon, when Bird played his ace card. Bringing up his guns to within eighty yards of the fort, he compelled the defenders to surrender. The chiefs had tried to restrain their warriors, protect prisoners, and distribute plunder equally among themselves, but discipline soon broke down. The Lakes Indians poured into the fort to seize as much in the way of prisoners and spoils as they could and thereby precipitated a general scramble. One American was killed, many were hauled away, and animals needed to replenish the army's provisions were wantonly slaughtered. Under entreaty, most of the Shawnees and Mingoes yielded their prisoners to the British, but by no means all. Among captives integrated into the Shawnee towns was a Mrs. Honn, who became a member of Blue Jacket's family.

About two days after the fall of Ruddell's Station the army appeared before Martin's Station, further south, and forced it to capitulate. The same disorder occurred, with painted warriors scrabbling for booty impervious to the directions of chiefs. But although two additional stations, abandoned by the Big Knives, were burned, there the campaign ended. The four hundred prisoners, men, women, and children, exacerbated the shortage of supplies, and many warriors, pleased with what had been achieved, had begun to disperse. Bird was back in Detroit on 4 August. His expedition had been a moderate success but may not have been a cause for celebration. Four years earlier such a blow would have cleared Kentucky. But now, after the settlements had multiplied, it merely stirred within the Kentuckians fear, anger, and the determination to have their revenge.

The war lasted another two and a half years. The Shawnees and their allies continued to scour Kentucky, harassing stations and cutting up forces that ventured outside them, and in June 1782 they defeated a large force of militia from the Wheeling area, which marched against the Wyandots and Delawares of the Sandusky. On that occasion, however, the Shawnees were led by Black Snake rather than Blue Jacket.[23]

With desperate courage the Kentuckians struck back, under leaders such as George Rogers Clark. Chillicothe, Pekowi, and Kispoko Town were destroyed in 1780, and when the Pekowis and Chillicothes built new towns on the Great Miami they too were razed to the ground in November 1782. Throughout all of these campaigns the Shawnees lost relatively few men in battle. Even if we include the members of the tribe who emigrated, Shawnee losses were easily compensated by the numbers of captured whites and a few blacks adopted by Indian families, and in 1781 and 1782 groups of Cherokees under a chief named the Swan also reinforced the Shawnee towns.[24]

But there was no doubt the Shawnees were suffering. The three invasions of their towns, in 1779, 1780, and 1782, ˉost them many possessions, some of their people, and one invaluable harvest, and it forced communities to uproot and rebuild their homes elsewhere. The Shawnee economy was tottering. It was true that the British still shipped goods across Lake Erie from Detroit, sent them up the Maumee to Roche de Bout, and then packed them overland to the Indian settlements, and no less was it true that the plunder brought back from raids helped substitute for the returns of trade and hunting. Nonetheless, the war disrupted hunting, and in addition to supporting their own people the Shawnees were forever provisioning the armed parties of Indian allies and British who passed back and forth through their villages on the business of war. Furthermore, above all the other western allies of the British the Shawnees remained woefully vulnerable to counterattack. They continued to urge the British and the Lakes Indians to redouble efforts to support the front line, and a blockhouse was erected in Wakatomica in 1780. Still, the Shawnees grew so anxious for the security of their noncombatants that they became increasingly reluctant to campaign far from home.

Col. Daniel Brodhead, who commanded the American forces at Pittsburgh, opined in 1780 that the Shawnees were "the most hostile of any savage tribe, and could they receive a severe chastizement it would probably put an end to the Indian war." His judgment was not inappropriate, but the tribe was unable to mount a single major offensive in 1781 or 1782.[25]

An example of the uncertainty paralyzing the Shawnee towns occurred in July 1782, when McKee and Caldwell gathered a force of Shawnees, Delawares, Mingoes, Wyandots, Miamis, Ottawas, Ojibwes, and Potawatomis, as well as rangers, and set off to attack Wheeling on the Ohio. Blue Jacket remained at home with a skeleton force to protect the Shawnee towns, but soon after McKee's force left, runners panted in with news that an army of Kentuckians was advancing with artillery. It was supposedly led by George Rogers Clark, who had invaded the Shawnee country in 1780 and was the most feared of all the Big Knives. There was particular alarm at Standing Stone, the most exposed town, and messengers were sent after McKee to recall him. In the meantime, Blue Jacket made a personal reconnaissance down the Great Miami toward the point of danger.

Six days later, Blue Jacket was back with disconcerting tidings. Clark was indeed on his way! In fact, the chief was mistaken. Clark had prepared some new row-galleys to patrol the Ohio looking for Indian war parties crossing to Kentucky. They were substantial vessels, over seventy feet long, shipping forty-six oars and a few pieces of artillery and capable of transporting one hundred men. Blue Jacket had watched one of these formidable vessels ascending the Ohio above the falls and disembarking some of its men near the mouth of the Licking. This was the place the Big Knives had used as a rendezvous for the previous invasions of the Shawnee country, in 1779 and 1780, and Blue Jacket had jumped to an erroneous conclusion.

The scare aborted the expedition against Wheeling. Caldwell and McKee returned and drew up a thousand men on the Mad River, ready to intercept Clark. When the Big Knives failed to appear, most of the chagrined warriors scattered into the woods to hunt. The campaign had turned into a fiasco, as the Americans learned from an escaped black prisoner of the Shawnees. He turned up at an American settlement in August and explained that he had been two years in Blue Jacket's family, "as much in character of a steward or manager as a servant." It seems that the chief employed him in his business enterprises.[26]

Fortunately for the Shawnees, in this instance something was salvaged. Caldwell took his rangers and three hundred Wyandots and Three Fires into Kentucky. On 19 August they administered a crushing defeat to the

Big Knives at the Blue Licks on the Licking. The battle, with a report that Kincheloe's fort in Jefferson County had also been burned, sent a shock wave through Kentucky. It "cast a gloom over the whole country," wrote one witness, and led many settlers to consider abandoning the frontier for safer parts. Blue Jacket must have felt himself cheated of sharing in the most striking Indian victory yet won on the Ohio.[27]

*    *    *

Then, suddenly, the redcoats stopped fighting. They talked about peace negotiations. Blue Jacket and other war leaders must have realized that they had inflicted considerable damage upon their adversaries. According to Andrew Steele, 860 effective men were killed or captured in Kentucky during the Revolutionary War, and if that figure was accurate, the addition of noncombatants would raise the total losses inflicted to over twelve hundred people. If the war on the Ohio was less effective than the Iroquois assault that rolled back and depleted the New York frontier, it was still one of the most destructive in the history of Indian-white warfare. Truly had the Shawnees and their friends made the settlement of Kentucky dark and bloody.[28]

Nevertheless, the Shawnees had failed, and Indians as astute as Blue Jacket must have known it. The tribe had been forced to retreat further up the Great Miami. Not so the Kentuckians. At the beginning of the war Kentucky's militia barely exceeded one hundred. In 1782 the number of settlements had increased, stolen closer to the Ohio, and contained some thirteen hundred men capable of serving under arms. One conclusion was abundantly clear: the Shawnees had lost the second war for their hunting grounds south of the river.

Unfortunately, that was not all. For the new United States was looking greedily at the Indian country north of the river, and Blue Jacket was about to be thrust into the greatest struggle of his life.

# 5

## Trouble Is Coming upon Us Fast

Blue Jacket may have been shut out of Kentucky, but in other respects he had survived the war relatively unscathed. His town had not been one of the six Shawnee villages torched by Big Knives marauding up the Little and Great Miami Rivers. But would there now be peace?

It was not until May 1783 that the Shawnees and Americans began to talk peace, and a fragile armistice was established through Maj. George Walls of Fort Nelson. Some Mingoes and Cherokees, living about the Shawnee towns, continued to commit occasional depredations, but the Shawnees themselves sat on their tomahawks and waited.

Of course, it did not last. In the treaty of Paris, concluded in September 1783, the British ended the war without making the slightest provision for their Indian allies. Indeed, they conferred sovereignty of the lands south of the Great Lakes and toward the Mississippi upon the United States and agreed to evacuate their western posts, Oswego, Niagara, Detroit, and Michilimackinac — posts from which they had been supplying the Indians. Later, when they had thought about it, the British protested that their agreement did not affect Indian claims to lands north of the Ohio. They said these lands still belonged to the Indians by virtue of the 1768 treaty of Fort Stanwix, and the Crown had merely ceded its own rights to the territory. Even this would not have absolved the British from failing to protect their allies in the treaty of Paris, but in any case the Indians did not see it the same way. Able leaders such as Blue Jacket and the Mohawk Joseph Brant said Britain had no rights in those lands to cede.

The people of the United States also viewed the situation differently from the British. They regarded the lands as the spoils of war and the treaty of Paris as its acknowledgment. Now the wilderness north of the Ohio belonged to the Americans by right of conquest. It could be sold to raise money for a needy government or to reward Revolutionary War veterans. Blue Jacket's people had fought a war to defend their hunting range south of the Ohio; but when the war ended they found the very ground they stood and slept on north of the river was also to be forfeit.

Indian anger soon forced the British to backtrack. Their officials advised the Indians to keep the peace but to remain united and assert their rights, hoping the United States would deal honorably with them. More, as Brant and others began to mobilize the Indians, the British tried to appease them. Sir Frederick Haldimand, governor of Canada, granted tracts of land in Canada to the Mohawks and their adherents, and the Crown eventually indemnified that tribe for its losses during the war. Haldimand also delayed evacuating the western posts, which continued to issue presents. Indian goodwill was still considered essential to the security of Canada, weakly defended as it was, and it ensured the health of the fur trade. So Lord Sydney, Britain's home secretary, authorized the retention of the posts, using the failure of the United States to live up to all its treaty obligations as justification. For the time being, the flags flying over those garrisons proclaimed to the Indians that the king had not entirely abandoned his native allies.[1]

Brant, whose sister had been a mistress to Sir William Johnson and who had gained a basic English education at the hands of missionaries, took the lead in organizing the Indian voice. He had been an important instrument of the intertribal confederacy brought into being by the British during the war and found no difficulty in putting himself at the head of a new union. The most ambitious pan-tribal confederacy yet put together by the Indians themselves began at a "congress" of tribes hosted by the Wyandots at Lower Sandusky in August and September 1783. Representatives of the Iroquois, Delawares, Wyandots, Three Fires, and a few Cherokees and Creeks were there, and a Shawnee deputation was led by Wryneck.

The confederacy committed itself to preserving the Ohio as a boundary between Indians and whites, as defined by the treaty of Fort Stanwix in 1768. Wryneck and his Shawnees did not dissent. They knew that Kentucky was gone.

But they agreed wholeheartedly when Brant declared that henceforth no business should be transacted except by the whole confederacy. There must be no more of one group of Indians selling the ground of another. Everyone had to be consulted if a sale was to be regarded as valid. "We, the Six Nations, with this belt bind your hearts and minds with ours," Brant said, "that there may be never hereafter separation between us. Let there be peace or war, it shall never disunite us, for our interests are alike. Nor should anything ever be done but by the voice of the whole, as we make but one with you."[2]

The Iroquois threw in another binding doctrine: the view that the land was the common property of all Indians. Tracts were not the exclusive property of those Indians who happened to reside on them or who hunted and fished in them. This was not, as some authors have stated, a general principle of Indian land tenure in the Great Lakes region. For Indians normally acknowledged the premier rights of existing occupants. Thus the Moravian Indians settled Ohio by permission of the Wyandots, and when the Shawnees and Delawares moved into the Wabash basin in the 1780s and 1790s they sought the consent of its owners, the Miamis. It seems that the notion that the land was held in common by all was a purely political construct of the pan-Indian movement. It was devised to ensure that no group of Indians could sell land without the authority of the entire confederacy.[3]

Blue Jacket's people knew all about Indians selling their lands. The Iroquois had done it in 1768. They also knew that the country north of the Ohio was in danger of being invaded by the Big Knives. For them the principles enunciated by Brant, that the lands were owned by all Indians, that they could not be sold except by the consent of all, and that the defense of the land was the responsibility of all, made obvious sense. Experienced in pan-tribal diplomacy for nearly forty ears, they eagerly embraced the new confederacy, and the next year their emissaries were in the South again, drumming up support for it among the Creeks and the Chickamauga Cherokees.[4]

We must assume that as a leading war chief Blue Jacket was party to this new round of Shawnee diplomacy. Since the war had ended, the principal authority in the Shawnee towns had returned to the civil chiefs, especially the Mekoches, who were responsible for conducting the tribe's negotiations. Hardman was dead, and the position of head civil chief of the Shawnees was filled by old Moluntha. Until his death in 1784, Wryneck, a Pekowi, seems to have been regarded as the premier war chief. But Blue Jacket was advancing to the fore, and even the British advertised the valuable service he had given them during the war. In 1784 Blue Jacket got a testimonial from them, under the signature of Sir John Johnson, the superintendent general of Indian affairs in Canada. Evidently it was little more than a letter of introduction, enjoining British officers to respect the bearer "as a soldier," but Blue Jacket was proud of it. Eleven years later he would be flourishing it "to show that he was a great man."[5]

Blue Jacket and the other Shawnees were true to the new confederacy. When Virginia's Indian commissioners tried to bring them to a meeting with Walls at the falls of Ohio in the spring of 1784, Moluntha and his Mekoches replied with dignity, promising to adhere to the peace and explaining that they would refer the American speeches to the full confederacy.[6]

Unfortunately, others buckled more easily. When U.S. federal commissioners treated with the Iroquois at Fort Stanwix in October 1784, they told them, "You are mistaken in supposing that . . . you are become a free and independent nation. . . . You are a subdued people." The commissioners demanded that the Iroquois nations cede all their claims to land west of the states of Pennsylvania and New York. If the shrewd and articulate Brant, versed in wrangling with white officials, had been there the result might have been different, but he was busy shifting his people to the Grand River in Canada. At Fort Stanwix the Iroquois not only capitulated to the demands of the federal commissioners but also allowed a commissioner for Pennsylvania to persuade them to part with most of their territory in that state.[7]

In January 1785 the same tactics were applied to the Wyandots and Delawares of the Sandusky, and to some Ottawas and Ojibwes, at negotiations at Fort McIntosh on the Ohio. They met with equal success, for the Indians agreed to surrender an enormous tract, what is now southern and eastern Ohio. Yet again, when the federal commissioners had concluded their business, Pennsylvania extinguished Indian rights in the state. To the Shawnees this was a particularly wounding betrayal because it had been these same Wyandots and Delawares who had hosted the intertribal congress in 1783 and promised to stand against further land cessions. Now they had secured their principal villages in northern Ohio but ceded the country occupied by the Shawnees. Blue Jacket's Town, Mackachack,

Wakatomica, the new towns of Pekowi and Kispoko established after the destruction of their earlier villages in the war, a mixed Wyandot-Mingo town, and possibly also Buckongahelas's Town, all lay in the northern part of the ceded area. Of the Shawnees' important settlements, only new Chillicothe on the St. Marys might have been on the Indian side of the boundary described by the "treaty" of Fort McIntosh.

The Shawnees were furious. They complained to Alexander McKee that the Wyandots and their friends had sold "the whole Shawanese country" and "themselves with it." Ominously they asked McKee to return some war belts and pipes they had deposited with him. "You now see trouble coming upon us fast," they explained. "We think it nigh at hand." After only two years of a truce, they were preparing to fight again.[8]

Blue Jacket was probably at the council held at Wakatomica on 18 May 1785, in which the Shawnees and their closest allies, Buckongahelas's Delawares, the Mingoes, and the Ohio Cherokees, reaffirmed the principles of Brant's confederacy: "The people of one color are united, so that we make but one man that has but one heart and one mind." They warned the Americans, through James Sherlock and other messengers from Kentucky, that "you are coming upon the ground given to us by the Great Spirit." The land north of the Ohio was sacred and could not be surrendered by the Shawnees. Intruders should beware because the nations of the whole confederacy "shall take up a rod and whip them back to your side of the Ohio." The Shawnees would hold no talks with the Big Knives, except under British auspices at Detroit, where the Indians would not be intimidated by American muskets.[9]

Bravely, if forlornly, the Shawnees kept faith with what had been solemnly agreed and done on the Sandusky almost two years before.

*   *   *

In January 1786 some 230 Shawnee men and women, most of them Mekoches, made their way slowly down the Great Miami. Their leaders were Moluntha, head chief of the tribe; Kekewepelethy (Great or Tame Hawk), known as Captain Johnny, and Aweecony, both prestigious war chiefs; Nianimsica; Wapachcawela; Red Pole, a relative of Blue Jacket; Nihipeewa; Nehinissica, one of the most respected of the younger chiefs; and Cawechile, the senior female civil chief. They traveled with heavy hearts, because they were going at last to treat with the American commissioners, at Fort Finney, a square stockade the Big Knives had thrown up at the mouth of the Great Miami.

They were doing it without the endorsement or support of the Indian confederacy, doing, in fact, what the Wyandots and Delwareas of the Sandusky had done. And yet this was the same Captain Johnny who had declared before Shawnee, Mingo, Delaware, Cherokee, and Wyandot listeners at Wakatomica only two months before that "one or two nations . . . cannot do anything without the whole [of the confederates] were there present." But here they were, on their way to see Richard Butler, Samuel Parsons, and their old enemy, George Rogers Clark.[10]

They had tried to hold out. The commissioners had summoned the Shawnees to Fort Finney the previous September, but representatives of the tribe had already called on the Iroquois near Niagara and heard Brant and Sayenqueraghta denounce the Fort Stanwix proceedings, proclaim them invalid, and declare they would lay Indian grievances before the American Congress. In September, after learning of the upcoming negotiations at Fort Finney, the Shawnees had invited Delawares, Cherokees, Wyandots, Potawatomis, Kickapoos, and Miamis to talks in Mackachack, and they had told the American messengers sent to them that they would attend a treaty only in the presence of all the tribes. They had no wish to negotiate at Fort Finney but hoped to organize a general meeting at Detroit. Complained Black Snake, "This is not the way to make a good or lasting peace, to take our chiefs prisoners [hostages], and come with soldiers at your backs."[11]

Yet the Shawnees had finally been forced to go to Fort Finney. Some of their warriors, visiting the fort, reported that other Indians were coming in, including the ubiquitous Wyandots and Delawares from the Sandusky, and Moluntha and his chiefs may have worried that whatever the Shawnees did, the Americans would find some signatories to a treaty. Nor were the Big Knives tolerating any prevarication. They summoned the Shawnees twice and then told them that the treaty would close unless the tribe arrived. The Shawnees were told they must choose now between peace and war. Moluntha remembered how the Shawnees had been isolated in 1774, and he dared not risk it. With most of his Mekoches he reached the fort on 15 January. They put a bold face on it, performing a traditional peace ceremony, but the hostility many of the warriors felt for the Big Knives and the treaty was plain enough.

When the event got under way on 26 January the commissioners adopted the same belligerent stance that had wrought the earlier treaties. The Shawnees had been defeated, and their British friends had ceded their lands to the United States. To avoid punishment, the tribe must cooperate and accept such boundaries as the Americans chose to give them.

"We do not understand measuring out the lands," replied Captain Johnny, the principal Shawnee speaker. "It is *all* ours!" The few trade goods the Americans were now offering should be given to "other nations." The Shawnees wanted peace and would surrender any white prisoners they had, but they would neither give hostages nor cede territory.

Momentarily the commissioners were disconcerted, but they soon struck back fiercely. If the Shawnees refused the terms, there would be war. "We plainly tell you that this country belongs to the United States. Their blood hath defended it, and will forever protect it." By some accounts the commissioners swept the Indian wampum from the table, trampled it underfoot, and abruptly terminated the council.

It was enough. The Shawnee chiefs capitulated, to the fury of some of the warriors, a few of whom quit the council in disgust. Six hostages were surrendered, and on 31 January marks were put to a treaty relinquishing almost the entire tribal homeland in southern and eastern Ohio. Moluntha, Captain Johnny, and Red Pole were among those who put their marks to the paper.[12]

The Mekoches were supposed to speak for the nation, but too often they had been traduced for giving way to the Big Knives, and so they were again. About 318 Shawnees eventually attended the treaty, about a third of the Ohio Shawnees and probably most of the Mekoches. They had not been authorized to sell the Shawnee country, country that had been given them by the Great Spirit, country the Shawnees could surrender only at the cost of Waashaa Monetoo's already wavering favor. Not only that, but the treaty flatly contravened the principles agreed on by the Shawnees and other Indians, that no land could be sold without the consent of all the tribes.

It was not surprising that most Shawnees disavowed the treaty. Old Moluntha's stock declined, while Captain Johnny, who had stood up to the commissioners, enjoyed greater prestige. Four years later, in an intertribal council, the great Ottawa Egushaway recalled that

> the commissioners of the United States came, as though to frighten our relations, and repeated to them the old stories that they had conquered all his children of every nation, and all our lands within the limits or bounds I have already mentioned; and they required the Shawanese nation to sign an acknowledgement thereof, and to give

hostages. What answer did the Shawanese give to this? Listen, whilst I repeat it to you! That man *there* before you, with the great plume on his head [Captain Johnny]. Look at him! He it was who spoke like a man in behalf of his whole nation, and on behalf of all nations here present.[13]

Moluntha was by no means blind to such reasoning. Three months after the humiliating treaty he joined the Shade and Red Pole in an appeal for British help: "We never have been in more need of your friendship and good offices. We have been cheated by the Americans, who are still striving to work our destruction, and without your assistance they may be able to accomplish their ends." But he clung to a thread of hope that peace might be preserved and was frustrated at his inability to lead his nation into a better relationship with the United States.[14]

The Shawnees may have been a small and relatively weak people, but they had not been defeated, and there was little likelihood of such a clumsy instrument as the treaty of Fort Finney being accepted. They promised to restore white prisoners, but few were returned, and the six warriors taken as hostages soon found ways to escape and return to their people. By June 1786 Moluntha, like Cornstalk before him, had failed to make a bridge between the Shawnees and the Big Knives. In a message sent to Fort Finney he admitted that

the nation is divided; that the people of Chillicothe will not hear reason. They will not give the prisoners up. In fact . . . a party of them are as much inclined for war as anything else. . . . They are fully of the opinion that their king [head civil chief] and sachems [chiefs] have sold both land and warriors, and are determined not to agree to what has been done. Molunthy gives us information of four men being killed by the Mingoes on the waters of the Muskingum. He says that he advised the Mingoes and Cherokees to be quiet, but they would not hear him. He desires us to have patience. He is striving all he can to fulfill the promises made to our chiefs [commissioners] at the council fire.[15]

If the treaty of Fort Finney had seized the land, it had been done at the expense of the peace.

*     *     *

There is a story that Blue Jacket was there when the treaty of Fort Finney was being negotiated. He was intrigued to learn that one of the

American commissioners was George Rogers Clark, who had burned the Shawnee towns in 1780 and 1782. Never having seen this famous adversary but respecting him as a fellow warrior, Blue Jacket approached the American officials. As if by instinct, he went straight to Clark and confidently observed, "This is the man!"[16]

Several unverified stories about Blue Jacket have been told, and this is one of them. No firm evidence of the chief's presence at the treaty has been found, and since he did not sign it, one suspects that he was not there and trusted to Red Pole and others for his information about what had transpired. Whatever Blue Jacket thought of the treaty, he was quick to take advantage of it. On 23 April the chief appeared at Fort Finney with his son Jim and conferred with the post commandant, Walter Finney. The Shawnees were well disposed to Americans, he said disingenuously, and if any Indians planned to attack the post he himself would give it timely warning. Of course, Blue Jacket wanted something. He said that Shawnee hunters would be in the woods about the fort during the summer, and he sought permission for them to come in and trade. Finney was happy to comply, and Blue Jacket was so pleased with his reception that he left Jim at the fort when he departed the next morning. The chief was soon spreading the word, and Shawnees were shortly arriving with their peltries. Jim left with one such party on 26 April, but within a month Shawnee hunters were bartering at the post on a daily basis.[17]

Such fraternization seemed to confirm that the United States had miraculously seized the lands north of the Ohio without bloodshed. The United States had created its first regular regiment of infantry to protect the frontier in 1784, but for a while it was little more than witness to an astonishing flood of white settlers heading west. Encouraged by the treaties, they swarmed down the Ohio, buying flatboats on the Monongahela or at Pittsburgh, and piloting them downstream for Kentucky. Josiah Harmar, who commanded the troops from Fort Harmar at the mouth of the Muskingum, reported that 631 boats with 12,205 people passed the garrison between 10 October 1786 and 15 June 1787. "The emigration is almost incredible," he said. Other pioneers made their way to Kentucky overland, along the Wilderness Road through Cumberland Gap, and surveyors and squatters were even venturing on the new lands north of the Ohio.[18]

Behind this optimism a new storm was rumbling, however. The Shawnees were thinking of war. Hitherto, the few raids being made into Kentucky or along the Kanawha had been perpetrated by Mingoes or a band of Cherokees living on Paint Creek, but now Shawnees began to join them, and their chiefs appealed to the other tribes to fight alongside. The Wyandots and Delawares of the Sandusky failed to respond, but in the summer several hundred Lakes Indians — Potawatomis, Ojibwes, and Ottawas — were in the Shawnee towns ready for war.[19]

Belts from the Shawnees and Buckongahelas's Delawares also reached the Wabash Indians, urging them "to destroy all the men wearing hats . . . who seem to be leagued against us to drive us away from the lands which the Master of Life has given us."[20] And not without effect. On 13 July an estimated 450 warriors "of different nations and tribes" even menaced Vincennes, aggrieved at the murder of an Indian by one of the Americans residing at the place. French leaders managed to get the Indians to disperse, while the American population sheltered in the fort, but the situation remained tense. One participant later named Blue Jacket as one of the chiefs, but the Indians seem to have been Wabash Miamis, Weas, Piankeshaws, and Kickapoos rather than Shawnees, and the identification is doubtful. Nevertheless, the Shawnee belts had probably helped feed the unrest.[21]

Even at that hour the war might have been stalled by Brant. He had been to England, lobbying for military support for the Indian confederacy. He had been fobbed off with blandishments that the king would continue to look to Indian welfare, little enough to carry home, but when Brant returned his was no counsel of despair. He did not want a war he doubted the Indians could win, but he believed a united front on the part of the tribes might force the United States to negotiate. He wanted to restrain the angry Shawnees while he got up another intertribal congress at their villages to make a joint resolution to the American government.

But early in October eight hundred Kentuckians under Benjamin Logan struck the first major blow, marching up the Great Miami as of old and falling upon Mackachack, on a tributary of the Mad River. Mackachack, as its name implied, was the principal town of the Mekoches, and here it was that Moluntha kept his residence. If there was one Shawnee division that had stood for compromise, it was the Mekoche, and if any chief had committed himself to peace, it was Moluntha. Now the Kentuckians charged in. The Indians tried to raise an American flag, but it was ignored. About a dozen warriors were killed, and some thirty women and children, including Moluntha's wife, the tribal female chief, were herded together as prisoners. Old Moluntha was also seized. He saw the ruin of his policy, but he had been a warrior in his time, and he was not going to show fear now. Col. Hugh McGary asked him if he had been at the battle of Blue Licks four years earlier. Moluntha had not been there, but he misunderstood the question and seemed to indicate otherwise. McGary, a hotheaded soldier whose irresponsibility had been a cause of that defeat, angrily felled the old chief with a hatchet and, as he tried to regain his feet, killed him with a second blow and scalped him. History had repeated itself. Moluntha, like Cornstalk, had pleaded for tolerance, and like Cornstalk, he had earned his reward.[22]

After looting Mackachack, the Kentuckians spread out, raiding the nearby Shawnee villages, burning and plundering. At none did they encounter any appreciable resistance, for the warriors had been scattered in their fall hunting camps and could not gather in time. Wakatomica, Pekowi, McKee's Town, and Blue Jacket's Town were destroyed, and when Logan withdrew it was estimated that twelve thousand bushels of harvested corn had been burned.

Some historians have blamed Indian raids for the resumption of warfare, but they have missed the context of the relationship that had developed between the Shawnees and the United States. A contemporary, William North, drew a fairer conclusion. "We . . . are taking their land from them," he wrote in the summer of 1786. "This they neither could nor would understand. The lands may be bought, but they will not be given to us." North was equally frank about the savagery of the campaign and its roots in the bitter feud that had developed between the Virginians and Kentuckians on one side and the Shawnees and Mingoes on the other, a feud in which memories of slaughtered friends and family fed atrocities on both sides. "The people under [George Rogers] Clark are back woodsmen," said North, "as much savages as those they are to fight against. An immortal hatred subsists in the heart of the one against the other, and whenever a Virginian back woods man meets an Indian he will kill or be killed."[23]

# The War for Ohio

Blue Jacket seems to have been one of the first to hit back after Logan's raid. His action may have been prompted by the Indian custom of taking revenge for injuries suffered or by a need for prisoners to exchange for the Indians carried off into captivity by Logan's army.

About October 1786 Blue Jacket is said to have led a raid on the small settlement of Drinnon's Lick in Kentucky. Only three men were living there, and one was out hunting when the Indians arrived. Blue Jacket was approaching the open gate with some warriors when they saw one of the remaining inmates, an Irishman named Jerry Hays, carrying a bucket to a stream. Hays flung himself at the gate to shut it, but the Indians forced their way through before it could be fastened and seized the unfortunate Irishman. His companion, Monroe, was slain as he tried to escape over the roof.

For a while the fate of Hays was in doubt, but Blue Jacket refused to allow the warriors to kill him. He said the prisoner was needed to carry some of the plunder, including a kettle, back to the Shawnee villages. Evidently none of the captors had an unambiguous claim on the prisoner, but once he had been brought back Blue Jacket's wife bought him for twenty gallons of rum. Renamed Little Horse, Hays survived to return to his own people, perhaps the following year. He was one of several who bore witness to Blue Jacket's kindness. The chief had many faults. He was acquisitive, certainly, and vain and ambitious, and he occasionally drank too much. But he was neither vindictive nor inhumane, and people of all races usually liked him. Rachel Reno, a black woman born in one of his towns, recalled simply that Blue Jacket "was a good Indian."[1]

During the ensuing months Blue Jacket's attention would have been absorbed by salvaging what he could from his ruined village, helping prepare his people for the winter, hunting, and interesting himself in the new intertribal congress that was being organized. Brant had planned to hold it in the Shawnee country, but that was now out of the question. The "council fire" was then moved to Brownstown, a Wyandot village at the mouth of the Detroit River, where it was afforded some security by the nearby British post at Detroit. Overcoming the difficulties of traversing a country now ravaged by war, Shawnees, Wabash Indians (such as the Miamis), Delawares, Ojibwes, Ottawas, Potawatomis, Mingoes, and nearly sixty Iroquois deputies assembled in November and December to reaffirm their alleigance to the confederacy and to repudiate the "conquest" treaties. Aware of the fragility of that unity, Brant spoke powerfully of its utility:

> Take but a cursory view of that large tract of country between our present habitations and the salt water . . . and consider the reason why it is not still inhabited by our own color. . . . We were the lords of the soil. The Great Spirit placed us there. And what is the reason why we are still not in possession of our forefathers' birthrights? You may safely say because they wanted that unanimity which we now so strongly and repeatedly recommend to you. . . .
>
> Therefore, let us profit by these things and be unanimous. . . . If, after that, the Great Spirit wills that other colors should subdue us, let it be so. We cannot reproach ourselves for misconduct. . . . If we make a war with any nation, let it result from the great council fire. If we make peace, let it also proceed from our unanimous councils. But whilst we remain disunited, every inconvenience attends us. The interests of any one nation should be the interests of us all. The welfare of the one should be the welfare of all the others.

In its address to the American government, dated 18 December, the congress explained that "when a division of territory is agreed to by some particular nations without the concurrence of the whole of our confederacy, we look upon it as illegal and of no effect." Consequently, the treaties of Forts Stanwix, McIntosh, and Finney were invalid, and it was necessary for the United States to renegotiate with the entire Indian union.[2]

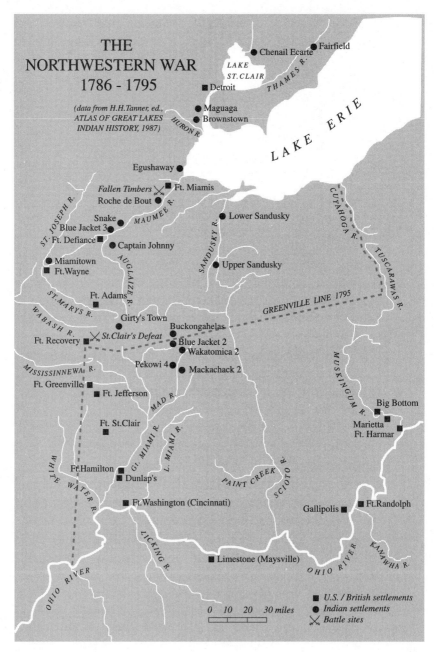

THE
NORTHWESTERN WAR
1786 - 1795

*(data from H.H.Tanner, ed.,*
*ATLAS OF GREAT LAKES*
*INDIAN HISTORY, 1987)*

LAKE
ST. CLAIR

● Chenail Ecarte    ● Fairfield

THAMES R.

■ Detroit

LAKE ERIE

HURON R.

● Maguaga
● Brownstown

Egushaway ●

CUYAHOGA R.

*Fallen Timbers* ✕ ■ Ft. Miamis
Roche de Bout ●

Snake ●          MAUMEE R.          ● Lower Sandusky
Blue Jacket 3 ●
ST. Ft. Defiance ■

ST. JOSEPH R.

SANDUSKY R.

TUSCARAWAS R.

■ Ft. Defiance    ● Captain Johnny

● Miamitown
■ Ft.Wayne

AUGLAIZE R.

● Upper Sandusky

ST.MARYS R.

■ Ft. Adams

GREENVILLE LINE 1795

WABASH R.

● Girty's Town
✕ *St.Clair's Defeat*          Buckongahelas ●
Ft. Recovery ■                  ● Blue Jacket 2
                                ● Wakatomica 2
                    Pekowi 4 ●
MISSISSINNEWA R.              ● Mackachack 2

MUSKINGUM R.

■ Ft. Greenville
        ■ Ft. Jefferson

MAD R.

                                                    ● Big Bottom
                                                    ■ Marietta
■ Ft. St.Clair                                      Ft. Harmar

Gt. MIAMI R.

L. MIAMI R.

WHITE WATER R.

■ Ft.Hamilton
    ■ Dunlap's

PAINT CREEK R.

SCIOTO R.

■ Ft.Washington (Cincinnati)

● Gallipolis ■    ■ Ft.Randolph

LICKING R.

KANAWHA R.

■ Limestone (Maysville)

OHIO RIVER

OHIO RIVER

0    10    20    30 miles

■ *U.S. / British settlements*
● *Indian settlements*
✕ *Battle sites*

*Map 2*

The Iroquois insistence that talking, rather than fighting, offered the best way forward may have seemed optimistic to the embattled Shawnees, but it was not entirely without effect. The American determination to settle Ohio was underscored by the Northwest Ordinance of 1787 and the creation of the Northwest Territory, but the United States government had too little money to embroil itself wantonly in a full-blown Indian war, particularly one with an extensive confederacy of tribes.

In October 1787 Arthur St. Clair, the first governor of the Northwest Territory, was authorized to renegotiate the disputed treaties. He was given $26,000 to confirm them. St. Clair was not permitted to give ground; in fact, he was to secure more land if an opportunity to do so presented itself. But the principle of "conquest" was to be abandoned, and henceforth land was to be obtained by purchase.

Still, Iroquois diplomacy moved slowly, and Blue Jacket and the Shawnees had serious practical problems to confront. Their provisions had been wasted by Logan's soldiers, and in the spring the uprooted Indians needed to build new, more secure homes. And not merely those whose villages had been burned, for Logan's expedition and the imminence of war meant that the headwaters of the Great Miami were no longer safe. The entire complex of communities there, Mingo, Delaware, and Shawnee, had to move.

The British helped a little. They were not going to fight alongside the Indians or encourage any hostilities that might involve Britain in a conflict with the United States, but they wanted the goodwill of the tribes. The redcoats could be relied on for some basic provisions, and Lord Sydney, the British home secretary, even sanctioned the issue of ammunition to give the Indians the means of defending themselves from attack.[3]

More important to the refugees was the hospitality of other Indians, in this instance the Miamis, who commanded much of the Wabash country. They offered asylum to the retreating militants of the Great Miami. From 1787 most of the Shawnees moved to the Maumee, close to the British supply line which ran up that river and near or among their Miami allies. By 1789 Captain Johnny, who was emerging as the tribal civil chief, had a town on the Auglaize River, just above its junction with the Maumee at a place known as the Glaize. Blue Jacket, Buckongahelas, and most of the other refugees made for the headwaters of the Maumee. There two streams, the St. Joseph and the St. Marys, met to form the Maumee, and there stood two important Miami towns that welcomed the newcomers.

One of the Miami towns, Kekionga, was situated on the west bank of the St. Joseph, at its junction with the St. Marys. Its leading chief was Pacanne, whom Blue Jacket knew from the days they had spent together with Henry Hamilton. The other was Miamitown, under another of Blue Jacket's old associates, Le Gris, and occupied the left bank of the St. Joseph in the fork that river made with the Maumee. It was in Miamitown that Blue Jacket built at least one residence, by the riverside. Here he was in a position to represent the Shawnees and concert policy with the Miami chiefs.

Other Shawnees built their own villages, at least one, under Black Snake, above Miamitown, and one or two below, headed respectively by Blackbird and the Wolf. Close to Blackbird's town, which was yet another Chillicothe, the allied Delawares put their village. The Miamis were themselves important and independent warriors, deeply distrustful of the United States, and they had had no truck with the "conquest" treaties. This influx of Shawnees, Mingoes, and Delawares, the core of the resistance to American expansion north of the Ohio, turned the Miami complex into the hub of Indian affairs for the next few years.[4]

A priority for Blue Jacket, of course, was the resumption of his business enterprises. We know he was successful because he was described in 1788 as "a Shawnese chief of considerable note and property," and a white prisoner who saw his home the same year described "a fine plantation, well stocked with cattle." In Miamitown Blue Jacket mixed with numerous traders operating out of Detroit, including the French Lasselles, the Adhemars, John Kinzie, the Rivards, George Ironside, and David Gray. Like them, he acted as a middleman between the rich Canadian merchants and the Indian hunters. The Indians supplied him with pelts and skins, which he exchanged for European manufactures he had obtained from the merchants.[5]

One who remembered this aspect of Blue Jacket's activities was Jacob Hubbs. Captured by the chief on some raid about 1786, Hubbs seems to have learned to respect Blue Jacket. The chief spared Hubbs abuse and put him to work in his store as a clerk. He even trusted him to make trips to Detroit to buy goods for resale in the Indian towns. On one of these visits Hubbs escaped, persuading someone to hide him in the town, but he boasted that he left with nothing that belonged to Blue Jacket.[6]

One reason why Blue Jacket and other Shawnee war chiefs muted their response to Logan's invasion and launched no major counteroffensive was the imprisonment of Logan's captives in Kentucky. Those prisoners included a Frenchman, a white woman who refused to leave the

Indians, the widow of Moluntha, and two boys who would later serve the Shawnees as English interpreters under the names Peter Cornstalk and James Logan. Negotiations for their exchange had begun as early as December 1786, but it was not until the following spring that Captain Johnny got the process thoroughly under way, using Daniel Boone, who then ran a store and inn in Limestone on the Ohio, as an intermediary.

In August 1787 talks reached a climax when fifty-five Shawnees under Captain Johnny arrived at Limestone to treat with Kentuckians represented by Logan, Boone, John Crow, and Isaac Ruddell. The Indians failed to bring enough white prisoners to surrender, many belonging to warriors who refused to give them up and some simply preferring the native life themselves. Nevertheless, Captain Johnny got all but ten of the Shawnee hostages released and cloaked the proceedings in a show of amity. Several other chiefs were present, including Black Snake, Wolf, Nianimsica, Lathensica, Pemenacawah, and Blue Jacket. Blue Jacket took advantage of the truce to take a son of Boone's hunting north of the Ohio.[7]

Yet fine and friendly speeches on both sides did not make the Limestone exchange more than an interlude in a cruel conflict. Black Snake (Peteasua), a tall, thin, but bighearted war chief, a militant of long standing, was at Limestone, but the spring of 1788 saw him with Blackbeard and a large war party of Shawnees, Cherokees, and Mingoes plundering flatboats on the Ohio. About the same time Blue Jacket raided into Kentucky.

In May 1788 Blue Jacket's party ran off some horses from Strode's Station on a fork of the Licking River. They retreated through rain and high wind toward the Ohio, and near Cabin Creek, above Limestone, Blue Jacket and one or two companions dried themselves by a tree stump they had set on fire and watched the back trail. Suddenly a pursuing posse swept toward them. As the whites advanced, shots were fired, but the damp powder prevented most from igniting. Blue Jacket scrambled down the high bank of the creek and then up a rise but then found himself being headed off by horsemen under one Andrew Hood. For a while the chief dodged about the trees, looking for an escape, but finally he realized it was hopeless. He threw his musket away and strode toward the Big Knives to surrender.

He was treated abominably. One Kentuckian struck Blue Jacket violently on the forehead, whether with a gun barrel or a hand is uncertain, and "raised a great lump as big as your fist. They knocked six rings out of his ear, which I picked up and kept," said a witness. A number of armbands were taken from the chief, and it was said that guns were fired at him, although they flashed in the pan without discharging. There was a brief discussion about whether the prisoner should be killed outright. Blue Jacket protested that he had only been taking horses and that no one had been killed on the raid, but sentiment was still strong against him. But Blue Jacket was in luck. No one fancied committing the deed in cold blood. Instead, the Kentuckians decided to take their prisoner into Limestone.

Here was hope, for Blue Jacket knew Daniel Boone, who lived in Limestone. He told his captors that he had taken Boone's son hunting and that Boone had once given him meat and tobacco. After eating, the chief was set on a horse and told to pilot the posse to the town. Christopher Wood remembered seeing the chief come in. He struck "a most singular appearance," with a ravenskin cap and spread wings upon his head. The party fell to carousing in Boone's tavern, drinking throughout the night, an activity in which Blue Jacket heartily participated, imbibing long drafts of whiskey. Before long the men were in a drunken stupor. John Hanks, who put up in another house, visited Boone's during the night and found the Shawnee war chief sprawled across Frank Jones of Cross Plains.

In the morning the captive was prepared for another journey. He wanted to carry his empty musket and appear as a warrior but instead was pinioned with a backpack strap. One witness recalled that Jimmy Bath "tied him . . . did it pretty roughly too. . . . B[ath] put the string round his neck, so that he couldn't get it over his head, and then tied a knot, and then jerked his arms back as far as he could and tied them above his elbow." According to a son of one of the party, some of the barely sober Kentuckians fired powder from their muskets at the helpless prisoner.

The halt for the second night was made at Robert Scouse's cabin, just below Bourbon in Kentucky. The place had only one small room, but Blue Jacket was placed inside, tied hand and foot and hobbled by a log chain. Those whites who could not share the hut bedded out beneath the stars, while those inside took turns to stay awake on guard. Old Stephen Riley, it was said, had been drinking. True or not, when his turn for sentry duty came, just before daylight, he was too weary to keep his eyes open. Blue Jacket, alert as a fox, saw his opportunity. He slipped the log chain, somehow freed his feet, and stole outside. But then Mrs. Scouse saw him and raised the alarm. The Shawnee chief bounded into the woods, while Scouse loosed his dogs and the men fell to their weapons to chase after him.

Blue Jacket had been more than forty years in this wilderness, and there was no catching him. He crossed a bear's trail, which threw off the dogs, and stripped off one of his woolen leggings to throw on a bush, probably to suggest a false trail. Various rumors of his escape reached the chastened backcountry men. Wood heard that Blue Jacket survived fourteen days on leaves and herbs, unable to free his hands, but stole a horse from Stockton's Station, near Flemingsburg (Fleming County), and used it to get home. Another participant said the chief reached the Indian towns with his clothing torn away and his body lacerated by bushes. Nonetheless, he escaped, and the captors had to content themselves with auctioning Blue Jacket's horse and gun.[8]

It was a close call for the Shawnee war chief but by no means his first. During his brief captivity it was noticed that Blue Jacket had a scar on his neck, and it was understood that he had been shot by a courageous pioneer woman during an Indian raid on her home on the Clinch or Nolichucky Rivers in what is now Tennessee.[9]

Blue Jacket's escape probably enhanced his reputation among the Indians, writing a dramatic finish to what had in fact been a rather disappointing raid. And there must have been other, more successful, forays, for the chief advanced in reputation. Some of his rivals, such as Black Snake, had their triumphs too, but by 1790 it was Blue Jacket, not they, who had become the premier war chief of the nation.

His elevation occurred at a critical time, for the prospects of the tribe, which had seemed to stabilize for a while, suddenly clouded. The hopes Brant and others had pinned on a renegotiation of the treaties crumbled, and the Indian confederacy fell with them.

\*    \*    \*

Blue Jacket and other Shawnee chiefs had been among the most fervent promoters of Brant's vision of unity, and their diplomats had added their voice to Iroquois embassies. In June 1787 a delegation of Shawnees, Iroquois, and Wyandots were in the South, at a Cherokee town on the Mobile River. They then divided, some to tour the Choctaw and Chickasaw settlements and others the Cherokee towns, before they reformed at Tuckabatchee, a Creek town in what later became Alabama.[10]

Yet while efforts were being made to extend the confederacy to the south, allies were falling away in the North. Between 1785 and 1789 the Iroquois of New York and western Pennsylvania ceded much of their territory to the United States, retaining only miserable reservations.

With the white frontier closing in around them, the vulnerable Iroquois grasped at such promises the Americans were prepared to make that their remaining land would be spared. Their support for the confederacy evaporated, and Brant, whose Canadian Iroquois held firm, angrily declared that they had "sold themselves to the devil." Once the dominant force in intertribal affairs, the Iroquois had been broken and intimidated. The battle was now moving west, leaving them behind.[11]

Worse, when the United States got around to renegotiating the conquest treaties it turned into a fiasco. Brant wanted the confederates to go to the council fire with an agreed position, but there was no agreement. Brant, supported by the Three Fires and the Sandusky Indians, favored a compromise boundary line along the Muskingum River. That would have meant the Indians relinquishing the land north of the Ohio and east of the Muskingum, but that ground was already well on its way to being settled by the whites. The territory north of the Ohio and west of the Muskingum, including the Shawnee country, would have remained in Indian hands. Unfortunately, even that compromise was too much for the Shawnees and some of their militant allies to swallow. They wanted the Ohio boundary, exactly as it had been established in 1768.

When Governor Arthur St. Clair convened the treaty council fire at Fort Harmar, instead of on a neutral site, Brant despaired and advised the Indians to boycott the entire proceeding. Most Indians did but not all of them. In December 1788 and January 1789 a diminutive but familiar party of Indians mustered at Fort Harmar: the Wyandots and Delawares of the Sandusky and a few Ojibwes, Potawatomis, Senecas, and Sacs. In two agreements they confirmed the treaties of Forts Stanwix, McIntosh, and Finney for the trivial sum of $9,000. "Their confederacy is broken," crowed St. Clair, "and . . . Brant has lost his influence."[12]

The treaties of Fort Harmar, concluded in January 1789, were condemned by the Indians who had declined to attend. Although most had stood firm, every display of disunity had been a powerful weapon in St. Clair's hands. Dismay spread throughout the supporters of the fractured confederacy.

It was compounded by the growth of American settlements on and north of the Ohio. In 1787 the Ohio Company bought the territory between the Muskingum and Hocking Rivers, and Marietta was established at the mouth of the Muskingum the following year. Over four million acres between the Little Miami and the Scioto were reserved for Virginia war veterans, and further west John Cleves Symmes and the

Miami Land Company secured three hundred thousand acres confined by the Little and Great Miami in 1788. On the backs of these transactions, small wooden settlements began to appear on the Ohio and to creep into the Miami valleys.[13]

Some Shawnees were giving up and moving to other parts. In 1787 and 1788 their old friend Louis Lorimier, a French-Canadian trader who had fought alongside the Indians in the Revolution, invited both Shawnees and Delawares to join him in Spanish Missouri. Some Shawnees heeded the call, and one band, under a fiery Kispoko war chief named Cheeseekau (the older brother of Tecumseh), settled among the Chickamauga Cherokees about 1790.[14]

These emigrations drained the Ohio Shawnees of much needed strength, but Blue Jacket, Black Snake, and other war chiefs elected to fight on, and they were bolstered not only by their usual Mingo, Delaware, and Cherokee allies but also by Miamis and Kickapoos and some Ojibwes and Ottawas.

The energy that filled the Shawnee defense of Ohio ran from many springs. For one thing, most Shawnee families had lost people in the war with the Big Knives. They had suffered greater casualties than any western nation save the Delawares and continued to do so: in 1789 Kentuckians attacked a Shawnee camp on the Wabash, killing eight adults and capturing two children. By Shawnee lights the souls of the dead cried out for retribution.[15]

Then, too, there was an undercurrent of religious nativism among the Shawnees, much of it tapped from Delaware prophets in the 1760s and 1770s. Most of those prophets had preached that the absorption of white culture by the Indians was displeasing to the Great Spirit, who manifested his anger by reducing the game or inflicting famines and disease upon the tribes. To reverse their decline, the Indians should resist the trappings of white civilization or drive it out. Although there are few clear references to this kind of nativism among the Shawnees between 1772, when the Delaware prophet Scattameck was living in a Shawnee town, and 1803, it likely had its adherents betweentimes.[16]

For the nativists white manufactures were pollutants, but most Shawnees coveted them and found war to be a ready means of acquiring them. Trade might be disrupted, but the plunder dragged from captured cabins, carts, and boats offered a lucrative substitute. This was one reason why the Ohio River traffic was so attractive to Indian raiders. Those heavily laden but lumbering, almost unmanageable, flatboats were prime targets. In

March 1790 a war party under Black Snake took two boats, one of which contained twenty-six horses, dry goods said to be worth £1,200 or more, and bags of cash and other commodities.[17]

Most important was the issue of the land. It was an economic and emotional issue and also a spiritual one. For after all, the land had been the gift of Waashaa Monetoo. It was a sacred gift. Some Shawnees had long suspected that they had caused the Great Spirit considerable grief. That, they believed, must have been why he had stripped the tribe of its former preeminence among the nations and afflicted it with so many vicissitudes. For many years Shawnees had hoped to put that dissatisfaction right, to please Waashaa Monetoo by reuniting the tribe in the Ohio country, one of its traditional homelands. Now, as the Shawnees retreated before the unyielding advance of the United States, that ambition looked increasingly impracticable. But to antagonize the Great Spirit even further by losing the land completely — that portended a terrible fate indeed. For some Shawnees there was but one option: to fight. To do less, to surrender the land bequeathed to them by the Creator, was to risk massive spiritual disapproval.

Just how determined Blue Jacket and others were became plain to the Kentuckians during another round of exchanging prisoners. The Big Knives had fifteen Indian prisoners, ten of them left over from the previous exchange of 1787. Ten were sent forward to the infant settlement of North Bend, carved out of the Shawnee country by the Miami Land Company, and in June 1789 John Cleves Symmes sent one of the prisoners, Peter Cornstalk, with an Indian named Manogrie and Isaac Freeman, a volunteer, to the Indian towns. He appealed to Blackbeard and other Shawnee chiefs to protect Freeman from harm and proposed another exchange of captives.

When Freeman's party arrived on the Maumee, it was Blue Jacket who took matters in hand. He offered Freeman the hospitality of his own house, and during his stay the messenger saw plenty of evidence of what Blue Jacket intended to do about the treaties of Fort Harmar. Packhorses plodded to the war chief's door, carrying five hundredweight of powder and enough lead for a hundred muskets. Freeman learned that similar deliveries from Detroit were reaching other fighting leaders, and on their arrival the chiefs raised British colors above their houses. He also heard that Blue Jacket and his colleagues were hoping to get two pieces of artillery.

There was another ominous sign. The war chiefs were taking precedence over the civil chiefs in councils and controlling the affairs of the nation. This plainly indicated that despite the treaties of Forth Harmar, the Shawnees were on a war footing.

Six white prisoners were found for Freeman to take back to North Bend, although two of them absconded the night before the party was due to leave the Indian towns. Once again, repatriating whites accustomed to the freedom of Indian life proved less than straightforward. The Shawnees also sent encouraging word to Symmes, and the result was that at a meeting at the mouth of the Great Miami in September 1789 the Indians obtained the release of ten of their people.

The chiefs were as amicable as the situation required, blaming their "foolish young men" for the raids, but they aired their differences all the same. "Now brothers," they said. "Let us try to settle all these misunderstandings, and touch not our lands. Then you will see that we will live in peace and quietness."[18]

But even as they spoke, Shawnee war pipes were circulating among the tribes, and their requests for ammunition were embarrassing the British at Detroit. No one knew the Shawnee temper better than Alexander McKee. He told Sir John Johnson that though Cherokees, Shawnees, and Miamis had been involved in the raids on the Ohio boat traffic it was the Shawnees who "publicly declare themselves at war with the Americans." He knew that Blue Jacket, Captain Johnny, and other leaders were preparing for a last desperate struggle to defend Ohio from invasion.[19]

# 7

# Tomahawks and Tobacco

It was probably in the spring or early summer of 1789, a few months after the disastrous proceedings at Fort Harmar, that Blue Jacket and other chiefs and warriors of the Shawnees made a bold decision. They might have been driven to the Maumee, and the plan to persuade the United States to annul the conquest treaties had failed, but they would reform the Indian confederacy and make another attempt to expel the invaders. The fight to save the Ohio country would go on.[1]

The leaders who committed themselves to this dangerous course included the tribal chief, Captain Johnny, and such men as Blackbeard, Black Snake, and Red Pole, but one was particularly important — Wawe-yapiersenwaw, or Blue Jacket. By this time he had become the premier war chief of the nation and more. Because the Shawnees were planning to fight, they removed tribal business from the hands of the civil chiefs and gave it to the war chiefs. In councils it was now the war chiefs who sat at the front, symbolizing their ascendancy. The elevation of the war chiefs made their leader, Blue Jacket, the most powerful figure in the nation.[2]

The task Blue Jacket and his people had set for themselves, the restoration of the Indian confederacy, was far from easy. The idea itself, of groups consolidating in the face of a common danger, was a simple one and as old as human history; but successful Indian confederacies of the past had been much more limited in area than the one envisaged by Brant and the Shawnees. To rebuild *that* confederacy, which proposed to bring culturally diverse and independent Indian peoples, scattered over enormous distances and imbued with distinct regional interests, into a union "of one mind and one color" was indeed a project of soaring ambition.

It should be remembered that the Indians spoke different languages. Shawnee was intelligible only to the Kickapoos, and then with difficulty. Beyond, Shawnee diplomats worked in a world of mutually unintelligible languages: Sauk, Miami, Ojibwe, Menominee, Delaware, Iroquois, Cherokee, Wyandot, Muscogee, and Winnebago, to name only the most important. Dealing with such elements, particularly in intertribal gatherings, was slow going and required skilled interpreters.

But language was only the most basic of many problems. These Indians lived far apart, separated by a rugged terrain, requiring long, difficult journeys by waterways or thinly marked paths. In 1792, when members of the Seven Nations of Canada (a group of Iroquois and Algonquians inhabiting the St. Lawrence Valley) reached an intertribal congress on the Maumee, "the greater part of them were almost naked," their provisions were exhausted, and some had died on a travail of many months. To coordinate such a confederacy and focus it to defend any one point required a colossal effort.[3]

In addition, these peoples were ruptured by long-running intergroup feuds, and they were highly decentralized societies in which chiefs had few powers, individual rights were well established, and control remained precarious. These were truly formidable difficulties, which had already frustrated men of the stature of Guyasota, Pontiac, and Brant, but the Shawnees saw few alternative options. They were being stripped of their country and their livelihood, and they could not defend them alone.

Then, Blue Jacket, no less than Brant before him, realized that the aid of a European power, which could supply guns, powder, lead, and other necessaries, was of paramount importance. That meant he had to cultivate the British alliance. Twenty years later John Norton, an associate of Brant, visited the Shawnees and heard that Blue Jacket "had been a brave and distinguished warrior, possessing strong natural parts that were now ripened by the experience of age, which perhaps had also damped the fire and enthusiasm of youth. He had long lamented the want of resources to carry on the war with effect, and at one time attempted to go to England to enquire what succour might be expected from that quarter, but was prevented from the want of pecuniary means."[4]

Perhaps Blue Jacket's plan to visit England failed, but among the western Indians there was no other chief so peculiarly fitted to finding out what the British were up to or of presenting to them the Indian case. His connections with the Detroit merchants were undiminished. Sadly, his influential and respected father-in-law, Jacques Dupéront Baby, died in August 1789, but if one door closed to Blue Jacket others were opening. The former ranger William Caldwell, once described as that "very very odd but very gallant fellow," had married the daughter of Baby and Susanne Réaume. Thus the wives of Caldwell and Blue Jacket were half-sisters, and Caldwell remained a significant figure in the Detroit community.[5]

And at Miamitown the Shawnee war chief was making new friends among the traders, many of whom fed him with the talk of the mercantile community. Chief among these new associates were the Lasselles, an enterprising clan of French Canadians based in Detroit. Two brothers, Jacques and Antoine Lasselle, were trading with the Miamis before the Revolution, until the war drove them out. Afterward they were back, not only Jacques and Antoine but also their brother Hyacinth (known as Tappon) and eventually the three sons of Jacques by his wife, Therese Berthelet, whom he had married in 1765 — Jacques Jr., commonly called Coco, François, and Hyacinth. Not only were the Lasselles related by blood or business to all the merchants dealing along the Maumee and the Wabash but they bore charmed lives among the Indians, coming and going as they pleased without fear of being attacked or plundered. They were the envy of the other traders.[6]

One explanation for this license was the friendship that developed between the Lasselles and Blue Jacket, a relationship illustrated by an incident of January 1790. The Shawnee chief was then hunting away from his Miamitown home. Antoine Lasselle, "a man of wit and drollery" according to one who knew him, was anything but good-humored at the time. A Wea Indian was accusing him of spying for the Americans, and Le Gris, the Miami chief, was reported to have sent warriors to apprehend him and bring him to Miamitown for questioning. Lasselle decided to confront his accusers. He armed himself with testimonials from some Eel River and other Indians of his acquaintance, as well as from French traders, and found Blue Jacket, whom he asked to act as an escort into the Miami village. The two arrived in Miamitown on 13 January, and the matter was quickly settled. Lasselle discovered that although rumors that he had been dealing with the Americans were part of village gossip, there was no truth in the story that Le Gris had ordered his arrest. The trader was able to restore his credibility, and on 19 January Blue Jacket returned to his hunting.[7]

In a short while Blue Jacket would be drawn even closer to the Lasselles. His daughter Mary Blue-Jacket married Coco Lasselle. The date of the event is not known. The two solemnized their union in St. Anne's Catholic Church, in Detroit, on 29 March 1801, but it certainly had an older history. Their first child, Anne Marie, known as Nannette, was born about September 1791, when her father was some twenty-four years old.[8]

From traders such as these, Blue Jacket learned much useful information. Not all of it was accurate, but it gave him new perspectives on the position of the Indians and briefed him for his meetings with British officials. He learned, for example, how much the Canadian merchants depended on the Indians and how mortally afraid they were of the tribes being driven out of the territory south of the Great Lakes. For traders needed Indians to bring in the furs. Montreal merchants were then estimating that if the United States gained control of that region they stood to lose not only an annual £30,000 worth of trade south of the lakes but also the £150,000 western and northwestern trade that ran from Montreal to Lake Huron but relied on Detroit for provisions. Using intermediaries such as Alexander McKee and Matthew Elliott, Blue Jacket was able to cite the interests of the fur trade as a reason why the redcoats should increase their support for the Indians.

Writers have often spoken of the British manipulation of the Indians and portrayed Blue Jacket's warriors as mere pawns in an imperial chess game, and it is true that some members of the British Indian Department had great sway with the tribesmen. As a Detroit correspondent wrote in 1788, "Mr. McKee is now at the Miamis [Maumee] River, and seems to possess an entire influence over the minds of the western tribes." The stream of influence ran both ways, however, and Blue Jacket and other chiefs were ever alert to the possibilities of persuading the British to help them resist the United States. The relationship between the British and various Indian confederacies was undoubtedly an unequal one, but to some extent each was a pawn of the other.[9]

The British were important, but having decided to resurrect the demoralized Indian confederacy, the Shawnees had first "to acquaint the other nations," as Black Snake put it. They planned to organize another intertribal congress at Brownstown, and wampum went out to the tribes, east, west, and northwest, inviting them to the "grand council."[10]

In such an arduous enterprise the Shawnees were able to deploy symbols of pan-Indian diplomacy that were now widely known. One was the tobacco pipe, or calumet. By presenting the calumet one group of

Indians signaled its wish to talk with another and enjoy a truce. The device checked violence between potential enemies, and although calumet bearers were sometimes attacked, they were generally respected. Thus when Shawnee diplomats proffered a pipe to invite others to join a confederacy or assist in a war, recipients smoked to signify their acquiescence. The calumet, or "quacah" in Shawnee, was a symbol of peace and fraternity and was featured prominently in tribal peace ceremonies, but it could also bind smokers against a third party.[11]

Blue Jacket, like other Indians, also used strings or belts of wampum beads during councils. The symbols on, or the colors of, the belts conveyed messages which bearers could interpret as required. A red belt commonly denoted an invitation to join in a war, but one carried to the Cherokees of the Little Tennessee by some Mohawks and Shawnees in 1776 was nine feet long, six inches wide, and made of purple wampum. Confederation or alliance belts could also be elaborate. One of unquestionable authenticity, dating from the 1770s, survives in the Merseyside County Museum in Liverpool, England. It consists of purple and white beads and depicts several sets of Indian figures holding hands.[12]

The most famous symbol of war was the hatchet, particularly a red hatchet or one accompanied by tobacco painted red. Indeed, so common were the twin tools of fraternity and conflict that whites manufactured them for the Indian trade as a single artifact, the tomahawk-pipe, in which the bowl was placed behind the head of the ax blade. But such symbols were constantly being improved. At this time pan-Indian diplomats were inventing new symbols to express their idea that the land was not held by individual groups or tribes but by all the Indians in common. Thus at a meeting near the Maumee rapids in July 1792, Iroquois spokesmen presented the western Indians not only with wampum but also "a dish with one spoon," which "signified the country was in common."[13]

The Shawnees had some immediate supporters for their plans to restore the confederacy. Their villages were hosts to a number of Mingoes, as determined as ever to resist the Big Knives, while southeastward, on the Scioto River, were a band of fiery Cherokees. These Cherokees had recently been inflamed by news from home, where even the peaceful Upper Cherokees of the Little Tennessee and Hiwassee Rivers had been abused by vengeful white backcountry men. Their venerated chief, Old Tassell, had been murdered the previous year. Now the Upper Cherokees were making common cause with the belligerent Lower Cherokees of the Tennessee, and the principal leaders of both groups, Little Turkey and

Dragging Canoe, had met the Chattahoochee Creeks in May 1789 and called for Indian unity throughout the South and for an appeal to be made for British arms. Such events did not improve the temper of the Cherokees on the Ohio, and they quickly fell in with the Shawnee initiative.[14]

More important than the Mingoes and Cherokees were the Delawares under Buckongahelas. Buckongahelas had shared many of Blue Jacket's fortunes and misfortunes. Like Blue Jacket, he had been forced from his home on the headwaters of the Mad River by Logan's Kentuckians and taken refuge on the Maumee, where he had established a village a little downstream of Miamitown. He distrusted Americans and remembered the fate of the Delaware converts in the Moravian mission of Gnadenhütten, both men and women. Ninety of them had been murdered by militiamen in 1782. They had been led out bound, one by one, and their heads crushed with a wooden mallet. Despite his somewhat fearsome appearance, with one of the split rims of his ears broken so that it trailed upon his shoulder like a long worm, Buckongahelas was normally a mild-mannered and affable man. But he stood solidly behind his Shawnee friends, and his stock was rising in Delaware circles. As one witness remarked, he was "a man among them as General Washington was among the white people."[15]

The Mingoes, Delawares, and Cherokees were Blue Jacket's firmest allies. Together this hostile nucleus amounted to six hundred warriors or more.

About the Wabash lived two thousand Miami-speaking Miamis, Weas, Piankeshaws, and Eel Rivers (about four hundred good warriors in all), who also distrusted the Americans, especially since some Kentuckians had made unprovoked attacks on some Miamis and Piankeshaws on the Embarrass River in 1788. Unlike the Shawnees, they had not yet been uprooted or severely handled by the United States, but the new American garrison in Vincennes and the influx of Shawnee and Delaware refugees told their own stories.

In the absence of Pacanne, who was in the Illinois country, the greatest voice among the Miamis was Le Gris, but he relied considerably on his brother, the Deer, and brother-in-law and head warrior, Little Turtle. Born about 1751, Little Turtle was disarming. He had "a countenance placid beyond description" and a pronounced sense of humor, but behind that facade dwelt an astute, intelligent mind. Le Gris, the Deer, and Little Turtle were willing to support the confederacy, and it was essential that they did so, for the Shawnees and Delawares were no longer standing on their own ground. Whatever might be said in intertribal councils about the land being held by all Indians in common, Blue Jacket and his Shawnees understood that they were living at the head of the Maumee by the sufferance of its owners, the Miamis. It was crucial that these formidable people be friends.[16]

A powerful triumvirate had developed in the area, a union of Shawnees, Miamis, and Delawares. Blue Jacket and the Miami chiefs usually issued what orders went from the confederates; sometimes Blue Jacket cosigned with Le Gris and sometimes with Little Turtle.

Yet beyond the upper Maumee support was thin on the ground. The Iroquois, who had led the confederacy until the treaties of Fort Harmar, had not even returned the Shawnee belts. Nor was there movement from the powerful Ottawas, Potawatomis, and Ojibwes. In fact, their most influential leader, the great Egushaway, advised his people "to sit still . . . and not trouble ourselves about the Shawnees, who alone are out in war."[17]

Disappointed in the responses to their wampum belts, Blue Jacket and his councillors decided to chase them up. They dispatched Black Snake with a delegation of Shawnees and Cherokees to find out what the Iroquois were doing. On 7 September 1789 Black Snake and his companions confronted Iroquois leaders at their council fire at Buffalo Creek near Niagara. They reminded their audience of recent American atrocities, reiterated their determination to renew the confederacy, and asked why the Iroquois had now turned their backs on the western tribes. "We now declare that we mean to adhere strictly to the confederacy by which only we can become a people of consequence," declared Black Snake. And in words the Iroquois had taught him, he pointed out that "the lands belong to us all equally, and it is not in the power of one or two nations to dispose of it." Joseph Brant responded with his usual good sense. Yes, it was a good idea to persuade the tribes to "put our heads upon one plank," but he cautioned the Shawnees against proceeding rashly into a war. If it came to a fight, so be it; but first the Indians must exhaust peaceful negotiation. "Our advice to you is the same as it was last fall, when we put the affairs of our confederacy into your hands," he said. "Let us go on with vigour, but with reason . . . the world will blame us for such actions as can only distress individuals or helpless people." Nevertheless, at least nominally the Iroquois gave the enterprise their blessing. Even the Senecas, represented by Farmer's Brother, agreed "that the uniting the Indians is for their own interest, which confederacy we do agree to, and wish to join and support."[18]

Although the Iroquois mission offered some encouragement, it gave little practical help to the Indians at the head of the Maumee, and attempts to organize a pan-Indian congress for August 1790 met irritating obstructions. Belts from the Miamis and Shawnees went as far as the Mississippi and the western Great Lakes, but as late as April Black Snake was admitting that he had not yet received answers from all the nations. Blue Jacket and Little Turtle were soon complaining that continued bad weather and the disruption caused by the import of hard liquor were also impeding important assemblies. Even Shawnee plans to revive their old dream of reuniting the tribe, this time at a new town on the Maumee, do not seem to have recalled those fellow tribesmen who had followed Lorimier to Missouri. Although some Shawnees boasted that "all the nations beyond the setting sun, being in number forty-eight large towns, were all under arms," there was a creeping despondency, a fear that no more allies were there to be made.[19]

Blue Jacket could count one success, however. He successfully frustrated an American attempt to drive a wedge between his Shawnees and the more moderately opinioned Miamis.

It had become clear to the United States that the treaties of Fort Harmar had not brought peace to the frontiers, and Governor St. Clair was authorized to send an envoy from Vincennes, up the Wabash, in an effort to reach the hostiles. His chosen emissary, Antoine Gamelin, knew that the Shawnees were intractable, but he hoped for favorable responses to his speeches from the Miami-speaking Indians. One of the Wea villages replied satisfactorily, but most of the Wabash Indians referred Gamelin to the Miami villages at the head of the Maumee, and on 23 April 1790 the messenger arrived in Miamitown on his errand of peace. Shawnees and Delawares were there too, of course, and on the following day Gamelin had to allow them to join his audience. But he exhibited the agreement of Fort Harmar and invited the Miamis to join in the peace and recall their war parties.[20]

Le Gris privately confessed himself to be pleased with the American overtures, and both he and Little Turtle warned Gamelin "not to mind" the Shawnees, for they had "a bad heart" and were "the perturbators of all nations." How far this was mere diplomacy is difficult to say, but Blue Jacket acted quickly to forestall a split and to prevent the Miamis from making a precipitate response. Marshaling the authority of the Shawnees and Delawares behind him, the Shawnee war chief invited Gamelin to his house in Miamitown on 25 April, and there he courteously but firmly told him:

> My friend, by the name and consent of the Chaouanons [Shawnees] and Delawares, I will speak to you. We are all sensible of your speech, and pleased with it, but after consultation we cannot give an answer without hearing from our Father [the British] at Detroit, and we are determined to give you back the two branches of wampum [delivered by Gamelin the previous day], and to send you to Detroit to see and hear the chief, or to stay here twenty nights for to receive his answer. From all quarters we receive speeches from the Americans, and not one is alike. We suppose that they intend to deceive us. Then, take back your branches of wampum.

Blue Jacket brought the Miamis into line. On the twenty-eighth Le Gris told Gamelin that he might return when he pleased, but his speeches would have to be forwarded to neighboring tribes and no "definitive answer" could be given without reference to the British at Detroit. The Miami chief asked for the wampum which Blue Jacket had ominously rejected and for written copies of Gamelin's speeches, and he promised that an answer would be returned to Vincennes in thirty nights. It had been decided that nothing would be done without Indian unanimity.

Yet Blue Jacket was unable to get Gamelin to Detroit, where the chief wanted to probe his motives with the aid of the Lakes Indians and British. The same day Le Gris gave his revised response to Gamelin, Blue Jacket again invited the envoy to his house for a business supper. There before other chiefs the Shawnee war leader "told me that after another deliberation they thought necessary that I should go myself to Detroit, for to see the commandant, who would get all his children [local Indians] assembled for to hear my speech." Gamelin was not going to be delivered to the British, and the next day he refused to go to Detroit. He had supplied his speeches, and they could be sent to Detroit if necessary. Faced with such obstinacy, Blue Jacket relented, rising to assure the stressed ambassador that he would not be forced to make the journey. "Our answer is the same as the Miamis," said Blue Jacket. "We will send in thirty nights a full and positive answer by a young man of each nation."

Undoubtedly Blue Jacket was eager to divine American intentions and to explain the Shawnee viewpoint. Before Gamelin left, he was again entertained at the war chief's house. Candidly Blue Jacket said his people doubted

the sincerity of the Big Knives . . . having been already deceived by them. That they had first destroyed their lands, put out their [council] fire, and sent away their young men, being a-hunting, without a mouthful of meat. Also [they] had taken away their women, wherefore many of them would, with great deal of pain, forget these affronts. Moreover, that some other nations were apprehending that offers of peace would, maybe, tend to take away, by degrees, their lands and would serve them as they did before. A certain proof that they [the Americans] intend to encroach on our lands is their new settlement on the Ohio. If they don't keep this side clear it will never be a proper reconcilement with the nations Chaouanons [Shawnees], Iroquois, Wyandots, and perhaps many others.

In this final statement, Blue Jacket omitted the Miamis from the list of major allies, which suggests that even at that time he was unsure about the steadiness of his Miami hosts. For all his apparent docility, however, even Le Gris left Gamelin in no doubt that the treaties of Fort Harmar had been made by unauthorized Indians and carried no credibility. Given the deep feelings of injustice nurtured by these peoples, nothing Gamelin said convinced them that they were safe trusting the United States.

For the moment the triumvirate at the head of the Maumee survived.

∗    ∗    ∗

In the spring and summer the Shawnees and their allies launched fierce raids against the river traffic on the Ohio. Although new American settlements north of the Ohio were little troubled, except by minor horse-stealing raids, the accumulating toll of the Indian attacks was ferocious. According to one Kentuckian, some fifteen hundred people in or traveling to and from the region were lost to Indians between 1783 and 1790, along with over twenty thousand horses and thousands of dollars worth of property. In 1789 Gen. Josiah Harmar, who commanded American troops on the frontier, transferred his main strength from the Muskingum to a new post at the mouth of the Little Miami, Fort Washington (Cincinnati). As Alexander McKee presaged, it was only a matter of time before those soldiers were unleashed against the Shawnees and other Indian belligerents.[21]

The indigent confederation government of the United States had not wanted a war, but it had participated in the headlong rush to dispossess the Indians and had bullied them from treaty to treaty.

Now the administration established under a new American constitution felt obliged to answer Kentucky's calls for protection. A desire to maintain prestige, a fear for Kentucky, in which separatist sentiment was already under way, and a cast-iron determination to possess the Old Northwest, all pushed President George Washington's government toward a full-blown confrontation with Blue Jacket's embryonic confederacy.

In May 1790 the secretary of war, Henry Knox, recommended a campaign to silence the hostiles at the head of the Maumee. He wrote Harmar in June: "Although the said Shawanese and banditti aggregately may amount at the excess of two hundred fighting men yet they seem sufficient to alarm the whole frontier lying along the Ohio, and in a considerable degree injure the reputation of the government. To form a defensive and efficient protection for so extensive a frontier against solitary or small parties of enterprising savages, seems altogether impossible. No other remedy remains but to extirpate utterly if possible the said banditti."

Knox badly underestimated the strength of the opposition — "the banditti Shawanese and Cherokees, and some of the Wabash Indians on the northwest of the Ohio" — but he was nevertheless right that the support for the Shawnees was yet small. The confederacy had not gained back the ground it had lost in 1788 and 1789. The ensuing military campaign could easily have gone Knox's way.[22]

But it did not. In fact, it delivered to Blue Jacket and his colleagues the military victory their confederacy sorely needed to restore Indian morale throughout the Old Northwest.

# 8

# We Are Determined to Meet the Enemy

It was a bigger army than Knox had originally intended, the force that Josiah Harmar led from Fort Washington that September, bound for the Indian towns at the head of the Maumee. Eventually the general fielded nearly fifteen hundred men, far more than Blue Jacket could have raised and a larger army than the Shawnees had faced on a single ground.

It was not a crack force, however. Over one thousand of the men were militia from Kentucky and Pennsylvania, ill-equipped, poorly armed, and of uncertain composition. Some were old, too old; others young and inexperienced. As a whole, the militiamen were disorderly and ill-disciplined. Some of their officers squabbled, and probably most of them knew that General Harmar held them in low esteem. Nor had Harmar any prospect of surprising his opposition, as his army moved ponderously up the Little Miami, then northwest across the Great Miami to the St. Marys, and upstream to its goal. With bellowing cattle bringing up the rear, hundreds of packhorses stumbling under baggage, creaking, heavily laden wagons, and artillery, the soldiers made an average of only ten miles a day.[1]

In any case, the expedition had been well advertised. In an effort to isolate the target, in September and October Governor St. Clair had hurried messages to Mingoes and Wyandots on the Sandusky, to Indians of the Great Lakes, and even to the British at Detroit, warning them that none but hostiles would be harmed; no one should interfere. As he told these Mingoes, "We are going to whip the Shawanese, and some others who are joined with them, but not a man shall disturb you."[2]

Not all of St. Clair's letters got through, but other information was filtering out. Alexander McKee was at the foot of the Maumee rapids, distributing the king's annual bounty to gathering Indians, when three Americans arrived with frightening stories. Between six and seven thousand men were marching for the hostile villages, where they intended to build a fort. Harmar's army also intended to build other posts, at the Maumee rapids and the Glaize and on the Sandusky and Cuyahoga Rivers. McKee felt chilled. The Indians could not resist such an invasion, and if those posts were built, the Detroit fur trade would be ruined.[3]

Early in October a diversionary American strike up the Wabash, which was designed to draw the attention of the Indians from Harmar's advance, stymied through lack of supplies. Thus Harmar pressed upon his adversaries unsupported, but it should not have mattered for he appeared to command overwhelming strength. But he had reckoned without, or underestimated, the resolution of his opponents. Blue Jacket and Little Turtle had no intention of running. They had decided to fight. As McKee wrote, "The Indians of that neighbourhood are too few to make much opposition. However, I understand they are determined to attempt it, and have asked the assistance of other nations, who seem to be too dispersed to be able to collect in a short time."[4]

McKee had put his finger on Blue Jacket's difficulties. Since the response to his diplomatic overtures during the past year had been spotty to say the least, the defense would now depend primarily on the triumvirate: the Shawnees, Miamis, and Delawares. But even these had scattered for the fall hunting. In fact, it was a party of Shawnee and Delaware hunters who had first spotted Harmar's army on 6 October, as it lumbered up the Little Miami. They noted its slow progress and compact formation and rushed home to tell the chiefs. Blue Jacket and Little Turtle soon had messengers flying frantically about the countryside, calling in the scattered warriors. Others were sent in all directions to carry desperate appeals for help to neighboring tribes. At the head of the Maumee there was an air of grim determination. Noncombatants were removed from vulnerable towns and sent northwestward to sanctuaries toward the Elkhart River. Traders were helped to remove their goods, except for powder and ball, which the chiefs commandeered. Miamitown, which was supposedly the principal target, was partly burned so that it would not shelter Big Knives. And scouts were sent to monitor Harmar's

WE ARE DETERMINED TO MEET THE ENEMY

advance. On 13 October one Shawnee scout was captured by horsemen protecting the flanks of the American army.[5]

Afraid the Indians would scatter, Harmar detached Col. John Hardin, who commanded the militia, to speed forward with six hundred men while the main force plodded on behind. But when Hardin reached Miamitown on 15 October it was empty. Morale was rising among the warriors, as reinforcements scampered in from all sides. Further down the Maumee, a British observer noted, "It is astonishing with what spirit and alacrity the Indians at this place prepare to go to the assistance of their friends." Yet with only six hundred men the chiefs still lacked the strength to make a direct attack on the American force. All they could do for the moment was to keep the enemy under surveillance, build up their manpower, and wait for opportunities to counterattack detached portions of Harmar's army. They had to watch helplessly as Harmar's main force forded the Maumee between Miamitown and Chillicothe and occupied Le Gris's village on the seventeenth.[6]

By the time Harmar himself arrived, Hardin's men were spreading out from Miamitown in a fever of looting. "Like a rabble [they] strolled into the neighboring villages in parties of thirty or forty after plunder." Harmar's militia followed suit and "picked up as much plunder as loaded some of them home." The army did considerable damage. The soldiers discovered several thousand bushels of corn in the environs of Miamitown and burned what they could not consume, but the general was becoming alarmed at the propensity of his men to disperse. He had cannons fired to recall scattered parties and issued an order requiring them to stay in camp.[7]

Formidable as Harmar's force was, it was constantly fragmenting and offering vulnerable targets, which must have given Blue Jacket and Little Turtle satisfaction. On 18 October, while the army ravaged Miamitown, Harmar sent thirty regulars, a few cavalry and mounted infantry, and three hundred militia to reconnoiter an Indian trail leading northwest. The soldiers under Col. Robert Trotter advanced a mile or so across the St. Joseph and overtook and killed two Indian riders. Even this incident was prophetic. Excited officers thundered after one of the Indians, leaving their men undirected, and a soldier who got separated was soon back, "much frightened" by seeing fifty mounted Indians. Trotter's force was provisioned for several days, but it scuttled quickly back to the main camp. Not only was Harmar extending his forces dangerously, but they were showing unsteadiness and indiscipline in the field.[8]

Blue Jacket's warriors were never far from Harmar's force, waiting.

They watched Harmar's men raze Miamitown to the ground and then move downstream to torch Chillicothe too, and they hovered about to run off army horses. In surrounding Harmar's positions, the war chiefs had spread their forces thinly, but on 19 October they struck lucky.

Smarting to redeem the reputation of the milita, Hardin led out Trotter's force again that day, along the same trail as before. He went ten to fifteen miles, beyond the point where Trotter had turned back, and then ran into a small force of Shawnees and Potawatomis. They may have been posted there in ambush, or their presence may have merely been chance, for there were few more than a hundred of them, and they were badly equipped. Many were without guns and had to use tomahawks, and some had no horses. Nevertheless, they knew their duty. The American force might have been superior in numbers, but it was also badly extended. One company lagged so far behind that a group of mounted Kentuckians had had to be sent back to look for it.

Hardin had deployed his men in columns. He believed the Indians would disperse, but Blue Jacket's warriors fired on the Big Knives and surged forward in a furious charge, and Hardin's militia crumbled. Those ahead turn tail, some without firing a shot and others discarding their guns after doing so. The men behind refused to come forward to help form a line. Only about ten militiamen supported the thirty regulars who bravely resisted the Indian onslaught. "They fought and died hard," testified a regular officer as he bitterly recalled how the Shawnees and Potawatomis cut his men to pieces. Total losses are unknown. Twenty-four of the regulars and forty of the militia did not make it back to camp, but a few may have been hiding in the countryside. Some Indians also perished. John Norton, who interviewed Shawnees twenty years later, implied that they had suffered losses in these "predatory onsets" before the main battle.[9]

No one recorded whether Blue Jacket was personally at the head of his warriors that day, but the tactics he and his fellow war chiefs had adopted were paying off. Harmar was making mistakes, not the least in misjudging his adversaries as well as his own men. The defenders, in contrast, were jubilant, their enthusiasm mounting. "The Indians are all in the highest spirits, and very confident of success," wrote Matthew Elliott, who was gathering information about the crisis from the Glaize further down the Maumee. Two Delawares were sent with captured scalps and "very smart" messages to encourage the Delawares and Wyandots of the Sandusky to break their neutrality.

Blue Jacket and Little Turtle were pleased to find that some rein-forcements were coming in from tribes whose support had previously wavered. The day after the skirmish with Hardin a group of Ottawas arrived, about the same time as some Sacs and Foxes from the Mississippi. They were short of powder and ball and had to join their fellows in making bows and arrows, but the swelling manpower gave the war chiefs more opportunities. So far they had been "bush fighting" and planning night attacks on Harmar's guard and cattle herd, but now the war chiefs were able to consider a more general engagement.[10]

In the meantime, Harmar had made Chillicothe his base of operations, and from there he dispatched parties to destroy the local villages. In all he claimed to have consumed or burned twenty thousand bushels of corn and destroyed three hundred houses in five towns — probably Kekionga, Miamitown, Chillicothe, the Delaware village, and perhaps Snake's Town. The Indians did not seriously impede these activities, but they lost two or three warriors in periodic skirmishing.[11]

On the morning of 21 October, believing his job to be done, Harmar withdrew from the ruins of Chillicothe and headed back for Fort Wash-ington, camping that day after a march of seven or eight miles. It was there that Hardin proposed returning to Miamitown with a detachment of troops. The night of the twenty-first and twenty-second was clear and moonlit, and Hardin believed that a returning strike force might catch the Indians off guard, perhaps salvaging what they could from what remained of Miamitown. Harmar relented, and sixty regulars, forty horsemen, and three hundred dismounted militia left camp at about two o'clock on the morning of 22 October. The head of the regulars Maj. John Palgraves Wyllys, commanded. Retrospectively, we can see that Harmar was at fault. Again he was detaching a part of his force in the face of an opposition that had almost certainly increased, and the bulk of his assault unit was drawn from militia who had already shown themselves to be unreliable.

It took Wyllys till sunrise to reach the Maumee. Again, the delays were blamed on the militia, but despite the late hour the Americans launched an attack, one that aimed to surround any Indians impudent enough to have reoccupied Miamitown. The Big Knives divided. A battalion of militia under Horatio Hall went to the left to cross the St. Marys River and hold the west bank of the St. Joseph below Kekionga and across from Miamitown. Its purpose was to prevent a retreat that way. The other force, regulars under Wyllys and militia under James McMullen, forded the Maumee below Miamitown and advanced on the Indian village from the opposite direction.

But the operation misfired badly. Hall's contingent crossed the St. Marys, but instead of moving quietly to their position they began firing on some Indians who had appeared further up the west bank of the St. Joseph. To make matters worse, Hall's men floundered after them toward Kekionga until enemy fire either forced them to cross the St. Joseph or run back the way they had come. Far from screening off Miamitown on that side, Hall's force was all over the place.

The premature firing in this quarter instantly alerted the Indians in Miamitown and sent them racing from the village — for the most part before the oncoming Wyllys could attack. Then began a confusing and fluid melee. Retreating from the town, some warriors fled into the St. Joseph while others retreated up that river, occasionally standing and retaliating. Excited, McMullen's militia whooped after the Indians, up the east bank of the St. Joseph and toward their right. A force of cavalry under Maj. James Fontaine also tried to advance, but it scattered after meeting heavy fire from Indians ahead.

Wyllys and his regulars were left behind, unsupported. This was exactly the situation the Indians had been waiting for, and they closed in for the kill. A large body of warriors, apparently from Wyllys's right, fired into the vulnerable regulars and then rushed them with tomahawks and war clubs. Most of the Americans, including Wyllys himself, were cut down, but a few saved their lives by flight. Some ran into the St. Joseph and others up the river after McMullen's militia.

The Big Knives had been very badly beaten. The progress of the militia upriver soon ended, and they fell back as the excited Indians gathered about them. Retreating, they fell in with the pathetic remains of Wyllys's detachment. Somehow the force regrouped in Miamitown and stood the Indians off. Blue Jacket and his warriors held back, waiting for another opening, but the Americans had had enough. They withdrew across the Maumee and hastened back to Harmar's camp.

The Indians knew they had won a victory. More than a hundred of Harmar's men were killed and missing, many of them regulars who had formed the most dependable part of the general's force. Harmar knew he had been thrashed too. When Hardin, who had twice urged his superior to actions that ended in disaster, entreated Harmar to allow him to return, Harmar declared that "he would not divide his army any more." Nor would he risk his entire force in a further adventure. Instead, it fell back to Fort Washington. Apologists might argue that his army had discharged its duty. After all, it had destroyed the Indian towns. But it had suffered total losses of 183 killed and missing, and it had tasted defeat. "The ill fortune of the affair breaks through all the coloring," remarked William Maclay of Pennsylvania. Harmar himself was equally frank. "Our loss is heavy," he told St. Clair, "heavy indeed. All their Great Kanhawa [Point Pleasant], their Blue Licks, Bouquet's [battle of 1763], &c. &c. &c. was a damned farce in comparison of this action."[12]

Blue Jacket was unable to mount an effective pursuit of Harmar's army. The Indian losses had been light. Only some ten or eleven men were killed in the two principal engagements, according to Matthew Elliott. And there were signs that the American force was close to panic. Blue Jacket later reported that Harmar had destroyed some of his baggage and thrown valuable powder into the river. Blue Jacket and Little Turtle wanted to maul the retreating army. They hoped to harry it, breaking off fragments small enough to attack, and, when the main body had been weakened enough, to attempt a major assault against it.

Seven hundred warriors assembled for that purpose on the evening of 22 October, many of them Ojibwes and Wyandots who arrived after Wyllys's defeat. Unfortunately, the Ottawas refused to fight, and during the following night there was an eclipse of the moon. In the morning Blue Jacket was still expecting further action and sent a runner pounding to the Glaize, hoping to inspire Indians there with news of the victory and the claim that so far only five Indians had been slain. But the Ottawas were insisting that that lunar eclipse vindicated their forebodings. Their warriors decamped without consulting their allies and went home, and other Indians followed. With their strength draining from them, Little Turtle and Blue Jacket had no alternative but to call off their attack.[13]

It was a pity because the American force was badly exposed, the column so straggling that Blue Jacket was disappointed it did not abandon its artillery. Nevertheless, even though the victory had not been as complete as the Shawnee war chief wanted, he must have been exhilarated by it. Never in his lifetime had the Shawnees participated in so signal a defeat of the Big Knives.

✳    ✳    ✳

Much of what has been written about Harmar's defeat has been overimaginative. Attempts have been made to credit the victories over Hardin and Wyllys to individual tactical masterminds, rather than to the corporate valor of the Indians as a whole. There are those who seek battlefield Napoleons behind every victory.

The strongest evidence for controlled movements on the field occurred in Wyllys's defeat, when the Indians appear to have held forces in reserve until the militia dispersed and then delivered their counterattack against the unsupported regulars. We do not know which Indians staged this assault. A Mohawk who lived with the Shawnees was killed in the attack, so the Shawnees were probably involved. Yet the Miami war chief Little Turtle seems to have been on the west, not the east bank of the St. Joseph and removed from the decisive charge. But the evidence in both cases is too frail to depend on. Moreover, the attack on Wyllys may not have been a coordinated tactical movement at all but the spontaneous and independent action of opportunist warriors. Indian armies lacked the tight discipline of regular American or British forces, but this sometimes gave them greater flexibility. Attacks were fluid, and warriors could exploit such weaknesses as an enemy might present without awaiting orders from commanding officers. It could have been just such an initiative that destroyed Wyllys.[14]

The credit that unquestionably rests with Blue Jacket, Little Turtle, and other leading chiefs is less the tactical manipulation of warriors in the engagements themselves than their overall supervision of the resistance. They had been confronted by an invasion of their towns by a powerful force, one much greater than their own, and they could have been forgiven for abandoning the villages and scattering. But Blue Jacket and Little Turtle held their ground. They called in and enthused their men, and they held a superior enemy under surveillance until opportunities to attack appeared. In time their courage and resolution had been rewarded.

The first army of the United States had been beaten, but Blue Jacket knew that another one would soon be standing in its place, ready to expunge national dishonor. He also knew that it was important to turn the victory to political account, and almost immediately he set off for Detroit. On 4 November he was standing before the commandant of Fort Detroit, Maj. John Smith of the Fifth Regiment of Foot, with his words being translated by Alexander McKee. The chief related his triumph over the Big Knives and reminded the redcoats of the political and economic value of their Indian allies. He also wanted them to honor their promises:

When our Great Father over the large lake [the king] was wont to chastize his rebellious children, who now call themselves independent

Americans, Governor [Henry] Hamilton gave us the hatchet. The Shawanese have long had the friendship of the English. They have always considered them as brethren. They accepted the hatchet when offered. They lifted it up in their brothers' cause. Their arm was upheld in defense of their Great Father and his obedient children. He commanded peace. The hatchet was buried when he spoke, but we were promised not to be forsaken. We now, Father, call for your assistance. . . . Send out your young men [soldiers] amongst our nations. . . . Send your trading men . . . amongst us. . . . 'Tis the interest of ye and us. . . . Protect the barter between the white and red people, and forsake not the trade that links us together in amity and interest.

Blue Jacket used every argument he knew, strategic, economic, and moral, to induce the British to help. He repeated the rumor that Harmar's expedition had intended not only the destruction of the Indian towns but also the removal of British "trading posts."

Blue Jacket warned that if the redcoats failed them, the Indians "must divide like a cloud separated by a whirlwind, and scatter away to the long-running and never-tired waters of the great Mississippi, and be no more seen among you." The Shawnees would join the members of their tribe already in Spanish Missouri, and all their usefulness to the British, as military allies and partners in the fur trade, would disappear with them.

The Shawnees had never sold Ohio, "by deed, treaty or other ways," the war chief insisted, nor — according to their own story — had the British, "when our Great Father over the wide waters gave peace to his disobedient [rebel] children." The Indians did not want war. With less than the truth, Blue Jacket went so far as to deny that the chiefs had authorized raids against the Big Knives, which he said had been the work of young, intemperate warriors fired up by American "encroachments beyond the Ohio." But all the Shawnees would defend themselves. "We as a people have made no war, but as a people we are determined to meet . . . an enemy who came not to check the insolence of individuals [raiders] but with a premeditated design to root us out of our land."

Blue Jacket wanted "assistance" to alleviate the wants of Indians whose villages had been destroyed and to protect them from further attack. He wanted corn to plant, food, clothing, and traders, and he wanted soldiers. The chiefs of the Shawnees and their allies were waiting for an answer.[15]

With McKee at his elbow to stoke up fears for the loss of Indian support, Major Smith was in a quandary. He had a few supplies to give and could promise the free passage of traders from Detroit, but on the question of direct military aid he was helpless. Smith warned Blue Jacket against unnecessary hostilities and sought refuge in his own lack of authority. He said he would send the Indian requests to the governor of Canada, Lord Dorchester, in Quebec, and so he did, dashing off a letter the very next day.

With that, and McKee's advice to relocate his people on the Maumee, nearer British supply lines, Blue Jacket had to be content. While the wheels of British colonial administration slowly turned in response to his speech, he busied himself getting Smith's food and clothing to his needy people, to rebuilding the burned towns at the head of the Maumee, and to planning the next campaign.[16]

As it happened, his appeal to the British yielded little more substance than that. In January 1791 Dorchester sent it to England but wrote Smith that he had "no power . . . to begin a war." Dorchester expected posts such as Detroit to repel any attack the Americans might make on them, but he could not authorize direct military action on behalf of Blue Jacket's embattled warriors. The most he could do, and the British government in Whitehall would agree with him, was to suggest that if invited Britain might mediate between the belligerents. It was in accordance with this idea that Dorchester set about finding what terms the Indians would require to establish a peace.[17]

The Indians' relationship with the redcoats had always been an unequal one. The British expected the tribes to help them win the king's wars, but much as they saw the value of the tribes to Canada, they were not ready to take the field for *them*. Blue Jacket, like Brant, had failed to move them on that.

But Blue Jacket did not wait for the redcoats to answer. As soon as he returned to his people about the ruins of Miamitown, he began assembling his forces again.

✳   ✳   ✳

One beneficiary of the rout of Harmar was the Indian confederacy. Nothing enthused ardent young warriors more than military success, and some now came forward. Ottawas and Wyandots from the Detroit region appeared in the allied ranks, as did even a few independent-minded men from the cautious Delaware and Wyandot communities on the Sandusky. In the spring St. Clair, governor of the Northwest Territory, complained that "nearly the whole of one" of the Wyandot towns south of Detroit had "joined the Shawanese, and a good many of the Delaware likewise."[18]

There was enough interest among the warriors for Blue Jacket to mount an unusual winter campaign against American settlements on the north side of the Ohio. As the Indians prepared, Blue Jacket and Le Gris issued firm instructions that no traders were to be allowed into the camps at the head of the Maumee, nor were those already there permitted to leave. They wanted no leaks of information. There was one exception to the ruling, however: Blue Jacket's friend Antoine Lasselle. In fact, the Indians trusted him so much they asked him to accompany their army as an interpreter. Antoine decided not to risk it, but he did undertake a mission for the chiefs. He went down the Wabash to prevent traders from carrying intelligence to Vincennes and to search for a man named Fouchet, whom the Indians wanted to question.[19]

The campaign itself presented Blue Jacket with different problems. For all their durability, man-for-man fighting prowess, flexibility, and skill in ambush, Indians found large-scale military operations difficult. Blue Jacket and Little Turtle never had the control enjoyed by American commanders. Although they could exert some discipline in the field, warriors prized their individualism and would seldom entirely subordinate themselves to authority. For that reason carefully laid ambushes or surprise attacks were often ruined by the premature actions of impetuous Indians, eager to display their martial valor or to seize prisoners or plunder. And there were other problems too: a lack of manpower that discouraged Indians from offering battle when heavy losses seemed likely; a technological disadvantage in fighting American armies equipped with artillery and bayonets and more firearms; and the lack of a commissariat, which forced substantial Indian forces to live off the land or disperse for provisions. In addition, Indians regarded spiritual support as essential, and unfavorable omens were always likely to intervene, just as Blue Jacket's plan to attack Harmar's retreating army had been scotched by the lunar eclipse.[20]

Nothing exemplified those difficulties more than Indian attempts to capture forts or blockhouses. Blue Jacket and Little Turtle had no artillery to knock holes in walls nor the men to storm resolutely defended palisades. They did not even have the logistical backup to maintain long sieges necessary to starve out obdurate garrisons. Rather, they were largely dependent on suddenly surprising defenders or, worse, trying to persuade them to surrender. This general inability of Indian armies to reduce even modest fortifications constituted perhaps the most severe limitation of their ability to make war.

Now those problems had to be faced again. There was some success on 2 January 1791, when some of Blue Jacket's newer allies, Delawares and Wyandots from the Sandusky, surprised a blockhouse at Big Bottom, near Marietta, on lands claimed by the Ohio Company. Some fourteen settlers were killed.[21]

Blue Jacket, Little Turtle, and probably Buckongahelas led their Shawnees, Miamis, Delawares, and about two hundred Potawatomis against the ground now claimed by the Miami Land Company. They attempted to capture Dunlap's Station on the east bank of the Great Miami, one of the weakest posts in the area. Looking at it on 10 January, Blue Jacket would have entertained some hopes of success at Dunlap's Station. It possessed ten cabins, their roofs sloping outward, vulnerable to fire arrows or direct assault; a mill; and three indifferent blockhouses with the spaces filled by a picket. Covering about an acre of ground, the plan of the station resembled a mutilated triangle. Round about, trees and underbrush had been felled but not cleared, and Indian attackers could find shelter there. They could also scale a nearby prehistoric earthwork to get a reasonable look into the defenses. The garrison was weak, as the Indians probably surmised. In fact, Lt. Jacob Kingsbury had only twelve regular soldiers and about twenty-two other men, as well as women and children, and not a single artillery piece.

But the attack went wrong from the beginning. On 8 January an advance party surprised some surveyors near the fort, killed one of them, and captured another named Abner Hunt. Unfortunately, one surveyor escaped into the fort, alerting it to the possibility of attack. About sunrise on the tenth Blue Jacket's warriors surrounded the station, and the miserable Hunt was used to summon Kingsbury to surrender. Not unnaturally, he refused, and the attackers fired on the fort for about twenty-four hours, wounding one or two defenders. Flaming arrows were shot into the cabin roofs but failed to ignite them, and in their frustration the Indians turned on the prisoner.

About midnight Hunt was pinned down naked a few hundred yards from the fort and tortured to death with fire throughout the remaining hours of darkness. His agonized screams tormented the helpless garrison but did nothing to weaken its determination to hold out. The warriors also destroyed the nearby cornfields, butchered most of the cattle, but had to abandon the siege. They withdrew about eight o'clock on the morning of the eleventh, apparently leaving two of their dead behind. The attack had failed, but the settlers were shaken, and the station was temporarily abandoned.[22]

Blue Jacket must have been disappointed, and in the spring the Shawnees returned to easier targets. They slipped by the stubborn settlements north of the Ohio to hit the river traffic. In March a large war party of Shawnees, Mingoes, and Cherokees ambushed a boat forty miles above Limestone. Fourteen men were aboard, and they repelled the attack with the loss of only one killed and two wounded, but an escorting detachment ashore suffered eighteen of twenty-one men killed. Four days later the Indians took two boats near the same spot. Many prisoners were killed, but some French captives were spared, perhaps because the war party included two French Canadians named Barron and La Chapelle. In further attacks, the raiders captured another boat, but their canoes were beaten off from one vessel, which lost three of its nine-man crew killed or wounded. Blue Jacket may have been involved in these severe strokes, but there is no direct evidence of it, and the Shawnee war chief Black Snake was particularly experienced in this type of work.[23]

If Blue Jacket was frustrated by his inability to clear the invaders from the north bank of the Ohio, President Washington, Secretary of War Henry Knox, and Governor St. Clair were also chagrined. Harmar's army had been sent against the Maumee towns to end precisely such raids as these. The war would have to go on.

No authentic portrait of Blue Jacket is known to exist. This sketch of a Shawnee warrior, drawn by Joseph Wabin in the Illinois country in 1796, is the earliest known portrait of a Shawnee. It shows the typical dress of the period, a blend of manufactured European materials and native styles. Note the imported shirt; the breechcloth, leggings, and blanket fashioned from trade cloth; the use of trade beads and silver for necklaces, arm bands, and ear and nose bobs; and the persistence of the Shawnee scalplock, the practice of distending the ears, and the use of bows and arrows. Courtesy of the Cliché Bibliothèque nationale de France, Paris.

*Kishkalwa, a Shawnee leader related to Black Hoof, painted about 1825. He exemplified the wanderlust of his people. After the tribe had been defeated by the Virginians in 1774, he left the Ohio country for what is now Alabama. Returning about 1790, he took little part in Blue Jacket's resistance but withdrew to Spanish territory in present-day Missouri. The portrait was engraved for Thomas L. McKenney and James Hall,* The Indian Tribes of North America *(1836–44).*

*Paytakootha (Flying Clouds), a Shawnee also known as Hahgooseekaw and Captain Reed. He spent several years living with the Chickamauga Cherokees on the Tennessee River but returned to Ohio in time to sign the treaty of Greenville in 1795. He had little standing among his people and was frequently drunk; in one revel in May 1795 he attempted to burn down Fort Defiance. After the treaty he left Ohio for Missouri. In this portrait he typifies early nineteenth-century Shawnee costume and wears a silk, linen, or calico shirt, a linen caped hunting frock, and a silk turban. Engraving in Thomas L. McKenney and James Hall,* The Indian Tribes of North America *(1836–44).*

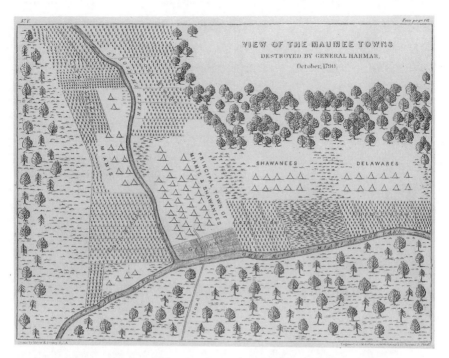

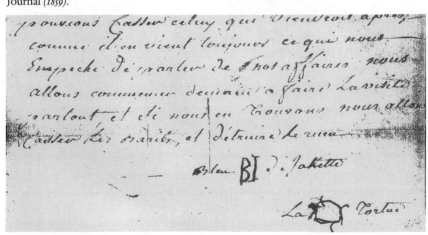

The Indian towns at the head of the Maumee, 1790. Miamitown, here correctly designated as a mixed village of Miamis and Shawnees, was the home of Blue Jacket from about 1787 until 1791. This was the scene of the defeat of Josiah Harmar's army in 1790. Map from Ebenezer Denny, Military Journal (1859).

Letter signed by Blue Jacket and Little Turtle in August 1790. It was written in French, probably by Antoine or Jacques (Coco) Lasselle. From Miscellaneous Intercepted Correspondence, 1789–1841, 2 August 1790, M588, roll 7, National Archives of the United States, Washington DC.

*Arthur St. Clair by Charles Wilson Peale. A distinguished veteran of the Revolutionary War, St. Clair served as the governor of Northwest Territory (1787–1802) and negotiated the treaties of Fort Harmar (1789), by which the United States claimed the bulk of Ohio from the Indians. When St. Clair led an expedition toward the Maumee towns to uphold the treaties in 1791, he was intercepted by the forces of Blue Jacket and Little Turtle and suffered one of the soundest defeats ever sustained by the American army. From an engraving in William Henry Smith,* St. Clair Papers *(1881).*

Gen. Anthony Wayne, *painted by Edward Savage. Despite a reputation for being egotistical, reckless, and imprudent, Wayne achieved the conquest of the Indians with consummate political and military skill. Failing to defeat Wayne in battle, Blue Jacket subsequently became a close ally and helped him organize the treaty of Greenville. Accession no. 1861.4, negative no. 6282, © Collection of the New-York Historical Society.*

*Dragoons breaking Blue Jacket's line at the battle of Fallen Timbers, 20 August 1794, as pictured by R. F. Zogbaum*
Harper's Monthly Magazine *(1896).*

*nthony Wayne and his staff negotiating with Indian leaders at the treaty of Greenville, 1795, a painting said to have
en made by one of the general's officers. Courtesy of the Chicago Historical Society.*

*Tecumseh, from an engraving in Benson J. Lossing,* The Pictorial Field-Book of the War of 1812 *(1868). Closely associat[ed] with Blue Jacket, Tecumseh later attempted to revive the intertribal Indian confederacy and became a substantial force [in] the War of 1812.*

*Tenskwatawa, formerly known as Lalawéthika, the Shawnee Prophet and brother of Tecumseh. When the Prophet returned from Indiana Territory to Ohio in 1805 to lead a religious crusade to revitalize Shawnee life, Blue Jacket was the only senior chief to support him. This is Henry Inman's copy of a portrait made from life by Charles Bird King but destroyed by fire in 1865. Courtesy of the National Portrait Gallery, Smithsonian Institution, no. NPG. 82.71.*

*Charles Blue-Jacket, son of George Blue-Jacket and grandson of Blue Jacket, in a photograph taken in Kansas. He showed the ability, strength of character, and entrepreneurial spirit of his grandfather and was widely admired by Indian and white associates. By permission of the British Library, no. AC8531 IX F183.*

# 9

# General Blue Jacket and Arthur St. Clair

The defeat of Josiah Harmar's army created outrage among Americans. The blame fell first on the commander, who was cleared by a court of inquiry, and then on the militia. In March the Congress of the United States approved preparations for another army of overwhelming strength to drive the hostile combination from the head of the Maumee and establish a post at Miamitown. The Shawnees knew there would be another battle too, and as early as April 1791 Captain Johnny was urging the tribes to send their warriors to repel another attack.[1]

The British, prompted by Blue Jacket's visit to Detroit, hoped to increase their standing by mediating a peace between the Indian confederacy and the United States. During that early summer of 1791, large numbers of Indians gathered at a storehouse Alexander McKee had erected at the foot of the Maumee rapids to receive the king's largesse. There were Ottawas, Ojibwes, Potawatomis, Wyandots, Miamis, Delawares, Mingoes, Shawnees, Cherokees, Conoys, and Nanticokes and even a delegation of Iroquois, including Joseph Brant. They accepted the annual presents distributed by the redcoats as proof of their goodwill and listened as McKee tried to find out what terms the Indians would stipulate for a peace. Blue Jacket may have been there. He and Little Turtle took shipment of some provisions from a Detroit merchant about this time.[2]

With Brant to counsel moderation, the Indians agreed that the territory east of the Muskingum would be surrendered in return for an American guarantee that the rest of the lands north of the Ohio, those west of the Muskingum, would be safe. It was decided that deputies from each of the nations, led by Brant, would carry these terms to Dorchester in Quebec. The deputies were also to reinforce Blue Jacket's call for increased British assistance, including the establishment of a fort at the mouth of the Maumee River. Brant and his colleagues presented the Indian proposals to Dorchester on 14 August, but to little effect. The governor of Canada was willing to consider establishing an advanced post on the Maumee and would defend existing forts, but redcoats would not turn out to help the Indians fight. Britain would mediate, however, when an opportunity arose.

Whatever Brant and the British might have supposed, the principal belligerents were thinking about war more than peace. Brant considered the Shawnees and Miamis "unreasonable." And although the United States preferred peace to an expensive war and sent envoys to the hostiles, its overtures were largely cosmetic. They contained no proposals that would have interested the Indian confederates, and it is possible that such missions were largely designed to inform the American public that peaceful initiatives had been exhausted and that a new military campaign was inevitable.

Blue Jacket spent most of the summer of 1791 assembling allies for the major assault that he felt sure was coming. War belts, hatchets, and tobacco painted red, all symbols of war, were circulated to summon warriors to Miamitown or to the confluence of the Maumee and the Auglaize, an area known as the Glaize, where Captain Johnny had his town. It was to the Glaize, upriver of McKee's depot at the foot of the Maumee rapids, that the confederacy was beginning to transfer its headquarters.[3]

A formidable force of warriors was brought together, but it kept dispersing to hunt and was forever decamping and reforming as one rumor succeeded another. It was a summer of scares, real and imaginary. In May and June and again in August two small armies of Big Knives advanced into the Indian country, the first composed of Kentuckians under Brig. Gen. Charles Scott, the second militia led from Fort Washington by Col. James Wilkinson. They struck at villages of Miami-speaking Indians and Kickapoos on the Wabash, Tippecanoe, and Eel Rivers and, according to one report, also destroyed a small Shawnee village in that neighborhood. Blue Jacket and his allies mobilized to intercept both forces, but they withdrew too quickly, and the disgruntled warriors had to disperse.[4]

Among other reports came one from a young Shawnee war leader named Tecumseh. He had been in the South, fighting under his brother Cheeseekau alongside the Cherokees, and had brought a party back north, through American lines. He arrived at the Glaize in August with an apparently unfounded story of American cavalry in the vicinity of the Mad River.[5]

Then in September, the Moon of Pawpaws, came the news that Blue Jacket had been waiting for. A great army, greater even than Harmar's, had left Fort Washington and was creeping toward Miamitown. Scott and Wilkinson had merely been diversions, entertaining the Indians until the big push could be prepared. Now it was finally coming.

The man George Washington and Henry Knox chose to redeem the honor of the republic was an aging veteran of the Revolutionary War and the first governor of Northwest Territory: Arthur St. Clair. He was instructed to advance on Miamitown, erecting a series of posts on his way, to defeat the Indians, and to build a fort that would dominate the strategic communication routes along the Wabash and the Maumee. At his service were two regiments of regulars, some two thousand levies enlisted for six-month terms but accountable to the federal government and army discipline, several hundred militia, and artillery. With such a force St. Clair considerably outnumbered his Indian opponents, and he should have been capable of doing the job.[6]

The commander was not without his problems, however, and they began with himself. Despite his experience as a major general, St. Clair was an indifferent soldier, and the burdens of the campaign were to damage his health. Suffering from a bilious colic, a rheumatic asthma, and gout, he was incapable of vigorous command. As one of his officers complained, "All the men that can possibly get in reach of him are scarcely enough to help him on and off his horse, and indeed, now a litter is made to carry him like a corpse between two horses."[7]

The army itself was poorly trained, undisciplined, and inadequately supplied. About a third of the soldiers were regulars. They were in reasonable order, but many of them were inexperienced recruits. The levies, who made up the bulk of St. Clair's force, had been idle in Pittsburgh for much of the summer, and now their enlistments were drawing to a close. As the weather and the provisions deteriorated, they grew more disobedient and unmanageable. Their officers detested their commander, Richard Butler, who stood second in command to St. Clair, and who, ironically, had once been a trader among the Shawnees and fathered Shawnee children. The men themselves were badly trained and, according to the adjutant general, Winthrop Sargent, displayed an "extraordinary aversion to service." Nor were the few hundred militia who marched with St. Clair any more inspiring. They were widely condemned as incompetent and unamenable, many were old, and some knew little of campaigning in the woods.

Compounding the deficiencies in personnel were the shortcomings of St. Clair's supply system, for the army lacked an effective quartermaster until September. Food ran low, and the lack of spare paper for the manufacture of cartridges prevented the men from practicing marksmanship. Despite the shortages, when the army eventually marched, it was accompanied by numerous civilians employed as packers, haulers, laundrywomen, cooks, and helpers. These included not only women but also a few children. Predictably, the force moved forward slowly, often hacking a path through thick woods to make way for the guns, carts, and pack animals groaning behind, or building bridges and forts.

More than two thousand men moved out of Ludlow's Station, a few miles from Fort Washington, on 17 September. Some days later the army was on the Great Miami, where it spent two weeks putting up Fort Hamilton. Early in October the troops were on the move again, but after advancing another forty-five or so miles north they halted while Fort Jefferson was built. Supplies were now being rationed, and the weather was turning cold, with rain, hail, and snow multiplying the miseries of the soldiers. The creeks began to ice over.

Discipline became more difficult. About twenty militiamen defected in a group and had to be rounded up. On 23 October three privates were executed. Some of the levies abandoned the army when their enlistments expired, and not all the losses were made up by the occasional arrival of new recruits. Most seriously of all, on 31 October sixty militiamen decamped, threatening to attack the supply convoys plodding along the communication line, and St. Clair had to detach his first regiment of regulars to protect it. This regiment had the best troops in the army and was still missing when battle was finally joined.

The American army encountered Indians from its first days, losing horses to raiders, but it blundered forward with little effective scouting. A militia party surprised a camp of five Indians on one occasion but failed to secure any of them, and the army lost a few men killed or captured on the march. The quality of St. Clair's reconnaissance should have improved at the end of October because a party of southern Chickasaws under Piomingo and George Colbert joined them. For many years the Shawnees would bitterly remember how the Chickasaws scouted for the Big Knives, but in fact St. Clair's Indian recruits made little difference. They were sent out and eventually turned up at Fort Hamilton the proud possessors of five enemy scalps. Unfortunately, they totally missed something far more important.[8]

In biting cold and flurries of snow Blue Jacket and Little Turtle were coming to meet St. Clair at the head of a thousand men.

*　　*　　*

The rendezvous for the Indian army was Miamitown, where Blue Jacket probably still had a base. There the warriors assembled. There were Shawnees, Miamis, Delawares, Mingoes, and Cherokees, of course — the nucleus of the confederacy — but also Wyandots, Ojibwes, Ottawas, and Potawatomis. In fact, Indians from these tribes of the Great Lakes made up at least half of the assault force. Nevertheless, the job in front of them was daunting. Prisoners and deserters brought in daily indicated that St. Clair had twenty-two hundred men, more than double the Indian numbers, with artillery to boot. Not all the Indians even had firearms, and many who did own muskets had traveled long distances to Miamitown, exhausting their supplies of powder and shot in hunting on the way.

But on 28 October Blue Jacket's principal strike force of about 1,040 men marched from Miamitown. Simon Girty, who watched them depart, wrote the same day that "the Indians were never in greater heart to meet their enemy, nor more sure of success. They are determined to drive them to the Ohio, and starve their little posts by taking all their horses and cattle."[9]

Doubtless, Blue Jacket and the other war chiefs had worked out their plans in councils. They might have opted for a defensive battle, such as the one that had given them a victory over Harmar, but the final decision was bolder. They would march to meet the Big Knives head-on in a major battle and hope to surprise them in a sudden dawn assault. The suggestion may have come from Blue Jacket or other Shawnee veterans, for it was an identical plan to the one they had tried seventeen years before. On that occasion the Shawnees had tried to stop an invasion of their country by striking at the Virginia army at Point Pleasant, and on that occasion too the Indians had approached their adversary, hunkered down nearby for the night, and then made a furious onslaught upon the enemy camp at first light. Blue Jacket, who had been one of the younger war chiefs at Point Pleasant, would have remembered that the Shawnees had failed, but failed honorably; this time morale was also tip-top, and he hoped for a better result.

Even in recent times much misinformation has been published about the leadership of the Indian force that attacked St. Clair. Today the common assumption is that the Miami Little Turtle exercised overall command of the Indian army, and this certainly seems to have been the view repeatedly put forward by the chief himself and his white son-in-law, the voluble but unreliable William Wells, who was also in the battle. Too often this assertion has been reproduced uncritically, as if it was not blatantly partisan, and some writers have used it to build a fictional career for the Miami chief, putting him at the heart of every notable Indian victory of the period, whether or not there was evidence of his being present.[10]

Little Turtle may have been given some executive authority during the campaign against St. Clair, but if he was the principal leader he said he was, it is strange indeed that some who were in that Indian army — independent witnesses with no apparent axes to grind — named Blue Jacket, not Little Turtle, as their leading war chief. Contemporaries believed them, and it was the Shawnee who enjoyed the greater reputation as St. Clair's nemesis and who, as far as our thin evidence allows, exercised the most authority when the confederacy mobilized again for subsequent campaigns.

The early "inside" evidence plainly declares for Blue Jacket. Soon after the battle, a Frenchman encountered some Indians who were returning in small parties from the fray and learned from them that "Blue Jacket the Shawnee commanded, and 600 of the Lake Indians, by which I suppose they mean the Chipeways and Hurons, were in the action, and their whole force was 1200." Ensign Turner, an American officer captured in the battle but later ransomed at Detroit, had ample opportunities to learn the identity of his principal Indian opponent. During his captivity he discovered "that the enemy in action amounted to fifteen hundred men under the command of Blue Jacket, and that they had nine hundred more at no great distance." Simon Girty, who participated in the action, told another American prisoner in 1792 that his brother James Girty commanded, "together [with] a Shawanoe Indian." Putting aside the familial loyalty in this account, it must also be taken to refer to Blue Jacket, who was the premier Shawnee war chief.[11]

Blue Jacket's leadership was generally accepted during the war. The British feted him as "General Blue Jacket," and American Quakers who visited Detroit in 1793 and met the chief acknowledged that he was credited with having been "in command at the defeat of St. Clair's army." American officers accorded him a celebrity not granted any other chief. They spoke of him as "the famous warrior at the defeat of G. St. Clair" and "the greatest warrior among all the tribes," while to General Wayne, St. Clair's successor, he was almost invariably "the famous Blue Jacket."[12]

Not until 1794 did the Americans appear to get an intimation of Little Turtle's claims. In a message of the confederacy chiefs, including Blue Jacket, Little Turtle is described, beside his name, as "the great Miami warrior and commander-in-chief of all the Indians in the action with General St. Clair." Whether this represented the views of all the chiefs, of the Delawares who carried the message, or merely of Little Turtle himself, in putting his name to the document, is difficult to say. But it alerted Wayne, who repeated the claim on at least one occasion. Nevertheless, in the preliminaries to the peace treaty that finally ended the war he found Blue Jacket so much the more instrumental of the two chiefs that he continued to regard him as the key figure. A dispatch written by Wayne in 1796 suggests that the dispute had, by then, become a personal bone of contention between the two great warriors. Among the Indians assembled for a delegation, Wayne reported, "is *the famous* Shawanoe chief, Blue Jacket, who, it is said, had the chief command of the Indian army on the 4th of November 1791 against Genl. St. Clair. The Little Turtle, *a* Miamia chief, who also claims that honor, and who is his rival for fame and power — and said to be daily gaining ground with the Wabash Indians — refuses or declines to proceed in company with Blue Jacket."[13]

It was Little Turtle's version, rather than Blue Jacket's, that subsequently passed into the literature on the Indian wars, but even then some battle veterans continued to name the Shawnee war chief as the most prominent leader. Among them was George Ash, a white man raised among the Shawnees, who gave one of the most interesting "inside" accounts of the Indian war. Recounting the attack on St. Clair's army, in which he participated, he said simply that "General Blue Jacket was our commander."[14]

Surrounded by such conflicting statements, spiced as they are by issues of tribal and personal honor, the serious historian cannot justly apportion credit between two such proven and distinguished leaders. Indeed, it would be misleading to make the attempt, for to assume that there was any commander in chief would be to mistake the typical nature of Indian leadership. There was no single mastermind behind the Indian campaign. These were democratic, not authoritarian, people, and their battle plans emerged from collective counsel. For the most part executive chiefs acted merely in accordance with that consensus. The important leaders, therefore, were less those who were delegated this or that task to perform than the chiefs who could win their points in council debates and turn them into policy.

In the early nineteenth century, when the case for Little Turtle was being circulated, some who had known the Indians well tried to explain this. The Indian agent John Johnston, who knew the Miami chief, wrote,

> There never was such a functionary as a Commander-in-Chief in any battle fought by the Indians of the N.W. They have no organization of the kind. Every tribe fights on its own hook, and I might say every individual, every man standing, lying, hiding, skulking, or running away as he chooses. The Delawares, Shawanoes and Wyandots has often told me that the remoter tribes, such as the Chippeways, Putawatimmies and Ottawas always ran off when hard pressed, leaving them to bear the brunt of the battle. . . . There is no punishment for cowards or deserters.[15]

With a little less exaggeration Henry Rowe Schoolcraft also felt bound to qualify the Little Turtle story:

> The principal circumstances connected with the battle are accurately remembered among . . . the Wyandots, a number of whom were present. According to their account the question of battle was determined in a public council of the tribes. The order in which they were to fight was arranged in this council on the evening preceding the battle. The Wyandots stretched to the west, the Delawares were placed next to them, the Senecas [Mingoes] next to Delawares, and so on, according to the arrangement agreed on by the chiefs. Little Turtle . . . did nothing but encourage the warriors.[16]

John Norton, who spoke to the Shawnees in 1810, also picked up something of the system as it related to the attack on St. Clair. He noted that "the chiefs" made the decisions, by implication in a council, but that the "lead" in the battle was "given to the Shawanons."[17]

The dispute between the two war chiefs was an unfortunate consequence of the battle, marring what was from the Indian point of view a tremendous performance. The only fair conclusion we can make about it, at this late stage, is that a council of chiefs was responsible for the planning, but that the two most significant of these leaders, and the ones people remembered, were Blue Jacket and Little Turtle.

But while these and other formidable captains led their warriors southeast, bent on a risky errand through snow and rain, Major General St. Clair torturously brought his army to the upper Wabash River. He pitched a camp there on the evening of 3 November. The site, in present Mercer County, Ohio, was some fifty miles short of his target, Miamitown. St. Clair chose a position on a rise overlooking the east bank of the Wabash. The water was perhaps fifteen yards across, but the Kentucky militia broke the thin ice and forded it, camping beyond the rich bottomland on an area of higher but level ground covered by an open wood. This force, about 320 strong, formed St. Clair's advanced guard.

Back on the eastern bank, the main army of 1,380 regulars and levies, with the camp followers, occupied an open space that was surrounded by woods and stood above a steep descent to the riverside. The troops were quartered in their tents in two lines parallel to the water. The lines were about seventy yards apart, and each was some 350 yards long. Gen. Richard Butler commanded the first line, closer to the Wabash, and Col. William Darke the second. The eight artillery pieces, mainly six-pounders, were divided equally between the two divisions. The right flank was covered by a corps of riflemen, some horsemen and pickets, and a party of horse was thrown out to the left.

It was not a particularly strong position, being surrounded by timber and confined in area, but St. Clair was not expecting an immediate attack.

But as St. Clair's force shambled into camp on that cold afternoon on 3 November Blue Jacket's spies found it. They hurried back. The Indian army had advanced in good spirits, the warriors singing their war songs, bands of hunters operating on the flanks, and scouts moving ahead. One who made that march was George Ash, the white Shawnee. He recalled:

The two armies met [approached] about two hours before sunset. When the Indians were within about half a mile of St. Clair, the spies came running back to inform us, and we stopped. We concluded to camp. "It was too late," they said, "to begin the play." They would defer the sport till next morning.

General Blue Jacket was our commander. After dark he called all the chiefs around him to listen to what he had to say.

"Our fathers," said he, "used to do as we now do. Our tribe used to fight other tribes. They could trust to their own strength and their numbers. But in this conflict we have no such reliance. Our power and our numbers bear no comparison to those of our enemy, and we can do nothing unless assisted by our Great Father above. I pray now," continued Blue Jacket, raising his eyes to heaven, "that he will be with us tonight, and" (it was now snowing) "that tomorrow he will cause the sun to shine out clear upon us, and we will take it as a token of good, and we shall conquer."

Before dawn the warriors were up, and as Blue Jacket had prophesied the weather had improved, and the snow had stopped falling. Remembering what Blue Jacket had said, the Indians took this to be a favorable sign. The war chief had prayed for them, and he had been answered. Clearly his power was strong, and the Great Spirit was with them.

About an hour before day [continued Ash] orders were given for every man to be ready to march. On examination it was found that three fires or camps, consisting of fifty Pottawattomies, had deserted us. We marched till we got within sight of the fires of St. Clair. Then General Blue Jacket began to talk, and to sing a hymn, as Indians sing hymns.

Blue Jacket was doing what Indian leaders did on every great occasion. He was using his influence with the spirits, an influence that had given him many previous successes, to seek assistance for his warriors in their coming trial. He performed a ceremony, but when Ash described it, his interviewer admitted that "I did not well understand."[18]

St. Clair's camp lay less than a mile upstream of Blue Jacket's, and the warriors soon covered the distance. They marched in files that made a half-moon formation. The Wyandots and Mingoes were on the right flank, and the Ottawas, Potawatomis, and Ojibwes guarded the left, both wings ready to sweep around the enemy force or to check any flanking movements against the Indians. In the center strode the warriors of the triumvirate, Shawnees, Delawares, and Miamis under Blue Jacket, Buckongahelas, and Little Turtle. As they closed in, they extended their front to prevent the Americans from gaining their rear.[19]

It was almost sunrise on 4 November 1791.

✳   ✳   ✳

The Indians were lucky. St. Clair's army had been singularly oblivious to signs of danger. Throughout the night some excited warriors had stolen around their camp, taking a few horses and occasionally drawing the fire of sentries. A band of volunteers under Capt. Jacob Slough had been out the previous evening looking for horse thieves. They returned to camp about midnight reporting that considerable numbers of Indians were in the woods, but no one thought enough of it to take suitable precautions. Just before sunrise the soldiers were turned out to parade under arms and then dismissed for breakfast without any realization that the Indians were gathering around them.

The sun had still to appear in the eastern sky when it began. From the open wood fringing the ground held by the militia across the river there rose an eerie sound, the Indian yell. Winthrop Sargent, the adjutant general, remembered that it was "not terrible, as has been represented, but more resembling an infinitude of horse bells suddenly opening to you than any other sound I could compare to it."[20]

Simultaneously, a heavy musket fire was directed against the militia. These worthies were fairly well posted but fired few shots in return and bolted for the main camp. They floundered across the river, scrambled up the opposite bank, and crashed through both lines of St. Clair's army, throwing the first into some confusion. This disgraceful flight did not serve the militia well. As they broke through the rear of the American camp they found Indians in the thick woods, encircling the enemy force.

As the militia fled, angry warriors plunged after them. Despite the cold, many of them were almost naked, painted red and black, and they shrieked fearfully. Butler's first line steadied and momentarily the Indians faltered. Colonel Semple "observed Major Ferguson preparing to fire his cannon on the Indians who were pursuing the flying militia, and soon saw him fire, which put them in great confusion, but they were soon rallied by their leader on horseback, dressed in a red coat."[21] One wonders who that Indian leader was, but the following year Blue Jacket enjoyed sporting a scarlet British military jacket, and it just could have been he.

Thus spurred on, the Indians chased the militia across the Wabash and then confronted Butler's line, standing some twenty-five yards distant, grimly but hastily formed with fixed bayonets. Rapidly the warriors filed left and right, enfilading St. Clair's entire camp and driving in his outlying guards. Within minutes they were ducking behind cover on all sides, almost vanishing in the foliage, but all the time training their muskets upon the confined space that contained the Big Knives and punishing them with a murderous cross fire.

St. Clair's aide recalled that the Indians "advanced from one tree, log or stump to another, under cover of the smoke of our fire. The artillery and musketry made a tremendous noise, but did little execution. The Indians seemed to brave everything, and when fairly fixed around us they made no noise other than their fire, which they kept up very constant and which seldom failed to tell, although scarcely heard."[22]

This, indeed, was no common performance. Well instructed by their chiefs, the warriors quietly settled down to their deadly purpose, coolly and accurately directing their fire against picked targets: the artillerymen in the center of St. Clair's lines and the officers. And the tactics worked. The defenders were sliced down at "a shocking rate," and as the gunners fell the canister and round shot projected by the artillery was subdued. Among the officers brought down was the gallant Richard Butler, knocked severely wounded from his horse as he tried to encourage his men. With the ranks of the officers thinning, some of the inexperienced soldiers began to panic.

If the Americans remained in their defensive posture, they would be cut to ribbons. St. Clair knew that. The general's gout was so painful that he could scarcely mount a horse, and two were shot from beneath him. Yet he was fortunate not to have been hit, perhaps because his plain coat and hat had masked his rank from Indian marksmen. St. Clair decided that a sortie from the left might turn the enemy's flank and break the encirclement. Colonel Darke's line made a bayonet charge. The warriors of Blue Jacket and Little Turtle melted before the assault, but as the Americans faltered in the thick cover, they closed in on them, firing from thickets and trees. In the words of one witness, "They seemed not to fear anything we could do. They could skip out of reach of the bayonet and return as they pleased. They were visible only when raised by a charge."[23] To avoid being cut off, Darke's men retired, and the battle continued as before. Increasingly desperate, the Americans made several such charges, but every time the result was the same.

At this point both sides were sensing an inevitability about the conflict. The Indians had not been in serious difficulties. During the sortie by Darke's men, the Wyandots and Mingoes had launched a frontal attack on the left of the unsupported American front line. Streaming over the embankment, they broke into St. Clair's camp, overrunning the artillery and axing men and women down. Vigorous counterattacks by Butler's men and the return of Darke's division expelled the invaders in ferocious close-quarter fighting and gave the Indians their only bad moment. The Wyandots and Mingoes angrily upbraided the Shawnees for inadequate support; on their part, the Shawnees appear to have believed their

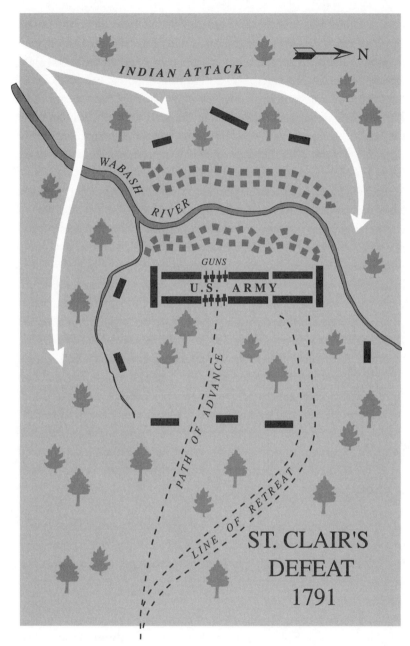

N

INDIAN ATTACK

WABASH RIVER

GUNS

U.S. ARMY

PATH OF ADVANCE

LINE OF RETREAT

ST. CLAIR'S
DEFEAT
1791

Map 3

incensed allies had made an imprudent forward movement, opening a gap between themselves and the Shawnees and almost accomplishing their own encirclement. But on the whole, Indian morale remained high. George Ash recalled a chief named Blackfish, presumably a Shawnee of that name, rallying flagging comrades with a shout of "conquer or die!" The chiefs could see that the American charges were ineffective and that the Big Knife army was relentlessly being pared down and contracting toward its center. As it did so, it offered a concentrated and ever easier target for Indian musket balls and arrows.[24]

Thrown back to defend the perimeter of the camp, St. Clair's soldiers were at a grave disadvantage. Hitting adversaries who were almost invisible behind their cover called for marksmanship the army simply did not have. As more Americans fell, the remainder began to disintegrate. Disorderliness, panic, and outright cowardice increased. Some men hid in the center with the wounded, looking for shelter from the bullets, and while there were many soldiers who bravely stood to their duty, others were overwhelmed with terror. They became "a mob at a fair," complained Darke, unable to "form in any order." Winthrop Sargent agreed. The men "could scarcely be led to discharge a single gun with effect," he said, and Ebenezer Denny described them as "perfectly ungovernable" and "incapable of doing anything." Dread now even stole into the hearts of the hitherto protected noncombatants, as they realized their lives were at risk. A surgeon's mate was slain as he dutifully tended the wounded. Desperate women, of whom there were many in the camp, ferreted shivering soldiers from beneath wagons or from holes to taunt them to fight.[25]

Eventually St. Clair was forced into a horrifying decision. The men were bullied into formation, and the badly wounded were told that to save what was left of his effective force the general was going to abandon them to the enemy, along with the artillery, tents, baggage, and equipment. If they could walk, they could try to join the retreat; if not, they must do the best they could.

Some of the most agile soldiers were then directed against the Indians surrounding the rear of the camp, with orders to cut through to the road along which the army had originally advanced. The warriors scampered out of the way as the Big Knives charged, and St. Clair with the remains of his force surged toward the road and began a mad flight for Fort Jefferson. It was about 9:30 in the morning and the battle had lasted only some three hours.

Those who escaped with St. Clair fled in total disorder. Some bravely helped their fellows along, but many ran headlong, discarding equipment, weapons, cartridges boxes — anything that threatened to impede their flight. On a road strewn with impedimenta, wounded and stragglers often limped along unaided. It was, Darke admitted, a scene of "confusion . . . beyond description." Sargent considered it a supreme disgrace. But there was little pursuit. Instead, the Indians fell upon the abandoned camp, ransacking wagons and baggage, butchering the wounded, both men and women, and mutilating their bodies. Some brandished their spoils or capered about in the cocked hats and uniforms of the defeated army.

Few of them had seen such a victory before. They captured eight artillery pieces, which they buried under logs or in swamps; two forges; two baggage wagons; a reported four hundred tents and marquees; twelve hundred muskets and bayonets; an estimated $33,000 worth of equipment and provisions; and many horses. The casualties suffered by St. Clair's force have never been accurately known. The most authoritative estimate was given by Adjutant General Sargent: 623 soldiers killed and captured and 258 wounded; 24 killed and 13 wounded among the artificers and packers; and 30 of 33 women killed — a total of 948 casualties. This may have understated the loss. Denny's count of the army casualties alone amounted to 630 killed or captured and 283 wounded. Remarkably, the Indian losses appear to have been light. None of the several accounts gave the killed at more than 35 men.[26]

In the long history of Indian resistance north of Mexico only once before had a victory of such magnitude fallen to the natives: the defeat of the British army under General Edward Braddock on the Monongahela River in 1755. Only two comparable battles would be fought in the years ahead: the destruction of American armies on the River Raisin and at Fort Meigs in 1813. If there was a zenith in the troubled story of the Shawnee stand for Ohio, it was surely that cold day on the banks of the Wabash when Blue Jacket and his allies utterly vanquished the first army of the United States.[27]

# IO

## All the Nations Are Now of One Mind

Within days of the electrifying defeat of St. Clair's army, a big, heavy Ottawa chief threw his immense influence behind the Indian confederacy in a council on the Maumee River. "You ought not to give peace to your enemy until they ask it, or until they first retire out of your country," said Egushaway. The Indians must "send deputations from each tribe to other nations, to present to them the scalps of your enemies, and to invite them to unite with you in the war."[1]

The greatest gifts the victory bestowed on Blue Jacket and his Shawnees were temporary security and credibility. For a short time the Big Knives had been beaten back, and there would be a respite until they could field another force. And now Shawnee emissaries had a tremendous story to tell as they toured the tribes. Everywhere there would be ardent young warriors deeply distressed that they had missed the battle, and everywhere there would also be doubters who were now having to admit that the Americans could be beaten and that the spirits seemed to favor the armies of the Indian confederacy. Never had the prospects for extending the union and welding it to Shawnee ambitions been rosier, and Blue Jacket seized the opportunity with both hands. In fact, if the near annihilation of St. Clair's army in 1791 was a military summit, the following year saw unusual political endeavors and achievements. It was the high-water mark of Shawnee diplomacy.

In January 1792 Blue Jacket was once again in Detroit talking with the redcoats. By then he knew that Dorchester had turned down Indian requests for direct military intervention, but there was still a lot the British could do to help. We have no record of what transpired this time, but Blue Jacket may have wanted additional ammunition to enable the Indians to withstand further attacks, and perhaps he urged the redcoats to arrest the rum trade, which was repeatedly reducing Indian armies on the Maumee to states of intoxication. The chiefs had stifled supplies of rum reaching the Indians from American settlements, but the Detroit trade was a continual embarrassment.[2]

Whatever Blue Jacket got for the confederacy, he spoke with unprecedented personal authority after his defeat of St. Clair, and the British fussed over him. It was rumored that he was awarded the commission and half pay of a British brigadier general, and people began to refer to him deferentially as General Blue Jacket. What lay behind these stories we simply do not know. They may have reflected nothing more than the testimonial he had had from the British as long ago as 1784 or the spanking red tunic with the gold bullion at the shoulders which he happily produced for gala occasions in the months that followed. In addition, he seems to have enjoyed some financial inducement from the British. Perhaps it was a small stipend, but if it was intended to bind him to the British interest rather than reward past services, the redcoats would find it singularly unsuccessful.[3]

It was probably while he was at Detroit that Blue Jacket sent his runners to the small community of Moravian mission Indians then settled on the Canadian side of the Detroit River. He warned that they "should not think that they alone could sit so quiet and see others go to war for them" and asked them to come and defend the Ohio. This was only one manifestation of the vigorous new canvass of the tribes being conducted by the Shawnees. Sometimes other Indians aided them. In the spring of 1792, for example, a Cherokee party under White Owl's Son, which had come north the previous year and fought against St. Clair, carried a Shawnee war pipe back to their people. The brother of White Owl's Son was Dragging Canoe, the formidable war captain of the Chickamauga Cherokees, whose villages were situated on the lower Tennessee River. Dragging Canoe personally took the cause of Indian unity to the Creeks and Cherokees in the early months of the year. But usually Shawnees themselves were at the heart of the recruiting. They went to the Iroquois to chide Joseph Brant and to the Great Lakes and the Illinois and Mississippi Rivers. Two of their envoys reached the Shawnee towns in Spanish Missouri, which Blue Jacket and his chiefs were considering making havens for their noncombatants while the warriors continued the fight to save Ohio.[4]

On these journeys the emissaries called upon the tribes to send their warriors to the Maumee, where they would be ready to meet the Big Knives if they advanced again. They were also organizing a great intertribal congress on the Maumee, which, they hoped, would tell the Americans "to abandon this side of the Ohio if they expect peace."[5]

Blue Jacket himself spearheaded the canvass. Today, when we think of an Indian leader carrying the message of unity across considerable distances, we think of Tecumseh, the Shawnee who rebuilt the confederacy in the years before the War of 1812. But in 1792 Blue Jacket followed that same course, in pursuit of the same vision. He carried a pipe and tobacco and speeches "to the distant western nations," inviting them to join the union. He went to the Great Lakes and the Mississippi, and his itinerary seems to have included the Potawatomis of the Illinois River and the Sac and Fox villages on the upper Mississippi, in what is now Illinois and Iowa. Evidently Blue Jacket had some success. According to his relative and close ally the Shawnee orator Red Pole, the Indians Blue Jacket visited requested that the pipe be returned to the confederated council fire on the Maumee "for all nations to come and take hold of it and to smoke with it, and desired us to be strong and hold fast our country." Blue Jacket was probably back about April, for a message sent to the British by the Shawnees, Delawares, and Miamis at that time mentioned that they had received satisfactory responses from the Ottawas, Ojibwes, Potawatomis, Foxes, Kickapoos, Weas, and Piankeshaws, some of the people Blue Jacket had visited. They were ready to march, the chiefs said overconfidently. "All the nations are now of one mind and resolved and able to defend themselves."[6]

When Blue Jacket and other ambassadors invited widespread tribesmen to join them, it was to the new headquarters of the confederacy at the Glaize that they were directed. Miamitown was now deemed unsafe, and in 1792 the principal allies completed their transfer to the confluence of the Maumee and the Auglaize, where a vibrant cosmopolitan community was in the making. The Glaize, as it was called, was a fascinating place in 1792, a rendezvous for powerful Indian war chiefs and British and French traders.

Captain Johnny already had a Mekoche town on the east bank of the Auglaize, just above its junction with the Maumee, but Blue Jacket created a separate town on the north side of the Maumee, about a mile downstream of the Glaize. In this, the military nerve center of the confederacy if there was one, several "fine" houses were built, one of them Blue Jacket's, while across the river, safe from grazing livestock, the cornfields were planted. Another eight miles down would have brought Blue Jacket to Black Snake's Town, while above he could find the homes of his important allies: Little Turtle's Miamis, on the north bank of the Maumee four miles above the Glaize, where Antoine Lasselle also made a home, and the principal town of the Delawares, under Big Cat, Buckongahelas, and Tetepachsit (Branching Tree), sitting on the west bank of the Auglaize, a little above Captain Johnny's. Sprinkled round about these important towns were small groups of other Indians, including Nanticokes, Cherokees, and Mingoes, who had thrown in with the triumvirate.

Not the least colorful figure in this complex was the Mohawk medicine woman Coocoochee. Her family had taken refuge with the Shawnees many years before, two of her sons lived in Blue Jacket's Town, and a daughter had married the British trader George Ironside. She herself inhabited a cabin on the Maumee, across from the mouth of the Auglaize, and it was a popular resort for Blue Jacket's men as they filed upstream on errands of war. Coocoochee was feisty but cheerful, but it was her reputation as a seer that attracted the warriors. If the old woman predicted success, the warriors crossed the Maumee in their canoes, some of them standing erect cradling muskets in their arms, in greater heart.

The traders were bound to the Indians by economic and social ties. Their center was the high ground within the southwest junction of the Maumee and the Auglaize. Ironside had a house and store there, and the other inhabitants included John Kinzie, married to a white girl taken by the Shawnees; a baker named Perault; Jacques Lasselle, Blue Jacket's son-in-law; and within a stockade James Girty and his Shawnee wife. Other traders located themselves further down the Maumee. John McCormick had a trading post on the north bank, near the rapids. His son Alexander used to tell a story of how Blue Jacket once came to the rescue of his father when a group of Indians began pillaging his store. The Shawnee chief drove the ruffians out in an instant.[7]

The advantages of this new position were obvious. It was farther from the enemy, more than one hundred miles from Fort Jefferson, the nearest American post, and some two hundred across country from Fort Washington. It was also closer to Detroit and convenient for McKee's depot at the foot of the Maumee rapids. Also downstream were valuable new allies: Egushaway's Ottawas near Roche de Bout and the villages of Delawares and Wyandots who had removed from the Sandusky.

Here, then, the Shawnees were not only close to British supplies but also to essential manpower. Within a short amount of time Blue Jacket could commonly assemble up to two thousand warriors. On the Maumee there were about three hundred Shawnee fighting men, more than three hundred Delawares and Munsees, one hundred Miamis, and one hundred Mingo, Cherokee, and Nanticoke warriors. And nearby they could call upon some two hundred Wyandots from the Maumee and Detroit Rivers and a large number of Lakes Indians — Maumee Ottawas, Ojibwes from present-day Michigan, and Potawatomis of the St. Joseph in southwestern Michigan and the Huron River flowing into Lake Erie.[8]

Back from his tour, Blue Jacket put himself into organizing that force. Occasionally small parties were sent to reconnoiter or harass the string of little garrisons between Fort Washington and Fort Jefferson. In June a party of Shawnees and Cherokees attacked Fort Jefferson, killing or capturing sixteen soldiers cutting hay outside the stockade. The greater problem, however, was holding together or convening a sufficient force to meet any major attack the Big Knives might make. Any unusual movements on the part of the Americans had Indian riders or runners scuttling up and down the Maumee, and some of them reached as far as the Ojibwe and Munsee towns on the River Thames in what is now Ontario.[9]

Brief reports of Blue Jacket's activities sometimes reached the publications of the day. "By a gentleman immediately from Montreal," ran one snippet, "we learn that about four weeks since the famous Indian partisan, known by the name of Captain Blue Jacket, was at Detroit with about 2000 men, waiting for the Americans to come out of the woods. It is believed at Montreal that in case the Americans do not go out, they will be divided into small parties to harass our frontiers." In September, when warriors arrived on the Maumee to attend the intertribal congress, the chiefs had even greater reserves of manpower. Nevertheless, an American newspaper exaggerated their strength greatly when it announced that Blue Jacket, Black Snake, and Egushaway commanded up to five thousand warriors![10]

Amid this excitement the Shawnees were also preparing for the intertribal congress, which they knew would be a major test of their influence. Blue Jacket's people were in no doubt about what course they wanted to follow. The treaties of Fort Harmar had to be nullified, and the proper boundary between the Indians and the Americans was the Ohio River. If the Big Knives did not agree to that, the war would continue. Some Indians agreed with the Shawnees outright, the Cherokees, Mingoes, and most of Buckongahelas's Delawares, possibly also the Miamis at the Glaize. But could they win the support of the entire congress? It was a congress composed not so much of young warriors, in whom military victories had kindled an extraordinary will to fight, but of older, wiser heads capable of weighing consequences.

There was doubt about whether Shawnee opinion would prevail. The Senecas were on their way to the congress, but they were firmly in the American orbit, and their chiefs had been entertained in Philadelphia in the spring. Brant was also coming and was known for moderation. He, too, had been speaking to the American administration and was practicing a delicate balancing act. He flatly told Washington and Knox that to achieve peace they must rescind the former treaties, something the Americans refused to hear, and he was now on his way west hoping to persuade the Indians to negotiate on the basis of a compromise line along the Muskingum River.[11]

Even in the west the Shawnees had important opponents. One was Egushaway, the civil and war chief of the Ottawas. A skilled diplomat, he had a tremendous influence with the tribes of the Three Fires — the Ojibwes, Potawatomis, and his own Ottawas. Henry Hamilton had described him as "a sensible Indian . . . more attended to than any of the Lake Indians," and the Moravian missionary David Zeisberger found him the chief "to whose hands everything must go." Egushaway expected the congress to declare for peace, and he was ready to support it. Indeed, some of the Ottawas even quit the Glaize before the congress opened, so tired were they of hearing the Shawnees "talking . . . so much for war."[12]

When a Mahican, Hendrick Aupaumut, reached the Maumee in July on a peace mission from the United States, he found few willing openly to contradict Shawnee opinion but considerable private dissatisfaction. A Wyandot declared that his people had not come to the congress merely "to attend to the voice of the Shawannese," and he intended to put it "under my feet." Even Big Cat of the Delawares said that though the tide was running for war, he was not personally inimical to peace. He advised Aupaumut to lay his proposals before the other Indians first and to build a bloc of support before approaching the Shawnees.

At this critical juncture in Shawnee affairs neither Blue Jacket, the principal war chief, nor Captain Johnny, the tribal civil chief, stood to the helm. They deferred to a younger man distinguished as a diplomat and orator, Musquaconocah, or Red Pole. He was a close relation to Blue Jacket, probably a half-brother or first cousin, and certainly a powerful ally. Red Pole shared some of his "brother's" vices and occasionally drank heavily. An American officer, Andrew Marschalk, who knew the two Shawnees in the summer of 1796, remembered how they retired to their temporary camp on an island at the foot of the Maumee rapids for a drinking bout. Still, when sober Red Pole was an amiable, urbane, dignified, and sensible man, intelligent and eloquent. It was probably for those qualities that he was chosen to superintend the congress at the Glaize, but he also seems to have been a Mekoche. The Mekoches claimed the right to negotiate for the tribe, at least in peacetime, and the selection of Red Pole may also have been a way of satisfying protocol.[13]

Hitherto, Red Pole has cut an obscure figure in the surviving documents of the period, but in 1792 he stands firm and clear as the master of ceremonies at one of the most remarkable intertribal congresses in the history of the Old Northwest.

＊　＊　＊

The gathering of an Indian congress was a slow business. In the summer Shawnee runners had gone out, trying to hurry delegates forward, but many did not begin their journeys until the corn had ripened. Some arrived sick, others late. On 15 September Captain Johnny went down to the foot of the Maumee rapids to welcome forty-five representatives of the Iroquois living within American limits, mainly Senecas, but the Canadian Iroquois under Joseph Brant did not make an appearance until the congress was over.

By the end of September, however, a remarkable gathering had taken place at the Glaize. There were Shawnees, Miamis, Delawares, Munsees, Mingoes, Cherokees, Conoys, and Nanticokes from the heartland of the confederacy. Wyandots, Ottawas, Ojibwes, and Potawatomis from the Great Lakes were also at hand, as were the Weas of the Wabash. Sacs and Foxes had traveled east from the upper Mississippi to reach the congress, as had Delawares and Shawnees from Missouri. Westward from New York had come Mahicans and the deputies of the Six Nations of the Iroquois and from the banks of the St. Lawrence members of the Seven Nations of Canada. The South, too, was represented, by Cherokee and Creek delegates, and there as observers and suppliers were also the omnipresent members of the British Indian Department under Alexander

McKee. All had been drawn together by Shawnee diplomacy and the luster of recent Indian victories.[14]

Finally, on 30 September, the Indians filed into one of the Shawnee villages at the Glaize, probably Captain Johnny's, and the proceedings began. The Shawnees and Miamis opened formalities, passing a calumet first to their "elder brothers" the Iroquois and Wyandots and then to other leaders of the confederacy. Red Pole held aloft the pipe Blue Jacket had carried west, with black and white strings of wampum, and welcomed the delegates. No other business was transacted that day, but Red Pole fired a warning shot. He cautioned his solemn audience not to heed the "bad birds who will corrupt your hearts, blind your eyes, and shut your ears against your true interests." His mind, if not his eyes, was on the Senecas, who he knew were here at the behest of the United States. They had made no contribution to confederate affairs in recent years, but they had been talking to the Americans and got an increase in their treaty annuities, and the Shawnees were deeply distrustful of what advice they had to offer.[15]

On 2 October, when Red Pole again stood before the assembled delegates, he launched a frontal attack on the Senecas. He reminded them of their former significance and their advice to the Indians to "be strong and united and to defend our country," and he said that both the western and southern nations were waiting to learn whether the Iroquois would attend the united council fire. The Senecas were "slow in coming," Red Pole complained, and had not concerned themselves with the confederacy for three years. "We have never seen you since that time," he informed them. "We suppose you have been constantly trying to do us some good, and that was the reason of your not coming sooner to join us. We shall now send these speeches to all the distant nations to acquaint them with this council, and of your being present."

Before the congress had opened, the Mahican Hendrick Aupaumut had fancied that he had cultivated a peace lobby among the Delawares, but now in public council Buckongehelas crushed any prospect of a wedge being driven between him and the Shawnees. "Don't think . . . that it was their [the Shawnees'] sentiments alone," he said. "All of us are animated by one mind, one head, and one heart, and we are resolved to stick close by each other and defend ourselves to the last."

Two days later the Senecas replied through their most spectacular speaker, Red Jacket. He tried to reassure the confederates. The Senecas did support the union and gladly smoked from Blue Jacket's pipe, and yes, during the past few years they had indeed been working to assist their western brethren. Now, however, they had to inform the Indians that the Americans were willing to talk to them. The victories over Harmar and St. Clair should not blind the confederacy to the need for peace. "Don't be too proud spirited and reject it," said Red Jacket. "The Great Spirit should be angry with you."

In itself this advice was entirely sensible, but it sounded disingenuous given by people who had been treating confidentially with the Americans in Philadelphia. Even the Seven Nations of Canada, who for the most part were Iroquoian peoples, reacted ambivalently to Red Jacket's discourse. They commended the peace initiative but wanted no independent dealings with the Americans, as the Senecas had undertaken. Chief Cochenawaga urged "all nations of our color in the island" to "be of one mind and strong." If the Americans wished to talk, "let us put our hands together and join as one nation. And if they do not agree to what we shall determine, let us all strike them at once."

Red Pole was less charitable. On 5 October he retorted to the Senecas fiercely, accusing them of duplicity. "You did not speak to the *real* purposes you came [brought] to this council fire. . . . I can see what you are about from this place. . . . You are still talking to the Americans. Your head is now turned toward them. . . . When you left your village to come here you had a bundle of American speeches under your arm. I now desire you, Brother, to lay that bundle down here, and explain what you have been talking with them [about] these last two years. . . . All the different nations here now desire you to speak from your heart and not from your mouth." So saying, the Shawnee orator picked up the strings of wampum upon which Red Jacket had spoken the previous day and threw them at the feet of the seated Senecas.

The Iroquois were visibly flustered and begged to withdraw to confer. "You have talked to us a little too roughly," complained Red Jacket. "You have thrown us on our backs." Farmer's Brother, another Seneca, picked up the rejected wampum, threw it over his shoulder so that it trailed down his back, and led the entire delegation into an hour of urgent discussion. When they returned, Red Jacket made a clean breast of it.

Yes, the Senecas had been to Philadelphia, but they had told President Washington that the western Indians were angry about the land. The Americans had said they would "satisfy" the owners of the ceded lands if they had been purchased from the wrong Indians. "He did not say he would give up the lands," Red Jacket conceded, "but that he would satisfy the Indians for them. That he wanted . . . the friendship of all his brothers, the Indians." Washington had promised to remove any military posts established on unceded Indian territory and wanted a peace conference. Then the Senecas handed over a tin case they had been given. It contained a map and several American speeches.

Even this failed to restore Seneca credibility. The following day the Iroquois delegation tried to avoid further public humiliation and did not attend the council fire; instead, they asked for a private conference in their own camp. There Red Pole, Black Snake, Buckongahelas, and a few others were served up a fuller and franker explanation of the Iroquois mission. The Senecas declared their faith in the justice of the United States, and while they agreed to support the majority will of the congress they strongly urged peace. These remarks found little favor. The Senecas were reminded that while they were talking peace with the United States, two armies of Big Knives had invaded the Indian country. "Brothers," they heard, "had the Great Spirit been favorable to them, instead of us, you would have found here their strong forts, and only a small remnant, or perhaps none, of your western brethren to deliver their sweet speeches to." Other nations, such as the Wyandots and Delawares of the Sandusky, had been temporarily duped, but the Americans "did not succeed so well with these nations as with our elder brethren [the Senecas], for you now see them strong in defending their just rights to this country. They put their [American] speeches at their back, and united themselves to us as one man."

It was obvious that the Senecas had underestimated the intense sense of grievance felt by dispossessed western Indians, such as the Shawnees, and their distrust of the United States. A war dance opened business on 7 October, and Red Pole dismissed the American overtures. "All the Americans wanted was to divide us," he explained, "that we might not act as one man." The Senecas had been naive, for the Shawnees knew full well what the Big Knives intended from the papers they had captured from St. Clair's army. If the Indians had been defeated, forts would have been built at Miamitown, the Glaize, and the mouth of the Maumee. Indians who resisted would have been driven away, and those who acquiesced would have had "hoes [put] in their hands to plant corn" for the Americans and been made to "labor like their beasts, their oxen and their packhorses." This was a disparaging reference to the efforts of missionaries to improve Indian husbandry and to convert warriors into farmers. As for the willingness of the Americans to pay more for the lands they had taken, Red Pole thundered, "We do not want compensation. We want restitution of our country." If the Americans were serious about peace, they had only to destroy their forts and restore the Ohio boundary as defined by the 1768 treaty of Fort Stanwix.

The congress closed a triumph for the Shawnees. They had agreed to meet the United States for peace talks at Lower Sandusky in the spring, provided that British officials were on hand to interpret papers and document the treaty of 1768, but they had harnessed the congress to their war aims — the Ohio boundary — and secured pledges of unity, even from the Senecas, who were entrusted with passing the Indian resolutions to the Americans. It is unlikely that the Shawnees and their allies seriously believed the Americans would meet their terms, at least without increased pain, but those declarations of support from the other tribes would enable the triumvirate to assemble the needed military force.

For a while the militants resumed their task of harassing the settlements and military posts north of the Ohio, but efforts to implement the decisions of the congress proceeded fairly quickly. Within days of closing the council Red Pole, Kakinathucca, and Black Snake called on Alexander McKee and formally requested British assistance in the forthcoming negotiations with the United States. When the American government received the news, Henry Knox also acted promptly, promising to appoint commissioners to meet the Indians the following year. Both sides undertook to curb hostilities during the intervening period.[16]

The Shawnee chiefs were elated by the unity displayed in the Glaize congress and were determined to carry word of it back to the "distant" nations and to add cement to the agreements and understandings they had already reached. Moreover, they wanted to extend that union and to fashion an even more formidable instrument of war.

Blue Jacket had toured the Northwest. Now it was the turn of his "brother" Red Pole, but he turned elsewhere, embarking on one of the most ambitious Shawnee attempts thus far to carry the message of unity through the broad lands of the South.

✳    ✳    ✳

With him went seven other Shawnees and the twenty-two-year-old white Shawnee George Ash, who had a tolerable facility with the English language. The prime intention was to strengthen bonds between the southern Indians and the northern confederacy and to stiffen resistance against the United States. Red Pole's message was simple. He warned his audiences about American land hunger and urged them to unite with their northern brethren, and he told them that supplies and ammunition might probably be had from the British in Canada. His clarion call came at a time when Hector, Baron de Carondelet, the new governor of Spain's possessions in the South, was himself worried about the threat from American expansionists and was also advocating a union of the southern tribes. He wanted to build an Indian buffer between the United States and the Spanish borderlands.

About the end of 1792 the Shawnees reached the villages of the Chickamauga Cherokees on the lower Tennessee, where the state lines of Georgia, Tennessee, and Alabama now meet. They were welcome here because the Chickamaugas had been battling the white settlement of Tennessee since Revolutionary times, and some Shawnees had been living among them since 1789 or 1790. Their leader, Cheeseekau, a Kispoko war chief who was the older brother of Tecumseh, had just been killed helping the Cherokees and Creeks to attack Nashville on the Cumberland. Red Pole's party called at one of the Chickamauga villages, Willstown, and said they would probably hold a public meeting there after they had visited the Creeks.[17]

Pressing on, the Shawnees arrived among the Creeks in January 1793 to find the nation in disarray. In 1790 some of the Upper Creeks, who lived in what is now Alabama, had been to New York under the leadership of the astute mestizo Alexander McGillivray. Eager to placate the southern Indians at a time when their resources were few and their army embroiled with the northern Indians, the Americans guaranteed the remaining lands of the Creeks in return for the cession of territory between the Ogeechee and Oconee Rivers. But many Lower Creeks from the Flint and Chattahoochee Rivers of Georgia were furious about the deal, and the area was further destabilized by the decline of McGillivray, who was on his deathbed when the Shawnees made their appearance.[18]

With some Cherokees and an interpreter in tow, Red Pole's party went first to the Lower Creek villages near the modern boundary of Georgia and Alabama, where the most extreme opposition to the treaty of New York was to be found. Their public meetings soon reduced James Seagrove, the United States Indian agent in those parts, to panic. He urged the Creeks to drive the northerners away and recklessly promised a horseload of goods for every Shawnee scalp, a stupid bribe which the Creeks realized could only have entangled them in embarrassing intertribal difficulties. Seagrove's fury increased after some Lower Creeks raided the store of his brother on the St. Marys on 11 March, killed a few people, and made off with large quantities of merchandise.

At Seagrove's behest, several Indians and whites did try hard to counteract the influence of the Shawnees. One, John Kinnaird, was reported to have ridden about the villages delivering pro-American talks, and another, a trader named Timothy Barnard, condemned the visitors in a public council. An Upper Creek chief known as the Mad Dog of Tuckabatchee threatened to give the northerners "their lesson" and to "send them home" when they came to his town on the Tallapoosa.[19]

Seagrove claimed that all but three Lower Creek towns finally rejected the Shawnees, and they were ordered from the nation, but there are reasons to believe he was minimizing Red Pole's success. On 12 April three Lower Creek leaders, one the prominent Ockillissa Chopka, wrote to the British in Canada. They said they welcomed the Shawnee call for unity but needed arms and ammunition to make war. In May, when the Shawnees returned to the Cherokees, they left the Creek country in an uproar. Disaffection was most evident in the Lower Creek towns of Osochi, Coweta, Broken Arrow, Yuchi Town, and Chiaha, but the Upper Creek village of Big Tallassee, where Hopoithle Mico (Tame King) had led opposition to McGillivray, was also hostile to the Americans, and Seagrove went so far as to recommend that the secretary of war send an army to subdue opposition. The governor of Georgia did field several hundred militia in June, but his force had no sooner invaded Creek land than it disintegrated.

The Shawnees left the Creeks closer to war than they found them, and late in May they were at Willstown, urging the Cherokees to attack the white settlements on the Cumberland. Presumably, Red Pole and Blue Jacket had decided that if they could provoke a southern war, it would both divert and drain the resources of the United States and force it to meet the Shawnee terms for peace on the Ohio. Some of the Cherokees were sympathetic to the Shawnees. Even Little Turkey, the leading chief of the more peaceful Upper Cherokees of Georgia, seized the opportunity to send a letter to the British along the lines of that already composed by the Creeks. Publicly, Little Turkey and his associates professed friendship to the United States, but privately they too were exploring the possibilities of armed resistance.[20]

The Willstown conference over, the Shawnees looked toward home. With them traveled an old Loyalist, George Welbank, who had been living with the Creeks and who now carried the letters the southern

Indians had written to the British. Some Creek and Cherokee supporters also journeyed north. But for some unknown reason, Red Pole chose to remain in the South. Perhaps he returned to the Tallapoosa, where some Shawnees still had settlements, and almost certainly he continued to promote Indian solidarity. But Red Pole did not see Blue Jacket for nearly two years.[21]

The Shawnees were an influence in the South, but their hopes were not to be realized. The southern Indians lived far from the battlegrounds of the North and were preoccupied by local issues, so it would have been difficult for them to send recruits to Blue Jacket's armies. The Shawnees likely saw their value as mainly diversionary. Yet there was to be no general war against the Americans in the South. Neither the Chickasaws nor the Choctaws responded when the Chickamaugas tried to persuade them to join a southern confederacy in 1792 and 1793, and both supplied scouts to the United States for use against the northern Indians. Some of the Creeks and Cherokees did assist the Shawnees, but both were riven with factionalism and neither had ready sources of arms and ammunition. The British were too far away, and Carondelet's policy of promoting a pro-Spanish confederacy of southern Indians was not favored by a prudent home government and soon ran out of steam.[22]

Nevertheless, the Shawnee diplomacy of 1792 and 1793 was truly impressive. The dream of Indian unity had been carried thousands of miles by durable Shawnee emissaries, through deep woods, over wide prairies, and along furious and twisting rivers, from New York to the muddy Mississippi, and from the warm, wet river valleys of Alabama and Georgia to the swampy Thames in Ontario. Hundreds of Indians had been brought to the Glaize, representatives from across a vast region, and persuaded to endorse the fight for the Ohio boundary.

Although the practical benefits were doubtful and had yet to be seen, it had indeed been a mighty effort. Today, whenever the struggle for Indian solidarity is aired, we think of the two Shawnee brothers, Tecumseh and the Prophet, who promoted pan-Indianism in the early years of the nineteenth century. Perhaps we ought also to remember their predecessors, the other Shawnee brothers, Blue Jacket and Red Pole, who championed the same cause two decades before. For if Tecumseh would prove himself to be the ultimate pan-Indian visionary, he merely trod a path well and bravely worn by his now forgotten mentors.

# II

## Just Rights and an Uncertain War

It was well that Blue Jacket and Red Pole prepared for war, because the prospects for peace were few.

The American government had no recipe for peace. It, too, knew there would be another battle. St. Clair's defeat might have shocked the nation and brought a storm of criticism about the war, its expense, its morality, and its ineptitude, but Washington and Knox resolutely planned the military conquest of the Old Northwest. Brushing aside the constitutional arguments against strengthening the army, they began raising a new force of five thousand men under Anthony Wayne and reformed the militia system. Wayne had his detractors, but he knew his principal business. His "legion," a self-contained army of infantry, cavalry, and artillery, was turned into a crack force. It boded ill for the Indians. They had always been inferior to the Americans in numbers and equipment and relied on superior fighting qualities to overturn the odds. By improving the quality of his troops, Wayne destroyed one of the few advantages Blue Jacket and his associates possessed.

These changes took time, and it was to buy that as well as to mollify critics of the war that the government engaged the Indians in unimpressive peace initiatives. Peace was desirable, of course, not the least to save the expense, but only if it was compatible with the white settlement of the Ohio country. That was the basis of President Washington's olive branch policy. There was never any question of returning to the Indians the land seized from them in the treaties of Forts Stanwix, McIntosh, Finney, and Harmar. It was already being sold off to land companies.

American peace initiatives simply emphasized that the United States desired no *further* territory from the Indians, at least none that they did not wish to sell, but the government eventually also dug deeper into its pockets to confirm the existing treaties. On 26 April 1793 the instructions for three peace commissioners, Timothy Pickering, Beverley Randolph, and Benjamin Lincoln, were dated. The commissioners were told to confirm the Harmar line, and $50,000 in goods and $10,000 a year in annuities were made available if the Indians did not regard the previous treaties as "a fair purchase," or if some Indians had been unjustly excluded from the benefits. Claims to some tracts intended for trading posts would also be relinquished, and the string of military posts the army had constructed in almost a direct line from Fort Washington toward the head of the Maumee — Forts Hamilton, St. Clair, and Jefferson — would be dismantled.

There was nothing here to attract the heart of an Indian confederacy victorious over two American armies. There were no real compromises. The only chink was a small one. The federal commissioners were authorized to retreat from the Harmar line, if necessary. Small pieces of ceded land that had not yet been sold to the speculators might be abandoned, but these were so insignificant that they would have made little difference to the general boundary line. Worse still, the United States wanted an *additional* 150,000 acres of Indian land so that the soldiers of George Rogers Clark, the fabled destroyer of Shawnee towns, could be rewarded!

Not surprisingly, the Americans expected the negotiations to fail. Although the commissioners were advised to weaken the Indians by trying to divide them, the government did not suspend military operations, as it had promised to do. During the spring and summer of 1793, men and supplies were pushed down the Ohio to Fort Washington (Cincinnati) and then up to the advanced posts.[1]

From May 1793 some two thousand warriors began gathering at the foot of the Maumee rapids, where they could feed on supplies from McKee's storehouse. They had come for preliminary discussions, before their representatives met the American commissioners at Lower Sandusky, and many had made long journeys to get there. Canada supplied 280 delegates from the Seven Nations of Canada in Quebec, and from what is now Ontario came Delawares and Ojibwes of the Thames and

50 Iroquois from the Grand River. The men of the Glaize were there and members of the Potawatomis, Ottawas, and Ojibwes from Michigan and Ohio. Senecas had returned from New York, and some Sacs from the Mississippi, but this time the tribes of the Wabash, Illinois, and Mississippi were generally poorly represented.[2]

The voices for peace here were few, however. Blue Jacket's people were fighting for their homes and a country where the Great Spirit expected them to live. If they let it go, against the wishes of Waashaa Monetoo, there was no knowing what dire consequences might attend the tribe. The military successes themselves proved to Shawnees that the Great Spirit was on their side, and some young warriors were so flushed with success that they were talking not only about regaining the Ohio boundary but also of securing payment for their lost hunting grounds in Kentucky. They were in no mood to compromise.

Some Indians did not agree with the Shawnees. Joseph Brant, the head of the Grand River delegation, was willing to cede land east of the Muskingum River and even some places west of it, such as Marietta, if they had become too extensively settled by white homesteaders. But his was a forlorn stand. Even this compromise came nowhere near the American position, while among the Indians it not only faced opposition from the powerful triumvirate, the Shawnees, Delawares, and Miamis, but also from another influential group of players — the British.[3]

The British did want peace, but they also wanted the Indian country left intact, capable of providing warriors for the defense of Canada if another war with the Americans occurred, and furs for export to Europe. They also wanted a peace that preserved their own standing with the Indians, and that meant playing an important role in the proceedings, one which was visibly valuable to the tribes. The British, then, posed as objective facilitators of the negotiations. They gave documentary proof of the 1768 line, victualed the Indians, and supplied interpreters, and they offered the American commissioners hospitality, protection, and passage on the Great Lakes. But they, too, had their agenda.

In reality, the British position was complex. St. Clair's defeat had awakened contradictory currents in their ranks. The official line underscored caution. The British must not be drawn into a war with the United States, and nothing should be done to color accusations that they were encouraging Indian hostilities against the Americans. Consequently, McKee was instructed that the Indians must be told that Britain would not give them direct military assistance in their dispute with the United States.

In some quarters, however, the Indian victories had stimulated dreams of a British resurgence in the West. One thinking along those lines was the bluff lieutenant governor of the new colony of Upper Canada (Ontario), John Graves Simcoe. Encouraged by the great victories, Simcoe hoped that the Americans would have to yield ground in the Northwest. Sometimes he even fancied that a successful Indian war, along with secessionism among disaffected backcountry men in Kentucky, Pennsylvania, New York, and Vermont, might one day return the West to Britain and confine the impudent new republic to the Atlantic seaboard.

Simcoe would have loved to have seen the Americans concede to the demands of Blue Jacket and his allies. He was interested in the creation of an Indian buffer state in the Northwest, between British and American possessions, and guaranteed by both powers. This idea was going around among British administrators at the time, and Simcoe envisaged that it could approximate the Indian country defined by Brant, with a boundary along the Ohio and the Muskingum. He knew so little about the aspirations of the United States that he actually believed the Americans might accept such a proposal, even one allowing the British to retain command of Detroit. The American government would have regarded it as preposterous, of course. From their perspective, it would have been tantamount to ceding territory, forgoing the settlement of the Northwest, and allowing the potentially hostile influence Britain exercised over the Indians to continue through Detroit.

Paradoxically, although Simcoe believed that Brant's hypothetical Muskingum line offered the best chances of securing an agreement with the United States, he threw British influence behind the Shawnees rather than moderate Indian opinion. This was because conversations with Alexander McKee had convinced him that the Shawnees and their immediate associates would simply refuse to give ground on the Ohio boundary and that Indian unity was paramount. Better that all the Indians backed the extreme position than that they fragmented. Simcoe therefore told McKee and his assistants to pressure Brant and others to fall into line with the Shawnees.[4]

The British were not the honest brokers they claimed to be. In June 1793 Simcoe urged his agent "to exert your ascendancy over the Indians in inclining them to accede to . . . offers . . . consistent with their safety and benefit, or to reject others, if they seem likely to prove injurious."[5] In other words, they were to be advisers, watching for anything contrary to the interests of the Indians — and the British.

In these circumstances, the honorable compromise Brant strove to find was doomed to failure. Unacceptable to the Americans and Shawnees alike, it was even targeted by its few friends, Britons such as Simcoe, who saw in it the germ of reconciliation. No, the war seemed set to last.

Yet among the Shawnees there were those who entertained hopes that the Big Knives might just agree to their terms. Captain Johnny coordinated the councils on the Maumee, receiving messages Indian runners brought in for the confederacy, consulting the chiefs, acting as their spokesman, liaising with the British, and attempting to placate the sensibilities of the different Indian nations gathering about the rapids. He hastened to reassure the prickly Joseph Brant, who arrived grumbling about the inadequacy of the condolence ceremonies that were supposed to welcome guests who had traveled a long way.[6]

Blue Jacket left him to it but stood at hand, monitoring the proceedings. He heard the reports of continued American military activities, which were supposed to have been halted by the peace negotiations, but although some Indians panicked and rushed home to guard their villages, Blue Jacket kept calm and did not take the threat seriously.

Blue Jacket learned that the United States commissioners had reached Niagara, where they were enjoying the hospitality of Simcoe and waiting for a ship to take them across Lake Erie to the venue at Sandusky. The Indians decided that two delegates from each tribe should go to Niagara to complain about Wayne's movements and to ensure that the commissioners had powers to treat with the tribes. The articulate and experienced Brant headed the mission, with a Shawnee leader named Canawya (Cat's Eyes).[7]

Blue Jacket embarked upon a mission of his own, a mysterious one, which remains unexplained to this day.

*    *    *

After outlining his views about the peace negotiations to Captain Johnny and his fellow chiefs, Blue Jacket left the rapids at the beginning of July and made for Detroit on the first leg of a journey to Montreal.

Perhaps there was private business on his mind, business concerning his trading connections with Canadian merchants, but he told Col. Richard England, the commandant at Detroit, that he wanted to see Sir John Johnson, the superintendent general of Indian affairs in Canada. The obvious conclusion is that Blue Jacket believed that now negotiations were under way, hostilities would be suspended for several months, giving him an opportunity to confer with Johnson about the interests of the Indians.

What these matters were there is no telling. Perhaps our only clue comes from John Norton, who interviewed Shawnee associates of Blue Jacket in 1810 and left one of the most reliable "inside" accounts of the war. He stated that Blue Jacket once "attempted to go to England to enquire what succour might be expected from that quarter, but was prevented from the want of pecuniary means." Sir John Johnson was exactly the person to approach about a passage to Britain. The fortunes of the confederacy were at a critical point, and the Shawnees expected that further military campaigns would be necessary. At the same time, news from Europe would have been unsettling. War had broken out between Britain and France, and we may be sure that Blue Jacket had heard something about it from his friends the Lasselles. It is entirely possible that he was worried about whether Britain had the ability to support the Indians while waging a major conflict on its own side of the Atlantic. Less than a year later, George Ironside and Ronald McDonald wrote from the Glaize that the Lasselles were sympathetic to France and had been lauding French power at the expense of the British. How such remarks preyed on Blue Jacket's fears at such a critical time may be imagined.[8]

All this is mere speculation, however. In truth, Blue Jacket's motives remain a mystery because he never got to Montreal. On 8 July he was in the British fort at Detroit, trying to persuade the impressive figure of Col. Richard England to find him a voyage down Lake Erie on one of the British ships. The colonel distrusted Blue Jacket because of his association with the French Canadians and endeavored to sway him from his purpose. The chief was too important, flattered England. He was needed at the rapids, and besides, before he went to Montreal he should consult McKee. Blue Jacket did not buy this reasoning. He was "determined" to go, reported England, haughtily replying that "he is a grand chief, and not under the control of any person."[9]

For a while the matter simmered because no ship was available, but the colonel scribbled an urgent note to McKee at the rapids. In the meantime, the Shawnee war chief looked up friends in the little town of wooden buildings clustered by the riverside. The same day he visited the colonel, he sought out some American Quakers who were in Detroit on their way to attend the peace commissioners at Lower Sandusky. One of them, Jacob Lindley, recorded meeting Blue Jacket and speaking to him through an interpreter. The chief was resplendent in his scarlet regimental coat and hat, and he acknowledged that the Quakers were men of peace and harmless. He expressed a wish that a peace would be established.

Probably Blue Jacket suspected the Quakers would try to divide the Indians and press them to accept any peace, and he remained friendly with them but noncommittal. On 9 July he called at their lodgings at Matthew Dolsen's tavern and spoke with the Moravian missionary John Heckewelder, as well as John Parrish, one of the Quakers. Heckewelder found the war chief cordial but "very reserved," while Parrish was impressed by this "intelligent person" and was encouraged to think a treaty could be signed. Blue Jacket "thinks a peace will take place," he said, "but that it is probable . . . the treaty will hold two months."[10]

As soon as Alexander McKee heard of Blue Jacket's plan, he asked the chiefs at the rapids to transmit a message asking their war leader to return. McKee had the note rushed to Colonel England and also warned a Detroit commissary, Thomas Duggan, to watch for Blue Jacket. Armed with the request of the chiefs, which reached Detroit about 12 July, England and Duggan spent two days trying to find Blue Jacket. England believed the war chief had gotten drunk somewhere. Duggan made the same charge, saying that Heckewelder and the Quakers invited Blue Jacket to dine with them but that he "got merry before dinner time and thought himself better engaged." These allegations appear to have been unfounded. John Heckewelder's diary for 13 July gave the true version: "Mr. Wilson and I, who were alone at home today, invited the great war chief Blue Jacket to dine with us. The conversation being of course on Indian affairs, we wished to hear his sentiments, and whether there was a prospect of bringing about a peace, but he conducted himself with that reservedness so peculiar to Indians and especially on such occasions." It was not until the morning of the fifteenth that England found Blue Jacket and delivered the message to him in the presence of two young Shawnees and Matthew Elliott. The chief instantly decided to return to the rapids and said he would set out the next day. In fact, he does not seem to have left until the seventeenth. Both England and Duggan were relieved. They believed Blue Jacket had been influenced by disaffected French. "I don't know if he has been tampered with or not," complained England, "but I have not the highest opinion of either his zeal or abilities. He certainly may do mischief, but I don't think he will do much good." Duggan believed that Blue Jacket's "son-in-law young Lasselle tampers with him as much as any one."[11]

One reason why the redcoats were so alarmed by Blue Jacket's un-scheduled visit to Detroit was that they were never able to control him. His loyalties were not to the British, of course. He acted for himself and those who were dear to him, certainly, and generally for the Indians as a whole, but he held no brief for the British. Nor did he rely purely on the British for his information. Unlike most Indians, he had many friends among the mercantile community, some of them Frenchmen, and had access to a broad range of opinion. This made him dangerous to the British. We cannot say what, if any, justification there was for the British fears on this occasion, but they proved to be eerily prophetic.

For the train of thought and action they indicated — the influence of the Lasselles and the weakening of Blue Jacket's faith in the redcoats — would one day help to bring about the end of the war in the Northwest.

∗   ∗   ∗

When Blue Jacket got back to the rapids before the end of the month, he heard that the negotiations were already in trouble.

On the formidably hot day of 7 July a group of fifty Indians under Brant and Cat's Eyes had met the American commissioners at Niagara, in the presence of Simcoe and other British officials. Tall and muscular, Brant was an impressive figure when he opened for the Indians, but his intelligent features bore a careworn expression, as if burdened by the magnitude of his task. He complained about the movements of the American army and reminded the commissioners that the land north of the Ohio was the "common property" of the united tribes. He wanted to know if Pickering, Randolph, and Lincoln had the power to run a new boundary line. What Brant did not do was interesting. He did not tell the commissioners that the Indians at the rapids were insisting that the Ohio was the only acceptable boundary. By using vaguer language, Brant prevented a premature rupture in the negotiations. Probably he was playing for the extra time he needed to convince the Shawnees and their allies to accept a moderate proposal.

The commissioners replied the next day, according to the Indian custom. The Indians were assured that hostilities had been suspended and that the commissioners were authorized to fix a fresh boundary. They did not elaborate on what that boundary might be but indicated that the Indians would not get everything they wanted. "We repeat," they said, "and say explicitly that some concessions will be necessary on your part as well as on our own in order to establish a just and permanent peace."

It was less than a candid statement about what the United States had to offer, but in substance it was language Brant understood. He gave his approval to the negotiations proceeding but made it plain the Indians would not be divided this time:

Our prospects, Brothers, are the more encouraging as our minds are now all one, and we are now all together as the Indians' deputies. Our first wishes in land affairs were that all the nations of the Indian confederacy should be together. It approaches now near to our wishes. The reasons why matters have not been properly transacted before are because those whom you treated with were but . . . a small part of the Indian confederacy. But now they are all about to assemble, business may be done, so we take you by the hand and conduct you to the meeting.[12]

That unity Brant had assumed soon fell about his ears back at the rapids. The Mohawk leader was criticized for his failure to stipulate that the Ohio boundary was a sine qua non for the meeting at Sandusky to proceed. In the hubbub Captain Johnny suggested that the chiefs of the confederacy split into two groups to confer. The divisions were predictable. The leaders of the triumvirate, with the Wyandots, formed one group, the Iroquois and the Ottawas, Potawatomis, and Ojibwes, for whom the modified boundary held fewer fears, the other.

On 26 July the discussion groups merged for a general meeting. The atmosphere was stark, and the Shawnee, Delaware, Miami, and Wyandot leaders appeared with pistols in their belts. To save further time, Egushaway and Brant, who were supporting the Muskingum line, suggested the American commissioners be brought to the rapids to negotiate, instead of Lower Sandusky. The Shawnee faction disagreed. Not only that, but Captain Johnny buried further argument. He flatly proclaimed that the Indians would demand the Fort Stanwix line of 1768. Another message would go to the commissioners to determine whether that was acceptable to them. If it was not, there was no point in going on.

The following day the confederacy sent its ultimatum: the Indians wanted the 1768 boundary and the removal of white settlers north of the Ohio. Brant seethed with fury and humiliation. He penned a protest to Alexander McKee, who was visibly in the confidence of the Shawnees and their supporters, and persuaded the Iroquois to refuse to sign the letter to the commissioners.[13]

According to some, the continued firmness of the Shawnees was encouraged by the appearance on the Maumee of a party of Creeks and Cherokees, accompanied by the Loyalist George Welbank. These were the warriors inspired by Red Pole in the South. The southern Indians were looking for British supplies, but they also brought stories of American encroachments on tribal lands in the South, which infused the northerners at the rapids with indignation. There were also wild stories about how many southern Indians might join in a war against the United States and unrealistic estimates of the amount of support to be had from the Spaniards, who still controlled the far South.[14]

The new delegation to the commissioners had none of the prudence of the old. It was headed by Captain Johnny and Buckongahelas. The Delaware war chief had been loud in his denunciations of Brant for not allowing the Shawnees to take the lead at the Niagara meeting, and he was a powerful supporter of the Ohio boundary of 1768.

Pickering, Randolph, and Lincoln had gotten as far as the Canadian side of the Detroit River and occupied Matthew Elliott's farm in what is now Amherstburg. It was there that Captain Johnny and his friends found them. They camped on Bois Blanc Island and on 30 July opened negotiations with the Americans, demanding clarification of the boundaries the commissioners were authorized to establish. The next day the commissioners replied. They were frustrated by these discussions with one Indian party after another and urged that they be allowed to address the full council without further delay. More specifically, they shot down any lingering Indian hopes of a peace based on the 1768 line. The former treaties were deemed satisfactory by the United States, and many settlers had made their homes on the ceded land north of the Ohio. It was now impossible to establish the Ohio as the boundary.

Facing the stony-faced Indian delegates Pickering said that "the concessions which we think necessary on your part are that you yield up and finally relinquish some of the lands on your side of the Ohio." By "some" land he meant the territory ceded at Fort Harmar, *plus* an additional tract claimed by George Rogers Clark and his soldiers. To sugar this pill, Pickering promised that "the United States would give such a large sum in money or goods as was never given at one time for any quantity of Indian lands," as well as "a large annuity" in perpetuity. If a new line had to be run, the commissioners would offer "generous compensation" and annuities.

Any remaining possibility for peace clouded over with this speech. Pickering made the most of the little he had to offer. He formally renounced the old American policy of acquiring land from the Indians by conquest. Pickering admitted that the king had not, after all, ceded Indian claims to the Northwest in 1783. "Of course he could not give it away. He only relinquished to the United States his claim to it." The Americans had merely gained the right of preemption or purchase should the Indians ever wish to dispose of their lands. "We now concede this great point," explained Pickering. "We, by the express authority of the President of the United States, acknowledge the property or right of soil of the great country above described to be in the Indian nations, so long as they desire it." Ten years before, such an attitude might have led to a sounder relationship between the Indians and the United States.

But in the summer of 1793 it thawed little ice. The council reconvened on the morning of 1 August, and Simon Girty, the infamous partisan of Revolutionary times, interpreted the reply of a Wyandot speaking for the Indians. Girty cut "a shocking figure," according to John Heckewelder, and the reply was as uncompromising. The Indians had made no valid treaties since 1768 and had sold no land north of the Ohio. The commissioners should go home and tell the president so. Matthew Elliott intervened at this point. He whispered to Captain Johnny that it sounded as if the Indians were breaking off negotiations, and the chiefs quickly modified the message. They asked the American commissioners to stay at Detroit a little longer while the delegation returned to the rapids. A reply would be made within a few days.[15]

Captain Johnny's party was at the rapids to report on the meeting on 5 August. Faced with the collapse of talks, the Indians tore at each other for a while. Brant was on the point of throwing up his hands in despair and heading for home until the Shawnees persuaded him to say. Finally, two days later, the newly arrived representatives of the Seven Nations of Canada said that they would not smoke the great pipe of union if it meant that they had to support the Shawnees in a war. They were not ready for that yet, they said; the business with the peace commissioners must be exhausted first. The stubborn Shawnees appeared to relent. They agreed that the Americans should be seen in a last attempt to reach a settlement.

It was then that Alexander McKee played a crucial hand. Each evening, after the day's discussions, the Shawnee, Delaware, and Wyandot chiefs habitually closeted themselves with McKee, Girty, and Prideaux Selby (also of the Indian Department) for private conversations. Brant, who was excluded, bitterly charged McKee with fostering extreme principles among the Indians, but the agent as vigorously denied it. He insisted that "all my endeavors were directed to accomplish a union" along the lines of Brant's Muskingum compromise. He in turn accused Brant of introducing divisions and of trying to bring the American commissioners forward before the tribes had concerted policy. Brant, however, was not alone in his view that McKee's overnight councils were directed against moderate opinion and hostile to full meetings with the commissioners.[16]

McKee's influence seemed particularly evident during councils on 9 and 10 July. On the first of the two days Brant seemed to have won a hard-fought argument with Captain Johnny. The western leaders eventually conceded that his Muskingum line was the best basis for negotiation. They told Brant that "your knowledge of the white people exceeds ours . . . you are from that enabled to form a better judgment of our affairs." The Mohawk went to his bed that night counting another victory in a long record of military and political triumphs.

To Brant's astonishment, the next day found the western chiefs as trenchant as ever. They would not move from the 1768 boundary, and Brant had no doubt who was to blame. Buckongahelas even pointed to McKee and remarked, "That is the person who advises us to insist on the Ohio River for the line." Without further argument, the Shawnees circulated a belt and a bunch of wampum, asking each nation in turn to signify its support by accepting it. Begrudgingly, the Ottawas, Ojibwes, and Potawatomis, along with the Seven Nations of Canada, submitted to the triumvirate, but Brant and his fellow Iroquois deputies declined. They moved their camp some eight miles downstream, declaring that they would meet the commissioners if no one else did.[17]

On 13 July the Indian response to the commissioners went out. It was signed by the Wyandots, Seven Nations, Delawares, Shawnees, Miamis, Ottawas, Ojibwes, Mingoes, Potawatomis, Conoys, Munsees, Nanticokes, Mahicans, Mississaugas (Ojibwes from the Thames River in Canada), Creeks, and Cherokees, and it fiercely presented the position for which Captain Johnny and Buckongahelas had fought. The document was impolitic, tactless, and unrealistic. It was almost foolish. But it was something more — the defiant and frank sentiments of proud, undefeated peoples, asserting their independence and sovereignty and rebutting the pretensions of those who would dispossess and humble them.

The Indians firmly rejected the American offer of money. "Money to us is of no value," they said, "and . . . no consideration whatever can induce us to sell the lands on which we get sustenance for our women and children." If the United States gave back the land it had taken, that money could be used to compensate the poor white settlers who would have to remove. As for the commissioners' call for concessions and their admission of the Indians' rights of the soil, the confederacy continued:

Brothers, you have talked to us about concessions. It appears strange that you should expect any from us, who have only been defending our just rights against your invasion. We want peace. Restore to us our country and we shall be enemies no longer.

Brothers, you make one concession to us by offering us your money, and another by having agreed to do us justice after having long and injuriously withheld it. We mean in the acknowledgement you have now made that the King of England never did, nor ever had a right to, give you our country by the treaty of peace [1783]. And you want to make this act of common justice a great part of your concessions, and seem to expect that because you have at last acknowledged our independence we should for such a favor surrender to you our country.

Brothers, you have talked also a great deal about pre-emption and your exclusive right to purchase Indian lands, as ceded to you by the King at the treaty of peace. Brothers, we never made any agreement with the King, nor with any other nation, that we would give to either the exclusive right of purchasing our lands. And we declare to you that we consider ourselves free to make any bargain or cession of lands whenever and to whomsoever we please. If the white people, as you say, made a treaty that none of them but the King should purchase off us, and that he has given that right to the U. States, it is an affair which concerns you and him and not us. We have never parted with such a power. . . .

We desire you to consider, Brothers, that our only demand is the peaceable possession of a small part of our once great country. Look back and view the lands from whence we have been driven to this spot. We can retreat no further, because the country behind hardly affords food for its present inhabitants. And we have therefore resolved to leave our bones in this small space to which we are now confined.[18]

There was a finality about the message. It concluded by stating that unless the 1768 line was accepted "our meeting will be altogether unnecessary." Upon receiving it the commissioners closed the negotiations and went home.

There was little surprise at the rapids, where tempers were fraying amid the heat, mosquitoes, and increasing sickness. In a concluding address

Brant wished the Shawnees and their allies well. "Since the council is now over," he said, "and you are come to a final resolution, we hope success will attend you. At this time it is not in our power to assist you. We must first remove our people from amongst the Americans, and if any choose to remain they must abide the consequences."

The divisions had become personal as well as political. The talking over, the Shawnees tried to raise a war party. They sang a war song and organized a dance in which a British officer, painted as an Indian, reportedly took part. The hatchet, that universal symbol of conflict, was passed around. The Iroquois representatives refused to take it and complained that in their opinion not enough had been done to reach a peaceful settlement.

Joseph Brant was derided by many westerners. Thomas McKee, the son of Alexander, called him "a Yankee rascal" but took care to make sure that the fierce Mohawk was not there to hear him.

Brant himself was no less bitter. Eight years later, long after he had discovered that even his Muskingum line would not have secured peace, long after the war had ended, he could not reflect on those days without anger. As he reminded some Ojibwes, "Had you listened to my advice instead of attending to that of the English and Shawanies the United States would have had their limits more circumscribed, and you would not have lost your country."[19]

The Shawnees and their allies had stood upon their "just rights," but now they were faced with what Brant called "an uncertain war."

# I2

## The Expedition to Fort Recovery

To Blue Jacket and the other war chiefs it was obvious what needed to be done.

Anthony Wayne's march north was marked by a line of forts, Washington, Hamilton, St. Clair, Jefferson, and, before the end of 1793, Greenville and Recovery. Wayne's army moved slowly but menacingly along them, toward the Indian towns. Fort Recovery (Mercer County, Ohio) was raised on the site of St. Clair's defeat and symbolized the reclamation of that bloodied ground. It was some ninety miles from Fort Washington and only sixty from Blue Jacket's headquarters at the Glaize.

Those posts were not in serious danger of being overwhelmed by warriors without artillery, but they were vulnerable. Whenever soldiers ventured from them to cut hay for their animals they were at risk, and the forts themselves were short of salted provisions and were dependent on the herds of cattle being driven along the communication line and on convoys of pack trains and creaking wagons. The small detachments of soldiers who accompanied those supplies, with the drovers and carters, were in danger whenever the forest closed in upon the thinly blazed paths.

The communication line was the weak link in Wayne's advance, for his ability to maintain large numbers of men in the forward posts depended on the regular movement of supplies. Successful onslaughts had been made on the line. On 17 October Little Otter, a dark-skinned Ottawa war leader from Roche de Bout, ambushed the road between Forts St. Clair and Jefferson with sixty warriors. In a sudden attack they captured twenty-two wagons and some seventy horses and killed or captured twenty-four or twenty-five of the military escort under Lt. John Lowry.[1]

The trouble was that to be effective the blockade had to be sustained, and the rupture of the peace negotiations in 1793 left the Indians disunited. Bad feelings, traditional fall ceremonies, the need to hunt, and drink peddled along the Maumee all disrupted attempts of the chiefs to raise men. Even in October, when Little Otter brought word that Wayne's main force had got as far as Fort Jefferson, urgency failed to concentrate sufficient minds. Tobacco painted red and scalps from Lowry's detachment were sent down the Maumee to the Great Lakes, and Egushaway himself made a round of the villages to urge the warriors to congregate, but only seven hundred had gathered at the Glaize early in November. Some of the Ottawas, Potawatomis, and Ojibwes said the Shawnees and their friends had brought the war upon themselves, and it was up to them to end it. Blue Jacket and the other chiefs were fortunate that Wayne's march was halted, not by the Indians but by sickness, bad weather, and inadequate supplies.[2]

During the winter and spring, however, the position of the Shawnees and their allies improved. Peace elements within the confederacy were silenced. The Iroquois made a final appeal to the United States, putting forward their best offer — the Muskingum line — adjusted to allow the Americans additional areas north of the Ohio, which had already been settled by the whites. Unfortunately, Knox responded without enthusiasm. Though he suggested that a meeting could take place in May, he refused to call Wayne off. Brant, whose proposal it was, felt piqued. In the spring of 1794 he fell back into line with the Shawnees and urged the other moderate groups, the Seven Nations of Canada and the Ottawas, Potawatomis, and Ojibwes, to fight for the Ohio boundary. For their part, the Ohio Indians also tried to repair their broken relationships with the Iroquois, offering those in New York an asylum in the West from the "large white beast" that was devouring their lands.[3]

Nearer home impulses to treat with the Americans were also suppressed. Early in January 1794 Blue Jacket, Captain Johnny, and leaders of the Delawares and Miamis sent four Delawares with an interpreter to Fort Greenville. Their task was to organize an exchange to secure the release of two Indian women held by the Americans, but it was hijacked by some moderate Delaware chiefs (perhaps Big Cat and Tetepachsit, or Branching Tree) who turned it into an unauthorized peace overture. When the envoys presented themselves before Wayne on 14 January, they asked for a peace parley. The general was suspicious and stated his terms firmly. The Indians must surrender all their prisoners at Fort Recovery within thirty days and recall their war parties before he would talk peace. Blue Jacket and Captain Johnny were equally astonished to hear what had been done in their names. Still, they put Wayne's message to a council. According to some evidence, there was a vocal peace lobby from the Miamis and Delawares, but the Shawnees stood firm, and British agents and Ottawas, Potawatomis, and Ojibwes later added their support. The peace initiative was crushed.[4]

There were other developments, even more exciting. Blue Jacket and the warriors were fired to learn that their British and Spanish "Fathers" were lurching to their feet! Blue Jacket's pleas that the British throw their hats into the ring, made over many years, seemed about to be answered.

It was the desperate struggle for survival being waged in Europe that engineered the change. It pitted Britain and Spain against France and made British Canada and Spanish Louisiana allies. Both were looking nervously at the United States, fearing that it would enter the lists against them, sucked in by maritime difficulties between the Royal Navy and American shipping trying to trade with revolutionary France. Spanish officials on the Mississippi awoke to the possibility of being attacked and began to foster pan-Indianism to strengthen their imperial possessions. In the fall of 1793 the Spanish brokered a rough alliance between the Chickasaws, Choctaws, Creeks, and Cherokees. The next year they reminded the Missouri Delawares and Shawnees that they stood to lose their haven if Spain was ousted and sent a war pipe and black wampum to "all the nations who live towards the setting sun." Tidings of the last reached the Glaize in May.[5]

But the redcoats were even more important. Sir Guy Carleton, Lord Dorchester, was back as governor of Canada, and he convinced himself that war with the United States was just around the corner. It was time to curry Indian support more strongly. On 10 February 1794 he made an intemperate speech to members of the Seven Nations of Canada in Quebec, predicting a war between the king and the United States within a year. He declared that the Americans had dishonored the treaty of 1783, and its provisions were therefore suspended. Dorchester reasserted British claims south of the Great Lakes and said the treaties the Americans had imposed upon the Indians after the war had infringed the rights of both the tribes and the king. He even went so far as to tell the tribesmen that a new boundary would be drawn between Canada and the United

States and that "what belongs to the Indians will of course be confirmed and secured to them."

This was inflammatory talk, and His Majesty's government in Westminster would disavow it, but for the moment it established a new climate in the Great Lakes region. Dorchester ordered Simcoe to transfer a detachment of the Twenty-fourth Regiment of Foot from Detroit to the Maumee rapids. It was a flagrant violation of the Peace of Paris, but Dorchester was smelling gunpowder, and Simcoe, ever ready to unfurl the British ensign in the Northwest, eagerly responded. His pulse quickened, and he began planning a campaign against Fort Washington in the event of war. On 8 April Simcoe arrived at the rapids to give the preparations his personal supervision. A new fort, Fort Miamis, was built on the north bank of the river, one and a half miles below McKee's storehouse. About 150 men garrisoned the post, with artillery. McKee's depot sat across the river, and nearer the rapids, and just above it, at Roche de Bout, an island in the Maumee (Waterville, Ohio), a corporal's guard was posted as an advance. And below Fort Miamis, in the mouth of the Maumee, Simcoe had Turtle Island fortified. As Indian spirits began to climb, Simcoe had Dorchester's speech read to some warriors at the rapids.[6]

Preparing his own campaign, an assault on Wayne's communication line, Blue Jacket had not neglected contingency plans. Talking it over with the Lasselles, he decided that if he was beaten he would withdraw to the Chicago region. But that spring of 1794 the prospect did not seem to be a bad one. The Indians were rallying, and the redcoats had not only built posts to secure the tribesmen's rear but seemed ready themselves to fight. Dorchester had pledged that if there was war, the British would not forget the Indian claim to Ohio.[7]

Waashaa Monetoo seemed to be smiling.

\*    \*    \*

Early in the year Blue Jacket began the difficult task of calling in the warriors of the confederacy. Again, there are few details of the personal journeys he made, of the tribulations of traveling in the spring by paths still obscured by ice and snow as they threaded through the broken wilderness of the Michigan region, or of the ceremonies and speeches he rehearsed in one village after another. All that survives is a bare statement that the Shawnee war chief toured the Ojibwes and other northern Indians, urging them to join their brethren in the Ottawa, Wyandot, and Delaware villages at Roche de Bout to make war on their enemies.[8]

These and other embassies brought a thousand warriors into Roche de Bout at the beginning of May, most of them members of the Three Fires. Usually Blue Jacket and the chiefs of the triumvirate remained at the Glaize, sending out parties to reconnoiter the American posts and pick up prisoners and deserters, but their runners were constantly on the path to Roche de Bout and the rapids, for it was there that McKee issued his provisions and the northern Indians mobilized. It was there that war chiefs such as Egushaway and Little Otter prepared parties to march upriver to join Blue Jacket's army. They smoked the Spanish war pipe, sent from Missouri via the Glaize, and they forwarded the wampum and tobacco summoning the warriors of the Great Lakes to fight. In this way calls reached the Potawatomis of the St. Joseph (Michigan), the Wyandots of the Detroit River, and the Ojibwes and Munsees of the Thames (Ontario), scolding slackers, and charging them that "none should remain behind." The trails were soon being worn by the feet of hundreds of grim warriors, heading for the Maumee.[9]

Blue Jacket and his supporters expected the redcoats to play their part too, particularly after hearing Simcoe's bellicose posturing. When messengers from the Glaize arrived at the rapids — with prisoners, intelligence, or entreaties — they usually carried something for the British. Early in May the Shawnees sent a prisoner to McKee. From him the Indians had learned that Wayne's principal force consisted of about two thousand men but that it was at Fort Greenville, stymied for lack of supplies. Wayne had no salted meat and only five head of cattle on hand, although convoys were expected. The prisoner also admitted that the most advanced post, Fort Recovery, was weak. It covered forty square yards and had blockhouses at each corner, but the pickets were low, and the garrison a bare 150 men. But two of the artillery pieces the Indians had taken from St. Clair and hidden had been discovered. Forwarding this prisoner to McKee, the Glaize chiefs urged the redcoats to "come and join us." Encouraged, the Indians intended to attack Wayne's communications and probably also to bring away the remaining artillery pieces.[10]

On 13 May more good news came. Some Shawnees and Delawares mauled an American supply convoy near Fort Hamilton, killing nine men. The Glaize chiefs sent six scalps down the Maumee, along with urgent pleas to the British for more provisions. "Make no excuses that you have not got it," they told McKee impatiently. Blue Jacket himself was in Detroit on 22 May. He may have conducted private business, but most likely he was also trying to get greater help for the Indian campaign.[11]

For all this, the Indian army formed painfully. The chiefs complained to McKee that proceedings at the Glaize were being disrupted by liquor which traders were still bringing up the Maumee and asked for the flow to be choked off. Other Indians gathered slowly. Even in June fresh bands of Wyandots, Munsees, Ojibwes, Ottawas, and Potawatomis were still dribbling toward Roche de Bout. Yet by then there were worrying indications that the Big Knives were ready to move against them. At Grey Eye's Town, one of the more exposed villages on the upper Auglaize, some Ojibwes and Potawatomis heard artillery fire on the night of 8–9 June, and Chickasaw scouts employed by the Americans were said to be hovering around. The next day some warriors from the Glaize investigated the reports and pronounced them false, but the scare helped spur the Indians into action. Blue Jacket sent part of his force from the Glaize to Fallen Timbers — not, it should be noted, the site of the later battle but another Fallen Timbers beyond Grey Eye's Town and on the line of march toward the enemy forts. Five hundred warriors at the rapids were also hurried to the Glaize, and McKee rushed urgent notes to sluggish Wyandot reinforcements downriver.[12]

Blue Jacket and the other chiefs wrestled with last-minute frustrations. Several whites attached to the British Indian Department, one of them Matthew Elliott, as well as some traders, had arrived at the Glaize, and a council convened in Captain Johnny's town decided to call upon them to join the campaign. Accordingly, a bunch of black wampum was handed to Elliott, inviting him and his comrades to accompany Blue Jacket's army. Britain was not at war with the United States, not yet, but Elliott and his associates felt that they had little choice but to accept. They togged themselves out as Indians to avoid being fired on by mistake and to escape the notice of the Americans.[13]

New arrivals had also to be welcomed, and on 15 June six hundred warriors fired a salute to a party of Wyandots and Ottawas marching proudly into the Glaize. Provisions were a greater vexation. Items from powder and shot to red paint had been furnished by the British, but food was scarce. Pork and flour had been exhausted, and the main staple was boiled maize. The Indian force, unlike Wayne's, would have to live off the land, and to ease the pressure on the game some war parties were directed to Fallen Timbers by an alternative route, straight from Roche de Bout rather than via the Glaize. One such detachment, led by Little Otter, bagged forty deer and five bears along the way.

So many messengers had been rushing back and forth that there was also a shortage of wampum. The Shawnees had difficulty making up a belt for Blackbeard to take to the southern tribes, and when the Mekoches applied to Blue Jacket for some wampum that he had, the chief insisted that he needed it for his own purposes. Relations between Blue Jacket and the Mekoches may have been deteriorating. Normally, the Mekoches superintended tribal affairs, but during military emergencies what authority there was was invested in the war chiefs. After several years of warfare in which Blue Jacket, the principal war chief, had consolidated his position as the most powerful Shawnee, resentment was beginning to surface among the Mekoches.

On 18 June 127 Ottawas from near the straits of Mackinac and Saginaw Bay Ojibwes made an eleventh-hour reinforcement. Blue Jacket learned that on their way upriver they had raped women in the Indian villages and pilfered property, taking advantage of the absence of the warriors. To protect the families of men out fighting the Americans, the Shawnee war chief sent word to Roche de Bout that no more parties were to be directed to the Glaize. Instead, they should proceed to Fallen Timbers along the path used by Little Otter. That done, Blue Jacket saw the bulk of his army strike out for Fallen Timbers on 19 and 20 June. Camping each day at one or two o'clock so that the hunters could bring in game, the warriors made Fallen Timbers by the twenty-third. Just over a thousand men were there. Spirits were high and the hunting had been good, but it was taking a toll of powder and shot, and the Indians grumbled that they had little tobacco.

Accounts of British participants suggest that Blue Jacket was the principal leader of the Indian force, and Jonathan Alder, a white Mingo in the army, flatly stated that "Chief Blue Jacket was Commander-in-Chief." Buckongahelas, we know, was supposed to have brought up the rear with a few hundred reinforcements, mainly Delawares, but he was delayed at the Glaize. Apparently, a sister of the Wyandot chief Roundhead and the wife of an interpreter, François Duchouquet, brought some rum to Buckongahelas's warriors and they were useless for a considerable time. The Delaware chief eventually got his force moving, but he would arrive too late for Blue Jacket's attack on Fort Recovery. None of the primary sources detailing the expedition refer to Little Turtle, but a small force of Miamis was present, and their war chief was probably one of them. Among the Ottawas, Potawatomis, and Ojibwes, who formed a large proportion of the main force, both Egushaway and Little Otter were prominent.[14]

Blue Jacket may have been the principal spokesman, but his position was far from that of an American or British commander in chief. The Indians did not fight that way. Their plans emerged from councils composed of the leading war chiefs and warriors, councils that were often heated and recriminatory. Blue Jacket commanded enormous influence in these debates, by reason of his experience, his successes, and his position as the leading Shawnee, and he enjoyed the confidence of powerful supporters such as Buckongahelas. But he could not always get his way, as his new expedition would vividly demonstrate. The army marching boldly toward Wayne's line of forts was the greatest yet fielded by the confederacy, but the divergent views of the leaders and the individual inclinations of the warriors in general signally weakened Blue Jacket's hand.

Fallen Timbers was about sixty-five miles south of the Glaize, and for a while Blue Jacket rested his men there, waiting for more reinforcements. On 25 June he learned that Buckongahelas was taking a more westerly route and planned to meet Blue Jacket somewhere near Fort Recovery, but fifty Ojibwes from Saginaw Bay joined him, and the next day the army marched to Kettle Creek, moving south by west in an impressive and frequently silent formation. The Indians rode or walked in twelve or so open files, carrying their rifles and muskets, with about fifty-five yards between each file. On the flanks and ahead moved lines of hunters, some of them extending several miles, bringing in game and doubling as scouts. These hunters later misled the Americans, who exaggerated the Indian strength and spoke of warriors marching in seventeen columns across a wide front, forming perfectly regular and square encampments at night.

Blue Jacket halted about noon, just beyond Kettle Creek, and waited for his rear guard, composed mainly of Wyandots, to come up. Two scouting parties were then dispatched, one to Fort Greenville, where Wayne had his main body, and the other to Fort Recovery, the forward American post. Near St. Marys Lake one of them ran into a party of enemy scouts, operating out of Greenville. These were mostly Choctaws, who, with some Chickasaws, were serving Wayne as auxiliaries, and in a brief skirmish a Choctaw was killed. The American party fell back to Greenville, but the Choctaw scalp found its way to Blue Jacket's encampment and was then passed to the rear to encourage stragglers. The first blood had been Indian, but it had not been spilled by the confederacy.[15]

During their advance the Indians were constantly troubled by news and rumors. A Seneca named White Loon arrived from the Ohio talking about many wagons and soldiers that were crossing that river bound for the forts, and a Miami brought word that some of their people had been killed by American rangers led by William Wells, who they had once regarded as one of their own. But these reports did not stay the Indian march, and Blue Jacket's strength was being swollen by fresh adherents. Forty Miamis and twenty-five Mingoes joined him as he left Fallen Timbers and on 29 June the arrival of ninety Wyandots brought the army to over twelve hundred men. Welcome as the recruits were, they increased the difficulties of the chiefs. More than one hundred warriors were without firearms, and the extensive hunting was depleting ammunition. In just one day two hundred deer and as many turkeys were killed to feed the marching warriors.

On 28 June, however, the campaign had struck another and greater difficulty. The Indians at last came upon the road that linked Wayne's forts, along which his precious supplies had to pass. When the tribesmen camped that evening the chiefs took additional precautions. The horses were hobbled to prevent them from straying, and the bells Indians generally attached to their animals were removed. A ten-man guard was posted on the road toward Greenville, where Wayne had his strength. Arms were put in order, and the war council met to determine the next move. That was when the trouble began.

Blue Jacket and the Shawnee, Miami, Mingo, and Wyandot chiefs wanted to continue south, evidently with the intention of circling around Greenville and then cutting its supply line. If Buckongahelas and his Delawares had been there to support them, they might have won the day, but perhaps half of the army was made up of Ojibwes, Ottawas, and Potawatomis, and they had different ideas. They turned in an alternative plan. Scouts had reported activity around Fort Recovery, the small advanced fort, and these Lakes tribes scented a convoy. A convoy meant plunder, probably some scalps, and little risk. It was not a sensible plan, however. Intercepting supplies at Fort Recovery would do nothing to damage Wayne's main communication line to the south of Fort Greenville, where he had billeted his legion. In contrast, cutting the road south of Greenville, as the Shawnees and their friends wanted, would have imperiled not only Wayne but Fort Recovery as well. Nevertheless, the Potawatomis, Ottawas, and Ojibwes insisted, and Blue Jacket and the other chiefs gave way. On 29 June the army headed in a westerly direction, toward the weaker post. A dozen warriors went ahead to try to secure a prisoner for purposes of intelligence.[16]

And so Blue Jacket returned to the scene of his greatest triumph, the victory over St. Clair more than two years before. The Indians camped a few miles from the fort, intending to rest before setting out early in the morning, as was their usual practice. Scouts reported that a pack train had reached Fort Recovery the previous night, and it was supposed that it would try to return to Greenville the following morning. Blue Jacket and the other chiefs planned to annihilate the returning train, and perhaps they also hoped to draw the garrison from the fort and to destroy that also. Their information was indeed accurate. A train of three hundred animals, escorted by ninety riflemen and fifty dragoons under Maj. William McMahon, had brought flour to the fort and was due to turn out at reveille for the return trip on 30 June. Nothing changed the American plans, not even ominous signs of lurking warriors. During the evening of the twenty-ninth members of Fort Recovery's garrison heard some distant gunshots, but they did not take them to mean anything more than a few raiding warriors or a lonely band of hunters. As dawn filtered over a landscape deceptively still, and a thousand Indians, stripped to breechcloths, painted black and red, and feathered and armed, slipped noiselessly through the woods toward the fort like specters, none of the Americans appear to have apprehended danger.

A Chickasaw spy left the fort that morning. He was soon back, tumbling in with the news that the forest was full of Indian signs. The soldiers found him difficult to understand and discounted his information. So complacent were they that just before seven o'clock the drovers took their pack animals from the fort to allow them to graze along the road. With its attendants, the convoy cantered across the two hundred yards of cleared ground around the post and disappeared from sight into the woods beyond.[17]

Whether all of Blue Jacket's force waited for the convoy is not known. The Shawnees were certainly there because one of the surviving drovers, James Neill, spoke of being captured by them. The luckless drovers and their herd were suddenly enveloped in a burst of firing and yelling, as the fierce warriors closed in. The fusillade was heard in the fort, where the commandant, Capt. Alexander Gibson, summoned the garrison to arms. Major McMahon gallantly led his troops out to support the herd, his dragoons in the front and the riflemen on foot behind. No sooner had the riders passed into the gloom of the woods than they were slashed to pieces by a furious fire from Indians hiding under the bank of a creek. Then angry warriors were on all sides of the stricken detachment, hacking them down with tomahawks and war clubs. The battered dragoons recoiled upon the foot soldiers behind, and the whole scrambled back in disorder, leaving the pack animals in the hands of the Indians.

Gibson had over one hundred men in the fort, and a substantial detail rushed out to aid McMahon. It advanced to the skirt of the forest on the brow of a hill before it, too, came under fire. The muskets of the soldiers barked in reply and briefly arrested the onslaught of the charging tribesmen, but then they fell back with the dragoons and riflemen. It became a rout. When the dragoons reached a creek above the post and came under the covering fire of the lower blockhouse, they made a brief stand, but although most of the soldiers streamed into the fort safely, they had been thoroughly worsted.

Thus far, Blue Jacket's ambush had been successful. In a scant fifteen minutes the Indians had seized several hundred animals, killed McMahon and a seventh of his force, and driven the others almost helplessly into the fort. Unfortunately, in their exhilaration some of the warriors now threw caution to the winds and made a full-blown attack on Fort Recovery itself. Blue Jacket, the Shawnees, and most of the other seasoned warriors of the Glaize watched in amazement as the inflamed Ojibwes and Ottawas sprinted toward the fort. The result was predictable. Some of the warriors got within sixty yards of the pickets, using tree stumps as cover, but the American muskets spat from the loopholes and canister shot and six-pound balls smashed into the native assault.

The attack was now beyond the control of the chiefs, and they had little option but to move up and support the Three Fires as they found a safer distance and opened a heavy fire on Fort Recovery. Some warriors shot down a few horses that had been left tied near the pickets, but most blazed away at the loopholes from which American marksmen were replying with no less energy. Jonathan Alder recalled that "an Indian that stood behind a tree close by asked me why I didn't shoot. He was loading and shooting as fast as he could. I told him I didn't see anything to shoot at. 'Why, shoot those holes in the fort,' said he. 'You might kill a man.'" Only rarely did good targets present themselves. At one time three men dashed from the fort to scalp an Indian who had fallen seventy yards distant, but no one hit them. The Indians persisted until the evening, when, wearying of their futile efforts, they withdrew to their camp.

That evening the Indians butchered some of the packhorses for meat and then set to a grimmer task. The night was dark and foggy, and the warriors had to use torches to steal toward the fort and search for their dead. Occasionally they drew potshots from sharp-eyed American sentinels, and Indian marksmen replied with covering fire. Some bodies were retrieved, but eleven were too close to the pickets and had to be left to be scalped by the whites when the Indian force eventually retired.

On the morning of 1 July the Indians again harassed the garrison with a desultory fire, but they quit about one o'clock in the afternoon. The fighting was over. It had not been entirely an exchange between the fort and the Indian army, for on both the thirtieth and the first the besiegers had been occasionally troubled by pro-American Indians, who had come from Greenville to find out what was going on. During these inter-Indian skirmishes both sides had a warrior killed.

The engagement at Fort Recovery left neither of the major belligerents totally dishonored. The Indians counted a victory in the earlier stages, capturing up to three hundred horses and some thirty bullocks, but they unequivocally lost the final round. The legion had twenty-one men killed, one missing, and twenty-nine wounded, in addition to the Indian scout slain on the first and casualties among the contractors of two killed, three captured, and one wounded. Blue Jacket's men lost about seventeen killed, only three of them in the attack on the convoy, and a similar number wounded. Most of his casualties were suffered by the Three Fires. The Indian wounded were put on biers or horses and returned to the Glaize, where they were transferred to canoes for shipment home.

Strategically, the slender fruits harvested in the assault on the convoy were surrendered by the premature abandonment of the siege. Of course, the Indians could not have damaged the garrison, but if they had maintained a presence they would probably have induced a relief force to leave Fort Greenville. When the legion's Indian spies brought word of the investment of Fort Recovery to the American commander in chief, he was ready to march to its aid. But Blue Jacket's prospects of meeting Wayne on anything like equal terms ended with the disintegration of his army. The significance of the debacle at Fort Recovery was not only that it handed the initiative to the Americans but that it sowed seeds of division among the Indians and fractured their unity.

The Indians buried their dead, wasted time turning over logs in the vicinity of the fort in a vain attempt to find artillery they had hidden after defeating St. Clair, and then withdrew east-northwest toward the head of the Wabash on 1 July. They also fell to mutual recriminations. The Shawnees and others condemned the Ottawas, Ojibwes, and Potawatomis for the foolhardy attack on the garrison, while the latter claimed they had been improperly supported. Some angry Lakes Indians accused the Shawnees of firing into their rear as they attacked the fort. Unity collapsed. The Ottawas, Ojibwes, and Potawatomis simply headed for home. Neither Blue Jacket nor any chief could prevent them from leaving, although the Shawnees, Miamis, and Wyandots wanted the army to stay together until Buckongahelas reinforced them. They still dared to believe the original plan practicable and talked about cutting the American supply line south of Fort Greenville and perhaps of drawing Wayne into the open. Later, American soldiers tracking the Indian retreat saw evidence of their fragmentation. They reported that trail crossed the St. Marys, which was low because of the lack of rain, and about eight miles from Fort Recovery it divided. One group of Indians (presumably the Lakes Indians) went almost due north, while the other (Blue Jacket) inclined to the right as if to avoid swampy ground.[18]

The defection of the Ojibwes, Ottawas, and Potawatomis cost Blue Jacket about half his force, and the arrival of Buckongahelas's detachment could not repair the damage. For a while the chiefs hoped to take a circuitous route around Greenville, with the Delawares forming the advance, but provisions were low and the number of warriors too few. The great Indian offensive crumbled, and as Blue Jacket turned dejectedly to the Glaize he must have pondered the hard work ahead. The confederacy would have to be repaired, and quickly, because a defensive battle against the full might of Wayne's legion was now almost inevitable.

\*   \*   \*

Things happened quickly after that. Frantic efforts were made to put the confederacy back on its feet. As Ojibwe, Ottawa, and Potawatomi warriors retreated past the Maumee rapids or through Detroit, alarmed British officials entreated them to rally to the defense of the Glaize. Some did so, even plunging back into the woods to resume the job of worrying Wayne's communications, but many others had had enough. When a deputation of Wabash Weas, Piankeshaws, and Kickapoos appeared at the rapids, probably looking for a share of His Majesty's largesse, Egushaway told them they should prove it by defending the Glaize from invasion.

Blue Jacket and the confederation chiefs thought the British also needed to improve their act. They were speaking more loudly, and although the corporal's guard had been withdrawn from Roche de Bout, Fort Miamis and the installations on Turtle Island were being strengthened. Yet for all that, the chiefs nursed nagging suspicions about their

British father. The Lasselles kept pointing out that the redcoats were fully engaged with France and were likely to lose the war raging in Europe. What, then, could such weak allies do for the Indians of America against the might of the United States? And had not the Big Knives and the French defeated the redcoats before, in the Revolution? These were worrying questions, and they undermined Indian confidence in the British. Now, faced with an impending thrust at their headquarters on the Glaize, the chiefs made another attempt to draw their British allies out.[19]

This time it was Little Turtle, not Blue Jacket, who went to Detroit. He wanted twenty men and two cannons for another campaign against Fort Recovery. Colonel England demurred. England had fallen afoul of the flamboyant Blue Jacket and distrusted him, but he was impressed by the Miami war chief, who "seemed the most decent, modest, sensible Indian I ever conversed with." Simple too, he must have believed, because although the colonel excused British inaction he "dismissed" Little Turtle as "seemingly contented."

McKee had a different view of Little Turtle. The Lasselles, he knew, had been trading with the Miamis for years, and he believed that Little Turtle, no less than Blue Jacket, responded to their baneful influence, commercially as well as politically. When the Miami war chief got back to the rapids from Detroit, carrying a letter of England's for McKee, the agent attempted to disabuse the colonel of his opinion of Little Turtle. England was unacquainted with his character, he said, for "notwithstanding the respectability of his appearance, [he] is as great a trader in rum as any amongst them, and he actually brought a considerable quantity from Detroit with him, with which he has made great numbers drunk and stripped them of their clothing for payment."[20]

Despite the efforts of Simcoe and McKee to stifle the flow of spirits into the Indian villages of the Maumee, the disruptive traffic continued. That chiefs such as Little Turtle, and probably also Blue Jacket, behaved so ambiguously, attacking the trade at moments of crisis only to profit by it as soon as opportunity afforded, sat ill with the frustrated British agent. The Miami war chief himself returned to the Glaize dissatisfied, however. He had not been as foolish as England supposed. The refusal of the redcoats to stand more firmly behind the Indians had seriously weakened his faith in continued resistance.

The summer failures now fell heavily upon Blue Jacket and his allies. On 4 August an American deserter, Robert Newman, reached the rapids with news that Wayne and his legion were marching up the Auglaize toward the Glaize.

For four scant but momentous years the Glaize had flourished, the focus of a community of Indians and French and British, the nerve center of the native confederacy. They had mixed freely, caroused and smoked together, bartered and gambled, and interbred, binding each other in kinship, friendship, and mutual well-being. They had exchanged blood, cultures, and ideas, and now it was over. The Glaize had to be abandoned, with the trading complex at the confluence of the Auglaize and the Maumee; and the villages, including those of Blue Jacket, Captain Johnny, Snake, Buckongahelas, and Little Turtle, hastily evacuated. Women, children, and aged warriors salvaged a few belongings and then poured downstream, passing Fort Miamis, to find sanctuary on the lower Maumee. Blue Jacket and the men assembled at the rapids, ready to make their stand.

Newman did not mislead the Indians. Reinforced by fifteen hundred mounted volunteers from Kentucky, Major General Wayne left Fort Greenville on 28 July. His army was some thirty-five hundred strong, larger than any force Blue Jacket could have raised, and it reached Fort Recovery the next day. The Americans built Fort Adams on the St. Marys and on 7 August reached the Auglaize River, which they traced downstream toward the abandoned Indian settlements. As it marched, the legion saw striking evidence of the sudden flight. Clusters of cabins crowned eminences on the banks of the river. Some, surely, were old and overgrown, but others had just been abandoned, the empty houses standing next to extensive ripening but neglected cornfields. Reaching the junction with the Maumee on 8 August, the Americans erected their main camp on the point overlooking the two rivers, each about 150 to 200 yards in breadth. Here the British and French traders had had their base, and here there was a view of the town of Blue Jacket and the other now silent villages around the Glaize. Some houses had been set on fire and were still burning. According to one of the soldiers with Wayne, "From the appearance of the Indian cabins, gardens, fields, etc. we are now in possession of, there remains no doubt but the enemy very lately left this place. Numbers of brass kettles are found in the weeds, and everything so situated as to wear the appearance of a sudden departure of the savages. . . . On an examination of the effects of the industry of the savages, I can say with propriety, their gardens produce vegetables equal to any I have ever seen."[21]

Once again, Blue Jacket and his Shawnees had been driven from their homes and surrendered them to the invaders. When the legion eventually resumed its advance, heading down the Maumee on 15 August, it found the villages of Blue Jacket and Black Snake, among others. The Americans noticed their rich stocks of food and the orchard of peach, apple, and plum in one town, possibly that of the Shawnee war chief. Probably they also discovered the base for Blue Jacket's trading activities because they described a few large storehouses containing account books, tools, and other items. Whatever, it was a lot to lose.

Yet the fighting spirit of Blue Jacket and his Shawnees had not been quenched, not yet. As the legion moved downriver, Blue Jacket and his people waited below, ready for their last battle.

# 13

## The Final Battle

The lower Maumee was a striking place, as beautiful a landscape as ever was painted, according to one who saw it that summer of 1794. The summit of Roche de Bout, a craggy island rising from the river, was cloaked in cedar. Upstream were the rapids, so often mentioned by correspondents of the day, while about the island the water slid over a stony bed to meander through cultivated meadows below, set against a backdrop of handsome eminences crowned in trees. Physically it suggested serenity, but the fifteen hundred or so men who formed a line there on 19 August stood to a grimmer purpose.

Blue Jacket's battle line stretched about a mile on the northwestern bank of the river, a little below Roche de Bout and two miles above the redcoat Fort Miamis. It stood in an oblique direction to the water, extending further from the river as it reached upstream. Blue Jacket's left, where his Shawnees were posted, was close to the steep riverbank and entrenched in the meadows near the home of a trader named John McCormick. His right, manned by the Wyandots and Three Fires, wandered into a thick wood with considerable undergrowth. It was from the many uprooted trees at this point, the legacy of some tornado, that the place received the name Fallen Timbers, although it should not be confused with the rendezvous south of the Glaize which the Indians had used marching against Fort Recovery two months before. It was *this* Fallen Timbers, on the Maumee, that people would remember, for here Blue Jacket would fight his last great battle. His formation was basically a sound one. It gave the defenders an opportunity to rake the front and flank of any enemy army advancing down the riverside. Strongly manned and stoutly guarded, it could have been a formidable obstacle.[1]

The men forming that line made an interesting composition. Most had been recently expelled from their homes about the Glaize, Shawnees, Delawares, Miamis, and Mingoes, but many were Wyandots, Three Fires, and Delawares from the lower Maumee, the Sandusky, and the Detroit. The provisions they drew from the British below, either at the fort or McKee's depot, gave them the means of holding their position without scattering to hunt, and their noncombatants were encamped at Swan Creek near the mouth of the Maumee. The great fighting chiefs of the confederacy were in that line, Blue Jacket, Buckongahelas, Little Turtle, Egushaway, and Little Otter.

There were whites in the line too, many full-blooded. Some, like Stephen Ruddell among the Shawnees, had been captives raised in native villages. Some were traders, tied to the Indians by economic interest and kinship. Blue Jacket's relatives, the French-Canadian Lasselles, were represented, at least by Antoine and possibly also by Jacques, Blue Jacket's son-in-law. Standing painted and feathered like other warriors, old Antoine had other reasons for putting himself in danger that day. Since Britain and France had gone to war the previous year he had been spreading anti-British rumors among the Indians. With Francis Lafontaine, a fellow trader, he had been telling them that Quebec was blockaded by a French fleet and that a French speech had been sent to the Iroquois, informing them that their old "Father" was once more on his feet and would soon be with them. Antoine's nephew Jacques had warmly expressed the opinion that such were the great resources of France that she could never be defeated. Both the Lasselles had magnified French successes in Europe and undermined Indian confidence in the redcoats. In Detroit they had finally been charged with the rumors, and they had protested their innocence and come to the Maumee to prove their fidelity to the British-Indian alliance.

There were others Blue Jacket was even happier to see in his line: fifty Canadian militia under William Caldwell, the famous partisan of the Revolutionary War. Fearing an attack on Fort Miamis, Colonel England had rushed reinforcements from Detroit: a handful of the Twenty-fourth Regiment of Foot under Maj. William Campbell, two howitzers with ammunition, a number of artificers to help strengthen the fort, and Caldwell's party of militia. Caldwell, like Blue Jacket, was a son-in-law of the late Jacques Dupéront Baby. Blue Jacket was married to Baby's Indian daughter; Caldwell to Susanne Baby, a daughter of Jacques by his French-Canadian wife, Susanne Réaume. Caldwell was therefore not only a capable frontier officer but connected to the principal Indian war chief and that part of the French-Canadian mercantile community loyal to the British. Colonel England's other reinforcements stuck to Fort Miamis, but Caldwell's men took their place on the right of Blue Jacket's line, with the Wyandots.[2]

Blue Jacket knew that the Big Knives were coming upon him in force. On 14 August a man named Christopher Miller had ridden into the Indian encampments at Roche de Bout. The Shawnees knew Miller. He had been captured by them while young and become one of their trusted warriors. Unfortunately, in February he had fallen into the hands of the Americans and began serving them as a scout and intermediary. Now Miller had come with a message from Major General Wayne, accompanied by a Shawnee prisoner the Americans had released as an act of goodwill. Wayne invited the chiefs to come to the Glaize to talk peace and promised that if they did so they could reclaim their villages and spare themselves a hungry winter. Blue Jacket had no intention of being brought to humiliating terms so prematurely, but he learned from Miller that Wayne's army was at the Glaize preparing to advance upon the Indian positions. The chiefs tried to buy time. They sent Miller back, urging Wayne to stay at his camp while the Indians assembled to discuss his proposals. On 16 August the chiefs sent scouts upriver and doubtless learned that Wayne had not been deceived by their answer. His forces were slowly descending the Maumee along both banks, coming toward them.[3]

Wayne's movements were soon confirmed. On 18 August, while the Americans were erecting Fort Deposit on the north bank of the river as a base for their final advance, some Delawares skirmished with Wayne's scouts. They brought away a prisoner, William May. He told the Indians that Wayne would attack within the next two days. It was probably upon receipt of this information that the chiefs called their final council of war.[4]

So much fiction has been written about this council that it is worth reciting the primary sources in full, vague as they are. What we have is consistent with the picture we have met before: the Indians laid their plans in debate, with Blue Jacket appearing to have been regarded as the premier war chief. On this occasion there was evidently great disagreement. Little Turtle, his faith in British support probably eroded by the opinions of the Lasselles as well as his own failure to get help from Colonel England, declared against giving battle at all.

This information comes from several sources. A Wyandot tradition of uncertain authority indicates that the Indians were divided over whether to attack Wayne's camp, as they had done St. Clair's, or to make a defensive stand. More authoritatively, Antoine Lasselle, who was captured in the ensuing battle, told the Americans that Little Turtle had complained to him on the morning of the action. He said the Indians were too weak to fight in any circumstance. He had advised the Indians to negotiate, but the Shawnees would not agree.

Many years later one of Wayne's young officers gave a similar story, one he had almost certainly also got from Lasselle. This version comes to us at least fourthhand and long after the battle, but although distorted and imprecise it appears to preserve a genuine recollection. Henry Rowe Schoolcraft, who told the story, reported:

> The Indians were led in this action by a chief called Blue Jacket, assigned by Little Turtle. But we have it from an officer of that campaign [Brig. Gen. H. Brady] that the latter strenuously opposed making a stand at Presque Isle [Fallen Timbers], and was not disinclined to peace. And it was currently reported and believed after the action that in consequence of this opinion high words had passed between the chiefs in a council preceding the battle, the Little Turtle maintaining his opinions in an argument containing expressions to this effect: "We have beaten the enemy twice under separate commanders. We cannot expect the same good fortune always to attend us. The Americans are now led by a chief who never sleeps. The night and day are alike to him, and during all the time he has been marching upon our villages, notwithstanding the watchfulness of our young men, we have never been able to surprise him. Think well of it. There is something whispers to me, it would be prudent to list to his offer of peace." On this he was reproached by one of the chiefs with cowardice. This put an end to the conference. . . . He [Little Turtle] took his post in the action, determined to do his duty.

The gist of this may have been true, and in subsequent reminiscences Brady directly referred to the episode again, specifically naming Blue Jacket as the chief who accused the Turtle of cowardice. We cannot take the incident further. From the evidence available it appears that Little Turtle opposed a stand but was overruled by the influence of Blue Jacket and the Shawnees. It was apparently with misgivings that some Indians manned the defense line on 19 August.[5]

The day itself proved to be a disappointment. A group of American volunteers under Maj. William Price rode close to Blue Jacket's line, close enough to see McKee's trading post in the distance, but they retired when they saw waiting Indians. Wayne and his legion did not appear that day. The Indians were restless. Expecting battle, many had fasted, attempting to purify themselves to appeal for the protection of the spirits. During the evening most of the warriors slipped back downstream, eager to assuage their hunger. It would not be until the following day that they met the Big Knives in battle.

＊   ＊   ＊

The morning of 20 August witnessed a fiasco. While some of the Indian army marched to the line, many frittered away valuable time stocking up on provisions from Fort Miamis. For one reason or another there were probably few more than five hundred men in place when the American legion suddenly appeared in midmorning. Wayne had caught most of his enemies napping. The left and center of the line, held by the warriors of the Glaize, seems to have been particularly incomplete. Blue Jacket had not had much chance of victory. Wayne brought a vast superiority in numbers and firepower, and during the battle shells and grape and canister shot rained upon the Indians. But that indisciplined dispersal of the warriors during the early hours of the day threw away what threadbare chances of victory they had.[6]

The day began with rain. As it subsided, yielding to a hot, bright sun, the legion left Fort Deposit in two columns and traveled four or five miles in good order. The right flank, including the legion's cavalry, was covered by the Maumee River, while on the left rode a brigade of the mounted volunteers under Brig. Gen. Robert Todd. The rear was secured by another such brigade under Brig. Gen. Joshua Barbee, and Major Price's mounted volunteers formed an advance.

Price's force first made contact with the left and center of Blue Jacket's line, secreted as it was in the high meadow grass toward the river and the thickening woods away from the stream. The Indian line was seriously undermanned there, but some Shawnees, including a party under Tecumseh, were in it and they rose, delivered a steady fire into Price's horsemen, and then ducked down to reload and fire again. Six of the Americans were killed, others wounded, and the remainder of the advance crumbled, fleeing in a confused panic. Exultant warriors broke cover to chase them. According to one exaggerated account, the Indians pushed forward as much as a mile on that flank.

Price's volunteers rebounded onto the legion's main force, there directed by Brig. Gen. James Wilkinson, Wayne's second in command. Then it fled through Capt. Joseph Brock's company and forced it to collide with the left of Capt. Howell Lewis's light infantry. This, in turn, was thrown into disorder and fell back about forty yards. For a moment the discipline and steadiness of the legion wavered, but then the leadership and training showed. Uriah Springer's battalion of riflemen reinforced Lewis and enabled him to regain his position, frustrating the Indians' efforts to turn the legion's flank.

At this point Indian reserves were needed to help the warriors hold their advantage, but they simply were not there. The Indian offensive on the left stopped short of Wilkinson's main force, perhaps as close as eighty yards, and merely delivered what the brigadier general termed "a feeble scattered fire, by which I had a few men killed." The Indians had also abandoned the cover of their original position and were wide open to a counterattack. Soon it came. Capt. Robert Mis Campbell with his dragoons came galloping through Wilkinson's flank, slashed through the thin timber along the riverside, and fell upon the Indian left some two hundred yards ahead. At the same time, the whole of the mounted volunteers, under Maj. Gen. Charles Scott, was dispatched on a circuitous route from the American left to enfilade Blue Jacket's right.

As the legionary dragoons clashed with the Indian left wing they met stiff resistance. Campbell and at least four of his men were killed or fatally wounded by Indian fire, and several others were brought down injured. The command of this force now fell upon Lt. Leonard Covington, who reputedly cut down two Indians with his saber. While the charge of the dragoons bogged down, the firing that had begun from the Indian left ran along the whole thin line of the confederacy, most briskly at its center, and both wings of the American army were engaged.

There is some controversy about Anthony Wayne's movements during the battle, including disagreement as to whether he ordered the general advance to drive the Indians back at bayonet point, or whether that initiative was independently taken by his subordinates, Wilkinson and Lt. Col. John Francis Hamtramck. The legionnaires were soon relentlessly pushing forward, piling through the fallen timbers, dislodging the warriors with their bayonets and driving them from ravine to ravine.

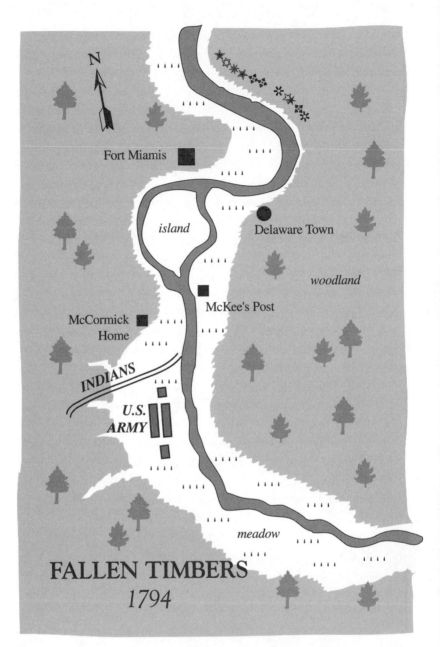

N

Fort Miamis

island

Delaware Town

woodland

McKee's Post

McCormick
Home

INDIANS

U.S.
ARMY

meadow

# FALLEN TIMBERS
*1794*

*Map 4*

Blue Jacket had lost the battle. Some individuals and groups resisted the legion's disciplined advance with courage and skill. On the left Tecumseh stubbornly tried to hold his ground, alternately falling back and making desperate stands until the danger of being outflanked forced him to retreat again. Further right the Indians also fell back, but the Wyandots and Caldwell's militia administered severe punishment to the oncoming legionnaries. They adopted firing lines. One line fired, then retreated through a second line to reload while it fired.

But it was hopeless. The Indians were pulling back along the whole line and soon were streaming in full flight toward Fort Miamis. There, at the redcoat fort, where they expected sanctuary, the most significant incident of the day took place. For as the defeated warriors clamored at the gates for protection, Maj. William Campbell peered over the stockade at the fierce painted faces and near naked oiled bodies thronging below and refused to let them in. He was in a very embarrassing position. His country was not at war with the United States, but here, in this remote spot of the empire, a war could have been kindled if Campbell played a reckless card. He made his decision. The gates remained closed, and the angry Indians swarmed around the fort and fled downstream.[7]

They never forgot it. Nothing rankled in the minds of the veterans of Fallen Timbers more than those closed gates. Nothing more forcibly demonstrated the fickle friendship of the redcoats. Years later, when a new conflict between the United States and Britain, the War of 1812, brewed, and when British agents again solicited Indian support, the memory of Fort Miamis was thrown back in their faces. Tecumseh mentioned it, and Kawachawan the Ottawa, and Nanaume, a Potawatomi, who remarked that the crumbling ruins of old Fort Miamis reminded him of the day the British had shut their gates against their friends.

Most important of all, Blue Jacket remembered it. Once, during the Revolution, he had been a stalwart ally of the British and done them good service. Of late his faith in them had diminished. Their help was always little and late, and the Lasselles were filling the Shawnee chief with stories of a French resurgence. But it was at the gates of Fort Miamis that Blue Jacket thought he saw the true measure of his British allies. "They have [had] often promised to help us," he recalled thirteen years later, "and [but] at last, when we could not withstand the army that came against us, and went to the English fort for refuge, the English told us, 'I cannot let you in. You are painted too much, my children.' It was then we saw the British dealt treacherously with us."[8]

After failing to gain admittance to Fort Miamis, the Indians sped six or so miles beyond, to Swan Creek on the northwestern bank of the Maumee, where their noncombatants were encamped. Here, where the modern city of Toledo stands, they took account of their disaster.

In some respects the engagement had not been a heavy one. Wayne had lost about forty-four men killed or mortally wounded and eighty-nine injured. Blue Jacket's losses were smaller — less than forty killed, including six whites, and one captured, none other than Antoine Lasselle himself. But these losses were concentrated in groups that had borne the brunt of the fighting. The Wyandots lost no less than eight leading warriors, including all the principal chiefs of the Sandusky Wyandots except for Tarhe, who was shot in the elbow. The two leading Ottawas, Egushaway and Little Otter, were wounded. Egushaway was hit in the head, and Little Otter had to be brought from the field on a white horse. The Shawnees also lost important men, and several Indians of various tribes were wounded.[9]

The fortunes of the confederacy had reached a pass. They had lost their homes on the Glaize, with their crops, and an important battle. Most crucial of all, they had lost much of their faith in their British allies.

*   *   *

While Blue Jacket's men regrouped downriver, Wayne halted his advance at the walls of Fort Miamis. For a while he blustered and demanded the surrender of the small post, but Campbell refused to be intimidated, and ultimately neither commander wanted the responsibility of risking a war. For several days Wayne wasted Indian villages above and below the fort, and then he withdrew to the Glaize.

The Big Knives completed their destruction of the towns of Blue Jacket and other chiefs near the Glaize. There were random acts of depravity, including the plundering of Indian graves, but the warriors could do little about it. Some sneaked back to harry the American force and snapped up the occasional deserter, but generally Wayne completed his work unmolested. He had erected Fort Defiance at the Glaize and soon set about building Fort Wayne close to the remains of old Miamitown at the head of the Maumee. Thus forts stood proudly on the sites of the two great headquarters of the Indian confederacy, impregnable to native arms and symbols of Wayne's victory.[10]

Blue Jacket's defeated followers dispersed. Those from afar returned home. The Indians from the Glaize survived the winter on British supplies, some at Detroit, but most, including Blue Jacket, Captain Johnny, and Buckongahelas, "hutted" on Swan Creek. A return of 15 September shows that 1,126 Delawares, 639 Shawnees, 355 Ottawas, 170 Munsees and Nanticokes, 83 Mingoes, 83 Miamis, 70 Iroquois, and 30 Cherokees drew rations there, and others were still coming in. At the beginning of December 300 Shawnee men, 370 women, and 279 children were at Swan Creek. Of these 196 were Pekowis, 224 Mekoches, 114 Kispokos, 292 Chillicothes, and 123 were described as "Wakatamakies," which signified Shawnees of various divisions from the former town of Wakatomica. They depended for their food on the flour, pork, beef, peas, butter, rice, and corn the redcoats shipped across the lake from Detroit and then rowed up the Maumee in light boats; for their protection they partly relied on a detachment of soldiers Capt. Thomas Smith commanded at a blockhouse on Swan Creek.[11]

Blue Jacket and his Shawnees had given more ground to the United States army, but now even they, the acknowledged heart of the Indian confederacy, were having to think hard. Were the British credible allies, when they had so often failed to provide more than token assistance to Indians in the field? And if they were not, was armed resistance still viable, or should the tribes come to terms with the Big Knives rather than watch them carrying torches to what villages remained in the former Indian country south of Lake Erie?

The Shawnee instinct was to fight on, and in the fall some warriors joined Delawares and other raiders in sporadic attacks that killed a dozen or more Americans around Wayne's posts. But across the confederacy Indians were tormented by doubts. Wayne knew it. On 12 September he sent a message to Swan Creek by an old Shawnee woman who had been for some months a prisoner of the Americans. It repeated his offer of the summer. The Indians could return to the Maumee, but they must bring in their prisoners and talk peace. Otherwise the war would continue, and the British could not protect them, as they had seen for themselves.[12]

The Wyandots of the Sandusky were the first important members of the confederacy to weaken. They had entered the war reluctantly in the first place, after Indian ambitions had been stirred by their great victories, but they had suffered grievously for it. The loss of so many of their head warriors at Fallen Timbers had also left a moderate, Tarhe, as the senior spokesman on the Sandusky. More important, the Wyandot villages were not directly threatened by the old treaties of Fort Harmar, but they were very exposed to American attack if the war went on. Encouraged by a mixed-blood Wyandot, Isaac Williams, Tarhe sent some men to sound out Wayne.

When Blue Jacket and the chiefs of the triumvirate at Swan Creek heard what the Wyandots had done late in September they urged Tarhe to "drop" his initiative. "You must not believe the Americans," they said, "for they only wish to decoy us into a snare with their fine speeches." They knew that Simcoe and Brant were due to speak personally at Swan Creek and wanted to keep the confederacy together at least until they had heard what the British and the formidable Mohawk had to say.[13]

Even among the Shawnees, however, there were some who wondered if Tarhe might have been right, and one mattered more than all the others: the leading war chief of the confederacy himself. From the Lasselles and other Frenchmen Blue Jacket was hearing of Britain's disastrous start to the European war and how the French were sweeping the British and Austrian armies before them. Thus the humiliation of the Duke of York's forces across the Atlantic even touched the Indians of the American interior. Another Shawnee friend of the Lasselles was described by Captain Smith at Swan Creek as "a great advocate for peace." The Indian openly claimed that the French were "likely to beat the English, who *would not assist the Indians*," and he admitted that "all the French in Detroit had told him so, *as well as Blue Jacket*."[14]

Indeed, in September Blue Jacket was himself considering going to Fort Defiance to speak with Wayne, along with some Ottawa and Potawatomi leaders. He decided against the trip when he heard that Simcoe and Brant were on their way to Swan Creek, but he still found a way to reach Wayne — through the Lasselles.

Antoine Lasselle, one of the patriarchs of the clan, had been captured at Fallen Timbers and was lucky to be in irons rather than swinging from the end of a rope. The day after the battle he was hauled before a five-member court supervised by Lieutenant Colonel Hamtramck and charged with spying. It was decided that he was an open opponent rather than a spy, since he had been discovered two hours after the battle, painted as an Indian and armed but hiding within the American lines. He was taken after a scuffle. Saved from the noose, Antoine became available for exchange. Upon hearing of his plight, the Indians furnished Tappon Lasselle with three white prisoners to take to Defiance to secure his brother's release. Blue Jacket charged Tappon with finding out from Wayne what reception the chiefs could expect if they went to the fort and whether their safety could be assured. Thus, while the Shawnee war chief remained at Swan Creek, he was already considering breaking with the British and making his peace with the Big Knives.[15]

Truly, the confederacy was tottering.

If anyone had the personality and imagination to allay Indian suspicions about the British, it was Lieutenant Governor John Graves Simcoe. Outspoken, enthusiastic, active, and bubbling with confidence and ideas, he was the man to make the best of a difficult position. When Simcoe arrived at Swan Creek on 27 September, about two thousand Indians lined the riverside to honor him. Three days later, Joseph Brant appeared with almost a hundred Iroquois and Mississauga warriors, hoping to breathe life into the creaking confederacy. In October Blue Jacket and the other Indians gathered at Brownstown on the Detroit River, the Wyandot village which everyone regarded as the symbolic capital of the confederacy, to hear what both men had to say. Brant urged them to stand firm. A year before he had stood for negotiations with the Americans, but then the Indians had been in a stronger position. Now, defeated, they were weak, and Brant believed they should be prepared to fight again. He said he would join them. The Mohawk's opinions were always authoritative, but it was Simcoe, the representative of His Majesty the Great Father, whose words really mattered.

Simcoe sensed the mood of betrayal in the Indians, and like Haldimand before him, he believed them entirely capable of turning on the British in their disappointment, but he had also dared to dream of restoring British sway over the Old Northwest and desperately needed the Indian confederacy to keep the vision alive. Furthermore, with relations between Britain and the United States still precarious, Simcoe recognized the continuing need to cling to an Indian alliance that protected the sovereignty and trade of the Canadian colonies. On 13 October he made light of the battle of Fallen Timbers in a speech to the Indians, dismissing it as "some trifling advantage [gained] over a part of your people in a skirmish." He said nothing about the incident at the gates of Fort Miamis, when the Indians had been refused admittance, but assured his listeners that he had now instructed the commandant of the garrison to fire on any American soldiers who approached it. Had Wayne's legion not retired, Simcoe would have reinforced the position, he said.

Simcoe told the solemn warriors to stay united, and he promised further British help, but Blue Jacket could not have failed to notice that the lieutenant governor carefully avoided undertaking to field men and guns, as the Indians wished. Blue Jacket needed artillery to reduce the posts which the Big Knives were sprinkling across the land, not just provisions and words of encouragement. When the Indians asked for that extra commitment the following day, Simcoe could do nothing more than agree to take the complaint to his superior, Lord Dorchester. In short, Simcoe spoke proudly, but his talk lacked substance and conviction.

The Indians said they would decide what to do in the spring, when a full congress would be convened at Brownstown. Until then they would remain united. Although many of the Indians intended to adhere to this schedule, the most skeptical of them were unimpressed. Brant reported the confused Indians in a "bad temper by not receiving any assistance from the English." Simcoe had simply failed to address that charge.[16]

The trouble was that although Simcoe respected and sympathized with the Indians, his hands were tied. He wrote to the Duke of Portland, a member of the British government, warning the Crown against sacrificing Indian support by a hasty abandonment of Fort Miamis and other western posts. Unfortunately, Britain was poised for just such a retreat. Dorchester's truculent tones of the previous February, which had so pleased Simcoe, had earned him a rebuke from London, and the year's campaigns in Europe had gone so badly for the British that they had no taste for conflict in America. The government decided to end its difficulties with the United States. In November 1794 Jay's Treaty was signed. Britain agreed to surrender the western posts they had held illegally since 1783. Their only provision for the Indians was that Canadian traders were to be permitted by the Americans to continue plying their wares south of the Great Lakes. For a dozen years Niagara, Detroit, Michilimackinac, and latterly Miamis had tangibly testified to the king's regard for his Indian allies. Now they were going.[17]

For the moment Blue Jacket was ignorant of this further example of British perfidy, but he had not been reassured by Simcoe's brave posturing. In fact, the influence of the Sandusky Wyandots and the Lasselles moved him more than the combined talents of Simcoe and Brant.

Still fretting about the danger to their homes, as well as to their hunters scattering across territory now dominated by the Americans, the Wyandots and Mingoes of the Sandusky had continued to communicate with Major General Wayne. They were denounced by the council of chiefs at Swan Creek and also by their Wyandot kinsmen on the Detroit River, who condemned their unilateral action and urged them to await the congress in the spring. From his new base at Swan Creek, Alexander McKee also railed at the people on the Sandusky, denigrating Isaac

Williams as an American agent who "cloaks himself in the character of an Indian."

Wayne, however, nurtured their interest tenderly. He suggested that the Harmar line of 1789, which posed no threat to the Sandusky villages, would be a basis for peace negotiations, and he promised that the Indians would not be punished if they came forward with prisoners. He also hinted that Britain was losing ground in its negotiations with the American diplomat John Jay in London and that neither Indians nor redcoats could prevent Wayne from cleaning out Swan Creek and Brownstown whenever he chose. Dutifully, Tarhe sent these speeches to his allies at those places, but they reproached him for breaking ranks with the confederacy. Tarhe held to his course nonetheless. By the end of the year he had sent further representatives to Wayne and promised to attend a peace treaty the next year. He was so afraid of the fury of the other members of the confederacy and the British, however, that he begged the Americans to erect a fort on the Sandusky to protect his people.[18]

The Wyandot initiative probably interested Blue Jacket, but it was the ubiquitous Lasselle family that he listened to most. Tappon rescued Antoine from the clutches of the Americans, and the former prisoner was back at Fort Miamis on 21 October, disheveled and subdued but safe. Antoine denied that he was carrying messages for Wayne, but he certainly lied. What he told Blue Jacket, who had asked the Lasselles to speak to Wayne on his behalf, or Little Turtle and Buckongahelas, whom he asked to meet him at Detroit, is not directly known. But we can guess. There is no doubt but that he told them that Wayne was honorable and would guarantee their safety and that it was in their interests to visit him.

The Lasselles had sharp eyes for profit. They believed that the United States would soon control the territory and were determined to protect their trade when that happened. Evidently Wayne had promised them a trading license to supply both the Indians and the new American military posts — providing they helped bring in the Indians for a treaty. Antoine was enthusiastic. His capture had seemed a disaster, but now it had put him in the way of stealing a march on the other Detroit traders. "If you come [to the American forts] you will do well in coming with the Shawanoes and Delawares," he would shortly write his nephew Jacques. "We will make a partnership for spirituous liquors. Money is to be made."[19]

The British hated the Lasselles but deeply feared their influence. Said one:

These scoundrels, bred amongst the Indians, masters of all their customs and prejudices, speaking their language and all its different dialects, keeping their daughters as wives, having in their employment a number of fellows, here called engagés, the last the most profligate and contemptible characters on earth, wretches desitute of every principle of common honesty or even humanity, equal to any crime, fearing nothing but a halter, appeared with their myrmidons at the action near the Miami painted and armed as if to assist their friends, whereas the end intended and obtained was to prevent the great majority of the Indians from coming into action.[20]

With some reason did the British dislike the Lasselles, for they made a difference. Back in Detroit, Antoine soon formed a trading company with Francis Lafontaine, John McGregor, and the métis Miami Jean Baptiste Richardville, among others, and put together a pack train of thirty animals. He left Detroit in November, heading for what is now Indiana and Michigan. In January Lasselle was at Fort Greenville, where Wayne had his headquarters, and with him were forty Indians he had persuaded to talk peace. They consisted of Ottawas under Kinouchamek (Fish), Ojibwes of the Mackinac region with their chief, Mashipinashiwish (Bad Bird), Potawatomis under Onanguisous (Wolverine), a few Sacs, and some Miamis from the Pacanne-Richardville faction. Lasselle received his reward. In no time he was erecting a storehouse at Fort Wayne and writing to his partners in Detroit for a new supply of goods.[21]

The arguments of the Lasselles and of French trading associates such as Jean Baptiste Laplante undermined Blue Jacket's belief in the British. At the same time, Wayne's sensitive pacification of the defeated tribes was evaporating his doubts about the reception he could expect at the American forts.

The beginning of the new year had brought reasons for optimism on the part of Wayne, but the core of the Indian confederacy had not to all appearances yet been broken. The Sandusky Wyandots and Mingoes had not been key players in the war, and although the Indians Antoine Lasselle brought into Fort Greenville claimed to represent all the Ojibwes and Ottawas of the Michigan area, as well as some Potawatomis, this was an exaggeration. Their story that Five Medals of the Potawatomis and Little Turtle had promised to follow was no more than mere rumor. Although these Indians came from villages that had supplied warriors to the confederacy, they were certainly not from its core.

From that core — the Shawnees, the Delawares of Buckongahelas and Big Cat, the Miamis of Little Turtle and Le Gris, the Ottawas of Egushaway, the Wyandots of the Detroit and the Maumee, and the Potawatomis and Ojibwes of the Detroit area — Wayne had as yet had nothing.

Then, at the end of January 1795, Blue Jacket, the most powerful war chief of them all, arrived at Fort Defiance.

# 14

## We Must Think of War No More

The party that arrived at Fort Defiance on 29 January 1795 was small but distinguished. Consisting of twenty Shawnees and Delawares, the Indian embassy included Blue Jacket, his sister, who was probably one of the tribe's female chiefs, and a Shawnee chief named Nianimseca, while the leading Delaware was a prestigious civil chief known to the whites as "the Grand Glaize King" and to the Indians as Tetepachsit, or Branching Tree. Stephen Young, a Stockbridge Mahican, accompanied them, probably as an interpreter.

They had four prisoners with them. Matthias Dawson and Susanna Baker had been captured about 1792, one on the Monongahela and the other in Kentucky. James Patten had been in captivity maybe a year longer, since his capture on the Muskingum, and Joseph Guy had been taken near Fort Hamilton the previous month. They all served several purposes for Blue Jacket. If prying British officials interfered with his mission, he could say that he was merely going to the American forts to exchange some prisoners. Once he got there, the captives would secure him a welcome.

Yet he moved cautiously, sending two warriors, a Shawnee and a Delaware, ahead with a flag of truce to signal his intentions. For the next leg of his journey, from Defiance to Greenville, where Major General Wayne had his headquarters, the chief had an escort of twenty men under Lt. Robert Lee. They arrived at the fort on 7 February.

Maj. John Hutchinson Buell was officer of the day at Greenville. He went out to meet the visitors and recorded his impressions in a diary the following day. "Blue Jacket is along," he wrote trumphantly. "He is the chief of the Shawnees and is said to be the greatest warrior among all the tribes." When Wayne turned out to meet his most celebrated opponent, he found the Shawnee's vanity and sense of occasion undiminished. According to Buell, "Blue Jacket was elegantly dressed with a scarlet [regimental] coat, two gold epaulets, a good woollen shirt, and his other dress compared. He had a sister with him, dressed equal with himself. The chief of the Delawares was dressed in the same uniform as Blue Jacket, but wore one epaulet." The single epaulet, of course, designated inferior rank in the British armed services.[1]

It had been a bold step for Blue Jacket, one that not only drew the full fire of the British, who simply regarded him as a turncoat, but also broke with the official policy of the confederacy and threatened to cost him the regard of his own people. The redcoats, of course, were fighting to preserve their influence among the Indians, and the confederacy, encouraged by the British, had agreed to wait until a full spring council could determine what action the tribes should take. But of all the tribes, the Shawnees were notoriously reluctant to treat with the Big Knives. After all, it was they who stood to lose the bulk of their country and they who had suffered most consistently in twenty years of warfare.

The Lasselles made no bones of it. They told the Americans that "all the tribes are for peace except the Shawneese, who are determined to prosecute the war." And this might not have been a big exaggeration. Some Shawnees were already bent on fighting again. Before the end of the year a joint Shawnee-Mingo delegation even set out to rouse the southern tribes to war, although it was dissuaded from proceeding by the Wyandot leader, Tarhe, who urged them to wait until the spring. Other Shawnees were talking about clearing out of the Ohio country rather than agreeing to sell it to the Big Knives. They planned to put the best of the winter hunting behind them and then to steal American horses to shift their families across the Mississippi in the spring.[2]

We can now appreciate what a serious step Blue Jacket had taken. By treating with Wayne he was risking his standing with the men upon whom he relied most — the Shawnee warriors. Not only that, but even if a peace were concluded, Shawnee custom would require him, as the senior war chief, to surrender his direction of the nation's affairs to a tribal civil chief, who would handle matters in times of peace. On the face of it, therefore, Blue Jacket seemed bent on self-destruction. By traveling to

Greenville he forfeited the regard of many of the warriors and paved the way for handing over power to the civil chiefs.

It was a decisive move and one Blue Jacket's family remembered with pride. One of his grandsons boasted, without complete inaccuracy, that his grandfather had been "the only chief who had the courage to go to the camp of General Wayne and sue for peace." Why, then, did he do it?

There is no doubt that he saw the will to fight on crumbling, even among his closest allies. The Delawares, for example, were thinking of moving to the White River (Indiana), the Illinois, or the Mississippi. Even the fierce Cherokees were weakening. They still had villages at the head of the Scioto and on Swan Creek, but before the end of 1794 some had tired and gone home to the warm banks of the Tennessee.

Then, too, Blue Jacket's faith in the redcoats had gone. He had seen the extent of their support and brooded over that humiliating fiasco at Fort Miamis, and the Lasselles and other French Canadians assured him that Britain was too committed to the European war to do anything for the Indians. A trader from the River Raisin area of Michigan, Jean Baptiste Laplante, was advising the Indians to make peace with Wayne at any price. He and other French settlers were claiming that the Big Knives and the French were one and could not be beaten. As for the British, they were not only weak but were also laying claim to land on the Raisin which the Potawatomis had given to the French settlers.[3]

The Wyandots and the Lasselles had also removed any doubts Blue Jacket had entertained about the reception he might expect from Wayne. Thus, when Isaac Williams had forwarded the speeches Wayne had sent to the Wyandots to Swan Creek, Blue Jacket had held several discussions with the courier, a Wyandot chief named Leatherlips. From all of this information, Blue Jacket deduced that if he went to Greenville his safety would be assured.

Finally, Blue Jacket saw advantages in being among the first, rather than among the last, chiefs to approach Wayne. By visiting Wayne early, he might prove himself useful in bringing about a general peace and place the American general under an obligation to him. That could pay dividends, to Blue Jacket personally and perhaps to his people. It was a gamble, but the Shawnee war chief saw the odds tipping in the favor of his enemies, and whatever jeopardy the mission had put him in, he looked at the United States and saw the future.

It was not until January that Blue Jacket bit on the bullet. On 1 January Wayne again wrote the Sandusky Wyandots, promising to build a post for their protection as they had requested and adverting to the party of Miamis, Potawatomis, Ottawas, Ojibwes, and Sacs Antoine Lasselle had brought into Fort Wayne on his way to Greenville. This information reached Blue Jacket and probably prompted him to action. Although none of the key members of the confederacy had yet approached Wayne, Blue Jacket made his decision. The Shawnees later told John Norton that Blue Jacket noticed the Indians were wavering and "thought he would not be the last to pay his addresses."[4]

Antoine Lasselle knew the trend of Blue Jacket's thought. On 31 January he wrote his nephew Jacques from the Maumee urging him to tell Blue Jacket not to wait any longer. "He must come absolutely with his band," Antoine said. "I give this notice as a friend, for I would not wish him to be the last a-coming." The Shawnee war chief had not needed that advice. Even before Antoine's pen had touched paper, Blue Jacket's party had left Swan Creek for Greenville.[5]

He had worked discreetly, avoiding the British and more obdurate chiefs and sounding out likely allies in covert private councils. Most of the Shawnees, including Captain Johnny and Blackbeard, were implacably hostile to treating with Wayne, but Blue Jacket found supporters among the Mekoche chiefs. He also bent some Delawares to his purpose, and probably those who accompanied him represented Buckongahelas, who had always been a close associate of Blue Jacket. As for the Miamis, those at Swan Creek belonged to the Le Gris–Little Turtle band and were few in number, and none followed Blue Jacket to Greenville. After the Shawnee's party left Swan Creek on 24 January, the Miami chiefs affected to disavow him. Little Turtle behaved shiftily. He disclaimed involvement in Blue Jacket's mission but then put himself out of the way in February, explaining that his absence need arouse no suspicions. He was visiting a brother, not going to Greenville. There are grounds, however, for believing these Miamis were secretly supporting Blue Jacket. Blue Jacket told Wayne that he represented "the chiefs and warriors" of "the Shawanoes, Delawares and Miamis," while Jacques Lasselle, who knew the Miamis as well as anyone, implied that the Shawnee war chief had Miami followers when he referred to "the Miamis that belong to him."[6]

Some of the French-Canadian traders were also privy to Blue Jacket's plan, for the chief carried secret letters from them to Antoine Lasselle, whom he expected to meet at the American forts.

On 8 February the two warriors met in council for the first time, face to face. Blue Jacket, we can guess, was at his fastidious best, and Anthony

Wayne knew that this was the man, if anyone, who could deliver him the peace. Nianimseca pulled out a copy of the speech Wayne had sent to Tarhe on New Year's Day and asked if it truly represented the general's sentiments. Wayne said that it did, and after some time Blue Jacket rose to reply on behalf of the Shawnees, Delawares, and Miamis. He claimed to speak "in behalf of the whole," something far less than the truth. The speeches Wayne had sent to the Wyandots had pleased the Indians, he said, and the "true character" of the British was now known to them. "Our hearts and minds are changed, and we now consider ourselves your friends and brothers."

In a few simple words, Blue Jacket surrendered the upper Ohio to his conquerors. "Elder Brother," said he, "we are well pleased with the time and place appointed for holding the general treaty [Greenville, 15 June], and will meet you here accordingly, and are ready and willing to sign the preliminary articles you propose for the cessation of hostilities and the surrender of prisoners. I have only to request that you will permit our flesh and blood [Indian prisoners held by the Americans] to come and stay with us."

Tetepachsit spoke for the Delawares the following day and got Wayne to agree that the Indians could come and plant corn about their old villages in the spring. Then, on 11 February, the chiefs signed the preliminary articles of peace. They were not committed to a particular boundary, but it was understood that the Harmar line would be the basis for negotiations. Rations of meat, flour, and salt were given the Indians, but in a private discussion with Wayne Blue Jacket wanted something else for his trouble. As Wayne reported,

> I observe that those great kings or chiefs, like children, esteem those trifles as objects of great price or value. They cost nothing, and they will have a good effect. Even the famous Blue Jacket appeared to set an inestimable value upon a piece of printed paper, enlisting him a war chief and directing the Indians to consider him as such, under the hand and seal of Sir John Johnston [Johnson], dated in 1784, which he produced at this place to show that he was a great man. In return I produced one of our commissions. The decorations struck him . . . and he expressed a wish that when he made peace he might be honored with one like that on parchment. His was only paper, and without much decoration.[7]

A piece of paper and flattering a proud leader did not cost Wayne much. Blue Jacket was simply looking to exchange his standing with the British, and their acknowledgment of it, for a like position with the Americans. On his part, Wayne was convinced he had secured much more, the peace. The most noted of the hostile chiefs had signed preliminary articles on behalf of the triumvirate. In letter after letter, to the outgoing and incoming secretaries of war, Henry Knox and Timothy Pickering, and to officers such as Hamtramck, Winthrop Sargent, and James O'Hara, Wayne wrote triumphantly of the submission of "the famous Blue Jacket." As he told O'Hara, his quartermaster, "The famous Blue Jacket has pledged himself as a man of honor and as a war chief that he will now make a permanent peace and be as faithful a friend to the United States in future as he has lately been their inveterate enemy. The whole of the hostile nations having now sued for peace, I only await the arrival of Tarhe's signal flag in order to issue a proclamation announcing the time and place for the treaty."[8]

For Wayne the war seemed to be over. But for Blue Jacket, who knew full well that he had not been authorized to make peace on behalf of the triumvirate, the road looked much thornier. He spent a few days about the garrison before leaving on 14 February with his entourage and a few released Indian prisoners. "We have had the famous Mr. Blue Jacket with us," wrote one observer a fortnight later, "and although he will speak no English he appears to be a good deal civilized."[9]

Blue Jacket knew what was waiting for him at Swan Creek: the fury of the British and a battle for the hearts and minds of the remaining confederates. Even now raids were in progress. Even as he spoke at Greenville, other warriors were raiding about the forts. Near Fort Hamilton four or five packers were killed. Blue Jacket had given his word to Wayne and had now to persuade those warriors to lay down their arms and to accept that they had been defeated.

When he left Fort Greenville, Blue Jacket knew he had lost the war, but he had yet to deliver the peace.

✳     ✳     ✳

Blue Jacket went home, preceded by his customary one or two heralds. From Greenville to Defiance he was again escorted by Lieutenant Lee, although the detachment of soldiers had been reduced to four by sickness. After two days at Fort Defiance, dining again in the officers' mess, the war chief headed down the Maumee on 27 February. When he reached Fort Miamis the storms of abuse he was expecting began to gather.

Some of them lashed Antoine Lasselle. As his nephew Jacques warned him, his actions had made a "great noise in Detroit, and a great number have wished that my uncle Antoine was scalped, saying that he deserved it. . . . I assure you, they talk very hard against you, my uncle Anthony."[10]

Blue Jacket was the other target, and he gave his own account to Wayne later in the year:

> I visited the British [he said], and was kindly received at their garrison on the Miami [Fort Miamis]. I was asked for news. I had none for them, except that of my kind reception from you. A Mr. Magdalen wrote from thence to Detroit that he had taken off my blue coat, which I had received from the Americans, and broke my gun, which he also falsely said was presented to me by General Wayne. I did not rest until I exposed this man and refuted his assertions.
>
> I informed all the Indians [at Swan Creek] of my full persuasion of the truth of the kind and benevolent intentions you expressed to me, and that they in due time would be convinced of the goodness of your motives. Mr. McKee invited me to his house and told me he was very sorry to find I had acted with such little regard for my people; that he ascribed my strange conduct to the instigations of some evil spirit who had led me astray from the plain good road and put me in the path which led towards the Americans.
>
> "The commission you received from Johnson," said he, "was not given you to carry to the Americans. I am grieved to find that you have taken it to them. It was with much regret I learned that you had deserted your friends, who always caressed you, and treated you as a great man. You have deranged, by your imprudent conduct, all our plans for protecting the Indians and keeping them with us.
>
> "They have always looked up to you for advice and direction in war, and you have now broke the strong ties which held them all together under your and our direction. You must now be viewed as the enemy of your people and the other Indians whom you are seducing into the snares the Americans have formed for their ruin. And the massacre and destruction of these people by the Americans must be laid to your charge."[11]

Evidently Blue Jacket did not exaggerate. McKee's son Thomas "declared that if ever he caught Blue Jacket he would kill him, as he was in a great measure the cause of the Indians coming in." Young McKee was notoriously intemperate. He had been preparing another scarlet coat, with gold epaulets, for Blue Jacket, and was said to have angrily thrown the epaulets into a fire when he heard of the chief's mission to Fort Greenville.[12]

The British had already betrayed the Indians by signing Jay's Treaty, surrendering their western posts to the United States, but out on the frontier, where the doings of diplomats in London had yet to be known, the redcoats and Indian agents demonized Blue Jacket and Antoine Lasselle. And not unjustly, for both now pulled in harness to persuade the Indians to attend the treaty.

In January Lasselle wrote his Detroit business partners from the Maumee, describing the good reception Wayne's officers were according the Indians at the forts and telling the traders to warn wavering Indians of the dangers of isolation.[13]

When Blue Jacket set to work he was even more potent. The Miamis and Delawares, if not all already behind his initiative, quickly fell into line with the agreement he had made. Tetepachsit, Big Cat, Peihetalmena, the Delaware civil chiefs, and their head warriors, Buckongahelas and Watepuckehen, applied to Wayne early in March to replant their old grounds at the Glaize to relieve them of further reliance on the British. Later that month the Miami leader Le Gris, "a sensible old fellow," according to Hamtramck, also agreed to abide by the preliminary articles signed by Blue Jacket's party.[14]

For the moment, however, Blue Jacket made little headway with the influential Ottawas under Egushaway and Little Otter, although other members of the Three Fires from further afield were going into Fort Wayne. He also encountered predictable difficulties with the Shawnees. Some quickly followed his lead and restored good relations with the Americans, visiting the forts looking for lost livestock or seeking permission to plant corn or tap the maples for sugar. But none of the Shawnee names thus mentioned in surviving letters and diaries — Pesekwassicsica, the Panther, Kanemissica, Nekskorwetor, and Pawotgue — are those of significant leaders. Blue Jacket did gain one valuable Shawnee ally, though. His half-brother, the respected orator and civil chief Red Pole, returned to the Maumee that spring after a two-year absence canvassing the southern Indians. Immediately he threw his not inconsiderable influence behind Blue Jacket's campaign.[15]

Blue Jacket had never needed Red Pole more. His visit to Greenville had shaken the Shawnees, but most could not bring themselves to make peace. Some, torn between the advice of their leading war chief on the one hand and that of their kinsmen in the British Indian Department on the other, even wrote to Joseph Brant and the Seven Nations of Canada for advice. There was furious debate about what to do. Yet even some of the Mekoches, traditionally the least warlike of the Shawnee divisions, complained about Blue Jacket's behavior, albeit for a different reason. They were annoyed that Blue Jacket had flaunted his paper testimonial before Wayne and claimed to head the nation. They protested that the Mekoches alone had the privilege of directing the tribe during times of peace, and they resented the efforts of Blue Jacket to prolong his wartime significance. Two Mekoche chiefs, Black Hoof and Red-Faced Fellow, made a "great noise" about the matter, blaming the British for having given a testimonial to one of their "younger brothers" and declaring that Blue Jacket "takes more upon him than he has a right to do" pretending to Wayne that "he was the principal of the Shawanoe chiefs and could do with them what he pleased." Although some Mekoches did finally follow Blue Jacket to Greenville, the jealousies he was arousing, both in and out of his tribe, did not help his attempts to broker a peace.[16]

Despite difficulties, Blue Jacket made progress. He circulated speeches and advice and put an end to a raid for which 150 men had collected. He told the Indians that they could be independent of the British and promised he could get Wayne to let them establish a village at the head of the Maumee, where Fort Wayne now guarded the site of old Miamitown. They would receive protection and could plant their old fields. Some Shawnees, Buckongahelas's Delawares, and probably the Miamis fell in with the idea, but Blue Jacket ran into problems getting an interpreter willing to make the trip. At first Jacques Lasselle was afraid to go with the chief, dreading British retaliation. He wrote Antoine, who was still with the Americans, asking him to interpret for Blue Jacket instead. Indicating the delicacy of the situation, Jacques warned his uncles not to tell the Americans about the stipend Blue Jacket still received from the British lest it might compromise him.[17]

But eventually Jacques threw in with his father-in-law, packing a horseload of trade goods, including spirits, to make his journey worthwhile. They arrived at Fort Defiance on 30 April: Blue Jacket, one of his sons, Jacques, and two warriors. The chief told Maj. Thomas Hunt that he had "had a considerable battle with McKee and the English" but had quit them and was going to Fort Wayne. He wanted to find a good place for a village before writing to General Wayne to get permission to settle and some seed corn. A diarist at the post wrote that "Blue Jacket is supposed to possess the greatest influence in his nation" and observed that Jacques was "certainly a very decent well-behaved fellow." The two dined with the officers, and Jacques lost no time in selling his wares at the post, even at inflated prices. Blue Jacket left for Fort Wayne on 2 May, but parties of Shawnees and Delawares were soon appearing at Fort Defiance to await word from the Shawnee chief. By 8 May several Shawnees, one of them Nianimseca, and four hundred Delawares under Buckongahelas were at the post, waiting. Canoeloads of them had paddled up the Maumee, a tribute to Blue Jacket's success in creating a peace party.[18]

The sixth of May found the Shawnee chief upriver, at Fort Wayne, conferring with Colonel Hamtramck. He explained that he had been "preparing the nations to attend the treaty," and as proof of his honesty he volunteered the information that he had been in receipt of a British allowance. This was something the Lasselles had advised him to keep to himself. They thought it would make the Americans suspicious of him, but Blue Jacket turned it to his advantage by pointing out that he had now sacrificed it by his actions. But he needed help to continue his work. First, if the treaty opened on 15 June as planned, he needed license to arrive late. Lord Dorchester was supposed to be visiting the western Indians, and there was still that congress which Simcoe and Brant were organizing. Blue Jacket had to be there to counteract British influence. Second, he wanted leave to establish a village near Fort Wayne, and he wanted corn to plant and provisions to help the Indians until their crops could be harvested at the end of the summer.[19]

Originally, Blue Jacket had expected to wait for Wayne's permission before locating his people near Fort Wayne, but Hamtramck, who commanded the garrison there, told him that the reply would surely be favorable. Consequently, after finding suitable places for villages, the Shawnee chief sent one of his warriors, Nekskorwetor, back to Defiance to tell Buckongahelas to come forward. Nekskorwetor arrived at Defiance on 10 May, and several hundred Delawares were soon heading up the Maumee to join Blue Jacket. Other Indians were also attracted by the idea of resettling the head of the Maumee. A Potawatomi from the Michigan peninsula called at Fort Wayne to confer with Blue Jacket, and later in the month Little Turtle's Miamis arrived. In short, Blue Jacket had transferred much of the triumvirate's strength from Swan Creek to Fort Wayne and from British to American protection.[20]

Hamtramck was right about Wayne's readiness to help Blue Jacket. He pinned much on the great chief's promises and soothed the shaky Wyandots of Sandusky by telling them that "Blue Jacket assures me that all the Indians from Swan Creek etc. will undoubtedly attend the treaty." When the Shawnee chief's requests arrived at Greenville, Wayne pounced on them. Everything Blue Jacket wanted would be granted: one hundred bushels of corn and as many provisions as could be mustered would go to Fort Wayne for the chief's following; Jacques Lasselle would be permitted to serve as Blue Jacket's interpreter; and the chief's plan to return to Swan Creek was endorsed, even if it caused him to be up to a week late for the peace conference. Blue Jacket anticipated Wayne's support. On 15 May he and Lasselle had left Fort Wayne, leaving instructions for Wayne's reply to be sent after him. He was bound for Detroit and Swan Creek, intent upon completing his work.[21]

These latest arrangements strengthened Blue Jacket's hand. Few Indians could now believe that the upper Ohio could be saved, but the Shawnee chief was offering places to build their villages, corn, provisions, trade through merchants such as the Lasselles, and treaty annuities. Unsatisfactory it may have been but preferable, perhaps, to a brooding exile, the uncertain support of the redcoats, and the dangers from American attacks.

Blue Jacket knew that three of the remaining pockets of resistance were particularly important: the greater part of the Shawnees, under Captain Johnny; the Ottawas of Egushaway, who was so influential among the Three Fires; and the symbolic leaders of the confederacy, the Wyandots of the Detroit River. Blue Jacket's messenger, Nekskorwetor, had been under orders to move on from Fort Defiance, carrying Blue Jacket's news downstream to Swan Creek. As the Shawnee chief followed, alongside the tumbling Maumee, he knew his words were going before him, reopening the debate and preparing the ground.[22]

But try as he did, Blue Jacket could not move all the recalcitrant Shawnees. Unfortunately, their belligerence had been reawakened by an untoward event that occurred on Paint Creek on 14 May. A Shawnee hunting camp under Pucksekaw (Jumper) had been attacked by a posse of white rangers led by Nathaniel Massie. The Indians were driven from their camp, losing their baggage and horses. Though the Shawnees counterattacked the next morning, wounding one of their enemies, the episode rekindled old enmities and sparked retaliatory raids north and south of the Ohio and into Virginia. Pucksekaw made two or three attacks in Randolph County, Virginia. On 13 July his warriors hit a homestead, killing two daughters of a settler and capturing the wife and two sons. This was not a climate conducive to Blue Jacket's appeal for reconciliation with the Big Knives.

In the end only 143 Shawnees attended the treaty of Greenville, a number which was swollen to a little over 200 by later arrivals, such as Pucksekaw. This amounted to about a fifth of the Ohio Shawnees. Even granting that some who stayed at home would have supported the treaty, probably less than half the Shawnees joined Blue Jacket's peace party, and the dissenters included such prominent figures as Captain Johnny, the war captain Black Snake, Blackbeard, and Kakinathucca.[23]

The closest military allies of the Shawnees also remained aloof. The Mingoes and the Ohio Cherokees both kept away from the treaty. The Cherokee leader, Coonaniskey (Big Spider), who lived at the head of the Scioto, told the Americans that he intended returning to his people in the South once the crops had been harvested.[24]

Blue Jacket was more successful elsewhere. Egushaway for one had already been listening to the Lasselles, and when Blue Jacket returned to Swan Creek, full of his additional assurances, the great Ottawa quickly threw in with the treaty party. He was a powerful recruit. As one at Fort Defiance remarked, Egushaway was still "the head chief of the Ottawas," and he had "much influence over the other tribes." Yet even he could not bring over all of his own tribesmen. Some Ottawas under Little Otter chose to remain within the British orbit.

At the end of May Blue Jacket recruited Jacques Lasselle for his last appeals for peace on a trip to the Detroit. There, on the doorstep of a fortress that had entered its final days under the British flag, he drew local Wyandots, Ojibwes, and Ottawas into his initiative. The Wyandots were the keepers of the confederated council fire at Brownstown and the custodians of the great wampum belt of union. Their support spoke starkly that the confederacy itself now stood for peace.

As Indian resistance to the United States crumbled, so too did the congress Brant and Simcoe had wanted. There was nothing to keep Blue Jacket from making his way to the treaty ground. It was agreed that the Shawnee chief would travel in advance, bearing letters to Wayne from the Wyandots, Ojibwes, and Ottawas. Red Pole and Egushaway would mobilize further parties at Swan Creek, while the Wyandots would assemble another at Big Rock near Brownstown. The whole would rendezvous at Fort Recovery, when Blue Jacket would lead them on their final journey to Greenville. As Egushaway addressed the American commander, "Brother, the Hurons [Wyandots], Ottawas and Chipeways [Ojibwes] will meet Jacques Lassell and Blue Jacket at Fort Recovery, from which place we will all go together to your place."[25]

Working from group to group and from village to village, Blue Jacket had kept his promise to Wayne. More than any other Indian leader, he had delivered the peace.

*     *     *

Few more important Indian treaties have been signed on behalf of the United States than the one negotiated at Greenville by Maj. Gen. Anthony Wayne. In one sense it was a victory for the Indian confederacy which had fought so hard to prevent it. Unlike the treaties before and after it, the treaty of Greenville brought together most of the tribes of the Old Northwest, rather than just the few whose village, hunting, and fishing sites happened to be on the debatable land. There were not only Shawnees, Miamis, Wyandots, and Delawares but also Ojibwes, Potawatomis, and Ottawas from the north, and Eel Rivers, Weas, Piankeshaws, Kickapoos, and Kaskaskias from the Wabash and Illinois Rivers.

In that sense the treaty was a victory for the confederacy, for it had argued that the land was held in common by all the tribes and was not to be regarded as the exclusive property of one tribe or another. At Greenville the United States — fleetingly, as it would prove — acknowledged that point and negotiated with all the tribes.

But in most respects the treaty was a total defeat for the Indians. The United States acquired two-thirds of the modern state of Ohio, the whole southern, central, and eastern sections of it. This was the land the Shawnees, Mingoes, Cherokees, and Delawares had occupied, defended, and bled for. Their defeat, in particular, was a big one.

Major General Wayne, a stoutly built, impressive man of fifty years, knew how to flatter his guests. He dressed in full uniform and saw to it that his officers did so, and he established a large council house in the middle of his garden at Fort Greenville. Above it he raised the white flag as occasion demanded, and he signaled daily assembly with a six-pounder gun. The gathering Indian leaders came in from their camps, which were sprinkled outside the stockade, and enjoyed being entertained by the general and his staff, up to sixty chiefs at a time. Dressed in their finery, the chiefs smoked their tomahawk-pipes and talked until the evening gun told them it was time to leave.

Formal proceedings were opened on 16 June, and by early the following month most of the Indians had arrived, including chiefs such as Tetepachsit, Buckongahelas, Le Gris, and Little Turtle. But the Shawnees had not arrived, and Wayne postponed the serious business. The Indians grew restless. A Potawatomi, the Sun, complained, "The days are long. We have nothing to do. We become weary and wish for home." But still Wayne waited, urging the growing congregation to be patient. He was sure Blue Jacket would come and just as sure that there could be no real peace without the Shawnees.[26]

Blue Jacket was late, very late, but he did not intend to forfeit the general's favor. The problems he encountered coordinating the march of his last followers were, however, considerable. After their councils at Detroit, Blue Jacket and Jacques retraced their steps to the Maumee and made their way to Fort Wayne via Defiance. Arriving at their destination on 25 June, nine days after Wayne had opened the talks at Greenville, Blue Jacket handed the speeches of the Detroit Indians to Hamtramck for delivery to the general. He picked up Antoine Lasselle as an additional interpreter and left for the rendezvous at Fort Recovery.

He got there on 29 June, but none of his parties had arrived. The Shawnee chief was surprised, for, as he told the post commandant, Lt. Samuel Drake, Red Pole's contingent was using horses. In fact, Egushaway's Ottawas were then en route between Forts Defiance and Adams, but Red Pole's Shawnees, coming from Swan Creek, the Detroit River Wyandots, and a group of Ojibwes and Ottawas coming from Detroit under the superintendence of John Askin, Jean Beaubien, and Louis Beaufait, had evidently not even begun their journeys.

Fretting at his delay, Blue Jacket spent a few days at Fort Recovery, hoping for news from his supporters and waiting for the rain to clear before he went on himself to Greenville. Then Drake got word from Wayne. He had received the speeches Blue Jacket had forwarded through Fort Wayne and knew Blue Jacket was gathering his party at Recovery. The chief breathed more easily now, reassured that Wayne understood what was happening. Instead of pressing on to Greenville, Blue Jacket decided to scout the back trail. He waited until Drake could furnish him with two horses from a newly arrived convoy and set off on 1 July, riding toward Fort Adams on the St. Marys.

Later that day his spirits rose when he intercepted Egushaway's people on the way. Hurrying them on, he sent a companion to look for Red Pole and stationed himself at Fort Adams, between Recovery and Defiance.

Egushaway reached Greenville on 4 July. He was unusually tactless, telling the general that he doubted the Shawnees and Detroit Wyandots would come at all, but Wayne dismissed it. Blue Jacket also sent a message to Buckongahelas and those of his allies already at Greenville. With a present of tobacco, he told them "to sit still and smoke; make themselves easy. He [Blue Jacket] will be with them soon."[27]

Yet two more weeks had to pass before the Shawnee chief met another of his contingents as he backtracked as far as Fort Defiance. This was the Detroit party of twenty-seven Ojibwes and Ottawas under a veteran Ojibwe leader named Omissas and the three white traders. He also encountered others bound for the talks, including a thirty-year-old British trader, George McDougall (a "rattle-headed, wild, volatile, though genteel man" someone said), who was, no doubt, interested in finding out how the treaty might affect the Detroit merchants. Blue Jacket began to worry about what had befallen Red Pole and the Wyandots, but he decided he could wait no longer. Leaving one of his men on the river, he traveled to Greenville with the Ojibwes, Ottawas, and traders and three Shawnees, arriving late on 18 July.

He was more than a month behind schedule and three days after Wayne had been forced to open full negotiations with the twelve hundred Indians camped about the fort. After drawing rations, the Shawnee chief shook hands with Wayne in the council house. Omissas spoke briefly, and then Blue Jacket candidly admitted that "my uneasiness has been great that my people have not come forward as soon as you would wish or might expect, but you must not be discouraged by these unfavorable circumstances. Some of our chiefs and warriors are here; more will arrive in a few days. You must not, however, expect to see a great number. Yet notwithstanding, our nation will be well represented. Our hearts are open and void of deceit."[28]

According to one of the traders, Blue Jacket was beginning to doubt that Red Pole would appear and said so. "However," he quoted the chief, "I have a bit of tobacco from them, and they sent me word they would come immediately, but I cannot assure you they will." But Wayne assured him that he understood the difficulties. He commended Blue Jacket's "great zeal and wish . . . to serve the [United] States." The next morning, when the two old opponents were able to meet privately, Blue Jacket elaborated on the problems he had faced but seemed more optimistic. "Brother," he said, "I am very happy that, notwithstanding all the difficulties and obstructions I had to encounter from my relations and others at Detroit, I have succeeded so far in bringing my people to you at this time. I expect intelligence this day of the approach of more of them. . . . I repeat my assurances of the sincerity of my sentiments and resolution to be, for the future, a steady friend to the United States."[29]

Blue Jacket's position at this time was certainly embarrassing. The events of the past year had shown that even stripped of the bedrock of his support — the Shawnees, Mingoes, Cherokees, and British connections — he probably exercised more influence and authority in the confederacy than any other of its leaders. Ojibwes, Ottawas, Delawares, Wyandots, and Miamis had also looked to his example, and significant opinion leaders, such as Buckongahelas, Egushaway, and the Detroit Wyandots, heeded his counsel. It was somewhat ironic, therefore, that he found himself at the peace conference with only a handful of his own people beside him. He was almost a chief without a nation.

Nevertheless, he took his place in the treaty council, and being the experienced intertribal power broker that he was, he insisted on proper Indian protocol. As a Shawnee, he sat with the Wyandots and Delawares, reminding all that "the Wyandots are our uncles, and the Delawares our grandfathers, and that the Shawanese are the elder brothers of the other nations present." And he requested that Wayne address the Indians through the symbolic head of the confederacy, the Wyandot nation, for "you know, also, that our uncles [the Wyandots] have always taken care of the great [council] fire, they being the oldest nation. Our eldest brother [the United States] will, therefore, address his words to our uncle the Wyandot, who will hand them round through the different nations." In such ways did the Shawnee war chief flatter and cultivate close allies. We can almost see the Wyandot chiefs, seated in their privileged spot and nodding solemnly at this recognition of their importance.[30]

The real issue, of course, was the treaty line, and on that question there was unfortunately little room for argument. The Americans may have managed the treaty of Greenville more soundly than they handled its predecessors. They assembled a representative body of Indians and avoided the common pitfalls. There were no undue issues of liquor to mellow the chiefs; no claims that the United States owned all the land south of the Great Lakes; no impossible demands that the Indians surrender those warriors guilty of outrages against white settlers, when the United States was itself unable to punish whites for robbing or murdering Indians; no vengeful bullying; no negotiations with one group of Indians to undermine the position of another; and no claims to the land based on the idea what it had been conquered in the Revolution and ceded by the British. Wayne worked with a far defter hand than that.

But the treaty of Greenville was still a conquest treaty, based on the naked inequality of power. The Indians did not want to sell their land. They had defended it, and lost, and would simply have to accept the settlement imposed on them.

Wayne put forward the terms of his treaty on 27 July, ten articles covering such matters as the surrender of prisoners, the licensing of traders, the right of the United States and the chiefs to apply to each other for justice against thefts or murders, and the Indian rights to hunt on the ceded land. The boundary was the main item. Timothy Pickering, the new secretary of war, had proposed the Harmar line as the basis for negotiation but had emphasized the need to secure a lasting peace. But in framing the treaty, Wayne exceeded his instructions, demanding a slightly more generous cession than the Indians had made before.

The line presented by the American general began at the mouth of the Cuyahoga River on Lake Erie, near present-day Cleveland, and ran upstream to the portage with the Tuscarawas headwaters. It passed down this river close to what is now Dover and then struck roughly west-southwest to a fork of the head of the Great Miami near the portage with the St. Marys. Instead of having the boundary descend the Miami to approximate the Harmar line, Wayne took it further west to Fort Recovery near the current Ohio-Indiana state line, and thence in a straight line to the Ohio opposite the mouth of the Kentucky River. This extended the Harmar cession to include what is now western Ohio and a strip of Indiana.

In addition, parcels of land at strategic sites on the Indian side of the line, deemed also to have been ceded in 1789, were confirmed, but here Wayne again went beyond the instructions from Pickering. He increased the number of these tracts and made them a necessary condition of peace. In the treaty the Indians surrendered sites from which they had once defied American authority, including the locations of Forts Wayne and Defiance and places such as the rapids and mouth of the Maumee. A block in southern Indiana, consisting of 150,000 acres, was reserved for the soldiers of George Rogers Clark.[31]

For this abject submission the Indians received $20,000 in treaty goods, plus perpetual annuities. The last amounted to $1,000 per annum to each of the Shawnee, Delaware, Miami, Wyandot, Ottawa, Ojibwe, and Potawatomi peoples and $500 for each of the Kickapoo, Wea, Eel

River, Piankeshaw, and Kaskaskia groups. It was a miserable sum, even judged by the land values of the day, but it represented the effective end of the Indians' fight for Ohio. This rich green and watered ground would now pass to other hands, and quickly. Peace would encourage a fresh tide of white settlers, one that ultimately swept aside even the Greenville line. In 1796 there were only 5,000 whites in Ohio. In 1810 there were 230,000 and ten years after, 581,000 — a rolling mass of humanity which the Shawnees and their allies simply lacked the power to halt.[32]

There was little opposition to the treaty. Most Indians had gone to it in the full knowledge that some approximation of the Harmar line awaited them. Blue Jacket, perhaps too eager to make himself useful to Wayne, made no objections. The joint response of the Wyandots, Shawnees, and Delawares, made on 29 July, was weak.

It was left to Little Turtle to mount the only spirited attack on Wayne's proposals. On 18 July he joined the Ojibwe leader, Mashipinashiwish, in condemning the old treaty of Fort Harmar. After conferring with the Kickapoos, Weas, Eel Rivers, and some Potawatomis, Little Turtle also objected to Wayne's extension of the boundary west of the Great Miami; to the tracts to be ceded at Fort Wayne and the Maumee portage; and to a proposal that the Indians provide hostages against the release of their prisoners. His stand was brave but futile.

Indeed, Little Turtle's fight was not a model of tact. He and the Wabash Indians were understandably trying to deflect the cession from their homes, but the Miami war chief's claim that his people's territory extended as far as the Scioto (he admitted that the Miamis "first saw my elder brothers, the Shawanese," there) sounded suspiciously as if he was trying to corner a lion's share of the spoils. Ottawas, Ojibwes, and Potawatomis also made doubtful claims to the ceded territory, and it was Tarhe, the Wyandot, who reminded the Indians of the philosophy under which they had all fought, that "no one in particular can justly claim this ground; it belongs in common to us all. No earthly being has an exclusive right to it." Although Little Turtle had wanted to unite the Indians behind his stand, his remarks had stirred dormant territorial rivalries.

On 30 July the Indians gave their assent to the treaty.

The following day Blue Jacket's last party came in: Red Pole with 88 Shawnees, 9 Iroquois [Mingoes?], 10 Delawares, and 8 Detroit Wyandots, including a headman named Tey-yagh-taw. In typical Indian fashion, Red Pole's progress had been leisurely. He had reached Fort Defiance on 21 July and spent three or four days there, mixing with the garrison.

Major Hunt was told that Red Pole was "the head chief of the Shawanoes," and he appeared to be "quite a manly well-behaved fellow." Apparently Red Pole liked Hunt, too, and invited him to observe a dance outside the fort. The chief's arrival at Greenville raised the total Shawnee representation at the treaty to over 140 and brought a respected opinion and powerful orator to the proceedings.³³

Red Pole opened the day's business on 2 August, but in truth there was then little more to be said. Blue Jacket, speaking on a blue string of wampum, asked Wayne to organize a visit to President Washington for "two chiefs from each nation," ostensibly "to see that great man, and to enjoy the pleasure of conversing with him." Likely, he was already intent on calling in favors. As for Red Pole, he made no difficulties about the treaty. On the final day of the talks, 10 August, he endorsed the peace terms as they stood and repeated Tarhe's warning to the Indians about squabbling with each other about the land. "The Great Spirit gave us this land in common," said he. "He has not given the right to any one nation to say to another, 'this land is not yours; it belongs to me.'" Red Pole also accepted the stewardship of the United States ("our father of the fifteen fires has adopted us as his children") and offered to leave "my aged father" as a hostage for the release of prisoners, an offer Wayne humanely declined.³⁴

The treaty was signed on 3 August 1795. The Shawnees observed Indian etiquette and signed after the Wyandots and Delawares. Red Pole, Black Hoof (Catecahassa), Kaysewaesica, Weythapamattha, Nianimsica, Long Shanks (Waytheah), Blue Jacket, Nequetaughaw (Nekskorwetor?), and Captain Reed (Hahgooseekaw) signed for the Shawnees. A special copy of the treaty was lodged with the Wyandots, and on the eighth the treaty goods were distributed, with medals for the chiefs. The final transfer of Ohio was presided over by 1,130 Indians: 143 Shawnees, 91 Ottawas and Ojibwes, 180 Wyandots and Iroquois, 381 Delawares, 240 Potawatomis, 85 Miamis, Eel Rivers, Weas, and Piankeshaws, and 10 Kickapoos and Kaskaskias.

The feelings of the Shawnees who had drawn a curtain over a drama in which they had been playing for half a century can only be imagined. In reality, the treaty merely confirmed conditions that had existed for several years. The Shawnee villages had long since been north of the Greenville line, and the treaty did not deny the Indians the right to hunt over the ceded area. But this land, which they believed had been a gift of Waashaa

Monetoo and in which they had wanted to unite their broken nation, had slipped from their control forever.

The compensation for that sacrifice, they soon learned, could too easily disappear. Flushed with twenty horseloads of treaty goods, Red Pole led a returning party into Fort Defiance on 23 August. Some of the Shawnees bartered their presents for liquor and became intoxicated. Had it not been for Major Hunt, who compelled the traders to restore the goods and trust to future fur deliveries for their payments, the warriors would have squandered what they had gotten from the treaty.[35]

For Blue Jacket, the great warrior of the Shawnees, the war was over. He stood high in the estimation of the new masters of the Old Northwest. He had his share of the presents and had been promised a house and an audience with the president. He planned to use that status to his advantage and for the benefit of his people.

Yet many former British friends now reviled him, his leadership had been rejected by a substantial portion of his nation, and the treaty had overthrown the work of a lifetime.

Not only that, but after many years at the helm of Shawnee affairs, he had by tribal custom to surrender his authority to the peace chiefs. Now in his fifties, the aging war chief was expected to step down, to let the spotlight fall on others, particularly the Mekoches, who held the senior civil offices of the nation.

As Blue Jacket had explained to Major General Wayne: "Elder Brother, and you my brothers present, you see me now present myself as a war chief to lay down that commission and place myself in the rear of my village chiefs, who, for the future, will command me. Remember, brothers, you have all buried your war hatchets. Your brothers the Shawanese now do the same good act. We must think of war no more."[36]

# 15

## Living with Peace

The war for Ohio seemed to be over. On 28 September the secretary of war informed the president that "the chiefs who signed the treaty are not numerous, but I observe among them the names of Blue Jacket, the great warrior of the Shawanoes, Misquacoonacaw [Red Pole], their great speaker, and Buckongelas, the great warrior of the Delawares, and of Augooshaway the Ottawa." In his view, they had the signatures that mattered.[1]

The treaty had been signed, and "the great warrior of the Shawanoes" should have been stepping down in favor of the civil chiefs of the nation. Yet he did not do so, even though other Shawnees resented his continued pretensions. Personal ambitions strongly influenced Blue Jacket's career during the next few years. The British had flattered him with uniforms and pieces of paper, even if they had never managed to control him, but the sway of the redcoats was visibly waning. Blue Jacket wanted similar privileges and recognition from the new power in the Old Northwest, the United States, and to win them he had to remain useful to Major General Wayne and his successors. Thus the Shawnee war leader continued to work hard, consolidating the peace, eagerly trying to prove himself the most valuable Indian friend of the American military. Sometimes he used the credit he accumulated to help his own or other tribes, but maintaining personal status was a major concern. Aging, a war chief without a war, Blue Jacket found it difficult to live with the peace he had helped to create.

Blue Jacket's first job was to bring more Shawnees over to his peace party. He left the treaty ground on 15 August, promising Wayne that he would put an end to Shawnee raids and get more prisoners released. He toured hunting camps, explaining the peace, often to those who had grown to believe the Ohio boundary to have been their inviolate right. He was not always successful. He found Tecumseh's party, probably on Deer Creek (Madison County, Ohio), but could not persuade him to go to Greenville. Elsewhere, though, he won adherents, among them Pucksekaw, the warrior who had led the raids in July. On 9 September 1795 Pucksekaw and up to seventy Shawnee warriors arrived at Greenville and surrendered four prisoners they had taken in the summer. Wayne was satisfied, and the day after he admitted Pucksekaw to the peace he wrote his daughter that the "last and most inveterate of all the savage tribes came forward yesterday, surrendered up their prisoners, and sued for mercy." Now he was sure the war had finished.[2]

The truth was that the Shawnees were still fiercely divided over the peace and were going their own ways. Captain Reed joined his kinsman across the Mississippi, and he was not the only one. Tecumseh took his band into what is now Indiana, first to the Whitewater River in 1796 and then to the banks of the White. A British faction under Captain Johnny still camped on Swan Creek, consuming McKee's rations. Despite Jay's Treaty and Britain's decision finally to relinquish western posts such as Detroit, the Indians on Swan Creek still had expectations of the redcoats. They had now been promised an asylum on Canadian soil, and the British were purchasing twelve square miles at Chenail Ecarté, north of Lake St. Clair, from the Ojibwes for that purpose. Captain Johnny's Shawnees were also fervently anti-American, and they passionately opposed Blue Jacket's surrender of Ohio. Stubbornly they refused to accept defeat and talked about resurrecting the great confederacy. The winter that followed the treaty of Greenville saw Captain Johnny's emissaries still circulating among the tribes, going north to the Ojibwes and south to the Creeks, calling on them to raise the hatchet.[3]

Despite such intransigent opinions, Blue Jacket hoped to rally supporters at a site he had chosen near Fort Wayne. Major General Wayne had promised both Blue Jacket and Little Turtle houses in the vicinity. He ordered Hamtramck, who commanded Fort Wayne, to ensure that the houses were "pleasing and comfortable," and the lumber for Blue Jacket's home was cut during the winter and drawn across the snow. Building was complete in April 1796. From this headquarters the Shawnee leader planned to organize the peace faction of the Shawnees, sustaining his personal authority by acting as a broker between the Indians and the Americans and by controlling the annual distribution of Shawnee treaty goods.[4]

Blue Jacket had always found fraternization with the whites easy, and he established good relationships with his former enemies. Early in 1796 the Morrison family, who had established themselves at the mouth of Hogan Creek on the Ohio (Aurora, Indiana), discovered that the Shawnee warrior had a hunting camp a little way up the stream. They struck up a friendship with him, and when Blue Jacket planned to visit the Detroit region in the spring Ephraim Morrison loaned him a saddle. Another family that spoke well of Blue Jacket was the Kelsays, who built a house in Warren County, Ohio, about 1797. The Shawnee chief often passed by with hunting parties and called in to share their hospitality.[5]

But even though trust slowly returned to the frontier, Blue Jacket understood that some of Captain Johnny's Shawnees were effectively tied to Swan Creek by their dependence on British rations. Peace now offered them access to their old planting grounds on the Maumee, but even if they sowed crops in the spring of 1796 they would have to wait till the end of August for a harvest. To counter this problem, Blue Jacket appealed to Brig. Gen. James Wilkinson, who stood in for Wayne while the commander made a trip east. Wilkinson agreed that it was advisable to wean potential hostiles from their British supporters, and he issued orders that the tribes might draw upon Fort Greenville for supplies until harvests and the issue of the first treaty annuities put them on their own feet. Consequently, Shawnees called at Fort Greenville through 1795 and 1796, collecting beef, bread, flour, pork, soap, mutton, salt, and whiskey. Red Pole was there in February, May, June, and July 1796, and Blue Jacket himself drew at least 115 pounds of beef and bread, 15 pounds of pork, 165 pounds of flour, 6 pounds of soap, 3 quarts of salt, and 3 quarts of whiskey between 24 April and 19 May 1796.[6]

Armed with concessions such as these, early fruits of Blue Jacket's policy of courting American favor, the Shawnee war chief risked a visit to Swan Creek in the spring, searching for recruits. His worth to the Americans was unquestionable. While he was at Swan Creek some disturbance arose between the white settlers and Indians near Fort Hamilton. Wilkinson wrote to Hamtramck at Fort Wayne and to Maj. William Winston at Fort Defiance with requests for Blue Jacket, Red Pole, and the Delaware Tetepachsit to come to Greenville to help restore unanimity. Red Pole had settled on the Auglaize River, about two miles above Fort Defiance.

Blue Jacket reached Fort Wayne on 14 April. He had come home by way of Fort Defiance and carried letters from Winston to Hamtramck, but it was only at Fort Wayne that he learned of Wilkinson's problem. He decided to go to Greenville immediately, and Hamtramck entrusted his dispatches to the Shawnee chief. "Blue Jacket is used to good company, and is always treated with more attention than other Indians," Hamtramck informed Wilkinson. "He appears to be very well disposed, and I believe him sincere." At the same time Blue Jacket sent a message back to Red Pole by means of Hamtramck's next courier to Fort Defiance. Plans had changed, Blue Jacket told his half-brother. Red Pole should not go to Fort Defiance, as the two had arranged, but proceed to Greenville, where Blue Jacket would meet him. Blue Jacket was at Greenville by 24 April and remained there through part of May, when Red Pole also arrived. It must be presumed the difficulties were sorted out because no more was said of them.[7]

Both Shawnee brothers also agreed to facilitate Wilkinson's next task. He was charged with supervising the transfer of Detroit and Fort Miamis to the United States, in accordance with Jay's Treaty of 1794. Though the British retained the right to trade with and supply the tribes, the surrender of these posts truly symbolized a further shift of power in the Old Northwest. Wilkinson ordered Hamtramck to take a detachment to take possession of the forts, but with a thousand pro-British Indians of different tribes still living on Swan Creek near Fort Miamis he invited Blue Jacket and Red Pole to accompany his expedition.

Hamtramck moved ahead of Wilkinson himself and headed for Fort Miamis in June. He halted at Fort Deposit on the Maumee to ease the fears of the Indians at Swan Creek, and it was there that Blue Jacket joined the expedition. While Hamtramck advanced on Fort Miamis, however, Blue Jacket remained at Deposit waiting for Wilkinson. The redcoats marched out of the little fort on 11 July, leaving Hamtramck to install a garrison under Capt. Andrew Marschalk. When Blue Jacket and Red Pole reached Fort Miamis, Hamtramck had moved on to Detroit, but the chiefs assisted Marschalk in dealing with the local Indians. Some 180 Shawnees and 30 Ottawas had gathered nearby, perhaps to witness the transfer of power, and Marschalk was under orders to provision them. No doubt Blue Jacket also used the opportunity to urge them to accept the olive branch now being waved by the Big Knives.

The two Shawnee chiefs were still at Fort Miamis when Major General Wayne arrived on 7 August. He had returned to the frontier and taken over Wilkinson's operation. During the three days he spent at the fort, Wayne's marquee was regularly visited by Blue Jacket, Red Pole, and other chiefs, all renewing their friendship. Wayne was bound for Detroit, but he invited the chiefs to visit the federal government in Philadelphia once they had collected their annuities. They accepted the new favor readily, and Red Pole, who had developed a friendship with Marschalk, asked the captain to go with them.[8]

Once the British had dutifully handed over Fort Miamis, Detroit, and Michilimackinac, those Shawnees still wavering between the old alliance with the king and a new relationships with the United States had to make a choice. Before the end of 1796 most Shawnees had thrown in with the peace party, but as if to demonstrate their independence of Blue Jacket, they built a new town on the upper Auglaize River (Auglaize County, Ohio). Named Wapakoneta (Man with a Club Foot), apparently after a real person, this village was situated just north of the Greenville line and a considerable distance from Blue Jacket's home near Fort Wayne. It was here that the Mekoches would recover their influence over the Shawnee nation, and Wapakoneta would be the effective capital of the northern Shawnees for forty years.

Only a few Shawnees remained within the British orbit. That year they harvested a crop on the bottomlands near the Maumee rapids, but after the British surrendered Fort Miamis, Captain Johnny, Blackbeard, the Buffalo, and Kakinathucca moved their "permanent" villages from Swan Creek to Bois Blanc, an island in the Detroit River, lying off Amherstburg (Ontario), where a new fort (Malden) was being raised as Canada's most important bastion in the West. The redcoats put a blockhouse and a storehouse on Bois Blanc, and Matthew Elliott issued supplies to the Indians there twice a week. The British Shawnees were supposed to transfer to Chenail Ecarté, the promised reservation, but for some reason they declined to do so. In 1797 they were with some Mingoes on Grosse Ile, another Canadian island in the Detroit, and between 1801 and 1805 they seem to have been located below the Maumee rapids.[9]

A powerful inducement to accepting the peace was the right to share in the annuities provided by the treaty of Greenville. They were due at Fort Defiance, and after his meeting with Wayne at Miamis Blue Jacket scurried home to Fort Wayne to assemble the American Shawnees for the distribution. On his way he passed the laden annuity wagons lumbering slowly to Defiance.

At Fort Wayne Lt. Col. David Strong was soon reporting that the

Shawnee chief was "very active" in preparing the Shawnees. Blue Jacket set out for Defiance on 26 August 1796, but when he arrived there the doleful new commandant, Capt. John Webb, had to tell him the goods had not yet appeared. In fact, some Shawnees who had been waiting at the fort had gotten so tired they had left to hunt. The distribution was certainly late, and the annuities did not arrive until the end of the month, two weeks behind schedule. Early in September some three hundred Shawnees were still on their way from Wapakoneta to collect them. Nevertheless, late or not, these spoils of peace strengthened Blue Jacket's position among the Shawnees. He had brought them the peace, and these were the rewards for those who had followed his lead.[10]

\*    \*    \*

At the treaty of Greenville Blue Jacket had requested Wayne to organize an Indian junket to Philadelphia. There were undoubtedly issues the chiefs wanted to impress upon their new "Father," and Blue Jackeet, at least, knew there was kudos in being received by the president. Although they had been embroiled in almost continuous warfare since 1774, no Shawnee leader had hitherto been feted in the capital of the new republic, and the trip to Philadelphia represented yet another tool in Blue Jacket's bid to remain at the head of his nation's affairs.

A shrewd operator, Blue Jacket was successfully maintaining his status without blatantly snubbing tribal tradition. A Pekowi, he had learned to tread carefully where the Mekoche prerogative of peacetime leadership was concerned. Blue Jacket publicly denied that he was the premier chief. That honor, he said, belonged to Red Pole. At this time Red Pole was certainly presenting himself as the head civil chief of the treaty Shawnees. He had the qualifications. The old civil chief, Captain Johnny, was still with the British, and Red Pole was the most renowned Mekoche supporting the peace. Furthermore, he was apparently a half-brother of Blue Jacket's. As we have seen, the evidence for this is opaque, but the conclusion most consistent with it is that Red Pole and Blue Jacket had the same mother and fathers from different Shawnee divisions, Red Pole's a Mekoche and Blue Jacket's a Pekowi. All of this was singularly convenient for Blue Jacket. By allowing his brother, friend, and ally Red Pole to stand as the senior chief, the war leader preserved tribal tradition *and* remained at the center of affairs.

When the Indian delegation bound for Philadelphia assembled in Detroit in September 1796 Blue Jacket and Red Pole were at its head.

Many of the other chiefs of the old confederacy were missing. Egushaway had died in the spring, and Buckongahelas had retired. The powerful Ojibwe, Mashipinashiwish, dropped out because of illness, and his people had to be represented by Muccatiwasaw (Black Chief). Asimethe was the Potawatomi spokesman, and the Miamis, Weas, Piankeshaws, Eel Rivers, Kickapoos, and Kaskaskias relied on an Eel River headman named She-mi-kun-ne-sa, the Soldier. Little Turtle, the Miami war chief, was supposed to go. Wayne distrusted him. The chief, said Wayne, "possesses the spirit of litigation to a high degree" and had possibly "been tamper'd with by some of the speculating land jobbers." But he was aware that Little Turtle's stock was rising among the Wabash Indians and would have included him but for his refusal to travel with Blue Jacket. As late as the previous year, Little Turtle had been willing to allow Blue Jacket to speak for him, but now he steadfastly declined to be part of a delegation dominated by the Shawnee war leader. Instead, he put his affairs in the hands of the Soldier and Red Pole.[11]

Christopher Miller, William Wells, and Whitmore Knaggs (a Maumee settler) served the chiefs as interpreters. Before they left Detroit, a group of land speculators, calling themselves the Cuyahoga Association, tried to curry favor with the Indians by providing money for drinks, but the chiefs had no intention of promoting further land transactions. They wanted to settle unfinished business relating to the treaty of Greenville, and on 3 October they left Detroit as passengers aboard the *Swan*, Captain John Heth. At Presque Isle Blue Jacket and his chiefs landed. They completed their journey overland by way of Pittsburgh.

About 28 November Blue Jacket found himself addressing President Washington in Philadelphia. "I need not tell you how long I was attached to my late British Father over the Waters of the Ocean," he said, "nor how often I fought his battles on the borders of our great Lake, for my name has been well known to your nation." The British had honored him. They had invited him to Quebec, and Sir John Johnson had given him a testimonial. Blue Jacket produced the paper to remind the Americans of their promise to supply him with something similar. "Father, when I fought for the British," said the war chief, "I fought with bravery and sincerity, but since I have found them carrying on a deception among us for many years past."[12]

Washington replied on 29 November. He advised the Indians to raise crops and animals, in the manner of the whites, and offered government support for such programs, and he remarked on the need for the Indians to punish any of their people who committed offenses against the settlers. Stolen property should be restored. As for the testimonial, the president would be happy to supply one.

If Washington believed that the Indian boundary had been settled to universal satisfaction, Red Pole soon disabused him. Either that day or the next he presented the complaints of the Wabash Indians that the line had been taken too far west and should have gone down the Great Miami to the Ohio. In due course the Soldier and other chiefs backed Red Pole's request for a modification of the treaty boundary.

The following day Red Pole took up the matter of crimes in the Indian country, mentioned by President Washington. He refused to countenance punishments as severe as hanging for such offenses as horse stealing but promised to discourage stealing and to attempt to restore stolen goods. With less than public spirit, he dwelled on the suits of clothes, saddles, bridles, rifles, ammunition, and other gifts the visiting Indians had been promised. He insisted that the same presents be accorded the absent Little Turtle and that dress coats be supplied to four leaders left at home. Blue Jacket, true to form, appealed to Captain Heth to witness the fact that he had lost considerable property in the war. He hoped that he would be allowed compensation, and not futilely it seems, because several years later the chief implied that he had received a pension from the United States.

Their principal business over, the chiefs took in the sights of Philadelphia while they awaited the president's responses to their requests. They were astonished to meet a delegation of southern Indians in Peale's Museum. The southerners included not only Creeks and such old allies as John Watts of the Chickamauga Cherokees but also Choctaws and Chickasaws, who had aided the Americans in the war. Two of the southern chiefs in Philadelphia, Piomingo and George Colbert, had actually served with General St. Clair. Nevertheless, no one was eager to reopen the wounds, and a second meeting was arranged, also at the museum. Finally, Blue Jacket and Red Pole asked the secretary of war, James McHenry, to convene a formal peace conference between the two delegations on 2 December. This gave both southern and northern Indians an opportunity to pledge themselves to brotherhood. Red Pole was the principal speaker for the northerners, but Blue Jacket gave his usual support. "You have heard our chief speak," said Blue Jacket. "What he says is permanent with us. I, as a war chief only, will back what he says and everything he undertakes."

The round of talks, visits, and dinners did not earn the Indians the revision of the Greenville line they had requested. On 8 December Washington maintained that as the treaty had already been ratified no changes to it were now possible. But the presents and testimonials the chiefs had wanted were on hand; a meager return, perhaps, but not unimportant to proud, status-conscious tribesmen. From the American point of view, the gifts were a small price to pay for the support they bought among influential leaders.

Tragedy struck Blue Jacket's party on the way home. The Indians reached Pittsburgh, where they were to embark on a vessel under a Captain Turner for the voyage downstream. Unfortunately, ice on the Ohio kept the boat at its moorings, and the Indians tarried about the town. About 17 January Red Pole fell ill, complaining of pains in his breast and head. Three American doctors, Carmichael, Bedford, and Wallace, attended him assiduously. They diagnosed a severe cold, but the chief's condition deteriorated. The Indians blamed no one. "Blue Jacket, in particular, acknowledges with gratitude that the kindest attention possible is paid to his sick brother," learned the secretary of war. But at nine o'clock on the morning of 28 January Red Pole died. He had not only been a respected chief but a popular one, and Blue Jacket and the other chiefs witnessed a satisfying funeral in the graveyard of Trinity Church in Pittsburgh. A headstone, possibly devised by James McHenry himself, boldly proclaimed: "Mioquacoonacaw, or Red Pole, Principal Village Chief of the Shawnee Nation, died at Pittsburgh, the 28th January 1797. Lamented by the United States." The words were still legible forty years later.[13]

When Blue Jacket boarded the boat for home early in February, he was a poorer man indeed. For Red Pole had not only been a brother but a brilliant speaker, an influential mind, and the staunchest ally and friend. His eloquence had been heard from Michigan to Alabama, and he had been able to call in favors of his own. Red Pole, for example, had preserved good relationships with Little Turtle long after the rift between the Miami and Shawnee war chiefs had become irreparable. Just as serious, it had been through the Mekoche Red Pole that Blue Jacket had been able to sustain his supremacy among the Shawnees. Now that partnership was over, and the other Mekoche leaders, over whom Blue Jacket had less influence, would be coming to the fore.

The death of Red Pole created genuine grief and shock among the Shawnees. It even sparked a wave of accusation and murder. Another

Shawnee, Pemenewa, died about the same time, and he, too, belonged to Blue Jacket's peace party. There were sinister rumors that pro-British Shawnees had been poisoning their political enemies through the use of witchcraft. Fingers pointed particularly toward an Indian named Wainway, who was said to have foretold the deaths of both Red Pole and Pemenewa. Soon Wainway was dead himself, slain by a Shawnee called Quilawa, who declared his victim to have been a witch. Then the right to revenge murdered kinfolk came into play. Wainway's uncle, Old Shade, shot Quilawa and was in turn slain by an Indian named Wessillawy in fierce revenge killings.[14]

Without Red Pole, it was left to Blue Jacket to assemble the Shawnees in June 1797 to hear his account of the trip to Philadelphia and to compose a reply to the president. Red Pole was dead, but for the moment Blue Jacket still held enormous sway in the nation. His standing with the Americans, reinforced by the gifts he had received from the president, was unequaled and could still be put to use, as the chief proved upon his return. He found the Shawnee economy in a poor state, and by May most of the people were surviving on boiled roots and herbs. Once again Blue Jacket interceded, persuading Wilkinson to issue further provisions to the tribe to tide them over until harvest time.[15]

But times were changing. Returning to the frontier, Blue Jacket learned that Anthony Wayne was also dead. His work, it was true, had been done, and Winthrop Sargent, the secretary of the Northwest Territory, had taken over the administration of the region. Yet the sudden death of Wayne, which had occurred on 15 December, when the soldier was a mere fifty-two years of age, was another harbinger of change. Blue Jacket and Wayne had understood each other. They had exchanged promises and kept them all, and it was upon Blue Jacket, more than any other chief, that Wayne had relied to influence Indian behavior. In Wayne Blue Jacket had lost a man who both respected and befriended him, a man of power and integrity. He never replaced him.

Two years after the treaty of Greenville, Blue Jacket still dominated Shawnee politics. He was still at the heart of Indian-white affairs in the Ohio country. Then his star began to fall, and quickly. Before the end of the year Wilkinson would be touring the region as newly appointed successor to Wayne, but it was Little Turtle who found a place in his entourage, not Blue Jacket.

With his Mekoche rivals seizing the reins of leadership in Wapakoneta, the Shawnee war chief was losing his grip.

## Uneasy Retirement

Blue Jacket was nearing sixty and had spent more than the last twenty of those years in continual armed conflict and political turmoil. Now he did what many sensible men do. He retired from public affairs to spend more time with his family and friends.

He abandoned his house near Fort Wayne and withdrew for a while to Wapakoneta, where he supplemented his farming and hunting by trade. It was not always to the benefit of the community. Like the Lasselles and Little Turtle, he trafficked in liquor. One observer, Jacob Burnet, remembered the chief importing whiskey in bulk from Cincinnati and getting most of the town drunk on it.[1]

About 1800 Blue Jacket moved again and established a joint Shawnee-Wyandot village on the American side of the Detroit River, opposite Grosse Ile and some two miles above the famed Wyandot settlement of Brownstown (Gibraltar, Michigan). Locally, his new home seems to have been called Tuage, but everyone simply referred to it as Blue Jacket's Town. There the chief cleared and fenced some land for cultivation. William Caldwell, a son of the famous partisan who lived on the Canadian side of the river, recalled that Blue Jacket "lived as well as white people, had cows, was a great hunter, and had plenty of meat, and was a trader too."[2]

To the end Blue Jacket kept his reputation for enterprise and hospitality. He mixed with the Wyandots at the nearby villages of Brownstown and Maguaga and with the trading community that still operated out of

Detroit. He was seen with the old British agents across the river, with the Caldwells and Babys, even with the McKees and Elliotts, who had so traduced him for destroying the Indian alliance with the king. Despite his heavy drinking, which destroyed his figure in his last years — "a large stout man," said one witness, and "very gross," another — people spoke of the chief with affection and of his excellent company and ready generosity. James Bentley often went by Blue Jacket's house during the severe winter of 1805–6 and was never denied admittance. The chief, Bentley said, "was very kind that cold winter in hospitalities to travelers — well remembers his large and cheerful fire when he called there."[3]

A pleasing glimpse of the Blue Jackets is afforded by the Presbyterian missionary Joseph Badger. The chief's youngest boy, George, intro-duced him. Blue Jacket had had George educated in Detroit. Many years later George's son remembered seeing his father's old schoolbooks and proudly opined that he had been the best educated Indian of his day. In 1800, when he was nineteen years of age, George reached the end of his schooling. His talents as an interpreter and interest in religion attracted the notice of a missionary, the Reverend Thomas E. Hughes. Hughes took the young man back to Virginia with him, and in 1801 the two returned to the West with Badger in tow. George visited his family, bringing both the missionaries with him.

Some of the Blue Jacket family were then living in Shawnee settlements on the lower Maumee River. On 11 September 1801 the party visited the home of George's aunt, probably the sister of Blue Jacket, on an island just below the rapids, where she lived with her two daughters. "Soon as we were seated," wrote Badger, "we were presented with a bowl of boiled corn, buttered with bear's grease. As the corn was presented, the old woman said, 'Friends, eat, it is good. It is such as God gives Indians.' This opened the door to preach." After patiently enduring the missionaries' proselytizing, George's aunt sent them happily on their way. They were soon on the west side of the river, at the home of George's brother, Jim Blue-Jacket, where they were supplied with "a good bed, and blankets all clean and wholesome." On 13 September the party "reached Captain Blue Jacket's seat about three miles from Brownstown, and were received by the old man and his wife with great cordiality. They lived in a comfortable cabin, well furnished with a mattress, bedding and blankets, [and] with furniture for the table, crockery, and silver spoons. Their crockery was equal to that of white people." After visiting Fort Malden and Detroit the missionaries returned to Blue Jacket's on 18 September. They "tarried with them," Badger said, and "had much talk with several Indian people about having schools, that they might learn to read, write and number with figures." Five days later, the missionaries began the return journey, and Blue Jacket and his wife accompanied their party as far as the Shawnee settlements on the Maumee.[4]

It was during this period that Blue Jacket lost the first of his children, Mary Louise Blue-Jacket, who had married Jacques Lasselle. The couple spent their time between the River Raisin, where they had a home, and Detroit, and in time gave the Shawnee war chief four grandchildren — Anne Marie (Nannette), born in 1791; Jacques, born in 1802; Susanne, born in 1804, and Julia, born in 1806. None of them really knew their famous grandfather. The eldest, Nannette, was schooled in Detroit until she was about six, when she was sent to a convent school in Montreal. When she returned about 1810, her grandfather and mother were both dead. Another of the grandchildren, Susanne, died at the age of two. Their mother, Blue Jacket's daughter Mary, died in Detroit on the morning of 17 June 1806, of what cause no one tells. She was buried the same day, near her daughter Susanne, in the cemetery of the Catholic church they had adopted as their own, St. Anne's, Detroit. Her husband, Jacques, a widower before he was forty, lived on the River Raisin until his death in 1815.[5]

In these years Blue Jacket continued to engage in business activities, and at least one witness remembered his capacity to drive a hard bargain. James Galloway Jr. was one of the early settlers of Ohio. Several of his descendants eventually spread some unreliable stories about the Shawnees, but this Galloway should not be confused with them. He sometimes embroidered his information and certainly got the best out of this story, but there seems to have been a solid foundation for most of what he said. Many years afterward he remembered strange meetings that took place at the house of his father, the elder James Galloway, on the Little Miami (Green County, Ohio) in the spring of 1800. Blue Jacket and another Shawnee chief boarded at the Galloway place for three weeks at the expense of a Kentucky syndicate of ten or so members. They wanted him to help them find a lost silver mine, rumored to exist in the wilderness south of the Ohio.

Old legends about the silver mines, said to be known to the Shawnees, had been going around Kentucky for some time. There were tales that a man named Swift had worked such mines in eastern Kentucky during the 1760s, but no one ever confirmed it. Now the syndicate and its representative Jonathan Flack drew up a contract with Blue Jacket and his associate which they hoped would lead them to the mines. Blue Jacket haggled with the prospectors for a considerable time, raising his demands as he saw their interest increase. He said he thought the mines were somewhere on the Red River, and he could take Flack and his comrades there. Finally, a deal was struck. The two Shawnees were given money, horses, and other commodities in return for their services.

As Galloway heard it, the expedition disintegrated into a farce. The chiefs and their wives were escorted to Kentucky, again at no expense to themselves. Then Blue Jacket went into seclusion, to purify himself and seek the assistance of his guardian spirits, and the hunt began in earnest. Days of fruitless search yielded nothing. The Shawnee chief told the chagrined prospectors that his eyes were not as good as they had once been, and he could not find the mines, but that his son knew where they were and when Blue Jacket got home he would send him.

Needless to say, the younger Blue Jacket never appeared, and the great mining adventure collapsed.[6]

*    *    *

One thing Blue Jacket almost always had was ambition, and even now it occasionally reasserted itself. When tension increased in the Indian country, the Shawnee war captain was usually ready to steal back into the limelight. Such opportunities occurred at the turn of the century, when fresh international contests and renewed anxieties for the land combined to disturb Shawnee councils. Once again, the Shawnees evoked the old ideal of pan-Indian action to deal with their stresses and talked about rebuilding a common intertribal policy. And once again, they called on the diplomatic talents of their greatest leader.

There were two major problems, both interlinked.

Across the Atlantic, in Europe, the war between Britain, the limited constitutional monarchy, and the French republic raged on. In 1796 Spain piled in, on the side of France, and the prospect of a new intercolonial war in America loomed. For Spain still commanded the Gulf coast and territory west of the Mississippi and was within striking distance of British Canada. If fighting broke out between them, say on the upper Mississippi, there was every chance that Indians would be dragged into it. In 1798 some tribesmen of the Fox and Wisconsin Rivers reported the rumors of war to the Ohio Indians, and the Shawnees revived their timeworn plan of orchestrating a common native response. By September their emissaries were at Buffalo Creek, Niagara, inviting the Iroquois to a new intertribal conference at Brownstown, the council fire of the old confederacy. In June 1799 those old allies, the Shawnees, Delawares, and Wyandots, were said to be considering uniting as one nation.[7]

Entangled with this was another concern, a growing Shawnee dissatisfaction over the land. The Americans were due to survey the Greenville line, and white settlers were spreading through what is now Ohio. Although the treaty of Greenville gave Indians permission to hunt over ceded areas, game always dwindled before the growth of white settlements. The spiritual attachment of the Shawnees to this ground was intense, for it had been the gift of Waashaa Monetoo, a refuge, and a place in which to unify their people. Nevertheless, that appeal was waning, and some Shawnees spoke of moving on, to somewhere that offered greater tranquillity and freedom of action and where the dream of reunification still had space to thrive.

But even if the Shawnees did cede their lands in Ohio, where was there such a haven? Spanish Missouri was one possibility. Aware of their vulnerability on the Mississippi at a time of international tension, the Spaniards had renewed their invitations to the Shawnees to move west. Yet another idea was an emigration north, into British Canada. In 1798 the Shawnees resuscitated Blue Jacket's old plan of visiting England to speak directly to the king and his government, and they sent word to Sir John Johnson through the Indian Department at Amherstburg. Now that war drums were throbbing, Sir John acted quickly to prevent the Shawnees from going over to the Spaniards. In April 1799 he assured the tribe that "they will always be sure of a peaceable asylum in the British government, and meet with that protection and aid their long and faithful service so justly entitle them." The Shawnees remained unhappy, however. They staged another intertribal council to air the matter, evidently early the following year, and in March 1800 made further representations to the British on behalf of the confederated tribes. They were being surrounded by whites, they said, and appealed to His Royal Highness the Duke of Kent, who they believed was visiting Canada at the time, to see them. Their plan to go to England was also refloated.[8]

Obviously Blue Jacket knew about these initiatives, and indeed he probably had a hand in launching them. Certainly when it came to approaching the Americans, the tribe had no illusions about which of their chiefs carried the greatest weight. In August 1799 the Shawnees informed white settlers in Ohio that they wished "to collect all the

Shawanese nation together in one town" and to "live without fear or disturbance from anyone" in a new home. In October Blue Jacket and another Shawnee chief went to Cincinnati, where they spent a few days in discussions with the new governor of Northwest Territory — none other than Arthur St. Clair, whom Blue Jacket had bested so convincingly many years before.

St. Clair thought the matter "little important in itself" and saw few serious implications for the United States. Blue Jacket sounded him out about a Shawnee plan to move to the Wabash, in fact near Fort Wayne, the area the war chief had originally chosen for his people after signing the treaty of Greenville. He also desired their annuities to be made available at Fort Wayne, rather than distributed, as they were then, at Fort Miamis. Blue Jacket explained that the land on the Wabash was claimed by the Miamis — there was no commitment there to the notion that the Indians held it in common — but that the Shawnees had already obtained their permission to settle. It would appear, therefore, that the tribe was debating whether their removal should put them under the protection of Spain, Britain, or the United States.[9]

Although St. Clair agreed to make Fort Wayne the distribution point for the Shawnee annuities, the Indians had still not resolved their dilemma when news of the Convention of 1800 reached the frontier. This was an agreement by which the United States and France cleared up some of their difficulties, and probably Blue Jacket's French-Canadian friends gave him word of it. The question it provoked in Blue Jacket's mind was whether the convention was the first step in the development of an alliance between the United States, France, and Spain, and, if so, whether it portended a new war between the Americans and the redcoats.

To learn something, Blue Jacket visited Maj. Thomas Hunt, who commanded the American garrison at Detroit, and enjoyed a long conversation with him. Hunt said he had heard of the Franco-American rapprochement from a Spanish post on the Mississippi. The Spaniards had said that Spain, France, and the United States now had common cause, and they asked Hunt if he could tell them of any British plans to attack their possessions on the Mississippi or to incite the Indians against them.

Hunt asked Blue Jacket to visit the British across the river and try to discover their intentions. In short, he was suggesting that Blue Jacket play the part of a spy. Unfortunately, if Britain and the Americans were going to fight again, the Shawnee chief had no desire to make a premature choice of sides. About 12 August he called on Thomas McKee. Alexander McKee, his father, had died the previous year, and Thomas, intemperate, loud-mouthed, and inebriated as he often was, now served as deputy superintendent of Indian affairs at Amherstburg. Blue Jacket represented himself as a friend to the British, purveying valuable confidential information. Drawing the agent aside, he requested him not to leak his source because Blue Jacket had things to lose from American resentment. He had an allowance from the United States, and George was still at school in Detroit. Blue Jacket told McKee about the convention and that the Spaniards had been communicating with Hunt. He wanted to know if the British expected a war with the United States or to recruit Indians for service against the Spaniards.[10]

Evidently McKee knew nothing of either, and Blue Jacket went away believing that nothing was afoot in that quarter. He probably reported back to Hunt. This behavior should not necessarily be seen as dishonorable. True, Blue Jacket played the friend to both parties, but he had grown old in Indian-white diplomacy. He knew full well that when the great white nations went to war, their least concern was for the welfare of the Indians, who had to look out for themselves.

The truth was that the continuing rumors of a war fueled Shawnee anxieties about the international situation and their own disenchantment with Ohio. They simultaneously worked to forge an Indian consensus in the Old Northwest and investigated the prospects for removal. Almost certainly most leaders wanted a united neutrality, free from dangerous entanglements with any of the contending powers, for if a war broke out the Ohio and Michigan Shawnees at least would find their towns sitting directly between the belligerents.

After probing Hunt and McKee, Blue Jacket went west. Almost certainly he visited the Shawnees in Missouri. They, if no one else, would have the latest information about what the Spaniards were saying to the Indians on the Mississippi, and there too Blue Jacket could assess the viability of Missouri as a refuge for the eastern Shawnees. In the spring of 1801, while employed in this or other work, he encountered a delegation of southern Cherokees near the mouth of the Ohio. They also appear to have been disturbed by the rumors, for they were on a mission to the Shawnees, whom they believed to be living on the Wabash. They wanted each of the northern tribes to send two chiefs to an intertribal gathering at the Cherokee towns in the South. Blue Jacket returned with the Cherokee party, conducting them to the Wabash by way of the Indian villages on the White River, where he probably seized the opportunity to discuss matters with Buckongahelas and Tecumseh, old acquaintances who had towns in the area.

On the Wabash the Cherokees assembled some northern representatives and set off with them for home, but Blue Jacket returned to his home on the Detroit. The new attempts at Indian unity were already floundering. The Iroquois wanted the tribes to meet at Buffalo Creek near Niagara, but the Shawnees, Ottawas, Ojibwes, and Wyandots were adamant that the recognized seat of the confederacy should continue to be Brownstown, the Wyandot village near Blue Jacket's own. On the Mississippi other problems had flared up when seven Potawatomis and Ottawas were murdered by a party of Sacs.

Probably Blue Jacket saw the importance of solving intertribal disputes in the West before the Indians relaunched their confederacy. He visited George Ironside at Amherstburg on 11 June and frankly declared his intentions. He planned to hold a multitribal congress at Brownstown in the fall, one that would draw Indians from far and wide, including delegates from the northern tribes, Chickasaws and Cherokees from the Tennessee River, and the wayward Sacs and Foxes. What was more, he and a companion, a Shawnee leader named Wathaiage, were leaving for the Mississippi directly and would bring the Sac and Fox delegates back with them. Blue Jacket evidently made the trip. He is said to have canvassed the Potawatomi villages on the Illinois River, but the final results of these intertribal deliberations are unknown.[11]

Both the Americans and the British distrusted the Indians, and the former even tried to discourage the Iroquois from participating in the new round of pan-Indian diplomacy. It was, in any case, probably aborted by the peace of Amiens, which brought a brief cessation of hostilities in Europe in 1802 and took much of the heat from the political situation on the American frontier.

Blue Jacket was soon back in his home on the Detroit River. For a while he lived there quietly, but if the troubles of the Shawnees had subsided, their basic dissatisfaction remained, and during the next few years tensions generally increased throughout Indian villages south of the Great Lakes.

*    *    *

In his lifetime Blue Jacket had seen the Indians weather many a crisis, including the Franco-British battle for the Ohio Valley, the arrogance of the conquerors toward the Indian peoples, and the American Revolution and a new set of victors, who blithely stripped the Old Northwest from the tribes. Now, in the nineteenth century, he would see another major flashpoint — the revival of American imperialism and the War of 1812. A man who kept an ear to the ground, Blue Jacket saw some of the storms brewing, but he could not have predicted their remarkable course or that they would have brought under his wing and patronage the two most remarkable Shawnees of the younger generation: Lalawéthika, who would call himself the Prophet, and his brother, the charismatic Tecumseh.

Of these swelling tensions, perhaps the most important was the reemergence of American land hunger, with its attendant series of shabby negotiations. The Greenville treaty had been and gone, but white settlers and speculators still wanted Indian land, and when Indiana Territory was formed in 1800 there were those who argued that the alienation of further Indian title was necessary for the political growth of the territory. It brought in settlers, expanding the population, and progress to statehood depended on population. President Thomas Jefferson was in office now, too, and after France secured Louisiana and the west bank of the Mississippi from Spain in 1800, he saw wisdom in strengthening the western borders of the republic against a notoriously aggressive nation. Securing Indian land in the West was one way of doing it.

Jefferson anticipated that the land could be taken from the Indians peaceably. As white settlements spread, the hunting would deteriorate, and the Indians would be willing to sell out and move to more remote areas. This process could be accelerated by establishing more "trading houses" or factories, which would attract the Indians from private traders because they would sell manufactures for furs at cost rather than for profit. The trading houses, however, were to encourage the Indians to "run in debt" so "that when these debts get beyond what the individuals can pay, they become willing to lop them off by a cession of lands." Finally, Jefferson was anxious to promote "civilization" among the Indians, to urge them to abandon the chase, and to make their living entirely from husbandry, stock raising, and domestic manufacture. In time, he supposed the Indians would forsake their old communal economies, take up individually owned homesteads, and integrate with their white neighbors. Agriculture, of course, was by no means foreign to the Indians, and those native communities long familiar with the whites had already adopted many of the practices of the Europeans, including stock raising. The "civilization" plan proposed accentuating this trend and completely overthrowing the Indian dependence on hunting. In the process, the Indians would gratefully sell their old hunting ranges to buy tools, crops, and stock. In short, Jefferson's administration was set upon a systematic seizure of Indian land.[12]

Jefferson had a zealous instrument in the governor of Indiana Territory, William Henry Harrison. He concluded seven treaties between 1802 and 1805, securing the southern part of what is now Indiana, most of the present-day state of Illinois, and parts of Wisconsin and Missouri. Eschewing the expensive precedent set by the treaty of Greenville, in which the United States had negotiated with all the tribes of the confederacy, these new treaties were targeted only on those Indians deemed to be the actual owners of the tracts concerned.

For that reason the Shawnees were not directly touched by the new wave of land deals, although they ceded their rights to a salt spring in the treaty of Fort Wayne in 1803. Blue Jacket himself was also party to the cession of a large tract in northern Ohio wanted by the Connecticut Land Company and the state of Connecticut. It was bounded by Lake Erie in the north and the Greenville line in the south and ran west from the Cuyahoga River to just short of the Sandusky. The Shawnees sometimes hunted in the area but had no villages there.

Nevertheless, on 4 July 1805 Blue Jacket and Black Hoof signed for the Shawnees when they and other leaders gathered at a diminutive post called Fort Industry, raised on Swan Creek at the instance of William Hull, governor of the new Michigan Territory. The Shawnees shared $1,000 in annuities with the Delawares, Munsees, Wyandots, and Mingoes, while the Three Fires of the Detroit netted $4,000 and a six-year annuity of $2,000. It was, in fact, a beggarly sum. The government acquired the land for half a cent an acre, although speculators would soon be demanding as much as $15 an acre for it, and the annuities themselves did not appear for two years.[13]

Soon the land cessions were spawning a new round of militant pan-Indianism, this time in the West, on the upper Mississippi, where the Indians were more remote from the centers of American power and less open to attack. The Indians involved included Dakota Sioux, Sacs, Foxes, Kickapoos, Potawatomis, Ottawas, and Kaskaskias, some of them tribesmen Blue Jacket had seen only three or four years before. The Shawnee chief may have been a minor stimulus to the movement, but no one now can possibly tell. What is clear is that the new confederates looked upon Blue Jacket's great confederacy of the 1790s, in which some had participated on the margins, for inspiration. They reproduced its language and ideology and talked about the common ownership of Indian land and the dish with one spoon.

The embryonic confederacy began to form in 1804 and from the summer of the following year incited the Indians of the Great Lakes and the Ohio country, including the Shawnees, inviting them to join in their plans to attack American garrisons. They persisted into 1807, showing considerable enterprise. In June 1805 and June 1806 their delegations unsuccessfully tried to tap the British at Fort Malden for aid, and in 1807 the Sacs and Foxes even approached White Hair's band of Osages, who had been traditional enemies of most of the confederated groups. Despite these efforts, the new pan-Indian movement traveled east badly, and nearly all of the Indians who had been at the core of the old confederacy, including the Shawnees, refused to countenance it.[14]

The new land cessions struck primarily at the Indians further west, but all the tribes between the Ohio and the Great Lakes were being blighted by another problem. The hunting side of their economies was floundering. Despite the development of stock raising among those Indian communities closer to the whites, the general importance of hunting was undoubted. It provided meat and other products, the skins to trade for essential Euro-American manufactures, and a way of life Indian men found fulfilling. But the demand for furs in Europe was slumping, and the wars there disrupted trade. The prices furs commanded fell, and Indians found themselves unable to provide enough for the goods they wanted. Their prosperity had become ensnared in the booms and slumps of the international market.

Then, too, the numbers of game animals were declining. Part of this was caused by overhunting by Indians confronting the falling value of their peltries, as well as by whites, and much simply was the historic retreat of wildlife before the increase of settlements and the spread of developed farming, which destroyed habitat and seized resources. Almost everywhere Indians were traveling farther and longer to hunt and were disturbed by the pauperization of their livelihoods. Some feared the spirits were angry with the Indians for overhunting and were withdrawing the game.

And poverty was bitterly sharpened by the trade in whiskey. It had been carried on by Indian middlemen such as Blue Jacket and Little Turtle, as well as by whites. Whoever sold it, more than whiskey flowed from the casks. Some Indians squandered their possessions and the fruits of their hunting and drank themselves into worthless stupors on the proceeds or turned on their fellows in violent, often murderous, rages. Everyone could see the effects of the trade, and Indians and whites made periodic attempts to crush it. From 1802 the United States outlawed the sale of whiskey to Indians, but it proved impossible to control the private traders. Apart from licensed traders, many illicit traders packed spirits to the Indians, and Jay's Treaty had protected the right of British traders to enter the Indian country from Canada. Occasionally Indian chiefs broke casks brought into their villages, but the trade and the disruption it caused continued to flourish.

A grim cycle was developing. Poverty made Indians desperate and demoralized. Some sought escape in drink, and many were tempted to sell more of their remaining asset, the land, in an effort to increase treaty annuities, but neither gave more than temporary relief. They made the situation worse. Other Indians, of course, were capable of more constructive approaches to their difficulties. Some began taking interest in the "civilization" policies supported by the American government and by some missionary bodies, including the Society of Friends in Philadelphia. One such party, consisting of Shawnees and Delawares, visited Washington in February 1802, looking for cattle and tools to help them build frame houses, improve the productivity of their agriculture, and raise more stock. The Shawnees — Black Hoof, Big Snake, Lewis, and Paumthe — were not interested in either giving up hunting or surrendering more land, as Jefferson would likely have wanted; in fact, they requested a new trade facility for Fort Hamilton. But they understood the need to get more out of their economy in increasingly difficult times.[15]

Given their problems, the direction being taken by the Wapakoneta Shawnees was logical, but was it the right one? It, too, created anxieties and insecurities. It raised important questions about cultural identity, independence, and the tribe's relationships to the dominant white society. These questions had a powerful spiritual import. All Shawnees stubbornly clung to their aboriginal religion and fully believed that the goodwill of the Great Spirit, Waashaa Monetoo, was essential to the material welfare of the tribe. For some Shawnees there arose a disturbing dilemma: what did it gain the tribe to harness the skills of the whites if by doing so they forfeited the favor of the Great Spirit, who had it in his power to degrade or destroy them?

The Shawnee relationship with the whites had been a long one. Their villages had provided white traders with bases, homes, wives, and métis children. They had adopted and integrated white captives wholesale, and during times of peace Shawnees willingly fraternized with white settlers, visiting farms and towns to barter, seek hospitality, look for gunsmiths, or hire out as guides or hunters. The Shawnees acquired much from the whites, selecting what they wanted, just as many of the newcomers, particularly the hunters, who borrowed Indian survival skills, foods, and modes of dress, took from them. Long before the end of the eighteenth century the Shawnees were to a large extent economically dependent on the whites for trade goods, clothes, and firearms. But for all that they were not whites, and they did not want to be whites.

In 1806 the Shawnee communities exhibited varying levels of white influence. Blue Jacket's band on the Detroit River, in Michigan Territory, had the most entrepreneurial leader of all. He had cleared land, raised stock, and trafficked in manufactures. His band, like the local Wyandots with whom they mixed, probably had superior houses and orchards. Similar developments had occurred among the Missouri Shawnees, who were mainly Pekowis and Kispokos. They had benefited considerably from intercourse with the French and American settlements at New Madrid, Cape Girardeau, Ste. Genevieve, and St. Louis and were described as a prosperous people, who raised cattle, hogs, and poultry and who stocked granaries and barns with the produce of the fields. Their homes were no longer bark-sided, as of old, but log houses, the uprights caulked with clay and some of them double storied.[16]

In Ohio the Shawnees, mainly Mekoches and Chillicothes, with a few associated Mingoes, lived at Wapakoneta (Auglaize County) and in a few settlements in what is now Logan County. Representatives of these villages went to Washington for economic aid in 1802. Their economies were not as sophisticated as those of their kinsmen in Michigan and Missouri, but they were probably superior to the livings that had been scratched out by the very first white pioneers of Ohio, who had built rudely furnished log cabins in clearings and supplemented meager crops of Indian corn by hunting, gathering, and keeping a few animals. The soil in Ohio was rich, and agriculture had developed rapidly among the white settlements after the treaty of Greenville. Crops diversified to include wheat, barley, oats, rye, hemp, and flax, and impressive vegetable gardens of turnips, pumpkins, peas, beans, and cucumbers and orchards of cherry, apple, peach, and plum were to be seen. Hogs and cattle abounded, and some farmers tried raising sheep. Mills replaced primitive methods of grinding corn, and farmhouses increasingly wore a prosperous appearance. They were frame built, with brick chimneys and occasionally with glass windows.[17]

These improvements were not lost on the Ohio Shawnees, whose own villages lagged behind. In Wapakoneta there were probably a few log houses with chimneys and a few cattle, but horticulture was generally organized in the traditional way. There were few fences to keep deer, horses, or stock from the crops, which sprouted in the bottomlands in what whites considered a disorderly manner, the pumpkins and beans growing amid the corn. The Indians had no plows, no mills to grind corn, no orchards, and no smithies, and there were no sawmills to provide for frame houses. It was this situation Black Hoof and his chiefs wanted to address on their trip east.[18]

Probably the most conservative Shawnee community in the north was the relatively remote village of Kispokos on the White River in Indiana Territory. Its chief was Tecumseh, but although he visited Ohio occasionally, he never participated in the tribal councils held at Wapakoneta.

Despite these developments, in 1806 the basic pattern of Shawnee society was still of long duration. It was a society in which men hunted and women grew crops and gathered fruits and which embraced a year divided between spring and summer planting in the permanent villages and fall and winter hunting in dispersed camps. The great changes in social structure, government, belief, and ceremony lay in the future.

Notwithstanding, the development of a syncretic culture and the openly avowed policy of some chiefs to accelerate it — at least insofar as the economy was concerned — did not go uncriticized. In fact, some of the more conservative Shawnees thought it was a cause of the tribe's misfortunes. For had not the traditional tribal culture been a gift of Waashaa Monetoo to his favored people? Surely to forsake it or to contaminate it with the gleanings of "inferior races" such as the whites amounted to an affront to the Great Spirit and risked dire consequences. Thus in this line of thought, the activities of Black Hoof and his associates at Wapakoneta were more than deeply suspicious. If they provoked the anger of Waashaa Monetoo, they were also dangerous.[19]

For some years this nativist argument was seldom made, or at least it had no powerful advocate. But then in 1805 something happened that shook the spiritual complacency of the Shawnees and powerfully testified to the Great Spirit's wrath and power to punish. And from that chaos came a new voice, that of Lalawéthika, the self-proclaimed Prophet. It was a voice that not only challenged the tribal leadership of the Mekoches at Wapakoneta, men such as Black Hoof, but also summoned the greatest Shawnee of them all from his retirement on the Detroit.

Now in his sixties and with a mere two years left to live, Blue Jacket returned to the forefront of Shawnee affairs.

# 17

## Voices from the West

The winter of 1804–5 was hard and cold, but the spring brought worse. A sudden savage pestilence began sweeping through Indian villages between the Great Lakes and the Ohio, cutting a swath of death. It struck the Shawnee and Mingo settlements in Ohio and scourged the Wyandots and Mingoes of the Sandusky River. In Indiana Territory, on the White River, it ravaged the Delawares and Shawnees, and in May it claimed its most celebrated victim, Blue Jacket's venerable old ally Buckongahelas. Whether it was smallpox or influenza is uncertain, but the epidemic reduced Indian towns to chaos as they grappled with this most faceless and terrible of foes.[1]

Indians as old as Blue Jacket had seen the like before. When smallpox had run through the Ohio Valley tribes between 1756 and 1764, Blue Jacket had been a mere boy. That epidemic had stimulated a religious awakening among the Delaware Indians. The spirits, they feared, were angry and were punishing the Indians for their sinfulness. Some Indians had searched for new sources of spiritual patronage to fight the crisis and flirted with Christianity as offered by Moravian missionaries. Some favored desperate reforms to regain sacred power, which included revitalizing traditional ceremonies of obeisance and purging their culture of supposedly alien elements to return it to a state that could command divine approval. Such contaminating elements, said nativist prophets, had been introduced by the whites.[2]

Now it was happening again, as terrified Indians looked into their own souls to seek the reasons for their persecution or into those of others for telltale signs of witchcraft.

Witches, whether men or women, were almost universally acknowledged by Indians to exist. All Indians invoked spiritual support by prayers, worship, sacrifices, and the manipulation of fetishes, but the power summoned by witches was malignant and was used to cause injury and death. Even the educated George Blue-Jacket, associate of Presbyterian missionaries, never lost his belief in these sinister beings. "This witchcraft has prevailed greatly, and been very common among our people," he told some Shakers in 1807, "and some of the white people have learned it and practise it, and it is a very wicked thing." The notion that witches were behind the epidemic produced some horrific scenes in several Indian villages, as witch-finders searched for scapegoats to put to death. The Wyandots of the Sandusky, for example, not only used witch-finders of their own, men such as Longhouse, but also tried to bring in more prestigious accusers from outside, such as Beata, a Delaware prophetess; Lalawéthika, the Shawnee prophet; and the Seneca, Handsome Lake.[3]

But disease was altogether too widespread and pervasive to be accounted for by the malevolence of a few individuals, and several prophets from different communities declared that the misery of the Indians arose less from witches than from the displeasure of the Great Spirit. To save themselves, the Indians must change and identify and remove the causes of offense. They must reform.

It was probably sometime early in 1806 that Blue Jacket heard the most famous of these new voices. He may have remembered the man, a dissolute drunken Shawnee waster named Lalawéthika, the Loud Mouth. Talkative he certainly was, but he was no hunter, and his war record had been poor. He had a certain standing as a physician, but few had hitherto entertained much of an opinion of Lalawéthika. Nor did his appearance suggest distinction, despite an unusual mustache. A slender man of middling height, he had drooping shoulders and had lost an eye.

Lalawéthika lived in the Shawnee village on the White River in Indiana Territory, a town founded and led by his older brother Tecumseh. Tecumseh had been one of Blue Jacket's best warriors in the war and was widely respected, but it was Lalawéthika who suddenly became the focus of attention during these difficult years. He claimed to be the medium of Waashaa Monetoo, the Great Spirit, and to have been told the means by which all Indians might save themselves from destruction. In 1806 the brothers began bringing their Shawnee band back into Ohio and settling it temporarily on Stony Creek (Logan County) while they prepared a new town near the site of Wayne's old fort at Greenville. There, they said, they would fulfill the old Shawnee dream of uniting the nation and lead it to grace according to the principles of the Prophet.

People were indeed astonished at the personal metamorphosis in Lalawéthika. He renounced whiskey and began to preach, admitting the error of his former ways. In his own words, he labored strenuously to convince his brethren that "they must change their lives, live honestly, and be just in all their dealings, kind towards one another, and their white brethren, affectionate towards their families, put away lying and slandering . . . never think of war again."[4] He condemned drinking, sexual excess and infidelity, violence, and the practice of witchcraft.

To encourage the excited Indians who gathered to hear him, the Prophet described the frightening penalties that awaited nonbelievers. The souls of those who confessed their sins and lived righteously would pass to a beautiful place, but those of sinners would be punished according to their particular vices. The drunkard, for instance, would be compelled to drink molten lead, while the totally incorrigible would confront an eternity of torment. The Prophet urged his audiences to reform their lives before it was too late, to confess, and to live according to his strictures. To symbolize their new state of grace they should forsake the guardian spirits that had guided them so poorly throughout life and declare a new allegiance to the Prophet. They must throw away the medicine packs and fetishes associated with those old guardian spirits.

These teachings tackled several of the major problems facing the Indians, especially the inebriation and violence so often found in the villages, but the Prophet had another important message. It was, undeniably, backward-looking, but it also contained an inescapable logic. If Waashaa Monetoo was punishing the Indians, their conduct must have become displeasing to him. To arrest that punishment and restore spiritual favor, it was necessary for the Indians to return to good behavior. The Prophet, like many Delawares before him, saw one cause for the anger of the Great Spirit: the melding of Indian and white cultures. He had created the Indians to be different from the whites, with different colored skins and distinct cultures. By neglecting old ceremonies, including forms of worship, and imbibing the ways of the whites, the Indians were effectively rejecting that bequest of the Great Spirit. Now they must unpick that cultural fusion and recover the virtues of their supposedly pristine ancestors.

From the beginning, therefore, the Prophet told the Indians to "live as did the Indians in olden days," reviving their distinct identities and in the process increasing their self-respect and independence of the white trade system. The Prophet did not incite hostilities against the whites. Rather, he preached a temporary coexistence. Soon, he said, there would come an apocalypse, and Waashaa Monetoo would transform the earth, overthrowing the whites and all those Indians who were becoming indistinguishable from them, and return the obedient Indians to a presumed halcyon past. To facilitate this event, the Prophet intensified his nativist message over the years to attack racially mixed marriages, fraternization with whites, and the use of white manufactures and provisions, including their clothing and foods.

Of course, white and native cultures had so intertwined on the frontiers that extrication was no simple matter. Religion gives us an example. The Shawnees had been resistant to the direct impact of Christianity. Although one group of Mekoches under Paxinosa, Cornstalk's father, had established good relationships with the Moravians since 1755, most had flatly refused to have any truck with missionaries. Hardman had checked the advances of the Moravians in 1773, and even when Black Hoof sought the help of the Quakers to develop the Shawnee economy at Wapakoneta he stubbornly refused to suffer any evangelism. Still, the influence of Christianity had not been stifled. It had even entered the teachings of the Prophet, largely because Lalawéthika drew nearly all of his ideas from the Delaware prophetic tradition, which had itself incorporated elements of Christianity, including the concept of Hell and the punishment of souls. Similarly, the Prophet's notion of the confessional had come to him from Catholics at Detroit via his Wyandot followers. Although the Prophet regarded white influences as pollutants, his was a syncretic doctrine, forged of white and native elements.[5]

Equally, the Shawnee economy, even in conservative bands such as Tecumseh and the Prophet's, was unalterably bound to that of the whites. It was not feasible to return to a self-sufficient past. Firearms, for example, were needed, as well as the means to shoot and repair them, and many of the conveniences in Shawnee villages had come from trade with the whites. Occasionally, fired by religious enthusiasm, some of the Prophet's followers endeavored to purge themselves of as many white influences as possible, but the ensuing hardships quickly dented the enterprise.

More generally, there was a constant tension between the dogma of the Prophet's religion and its actual practice. Tecumseh's preference for aboriginal clothing and foods attracted notice, but he also understood the value of having a trader at his village. The Prophet railed against the keeping of livestock, other than horses, and condemned the consumption of beef and pork, but he was unable to prevent needy followers from butchering the hogs of white settlers for food.[6]

When the Prophet and Tecumseh came back east they were not blessed with a welcome from all the Shawnees in Ohio. The principal Shawnee village, and the one from which the tribal council operated, was Wapakoneta. There the Mekoches had reasserted their traditional leadership under a feisty little wizened warrior named Catecahassa, or Black Hoof. He had distinguished himself on the war trail and claimed to have fought against Braddock's army in 1755, but now he stood as the head civil chief of the nation, aged but determined, and as formidable in debate as ever. Black Hoof jealously guarded the right of his Mekoches to direct the Shawnees in peacetime. He had been among those who objected to Blue Jacket acting for the tribe in the negotiations with Wayne, and since the retirement of the great war chief and the death of Red Pole, he had run things pretty much to his satisfaction. Now, he looked with dismay as the Prophet and Tecumseh, members of the Kispoko division, the "younger brothers" of the Mekoches, returned from the West and tried to gather the Shawnees around themselves at the behest of the Great Spirit himself. Why, the Prophet had never been a chief, and Tecumseh, although the head of his own band, had never been there when the tribal council discussed affairs in Ohio. Little Black Hoof set his jaw grimly. These Kispokos, he decided, were not going to pull the leadership of the Shawnees from beneath him.

There was another reason why Black Hoof and his fellows — chiefs such as Black Snake, Shemenatoo (Big Snake), Piaseka the Wolf (Cornstalk's son), Dameenaytha or Butler, and Chaukalowaik (Tail's End) — saw the Prophet as a threat. For it had been they who had set afoot a plan to develop the Shawnee economy in Ohio, to modernize their agriculture, and to raise extensive stock. They had visited the East in 1802 in search of help for these programs from the American government and the Society of Friends, and in the winter of 1806–7 they would be back again. Among the encouragement they then received was the news that a Quaker, William Kirk, would be sent to Ohio with funds to help the Indians.

The Prophet regarded Black Hoof's policy as blasphemous, a repudiation of the will of the Great Spirit. Lalawéthika denounced Kirk as a master, sent by the Americans to turn the Shawnee warriors into women by setting them to labor in the fields, and a decade later he and his followers refused to live at Wapakoneta for the same reasons. The way of the hunter and the warrior had been bestowed upon the Indians by Waashaa Monetoo, and to adopt the customs of whites merely risked his fury. As they explained to Governor Lewis Cass of Michigan,

> Our brothers the Macojacks [Mekoches] . . . now live like you whites. They cultivate their fields. We cannot do it. We want to live as we have been used to do. We want to hunt game. . . . He [Waashaa Monetoo] made the women to raise corn. He made us men to hunt. We can live no other way. You would think it hard to be compelled to live as we do, to live by hunting. You could not do it. . . . We cannot live as you do. . . . We wish to live as our fathers have lived before us. . . . We cannot live with our brothers the Mackajacks. They do not live as their forefathers used to live.[7]

Black Hoof and the Prophet were divided by policy, and Black Hoof resented the younger man's pretense to leadership. More than that, he saw the westerners as a destabilizing influence, all the Indians moving to and fro to hear the Prophet speak, not just Shawnees but also Wyandots, Ottawas, and others from further afield. They disturbed the white settlers making their homes in the new state of Ohio and the good relations those pioneers enjoyed with Black Hoof and his people.

So when the Prophet and Tecumseh returned to Ohio, their welcome was far from a fulsome one. A small band of Wyandots under Roundhead, who lived on the upper Scioto River, fell beneath the Prophet's spell. There were at least a couple of small Shawnee villages in what is now Logan County, Ohio, about two miles from each other, near present-day De Graff. The headman of one of these villages was a "Captain John," a "naturally . . . able and likely man" who could "talk tolerable good English." He was probably the same Captain Johnny who had once headed the Shawnees alongside Blue Jacket, but he paid little heed to the Prophet. The other Shawnee community in Logan County, established just a few miles inside the Greenville cession, was on Stony Creek. It offered the Prophet and Tecumseh hospitality while they prepared their new town at Greenville, but their chief, Lewis, was a man of little influence.[8]

Most of the Ohio Shawnees, who lived in the neighborhood of Wapakoneta, stuck with Black Hoof and their other chiefs. Relations between the parties of Black Hoof and the Prophet deteriorated. They sank to an all-time low in 1807, after the Prophet denounced his political enemies as witches and two men from Wapakoneta were murdered by his followers. Civil war was a distinct prospect.

A consolation for Black Hoof had been the Prophet's failure to win over the significant Shawnee chiefs — until the middle of 1806. Then the proud Mekoche leader heard disturbing news. His old rival, and the most famous man in the nation, had thrown in with the reformers. Blue Jacket had left his town on the Detroit River to put himself at the head of the Prophet's party.

\*　　\*　　\*

From his home on the Detroit, across the river from the British post of Fort Malden and south of Detroit itself, the capital of the recently formed Michigan Territory, Blue Jacket was in an excellent position to pick up news. That summer of 1806 there was plenty of it about, and much of it concerned war. A delegation of Sacs and Potawatomis, members of the militant confederacy developing on the upper Mississippi, arrived at Fort Malden looking for British assistance against the United States. Their messengers also called on possible Indian allies. They were said to have inflamed warriors around Michilimackinac, but the Shawnees, Wyandots, and Delawares steadfastly declined to be drawn into hostilities.[9]

Most of this must have come to Blue Jacket's ears, and that summer he was in Detroit, delivering a speech to Governor William Hull, probably on the subject of the agitation. Then he journeyed south into Ohio and brought his news to the Prophet's party on Stony Creek. Blue Jacket found the Indians there worried. The Wapakoneta chiefs had been defaming the band to the American Indian agent at Fort Wayne, William Wells. They had told him the Prophet was building a town at Greenville, on ceded land, and that he was alarming the white settlers, and they wanted him driven away. Other figures were maligning the reformers too, and there had already been some difficulties with settlers in the Mad River district. In view of the disquieting rumors Blue Jacket had heard in Detroit, it may have been he who advised Tecumseh and Lewis to take their case to Chillicothe. Direct talks with the governor of Ohio, Edward Tiffin, were the best means of reassuring the whites that the reforming Shawnees intended no harm.[10]

Blue Jacket went with them. Tecumseh and Lewis were also accompanied by two young men of Blue Jacket's band, who served the deputation as interpreters. One was John Logan and the other Blue Jacket's son George. In a speech made to Governor Tiffin on 11 August 1806 the chiefs declared that there was no truth to the rumors that the reformers were preparing for war. They had been victims of "malicious lies" invented by Black Hoof's faction and by some of their white friends, François Duchouquet, Frederick Fisher, and William Wells. The Prophet wanted nothing more than to gather the Shawnees together so that they could be kept "in good order" and reformed. The chiefs said that they intended to proceed to Detroit to reassure the people there, and it seems their sentiments were entirely acceptable because Tiffin took no further notice of the matter. In the ensuing winter and spring Tecumseh and the Prophet moved their band to Greenville, where they had built an elaborate town of some sixty houses. The reasons for selecting a site near the old fort, now merely an overgrown ruin, are unknown, although the Prophet several times said that the Great Spirit had directed him to the place. Equipped with a large council house and a meeting ground, Greenville was founded on hope. It was to be the Mecca of the new religion of the Prophet and an instrument of Indian salvation.[11]

Blue Jacket was a major fillip to the Prophet's people. He was their one widely recognized leader, as the chiefs of Wapakoneta admitted. At Greenville, they said, "there is not half as many of our nation . . . as there is here, and none of our principal chiefs . . . but Blue Jackett, who we do not consider as a chief as he does not come to our council." No less significant than the prestige he brought was Blue Jacket's ability to get first pick of the tribal annuities because they had begun to be issued at Detroit, only a few miles north of the chief's home. In this respect Black Hoof's fears were realized. Blue Jacket seized more than his fair share of the 1806 annuities on behalf of his own and Tecumseh's band.[12]

The old war chief was a shadow of his former self. He was in his sixties and profoundly overweight, but he was still dignified in appearance and effective in debate, and his standing and experience were second to none. Soon people were beginning to speak of him as the leader of the reformers. Black Hoof and Black Snake, the most important chiefs at Wapakoneta, referred to Blue Jacket as "the head of the [Prophet's] party," while William Hull described him as "the friend and principal adviser of the Prophet." Some Shakers, led by their curiosity to visit Greenville in 1807, found Blue Jacket installed there as "the principal chief."[13]

But why was he there at all? On the face of it, Blue Jacket's support for the Prophet and Tecumseh is a paradox. After all, in very many respects he epitomized what the Prophet condemned. He drank and peddled whiskey, which the Prophet wanted prohibited. He traded in the European manufactures which the Prophet insisted were weakening the independence of the Indians, and he farmed and lived much in the white style, a style the Prophet affected to despise. Blue Jacket not only fraternized with whites but also drew them into his family. His wives had been whites, and his children were mixed-bloods. In fact, Blue Jacket represented that very fusion of blood, culture, and attitudes which the Prophet denounced as offensive to the Great Spirit. Yet here he was, apparently unrepentant and simultaneously maintaining his comfortable lifestyle on the Detroit River. Why?

It would be a mistake to presume that everyone who supported Lalawéthika and Tecumseh during their brief spell in the limelight subscribed to the religious tenets of the movement. That was manifestly not the case. Even the brothers themselves understood that compromises were necessary, and Tecumseh was particularly sensitive to pragmatic considerations. Though he accepted many of his brother's pretensions and teachings, he was no slavish adherent. For example, he rejected the Prophet's notion that a coming apocalypse would ultimately solve the problems of Indian-white relations.

More generally, support for the brothers in no way implied an automatic acquiescence in the Prophet's doctrines. For many — men such as the Potawatomi Main Poc, who believed his own religious powers quite equal to those of the Prophet — the brothers were powerful friends and allies who could be used to achieve standing ambitions of their own. Stimulated largely by the threat of American land hunger, tribesmen on the Illinois and Mississippi had been plotting against the United States before they had heard of the Prophet or Tecumseh, and many of them welcomed the Shawnees as allies. In the South, too, where Tecumseh eventually found some of his most enthusiastic supporters, recruits came from diverse quarters. There were religious zealots such as Josiah Francis and High-Headed Jim, but there were also men such as Peter McQueen, the materially minded mestizo war captain, whose motives were more personal and political.

And so in the early days of the movement of Tecumseh and the Prophet, Blue Jacket illustrated its capacity to attract differently minded men and women, people who saw advantages in one way or another.

Blue Jacket probably saw the sense in much of what the Prophet said, but we cannot suppose that these arguments were sufficient inducements for the most sophisticated of all Shawnees. We can, however, only guess at his motives. We know he was ambitious; he always had been. We know, too, that he was isolated, living apart from the center of Shawnee affairs in Ohio and seldom attending their tribal council. The most likely explanation of his interest in the Prophet is that he saw in him a way to recover influence and power. It was his final attempt to challenge the supremacy of Black Hoof and other old Meckoche rivals.

The extent of Blue Jacket's involvement is reflected in records made by the Shakers, that abused Protestant sect founded by Mother Ann Lee, who was held to have been a female Christ. The Shakers had founded a new community at Turtle Creek, Ohio, about seventy miles from Greenville. Their codes embraced many parallels to that of the Prophet, including temperance, simplicity in dress and manner, the communal possession of property, the use of the confessional, and a commitment to peace. Unlike most whites, the Shakers were also disposed to believe that the Prophet was a true witness, set up by God, and to satisfy their curiosity about the Indian reformers they made several visits to Greenville in 1807. Their accounts make it clear that not only Blue Jacket but other members of his family were spending time in the Indian Mecca.

In March three Shaker brethren, Richard McNemar, Benjamin Youngs, and David Darrow, braved a cold spring, with snow and rain, to spend two days in Greenville, and they left us our most detailed portrait of it. They found it on a fork of Greenville Creek and evinced great satisfaction at the religious atmosphere that prevailed throughout. The council house and meeting ground ran east to west, with their southeastern and northwestern corners reserved for prayers made at the rising and setting of the sun, when the Great Spirit was deemed to be closest. The dramatic reveries of the Prophet, the Shakers later found, could endure the night through, but other speakers uttered public prayers daily, and at every pause the inhabitants would signify their assent with a firm "seguy." The community struck the Shakers by its gentility, orderliness, and profound religious character. "The very air," they said, was "filled with His fear and a solemn sense of eternal things, and this light shines in darkness, and the darkness comprehends it not."[14]

The Shakers found Blue Jackets much in evidence. George, one of only two English speakers in the village that March, they decided made an excellent interpreter, and it was he who was their principal chaperon.

George was "a likely sensible man," the Shakers wrote, and normally lived on a farm near Detroit, with his wife and two children. "He treated us with great kindness," they testified. George may have boasted an education in Detroit and had mixed much with Presbyterian missionaries, but he greatly admired the Prophet. White ministers, he explained, "call it foolishness," but Lalawéthika "was still seeing more and more wonderful things, which he taught the people." Not only that, but in the opinion of George and the other Indians the Prophet was displaying a quality they had rarely encountered in American ministers: sincerity. He preached against drinking spirits and abided by his counsel. In contrast, Hughes, the Presbyterian missionary who had been George's former employee, "would drink whisky after he had done preaching," as well as condone it in others. George had imbibed many Christian beliefs but was ready to reconcile them with his support for the Prophet. Christ, he believed, had tried to reform the whites; now, the Prophet was preaching to the Indians.

On 24 March the Shakers spoke to Blue Jacket himself, along with other notable leaders, in the chief's tent in the village. They dwelled on aspects of the Prophet's religion, including the use of the confessional and Lalawéthika's supposed ability to detect witchcraft and sin in evilly disposed persons. Although the epidemic that had spawned the revival of Indian prophecy was petering out, it was obvious to the Shakers that Greenville was powerfully charged with religious fervor.

A pleasant relationship developed between the Prophet's reformers and the Shakers, and several groups of Indians went to Turtle Creek to observe the Shaker ceremonies and way of life. More practically they also hoped to receive gifts of provisions. Food was scarce at Greenville, which was supporting not only the indigenous inhabitants but also the many Indian pilgrims crowding into the village to listen to the Prophet. One of the parties of Indians that visited the Shakers spent five days at Turtle Creek between 29 August and 3 September 1807. It was accompanied by an interpreter the Shakers called Nancy. She was possibly Blue Jacket's lost daughter.

Nancy was Blue Jacket's youngest child by his wife, Margaret Moore. The chief never saw her grow up because Margaret, a white woman, returned to her people in Virginia while she was pregnant. In due course, Nancy turned into a woman, married one James Stewart, and eventually gave him four children. Then, for some unknown reason, the whole family returned to the Ohio frontier. With Margaret as the matriarch, they settled in Logan County, mixing with both Shawnees and whites and renewing old friendships. The date of their return is not known, but it was probably about 1804. In 1810 the Shawnees granted the family a tract of their land to live on.[15]

Nancy Blue-Jacket, or Nancy Stewart, as people in Ohio remembered her, would have possessed a facility with both English and Shawnee, English from her upbringing and Shawnee from her mother and the Indians she met in Logan County. The Shakers said that Nancy the interpreter was "a bold advocate" of the Prophet's religion but somewhat resentful of the ill will borne it by some of the local whites. If the settlers attacked the Indians, she said, there would come a day of judgment, and all of them would be swept from the face of the earth.[16]

If Nancy the interpreter and Nancy Blue-Jacket were identical, the Prophet must have been having a remarkable impact on this, arguably the least conservative of Shawnee families.

*    *    *

When Nancy complained of the hostility of some of the local pioneers she had a good point.

Blue Jacket and Tecumseh had visited Governor Tiffin of Ohio in Chillicothe in 1806 and assured the Americans of their peaceful intentions, but the effects of their mission were only temporary. Before long, fear-ridden rumors about the Greenville Indians were again flitting to and fro, and many hard words were spoken against them. In the late summer of 1807 the tension reached crisis proportions. An army of militia threatened to descend upon the small Shawnee town, and once more Blue Jacket stepped forward to restore order. It was to be his last public service, to either Indians or whites.

The Shawnee reformers certainly distrusted the whites and wanted to disentangle aboriginal and American influences, to unpick the threads that were fusing the cultures of natives and newcomers. But the Prophet was not inciting warriors to attack the Americans. On the contrary, he had the notion that one day the Great Spirit would do the job for him, carrying the whites, and Indians who resembled them too closely, away in some great cataclysm. In the meantime he wanted to live peacefully with his white neighbors and concentrate on forming a model religious community at Greenville, one that would proclaim his gospel to Indians abroad.

Nevertheless, the settlers' fears of the Indians at Greenville were entirely understandable. They were largely ignorant of the motives of the

Indians, and some of the outlying farms and settlements, such as those on Ohio's Mad River, were isolated and vulnerable, hewn from extensive broad-leafed forests that afforded excellent cover for approaching enemies. Men tending their crops were easily surprised, even if they kept muskets or rifles nearby, and there were insufficient blockhouses to shelter fleeing settlers. A pioneer named John Boyer had been slain in his field in May, near the line between Champaign and Miami Counties in Ohio. He had been shot, tomahawked, and scalped by stray Potawatomis, and for a while the frontier had been in uproar.

Those tensions increased. Throughout 1807 the Prophet sent messengers to tribes far and near, inviting them to visit him and to hear the words of the Great Spirit that they might take them back to their peoples. These messages ran northeast to the Iroquois of New York, north into what is now Ontario, west as far as the upper Mississippi, and northwest along the upper Great Lakes and into present-day Minnesota and Manitoba. Hundreds of Indian pilgrims answered them: Sacs, Foxes, Menominees, Kickapoos, Winnebagoes, Ottawas, Potawatomis, Ojibwes, and Wyandots. The strange warriors filling the Indian trails to Greenville showed no hostility to the whites. Even William Wells, who had little good to say about the Prophet, admitted that his followers were merely "religiously mad." But their numbers and their congregation at Greenville frightened the exposed white settlements in Ohio, and Wells urged the American government to disperse the Prophet's band.[17]

In June another ingredient was suddenly poured into this inflammable mixture. The *Chesapeake*, a vessel of the United States Navy, was intercepted by a British frigate, the *Leopard*, in search of deserters off the coast of Virginia. When the American commander refused to permit his ship to be searched, the British fired on it, killing or wounding twenty-one men. This latest in a line of maritime disputes between the two countries brought Britain and the United States to the brink of war. Americans, raised to fury by the insult to the American flag, called for satisfaction. On the Ohio frontier memories of Indian war parties, armed with British muskets and backed by British bayonets, were revived. Soon British intrigue and the hostile influence of British agents were being seen behind every act of Indian hostility, and some settlers began defaming the Prophet as a tool of the redcoats. Greenville was now not merely a concourse of strange tribesmen from far and wide, a rallying point on land the Indians had already ceded to the United States. It was also a nest of foreign agents.

In August American militia officers of Champaign and Green Counties resolved to raise more blockhouses and establish a committee of safety. A small party of men, led by William Ward and Simon Kenton, also set off for Greenville, accompanied by interpreters, to see whether the Indians gathered there were coming toward the settlements and, if possible, to parley with the chiefs. They reached the town on 1 September but found that most of the Shawnees and all their chiefs were absent, most at Detroit collecting annuities or with the Shakers at Turtle Creek. After speaking to a French-Shawnee métis trader and some of the Potawatomis who were among the several hundred distant Indians there, the whites withdrew. They had not been reassured.[18]

Far from it. Upon reviewing their position, Ward and his fellows decided to raise fifteen hundred or more men to march out, at least to scare the Indians and perhaps to disperse them. One Elias Langham, who had been sent by the governor of Ohio to assess the situation, returned hotfoot to Chillicothe. Ward and the other militia officers were already gathering arms, and they wanted the governor or his representative to be on the spot when the army marched. The prospect of a clash between militiamen fearful for their homes and a religiously charged body of armed Indian warriors was gathering.[19]

For a time Blue Jacket had been blissfully unaware of the sudden squall whipping up around Greenville. While Nancy had gone to Turtle Creek with one party of Shawnees, he had taken another to Detroit to collect the year's annuities from Governor Hull. Probably Tecumseh was with him, although if so the younger chief did not come to the attention of the governor on this occasion. Blue Jacket had a surprise when he called on Hull and engaged him in a long conversation. Hull read a speech to the Shawnee chief. It had been made by an Ottawa leader known as the Trout to his people at Arbre Croche, Michigan Territory, back in May, but it was claimed to have been a message to them from the Prophet.

Unfortunately, as an embarrassed Blue Jacket was unable to deny, the speech was less than complimentary to the United States. The Americans, the Prophet was supposed to have said, were "the scum of the great water when it was troubled by the Evil Spirit," who pilfered their land, intoxicated them with whiskey, and cheated them in trade. Hull accused the Prophet of fomenting anti-American sentiment and demanded an explanation.

Almost certainly, the speech which the Trout had carried to his people did come from the Prophet, at least in substance. The Trout was one of the many pilgrims attracted to Greenville. About the time the Trout had been listening to the Prophet the Shawnees had been disturbed by rumors that the United States was about to suspend treaty payments to the Indians and to demand another land cession. There were also stories that the Americans intended to enforce an acculturation program, building houses for the Indians and setting the tribesmen to work for wages to pay for them. These ideas may have sharpened the Prophet's dislike of the Americans, even though he had no plans to attack them or to conspire with the British against them. Nevertheless, the speech was inflammatory, and Blue Jacket knew it.

Talking to Hull in Detroit that August the old war chief took the easiest way out. He simply denied the authenticity of the speech. He told Hull that "he knew all the speeches the Prophet had sent to the different nations," and the Trout's was not one of them. The Prophet "was a friend to the United States, and had ever advised all the nations to be friendly. That his object was to induce them to abandon the use of ardent spirits, and unite together, and preserve themselves as a nation." And to prove his own credentials, Blue Jacket pulled out a "very honourable" certificate he had wheedled out of President Washington in 1796 and pledged his friendship to the United States.[20]

Blue Jacket returned to Greenville during the first days of September. On his way he conferred with the Wyandots at Brownstown, where the council fire of the old confederacy had been kindled. There was much to discuss: the war talk among the Indians of the upper Mississippi, the rumors of a new war between the Americans and the British, and the difficulties of the Prophet. Blue Jacket was no inexperienced hothead. He had no illusions about the Americans, but no more did he trust the British, who had been fickle allies in the past. But whatever the Indians did, he was sure they should do it together.

Blue Jacket thrashed out matters with the Wyandots, searching for a policy around which the local tribes could rally. If the redcoats and the Big Knives went to war, one or the other of them would surely try to draw the Indians into the conflict. The Wyandots reminded Blue Jacket that the British had turned the Indians on the French and then the Americans and that during the war against Wayne the redcoats had urged the Indians on, telling them "that if they would turn out and unite as one man they might surround the Americans like deer in a ring of fire and destroy them all." But in the end the British had always let them down. In 1794 they had even closed the gates of Fort Miamis to their defeated warriors. No, in the opinion of the Wyandots, there was no good to be had from joining in a new war. The tribes should stay neutral.

It was true that the Indians had grievances, and the Wyandots remembered many attempts to halt the erosion of tribal lands. They spoke of the Royal Proclamation of 1763, when the British unsuccessfully forbade the colonists to cross the Allegheny Mountains into unceded Indian country. There were problems still, and many Indians were angry that the United States was building more garrisons, such as Fort Dearborn on the Chicago River. But these difficulties were not likely to be solved by another war. The Wyandots advised the Shawnees at Greenville to use their influence and their speeches to urge the Indians to remain united but also at peace.[21]

There is no reason to suppose that Blue Jacket did not wholly endorse this policy, for both his town on the Detroit River and Greenville were situated on ground over which any war between the Americans and the British must be fought. Armies marching to and from Canada would have passed through or by them, and the Indians could not afford to make enemies of either party. Peace was obviously desirable.

As it was, the threat of war and the animosity of local whites had convinced Tecumseh and the Prophet that Greenville was no longer suitable for them. Despite the effort they had put into building the town, they decided to move to the Wabash in the spring. The idea was likely to have been put into their heads by Blue Jacket, who had planned to concentrate the Shawnees on the Wabash himself, once in 1795 and again four years later.

That decision must have seemed a sensible one when Blue Jacket reached Greenville and found himself embroiled in the new crisis with the settlers in Ohio. Fortunately, at this stage Thomas Kirker, who was acting as the governor of Ohio while Tiffin was in the Senate, moved faultlessly. In response to early warnings about Greenville, he had already issued a speech to all of the Ohio Indians, cautioning the tribes not to be misled by any British agents and expressing his concern at the assemblage at Greenville. As soon as his informant, Elias Langham, hurried into Chillicothe with news that the settlers on the Mad River, a few miles east of Greenville, were planning on marching 1,500 men to intimidate the Indians Kirker acted. On 9 September the governor sanctioned the muster, summoning 1,460 officers and men to be ready to move within ten days.[22]

Kirker, however, had also been listening to good advice. William

Creighton of Chillicothe had pointed out to him the danger of antagonizing Indians who were not known to be definitely hostile. Creighton doubted that the warriors at Greenville intended harm to the whites, and he suggested that before any extreme measures were taken one or two "active intelligent discreet" men be sent to ascertain the real temper of the Indians. Consequently, early on the morning of 13 September, shortly after Blue Jacket had returned to Greenville, two representatives of the governor rode into the Indian village: Thomas Worthington and Duncan McArthur, along with an interpreter, Stephen Ruddell. It was a judicious action, and one that gave Blue Jacket and Tecumseh the opportunity to avoid trouble.[23]

Some two hundred Indians packed the council house and doorways to hear what the visitors had to say. They listened while the Americans reminded them how flimsy British friendship had been in the past. A war between the United States and Britain was likely, but the Indians had best stay out of it. Neither they nor the redcoats could defeat the Americans. Worthington and McArthur also wanted to know why the Prophet had established his town on land ceded to the United States at the treaty of Greenville and whether it was true, as some said, that he served the British. They warned that the governor of Ohio was even then raising a large army, but before he used it he wanted to know what the Indians intended.

The news of that army concentrated Blue Jacket's thoughts. The chiefs invited their guests to remain with them until the following day, when a formal reply to their speech would be delivered. As the meeting broke up, however, they lingered in conversation. Blue Jacket explained that the Trout's talk, which had been published in several American newspapers, had not been genuine, and he assured the governor's emissaries that there was no cause for alarm. Worthington and McArthur said that they had intended mentioning the Trout's speech the next day, but since Blue Jacket had introduced it, they would deal with it now. Ruddell was asked to translate the speech from a newspaper copy for the listening chiefs. He did so, and the chiefs agreed that it was bogus. Lalawéthika himself "seemed to resent it as a slander" and claimed that people told lies about him. One of them was Frederick Fisher, who had accused the Prophet of saying that he could "turn the Americans over like a basin of water."

The morning of 14 September saw the Indians and their visitors back at their places in the council house, and Blue Jacket rose to deliver the chiefs' official reply. He spoke, he said, for all the Indians then at Greenville, including members of the Shawnees, Wyandots, Potawatomis, Ottawas, Ojibwes, Winnebagoes, Menominees, Sacs, and others. They all agreed with the advice given Blue Jacket by the Brownstown Wyandots about eleven days before and by Worthington and McArthur themselves. They were not agents of the British and did not intend to be but would stand neutral in any war waged by the Americans and British. Blue Jacket pointed out that the Indians were not afraid of the Americans, and if trade was cut off from them they could still subsist using bows and arrows to hunt. They simply wanted peace. Blue Jacket admitted that the building of Fort Dearborn had irritated some Indians and that he could not speak for all the Indians on the upper Mississippi or those with the British. But "the sentiments of those who sit before you" were clear: "The white brethren are going to war. Their red brethren have formed a determined resolution to interfere no way, but to sit still and mind their own concerns."

Blue Jacket explained that part of the Indians' bad press originated with William Wells, the United States Indian agent at Fort Wayne. He asked the governor to intercede for them with the president and to have Wells dismissed and replaced.

Worthington and McArthur were satisfied. They replied that Wells could be removed only if serious charges were proven against him, and on the matter of Fort Dearborn nothing could be done. The Indians had ceded the site of the fort to the United States in the treaty of Greenville. But Blue Jacket's professions of peace impressed them. Would the Indians send their chiefs to Chillicothe to repeat those assurances to the governor?

Blue Jacket and Tecumseh agreed. They had been to Chillicothe before and would do so again. The effects of Blue Jacket's speech and the behavior of the Indians generally were plain enough in the report which Worthington and McArthur later made. "After the most strict enquiry," they wrote, "we could hear of nothing which left a doubt in our minds as to their sincerity. There was no hostile appearance. Their women and children, of which there was about 250, were with them, engaged generally in their ordinary labour. We were treated with great hospitality and kindness in their way from all, both strangers and foreigners . . . we were unable to find one single fact on them which wore a hostile appearance."

It had taken courage for Worthington and McArthur to put themselves at the mercy of supposedly hostile Indians in the cause of peace, and Blue Jacket and Tecumseh could do no less. With Roundhead, the Wyandot leader, and Panther, they left Greenville on 16 September, escorted toward the Ohio capital by their late guests. Two days later they arrived at Chillicothe, and Blue Jacket found himself lodging at Adena, Worthington's new freestone home half a mile north of the town on the brow of a wooded ridge.

Governor Kirker decided that the best way to restore confidence was for the Indians to address the public directly, and on 19 September Blue Jacket and the other chiefs followed Worthington and McArthur into the Chillicothe courthouse, which was crowded with anxious and curious citizens. According to the *Chillicothe Fredonian*,

> On Saturday morning last the Governor, attended by Blue Jackett, a chief of the Shawnee nation, with three other chiefs, entered the courthouse and were engaged in a talk till very late in the afternoon. The manly, firm and majestic deportment of these hardy sons of nature were well calculated, from the recent alarms, to attract the attention of the citizens. Vast crowds flocked to the courthouse, led thither by curiosity and the novelty of hearing an Indian address. Their manners were familiar, unassuming and engaging. Their delivery was cool, dispassionate and rational. They frequently appealed to the Great Spirit, the author of their existence, for the rectitude of their intentions and the truth of what they advanced.

The Indians were seated in the jury box, Blue Jacket and Roundhead to the left and Tecumseh and Panther to the right, with Governor Kirker occupying the clerk's seat between them. The governor opened the meeting, with Stephen Ruddell on hand to interpret. Blue Jacket then rose to speak. This was his last important public speech, but he looked the part. Watching him, Thomas Spottswood Hinde, who was scribbling notes of the proceedings for the local newspaper, saw "a venerable and very old looking Indian, but very grand and stately," and thought his "looks indicated simplicity and sincerity." Another witness remembered Blue Jacket as "the leading councillor on the part of the Indians. He was then an old man, an eminently dignified speaker, and of calm, persuasive eloquence."[24]

Reflecting wistfully on more than sixty years of bloodshed, Blue Jacket steadily recalled the fierce conflicts that had enveloped the Ohio country since the days when French and British armies had squabbled and bled over it. The Indians had always been involved, but to little profit. Now another war was coming, but Blue Jacket said the Indians wanted no part of it. As reported by the *Fredonian*, Blue Jacket staunchly supported Indian neutrality:

> They [the Indian chiefs] complained much of the whites making encroachments upon their territory, and of a few individuals who had made sale of lands beyond the line of demarcation, but their dispositions towards us appeared friendly. Blue Jacket observed, "We have deluged the country with blood to satiate our revenge, and all to no purpose. We have been the sufferers. The Great Spirit has shown us the vanity of these things. We have laid down the tomahawk, never to take it up again. If it is offered to us by the French, English, Spaniards, or by *you*, our white brethren, we will not take it."

Now, the Indians wished to serve Waashaa Monetoo in peace, and they were doing so at Greenville. There was no justification for this alarm among the whites, Blue Jacket said. The Indians wanted merely to worship in peace and friendship. In these protestations, the old warrior grew emotional and his voice faltered. He sat down.

Kirker was impressed. Speaking on behalf of the state of Ohio, he replied that he was pleased to learn that the Indians had abandoned war and that they were simply serving the great and good spirit. He wished them good fortune and assured Blue Jacket that the whites had no desire to disturb the Indians in their worship.

Then Tecumseh stood. Impassioned and fluent, the handsome young chief supported Blue Jacket's insistence that the Indians meant the whites no harm. He blamed the bad rumors on the jealousy of the Shawnee chiefs at Wapakoneta and on the whites they had prejudiced, men such as William Wells. Black Hoof and his chiefs had lost some of their best warriors to the community at Greenville. He said that Wells was abhorred at Greenville and ought to be replaced by an honest man. The settlers would have pricked up their ears when Tecumseh broadcast his plan to evacuate Greenville and establish a new town on the Wabash in the spring. He hoped the United States would maintain a store there, managed by some such upright person as Stephen Ruddell.

When the meeting ended, Blue Jacket and Tecumseh emerged triumphant. Kirker disbanded the militia and reported favorably to President Jefferson. The Indians, he wrote, "gave me every satisfaction I could ask. . . . I sincerely believe these people are injured . . . there does not appear on strict examination anything against them. On the contrary, their lives are peaceable, and the doctrines they profess to practise are such as will do them honor if they continue to be sincere." On the Mad River, settlers returned to their hastily abandoned farms, while at Greenville the Indians dispersed for their fall hunt in the knowledge that they were not going to be attacked.

For Blue Jacket and Tecumseh the trip to Chillicothe had been a nostalgic one, as well as a mission of peace. Tecumseh was born on the Scioto River, and Blue Jacket had had a town there for many years before the Revolution. From Worthington's home on the ridge Blue Jacket could gaze eastward toward and beyond the Hocking hills, a lush, green, and well-watered land he had known in his youth. It was a land the Shawnees had once ruled but since lost.

Blue Jacket's career had been remarkable and in great part successful, certainly from the personal point of view. He had risen to become the most influential Shawnee of his time, perhaps of any time before him, and he had won unprecedented military and diplomatic victories. In that process he had made a comfortable living, raised a distinguished family, and achieved widespread recognition. Yet he had been unable to save Ohio for his people, and there were probably times when he felt it keenly.

Thomas Spottswood Hinde, who had admired the aged warrior in the Chillicothe courthouse, collected a story that may have contained a grain of truth. According to him, one morning Thomas Worthington rose early and was surprised to find one of his Indian guests on the porch, gazing silently over the valley with tears on his cheeks. Blue Jacket explained that he had been thinking about all the blood shed in defense of the land these sixty years gone.

"It affects my heart and fills it with sorrow," said the old chief. "Now I am a very old man, and will soon pass away like all the rest. I desire to live and die in *peace*!"

# Conclusion

Blue Jacket's hope was fulfilled. He did not live to see the outbreak of the next major conflict in 1811, when the Prophet threw his fervent warriors into what would be remembered as the battle of Tippecanoe. No contemporary record marked the passing of the veteran war chief, but from what was said later it seems that he died in his village on the Detroit River in the early part of 1808, while Tecumseh and the Prophet were establishing their new town on the Wabash in Indiana Territory.[1]

He left a widow, a former wife, two daughters, and three sons.

His white wife, Margaret Moore, and the children Blue Jacket had had by her, Joseph and Nancy, all survived him. Joseph had never left the Indian country, a fact singularly advertised by his appearance. According to one who knew the family, Joseph Moore

> was brought up by his father among the Indians, and was a pretty fair specimen of the aborigines of the wild woods — dressed in their style, with buckskin leggins and moccasins, a blanket belted around the waist, and silver brooch for fastening over the breast. He had been subjected to the cruel and barbarous custom of cutting the rim of the ear from top to bottom, so as to hang apart from the ear, suspending a weight thereto for the purpose of making it distend as much as possible while healing. He had but one of his cut, for the reason, he said, that they could have but one cut at a time, as they could lay only on one

side. Before his one ear got well, he got out of the notion of having the other cut.[2]

Joseph's mother, Margaret, his sister, Nancy, and her husband, James Stewart, returned to Ohio about 1804 and renewed their acquaintance with the Shawnees. The Shawnees welcomed them with their usual hospitality, and the Wapakoneta chiefs granted both Nancy and Joseph tracts of their land in Logan County in October 1810. Each tract consisted of 640 acres and was situated on the banks of the Great Miami, just north of the Greenville line, Nancy's on the east bank and Joseph's opposite, on the west bank. Margaret Moore was awarded a jointure from her daughter's tract.[3]

The family presented an interesting bridge between the Indians and neighboring white settlers. Nancy, her mother, and husband were all members of the Christian Church Muddy Run Meeting House on the Mad River in Logan County, downstream of West Liberty, and were eventually buried there.

Joseph died sometime between 1813 and 1817, and when the Shawnees concluded a new treaty with the United States in 1817 it was only Nancy they attempted to protect. The treaty reserved "to Nancy Stewart, daughter of the late Shawanese chief Blue Jacket, one section of land, to contain six hundred and forty acres on the Great Miami, below Lewistown, to include her present improvements, three quarters of the said section to be on the southeast side of the river, and one quarter on the northwest side thereof." It seems, therefore, that Nancy exchanged some of her old tract for a portion of Joseph's, across the river, probably because of the improvements he had made. Three years later, in 1820, Nancy and her husband successfully petitioned the United States for permission to sell the tract. John Johnston, an Indian agent for the Shawnees, supported their application, describing the family as "very industrious, honest and well behaved people" who found "their Indian neighbors . . . very troublesome in consequence of their relationship, frequently as is their custom living on them for weeks at a time, consuming in idleness their subsistence."[4]

Nancy remained in the area, well respected, and died toward the end of 1840, a decade after the death of her husband.[5]

Blue Jacket's widow, the métis daughter of Jacques Dupéront Baby, lived to an advanced age at her husband's town on the Detroit but emigrated west of the Mississippi with her son Jim and the Huron River Wyandots in 1853. She died in Kansas.[6]

Of Blue Jacket's four children by this wife, one, Mary, predeceased him, dying in 1806. The other known children by this marriage were Jim, Sally, and George Blue-Jacket.

Jim was living on the lower Maumee in 1801 but later removed to the vicinity of his parents' home on the Detroit River. The younger brother, George, had a farm and a family near the mouth of the same river at the time of his father's death. George's brother-in-law Jacques Lasselle tried to secure this land for him on 14 December 1808 by filing a claim to preemption rights on the eighty-acre riverside plot with the Detroit Land Office. The application was made on George's behalf, and Lasselle made a down payment of forty dollars.[7]

Then the War of 1812 and Tecumseh's rebellion against the United States intervened.

It was only after Tecumseh moved to the Wabash that he undertook the mammoth task of organizing armed resistance to further American expansion. One early historian credited Blue Jacket with having put Tecumseh up to the idea, but during the period in which that chief had helped direct the Shawnee reform movement and for a short time after it had been peaceful. In 1808 the British began to recultivate the Indians as military allies, certain that the war looming with the United States would endanger Canada. The redcoats were particularly attentive to the Shawnees, remembering their role under Blue Jacket. "*They* are men that can be depended on," wrote the Indian agent William Claus. Sir Francis Gore, lieutenant governor of Canada, informed his superior that "this nation of Indians have been represented to me as having heretofore preserved a decided superiority in the general councils of the western confederacy, and as having a commanding influence in all their measures." Yet although they poured flattery on Tecumseh, when they finally got him to Fort Malden in the summer of 1808, he kept the British at arm's length.[8]

Similarly, when Sacs and Winnebagoes planned attacks on United States garrisons early in 1809, Tecumseh and the Prophet sympathized with their concern at the growth of American power but do not appear to have given them any support. Tecumseh visited these same tribes on the upper Mississippi in June 1809. He evidently invited them to come to hear the Prophet on the Wabash, but he also participated in a general council in which the Indians made some show of renouncing their former hostility to the Americans.[9]

Tecumseh's shift to a war plan was partly influenced by the western tribesmen with whom he mixed more freely after his move to the Wabash but was largely the work of the treaty of Fort Wayne (1809), by which Governor William Henry Harrison secured large tracts of Indiana Territory from the Indians. Determined to resist the cession, which Indian agent John Johnston broached to the Miamis in open council as early as June 1809, Tecumseh planned to mass warriors about his village on the Wabash to resist further white settlement. Beginning in the summer or fall of the year, he systematically canvassed the tribes, urging them to remove to the Wabash, or at least to support his confederacy. American land purchases, the encroachments of whites on Indian lands, and government promotion of the "civilization" program had been creating opposition to the United States for several years, particularly among the western tribes of the upper Mississippi and the Upper Creeks of the South. Tecumseh and the Prophet began to draw these strands together, trying to weld them into a cohesive force.[10]

At this time Tecumseh drew heavily from the example of Blue Jacket. Indeed, Tecumseh was merely attempting to restore the great confederacy of his youth, the confederacy of Blue Jacket, Red Pole, and Captain Johnny. He approached the Wyandots, who kept the wampum belt that had symbolized the previous union, and asked them to produce it anew; he reiterated the old doctrine that the land was owned in common by all the tribes and could not be sold by one group or another; and he and his emissaries traveled far and wide, to the Iroquois of New York, to the tribes of the South, to the Indians of the Great Lakes and the Mississippi, and throughout Ohio, nearly all of them trails already worn by Blue Jacket and Red Pole and other Shawnee diplomats of earlier generations.

Today, Tecumseh is deservedly remembered as the ultimate symbol of the search for Indian unity. He was a man of enormous talent, energy, and commitment, and he impressed people tremendously. The Reverend William Winans, who watched Tecumseh addressing Harrison in Vincennes in 1810, recalled:

> Tecumseh spoke first. He was as fine a looking specimen of man as ever I beheld. In both his form and feature, he was as near perfection of manly beauty and symmetry as I could imagine. He was very light in his complexion for a full-blooded Indian. He was calm, self-possessed and dignified, without any air of assumption or self-importance. He was modest, without timidity, and, in general, courteous without

sycophancy. He was simple and deliberate in his speaking, but by no means tame and common-place. He was one of Nature's true noblemen, and I think in its highest class.[11]

But Tecumseh was distinguished by the effort, passion, and versatility he brought to the cause, rather than for originality. Blue Jacket and others had been there before him, and he must have been a great inspiration to Tecumseh. In the last years of his life Blue Jacket had made many journeys and sat beside many campfires with Tecumseh, as a friend, adviser, and comrade. He must often have spoken of his attempts to build his confederacy and of the great intertribal congresses and the battles won and lost. A picture comes to mind, romantic and imaginary perhaps — a picture of a graying old man who had once been the first of his people sharing his experiences and thoughts with a rising young zealot who commanded the future. Surely, it is a picture that embodies truth. When Tecumseh finally committed himself to rebuilding the confederacy, and throwing it against the invaders, who can honestly deny that Blue Jacket was in his thoughts?[12]

The younger Blue Jackets continued to associate themselves with Tecumseh's activities even after the death of their old patriarch. One of Jim Blue-Jacket's sons may have accompanied Tecumseh on his canvass of the southern tribes in 1811 and 1812, and when the United States declared war on Britain in the summer of 1812 and Tecumseh arrived on the Detroit frontier to join the redcoats against a common enemy, both Jim and George Blue-Jacket became valued members of the Shawnee chief's forces.[13]

In allying himself with the British, Tecumseh expected the redcoats to help him drive the Americans back to the Ohio in return for his assistance in defending Canada. In short, Tecumseh's was a last-ditch attempt to restore Ohio, Indiana, and Michigan to Indian control, to realize the old dream of Blue Jacket and his confederates. The Blue Jacket boys fought alongside Tecumseh with courage and humanity, and their father would have been proud of them. After John Logan, a Shawnee interpreter of the Blue Jacket band, was slain in a skirmish with the Americans at Brownstown on 5 August 1812, George was enrolled in the British Indian Department to fill his place and held the post during that and the following year. He helped Tecumseh ambush another American force on 9 August and was hit in the shoulder during the fierce fighting.[14]

Like their father, the Blue Jackets made war without gratuitous malevolence. Indian leaders had little control over the treatment of prisoners, who were regarded as the property of individual captors. Moreover, it was customary for the relatives of Indians killed in battle to demand the death of prisoners in satisfaction. Nevertheless, during the War of 1812 Tecumseh enjoyed a reputation for protecting prisoners, even though he was not always able to prevent them from being killed.[15]

In this he was supported by the Blue Jackets, even in the chief's absence. Such an occasion occurred in January 1813, when the British and Indians crushed Brig. Gen. James Winchester's army on the River Raisin, a battle that cost the United States more soldiers than St. Clair's defeat. Local tradition claimed that young George was staying at the house of his brother-in-law Jacques Lasselle at the Raisin when the American advance surprised the settlement on 18 January and credited him with crossing the frozen Detroit River that bitter night to carry the news to the British at Fort Malden. Probably Col. Henry Procter, the British commander on the Detroit, got the news from several sources in the early hours of the nineteenth. The Indians and British counterattacked on 22 January and annihilated Winchester's force, but Jim and George Blue Jacket saved the life of Whitmore Knaggs in the battle. He was an old Maumee settler well known to the Blue Jacket family.[16]

Tecumseh was away when the battle of the River Raisin was fought, but he was on hand to help besiege Fort Meigs on the Maumee River in May 1813. An American relief force was cut to pieces, but Tecumseh successfully halted the wanton massacre of prisoners. The chief also intervened to stop the abuse of four Wapakoneta Shawnees who had been captured in American service. The Indian allies of the British were diverse and volatile, and to ensure that the four remained unharmed, Tecumseh put them in the charge of the Blue Jacket brothers. The brothers gave the prisoners a musket and a pistol, and Jim even escorted them safely back to Wapakoneta.[17]

It is even possible that some of the spontaneous acts of altruism ascribed to Tecumseh stemmed from his friendship with or the influence of the Blue Jackets. For instance, despite allied pillaging of some settlers on the River Raisin during the war, Jacques Lasselle was able to remain in the vicinity. The Indians and British left him alone. Jacques, known as Coco, was the son-in-law of old Chief Blue Jacket and the widower of his daughter Mary. The Lasselles believed that Jacques's survival was owing to the personal protection of Tecumseh. Similarly, Tecumseh intervened to spare Father Gabriel Richard of St. Anne's Church, Detroit, from imprisonment by the British during a period in which they wrested Michigan Territory from the United States. Richard was popular among local Indians and may have had a claim on Tecumseh for that reason; but Jacques Lasselle and Mary Blue-Jacket had also been the priest's parishioners. Richard had baptized one of their children, and he had buried Mary in 1806.[18]

Jim and George were not the only children of Blue Jacket who were swept up in the War of 1812. Their sister Sally was with the Shawnees who, with other Indians under Tecumseh, supported the British in the conflict. The Blue Jackets were an interesting brood, and their lives often took surprising turns. Nancy headed out for Ohio and her father's people after being raised and married in Virginia. George, interpreter, farmer, and aid to missionaries, was also strong in battle. And Sally, too, had unusual experiences. For her the war brought a ghost from her past.

Sally had probably been born about 1778 and was little more than a girl when her pleasing and unusually fair features had attracted the attentions of a young British redcoat, William Charles Shortt. Perhaps he noticed her hanging around Detroit or visiting Fort Miamis, for it was Shortt's regiment, the Twenty-fourth Regiment of Foot, which garrisoned the British fort on the Maumee in 1794 and 1795, during the heady days when Blue Jacket was organizing resistance to General Wayne. Shortt had entered the regiment as an ensign but was promoted to captain on 9 July 1794. He must have seemed a gallant fellow to the chief's daughter. They enjoyed a relationship, and Sally gave birth to a son. Shortt himself returned to England, but the boy remained with his mother and was ever after known as Thomas Shortt. Sally married a man named Wilson, probably a trader, and it was by the name Sally Wilson that she was remembered.

Sally must have thought that Captain Shortt had left her life forever. The outbreak of the War of 1812 found her living with her father's band on the Detroit River, and, like the others, she was soon having to shift her home here and there according to the fortunes of the fighting. In May 1813 the band settled on Grosse Ile, in the Detroit River. Sally and George took over the abandoned farm of a William McComb on the island, housed their families there, and raised crops. Occasional councils on the island diverted attention, and Sally also enjoyed visits from her great friend Catherine Walker, the daughter of an Irish trader and a Wyandot woman. In the summer there was suddenly something different to talk about. The Forty-first Regiment of Foot, which manned Fort Malden, was being reinforced, and among the new arrivals there appeared none other than William C. Shortt, now a lieutenant colonel.

Shortt had returned to America and joined the Forty-first Regiment in 1803. It was in that corps that he reached the rank of lieutenant colonel, in 1812. Shortt arrived at Fort Malden with a new wife, one Jane Crooks, whom he had just married at Fort George, Niagara, a woman related to Henry Procter, who commanded on the Detroit. Whether Sally had much to say to Shortt or even met him is uncertain. His days were few, for he was killed on 2 August 1813, gallantly attempting to storm Fort Stephenson on the Sandusky River.

Little is known about the rest of Sally Blue-Jacket's life. She evacuated Grosse Ile when the British and Indians retreated from Fort Malden in September but remained with the remnants of Tecumseh's band in Canada long after the war ended. Under a British statute of 1823 she was awarded £6.18s.od., but although she went to the British agent, George Ironside, to collect the money, no one remembered that she got it. Her last days, and those of her son Thomas Shortt were spent with her brother Jim and the Wyandots in Michigan. A grandson, Joseph Shortt, born about 1833, died in Kansas about the 1860s.[19]

Sally's brothers, Jim and George, got little from the war either. At the end of it, Tecumseh was dead, killed in battle, his confederacy had fallen apart, and the hope of an Indian resurgence in the Old Northwest was extinguished. Now the war for the Ohio country was truly over. In other respects, the war changed relatively little, with the peace of 1814 merely restoring the status quo of three years before. The dispossession of the Indians continued unabated, and the Blue Jackets were unfortunate enough to witness it.

Jim returned to life on the Detroit River. He married a Wyandot and moved to Flat Rock Reservation, which was established in 1818 on the lower Huron River in Michigan. The reservation was terminated by treaty in 1842, and the Wyandots were assigned lands in Kansas. Jim, his mother, and family went with them, via Cincinnati and Kansas Landing, Missouri. There, Jim's wife, who had been ill since the early spring, died in August 1843. Jim himself reached Kansas, where he died about two years later. He was survived by his son, Jim Jr., and an unmarried daughter.[20]

George also saw the decline of the aboriginal East. After the war he returned to farm the plot of land that Jacques Lasselle had tried to secure for him in 1808. Unfortunately, George believed that the United States would not grant a patent for the land to someone whose support for Tecumseh and the British had been notorious, and he relied on the Lasselles to handle the paperwork. As long as Jacques lived, George's well-being was assured, but when Jacques died in 1815 his younger brother François took over the administration of his estate. Somehow François maneuvered George out of his land, and although a friend of the Blue Jackets, the merchant George McDougall, tried to help, George left the Detroit in 1822 and moved to Ohio. The British did little better for George. He was awarded almost £25 as compensation for his war losses, but again, as in the case of his sister Sally, there is doubt about whether he ever received it.

George spent the rest of his life with the Ohio Shawnees, among whom he was respected as the most educated man of the tribe, at least in the white man's sense of the word. But the Shawnees, no less than the Wyandots, were losing their ancestral lands. In 1817 a treaty confined them to three reservations in Ohio, the lot summing only seventy-five or so square miles, and between 1831 and 1833 they, too, were induced to leave the East for homes in Kansas. George did not live to see the final removal. He died at Wapakoneta in 1831, but his wife and their numerous children emigrated. George's widow died in the West in January 1844.[21]

The younger Blue Jackets reflected the world of ethnic diversity inherited from their father. He had mixed freely with Indians and whites and imbibed habits, attitudes, and aspirations from both. All of Blue Jacket's children were mixed-bloods. All the girls married whites. Most fitted as easily into white as Indian communities. Nancy's transition from Virginia to Shawnee society and Mary's from Indian to French Canadian are perfect illustrations.

Blue Jacket's lifestyle, economic adventurousness, and interest in the formal education of the whites place him at the cutting edge of the gradual evolution of Shawnee culture. In this respect he contrasts with Tecumseh. Tecumseh was a rather conservative Shawnee, the very embodiment of the old-style warrior and hunter, who exemplified their finer qualities of bravery, generosity, and communal spirit. At least as influenced by the Prophet in his final years, he regarded white culture with suspicion. Tecumseh and the Prophet attempted to disentangle Indian and white cultures, as far as it was practicable, and hoped to achieve prosperity by self-sufficiency, restoring an equitable balance between hunters and game, independence, and the recovery of sacred power. Blue Jacket was also religious and a fine warrior and hunter, but he was also entrepreneurial. He sought prosperity through the reverse process, by embracing what improvements the whites could offer and by mastering the skills that were necessary for success in their world. This was a perspective Blue Jacket passed to his children.

No better example of this newer type of Shawnee could be found than the chief's grandson Charles Blue-Jacket, one of the several sons of George Blue-Jacket. George had the boy educated in a mission school near Fort Meigs (Toledo, Ohio) and then with the Quakers at Wapakoneta, and later he completed his schooling of his own volition at the Shawnee Baptist Mission in Kansas. Showing that strain of self-improvement which had marked the Blue Jackets. Charles became a highly successful stock raiser and fruit farmer in Johnson County, Kansas. He built a substantial two-story house and was widely admired by neighbors of all races. A licensed Christian preacher, Charles never lost interest in more traditional Shawnee culture and supplied information about it to the missionary Joab Spencer and the ethnologist Lewis Henry Morgan. During the Civil War he served the Shawnees as elective head chief and commanded an Indian company. Later Charles removed to Indian Territory (Oklahoma), where he died on 29 October 1897. He was greatly missed in Kansas and was enthusiastically welcomed when he made a return visit not long before his death. Recalling him, Joab Spencer said, "I can think of no one who, taken all in all, had more elements of true dignity and nobleness of character. He was my interpreter, and I never preached through a better."[22]

Yet in many, perhaps most, ways Tecumseh and Blue Jacket were alike. Like Brant before them, they both gave their lives to the defense of an Old Northwest under the suzerainty of the Indians, strove for the intertribal cooperation necessary to make effective resistance, and attempted to fashion great confederacies. They fielded large forces, and although they were eventually defeated, they had both known victories. Tecumseh was elevated into the American pantheon, but Blue Jacket shared the fate of the majority of eighteenth-century Indian leaders. He was more or less forgotten.

Today, most people's perception of American Indian armed resistance, itself only part of a complicated history, is extremely limited. It is the warriors of another age who are remembered — men of the later nineteenth century, whose fame has benefited from the growth of the popular press, the cinema, and improved communications. Yet Blue

Jacket's followers accounted for more American enemies in serious battle than the forces of Cochise, Red Cloud, Crazy Horse, Sitting Bull, and Geronimo put together, and his vision of intertribal unity was much keener and more sophisticated. Of course, we are all products of our own times, but when the long roll of Indian notables is called, surely the name of Waweyapiersenwaw, or Blue Jacket, deserves to find its place.

# Abbreviations

The following abbreviations have been used in the notes and bibliography.

| | |
|---|---|
| *ANB* | *American National Biography* |
| *ASPIA* | *American State Papers, Indian Affairs* (1832–34) |
| *ASPMA* | *American State Papers, Military Affairs* (1832–61) |
| BHC | Burton Historical Collection, Detroit Public Library |
| *Clark Papers* | *George Rogers Clark Papers*, ed. J. A. James |
| *DAR* | *Documents of the American Revolution*, ed. K. G. Davies |
| *DCB* | *Dictionary of Canadian Biography* |
| IHS | Indiana Historical Society, Indianapolis |
| *JP* | *The Papers of Sir William Johnson*, ed. A. C. Flick, et al. |
| *MPCPA* | *Minutes of the Provincial Council of Pennsylvania*, ed. S. Hazard |
| *MPHS* | *Michigan Pioneer and Historical Society Historical Collections* |
| OHS | Ohio Historical Society, Columbus |
| *Pennsylvania Archives* | *Pennsylvania Archives*, ed. S. Hazard, et al. |
| SHSW/D | State Historical Society of Wisconsin, Madison/Draper MSS., cited by volume, series [denoted by a letter or letters], and page |
| *Simcoe* | *The Correspondence of Lieutenant-Governor John Graves Simcoe*, ed. E. A. Cruikshank |
| *TPUS* | *The Territorial Papers of the United States*, ed. C. E. Carter and J. P. Bloom |
| U.S. SOW/LR/R | United States of America/Letters Received by the Secretary of War, Registered series |

| | |
|---|---|
| U.S. SOW/LR/U | United States of America/Letters Received by the Secretary of War, Unregistered series |
| U.S. SOW/LR/IA | United States of America/Letters received by the Secretary of War relating to Indian Affairs |
| *VSP* | *Calendar of Virginia State Papers and Other Manuscripts*, ed. W. P. Palmer |

# Notes

## Introduction

1. Notable among them are Robert Van Trees (Terry Morris, "The Mystery of Blue Jacket," *Dayton Daily News and Journal Herald*, 24 August 1987; "Fact, Not Fiction: Marmaduke Swearingen, Shawnee War Chief?" *Mercer County Chronicle* [Coldwater OH], 6 September 1990; Robert Van Trees, "Historian Re-examines the Blue Jacket Legend," *Northwest Journal* [Fort Recovery OH], 6 April 1992; and Bob Roberts, "Bluejacket Myth Exploded," *Journal Herald of Northwest Johnson County* [KS], 20 April 1994); Floyd Barmann, director of the Clark County Historical Society in Ohio (Bill Monaghan, "Would the Real Blue Jacket Please Step Forward?" *Ohio News-Sun* [Springfield], 12 December 1991); and Ray Crain ("Blue Jacket Lore White Man's Tale, Historian Says," *Dayton Daily News*, 15 December 1991; Bill Monaghan, "Blue Jacket Controversy Lives On," *Ohio News-Sun*, [Springfield] 10 February 1992; and "Historians Doubtful Blue Jacket White," *Daily Standard* [Celina OH], 13 June 1992).

2. Tanner, "The Glaize in 1792"; Reginald Horsman, "Weyapiersenwah," DCB 5 (1983), 852–53; Stevens, "His Majesty's 'Savage' Allies," 1947–48; and Thrapp, *Encyclopaedia of Frontier Biography*, 1:129–30.

3. For a conscientious review of the controversy, see Johnson, "Testing Popular Lore."

4. Thomas Swaine to Anthony Bartlett, 27 February 1795, Northwest Territory Collection, IHS; Andrews, "Shaker Mission to the Shawnee Indians," 119, 126–27; diary of Jacob Lindley, 1793, MPHS, 17:606; Jacques Lasselle t o Antoine Lasselle, 20 February 1795, Wayne Papers (2).

5. Thornbrough, *Letter Book of the Indian Agency at Fort Wayne*, 78; land grants to Nancy and Joseph Moore, 2 October 1810, Recorder's Office, Logan

County, Bellefontaine OH; John Wingate to William Henry Harrison, 15 June 1813, Harrison Papers (1); Moore, "Early Recollections of Nancy Stewart," 328.

6. For examples, see Calvin M. Young, *Little Turtle (Me-she-kin-no-quah), the Great Chief of the Miami Indian Nation* (Greenville OH, 1917); Anson, *Miami Indians*; Carter, *Life and Times of Little Turtle*.

7. Francis Gore to James Craig, 8 April 1808, Canada/Indian Affairs Papers, 2:843; Schutz, "Study of Shawnee Myth," 523; Lasselle to Thomas Jefferson, 12 June 1806, *TPUS*, 10:57.

8. Buell, "Fragment from the Diary," 268; Anthony Wayne to John F. Hamtramck, 25 February 1795, Wayne Papers (1); George McDougall to William Woodbridge, 26 February 1820, Woodbridge Papers.

9. Wayne to James McHenry, 3 October 1796, in Knopf, *Anthony Wayne*, 532.

10. Harrison to Henry Dearborn, 3 March 1805, in Clanin et al., *Papers of William Henry Harrison*, reel 2:104. See also documents in reels 2:235 and 4:58. For differing interpretations of Wells, see Woehrmann, *At the Headwaters of the Maumee*; Hutton, "William Wells"; Dowd, *Spirited Resistance*, chap. 7; and Sugden, *Tecumseh*.

11. Little Turtle quoted in Volney, *View of the Soil and Climate*, 356–57, and Hopkins, *Mission to the Indians*, 63–66. Wells wrote an account of the Indian wars about 1812. It was published in part as "Indian History, from the Ms. of William Wells," *Western Review and Miscellaneous Magazine* 2 (1820): 201–4, and since as Beckwith, "Fort Wayne Manuscript," and it was also the basis of William Turner's "A Description of the Emigration, Habits, &c. of the N. Western Indians," Ayer Manuscripts, Ms. 689, vol. 10. The published tradition seems to have influenced the remarks of Schoolcraft, *Travels*, 40, 42, as well as the reminiscences of Spencer, *Indian Captivity*, which appeared in 1834. Students are warned that Dresden W. H. Howard, "The Battle of Fallen Timbers, as Told by Chief Kin-jo-i-no," *Northwest Ohio Quarterly* 20 (1948): 37–49, is fictitious.

## *1. Blue Jacket's People*

1. This, and the plural "saawanwaki," were the words used in the 1930s (E. W. Voegelin notes, Voegelin Papers).

In 1824 and 1825 Charles Christopher Trowbridge preserved accounts of Shawnee life by Tenskwatawa (formerly Lalawéthika), a Kispoko Shawnee, and Black Hoof, a Mekoche. They were published as *Shawnese Traditions* by W. Vernon Kinietz and Erminie Wheeler Voegelin. Contemporary references to Shawnee culture can be sampled in Smith, "Shawnee Captivity Ethnography," and Sugden, *The Shawnee in Tecumseh's Time*. Scholars should be aware that much of the Shawnee material in Johnston, "Account," was lifted from a then unpublished manuscript Benjamin Hawkins had written about the Creek Indians; that the description of the Shawnees in Thomas Ashe, *Travels in America* (London: William Sawyer, 1808), is copied from Baron Lahontan's account of the northern Algonquians in his *New Voyage to North America*, published in translation in 1730; and that the Shawnee data Timothy Flint evidently gathered from Daniel Boone was promiscuously integrated with Miami material in Flint's *First White Man of the West*. William Wells's description of the Miamis, from which Flint drew his information, was itself published as Beckwith, "Fort Wayne Manuscript." The contemporary Shawnee references should be compared with the more detailed findings of later fieldworkers, but account must always be taken of the considerable changes that occurred in Shawnee society during the nineteenth and twentieth centuries. Most useful of the later studies are the account in White, *Lewis Henry Morgan* [1859]; M. R. Harrington, Ms., "Shawnee Indian Notes" [1909–10]; the various contributions of Charles F. (Carl) and Erminie Wheeler Voegelin [fieldwork, 1933–35], especially the latter's "Mortuary Customs of the Shawnee and Other Eastern Tribes"; Alford, *Civilization*; and Howard, *Shawnee!* (based on fieldwork, 1969–74). The best overall account of Shawnee culture is Schutz, "Study of Shawnee Myth." Jerry E. Clark's brief *Shawnee* rests substantially on his previous dissertation, "Shawnee Indian Migration."

2. For creation myths, see Mekoche speech, March 1795, Claus Papers, 7:124; account of Lewis Rogers, 1812, Schoolcraft, *Information Respecting the History*, 4:254; Johnston, "Account," 273, 275; Kinietz and Voegelin, *Shawnese Traditions*, 1–8, 60–63; and Spencer, "Shawnee Indians," 383, 394. The typescript "An Indian's Own Story," supposedly written by George Blue-Jacket and filed in the U.S. History Manuscripts, also refers to creation stories, but it appears to be fraudulent. It is factually incorrect, and the Shawnee words it contains are all taken from Johnston, "Account."

3. Mekoche speech, March 1795, Claus Papers, 7:124. Other Mekoche statements to the same effect can be found in Dawson, *Historical Narrative*, appendix; and the speech of Blackbeard, 1807, Shawnee File.

4. The evidence about divisional responsibilities is contradictory. John Johnston, who was sometime U.S. Indian agent to the Shawnees, assigned the Mekoches the priestly functions of the tribe, but Tenskwatawa, who detested the Mekoches, told Trowbridge that they had bungled the business so badly that it had been transferred to the Chillicothes. There is no doubt, however, that the Mekoches claimed and expected political preeminence: "We told you [the British] we were the king tribe and none but a person of our tribe could be made a king" (speech of Mekoche chiefs Black Hoof, Red-Faced Fellow, and Wolf, March 1795, Claus Papers, 7:124). See also Johnston, "Account," 275; Kinietz and Voegelin, *Shawnese Traditions*, 6, 8; Williams, "Journal of Richard Butler," 145; George Ironside to Alexander McKee, 6 March 1795, Canada/Indian Affairs Papers, 9:8840. The statements on this subject in Alford, *Civilization*, 44, although often quoted, are not valid for the eighteenth century.

The early history of the Shawnees is treated by Voegelin, "Some Possible Sixteenth- and Seventeenth-Century Locations"; Witthoft and Hunter, "Seventeenth-Century Origins"; Voegelin and Tanner, *Indians of Ohio and Indiana Prior to 1795*, vol. 1; Clark "Shawnee Indian Migration"; and Schutz, "Study of Shawnee Myth." Schutz deals extensively with the subject (pp. 305–466) and argues that before their seventeenth-century residence on the Ohio the Shawnees had occupied the South. Based on scattered references to groups who may have been Shawnees, he places them on the Savannah River in the sixteenth and early seventeenth centuries and contends that they were eventually forced to the Tennessee and Cumberland valleys, from where they were expelled by the Cherokees and Chickasaws. They then occupied the Ohio, where the historical record takes them up shortly after the middle of the seventeenth century. The language and culture of the Shawnees indicate an origin nearer the Great Lakes, but Schutz's theory of an early southern location for the tribe is supported not only by its nomenclature, which signifies "southerners," but also by eighteenth-century Shawnee traditions, which proclaimed a southern origin (Mekoche speech, March 1795, Claus Papers, 7:124). If the hypothesis is correct, those Shawnees who settled the Savannah region in the 1680s, dislodging the fierce Westos before being driven out in their turn by the English and Catawbas by the 1720s, had reoccupied an old homeland rather than claimed new ground.

5. Jones, *Journal of Two Visits*, 52–54. For chieftainship, see Jones, *Journal of Two Visits*, 73; John Slover's narrative, 1782, *Pennsylvania Archives*, 2nd ser. 14:722; Stephen Ruddell to Benjamin Drake, January 1822, Tecumseh Papers, 2YY120; Kinietz and Voegelin, *Shawnese Traditions*, 11–13, 15, 17, 19; John Johnston to Daniel Drake, 14 December 1831, Tecumseh Papers, 11YY18; White, *Lewis Henry Morgan*, 46–48; and Graham Rogers interviewed by Lyman C. Draper, 1868, Draper Notes, 23S166.

6. Among sources indicating the supremacy of the war chiefs during periods of conflict are Henry Bouquet to Thomas Gage, 15 November 1764, MPHS, 19:280; the speech of Blue Jacket, 2 August 1795, ASPIA, 1:579; and the speeches of Yealabahcah and Tenskwatawa, 1816, Cass Papers.

7. Kinietz and Voegelin, *Shawnese Traditions*, 9–11, 55. The Mekoches deferred to the Iroquoians with bad grace, declaring that while the Iroquois claimed to be the "oldest tribe" they "have no pretensions to it," but they acknowledged a debt to the Delawares, who had given hospitality to the Shawnees during their residence in the East (Mekoche speech, March 1795, Claus Papers, 7:124).

8. Material on the summer villages and work of the women comes from James Logan to George Thomas, 19 July 1742, Logan Letterbooks; Darlington, *Christopher Gist's Journals*, 44; Jones, *Journal of Two Visits*, 52–54, 56, 58; Filson, *Discovery*, 102, 105; *Old Record of the Captivity of Margaret Erskine*, 20; Beckner, "John D. Shane's Interview with Benjamin Allen," 74–75; Edgar, *Ten Years of Upper Canada*, 345, 349, 352, 354–55, 358–60, 364, 378; Johnston, *Narrative*, 28–29, 37–38, 46, 59; Spencer, *Indian Captivity*, 91–92; Perrin du Lac, *Travels*, 45; Andrews, "Shaker Mission to the Shawnee Indians," 126; Klinck and Talman, *Journal of Major John Norton*, 188; *Missouri Gazette*, 14 March 1811; Kinietz and Voegelin, *Shawnese Traditions*, 33–34, 38, 48, 49; John Johnston to Benjamin Drake, 30 March 1833, Tecumseh Papers, 11YY19; Harvey, *History of the Shawnee Indians*, 146; McCoy, *History of the Baptist Indian Missions*, 530; Alford, *Civilization*, 15–17; Voegelin, "Place of Agriculture"; and Howard, *Shawnee!*, 79–80.

9. George Croghan to James Hamilton, 16 December 1750, MPCPA, 5:496; Filson, *Discovery*, 102; Spencer, *Indian Captivity*, 67; Kinietz and Voegelin, *Shawnese*

*Traditions*, 48–49; Harvey, *History of the Shawnee Indians*, 146–51; and Harrington, Ms., "Shawnee Indian Notes," 45–46.

10. Harvey, *History of the Shawnee Indians*, 146. Examples of descriptions of the appearance of Shawnees are Cresswell, *Journal*, 49–50, and Wallace, *Thirty Thousand Miles with John Heckewelder*, 313.

11. Shawnees to James Hamilton, 8 February 1752, MPCPA, 5:569.

12. *Niles' Register* 32 (1827): 359–60 (quotation); Thomson, *Enquiry into the Causes of the Alienation of the Delaware and Shawanese Indians*, 23; Edgar, *Ten Years of Upper Canada*, 349; and Spencer, *Indian Captivity*, 109. Valuable accounts of the Indian trade and its role in British-Shawnee relations can be found in Hanna, *Wilderness Trail*, and Downes, *Council Fires*.

13. Kinietz and Voegelin, *Shawnese Traditions*, 16–17, 62.

14. Kinietz and Voegelin, *Shawnese Traditions*, 2, 35–46, provides the basis for my discussion of religion and witchcraft among the Shawnees. For the sacred bundle, see Kinietz and Voegelin, *Shawnese Traditions*, 55–57; Flint, *First White Man of the West*, 140 (quotation); and Howe, *Historical Collections of Ohio*, 32. Flint got material from Daniel Boone, once a prisoner of the Shawnees (pp. 131, 139, 141, 144, 147–48, 153), but he was not a reliable chronicler and is subject to the reservation made against him in note 1, above. See also Jones, *Journal of Two Visits*, 62; Edgar, *Ten Years of Upper Canada*, 376; Gregg, *Commerce of the Prairies*, 386–88; and "Motshee Linnee, the Bad Man," one of the "Indian Tales" collected by Trowbridge. Shawnee burial practices reflected their beliefs about the journeys of souls to the afterworld. Mourners walked around the grave westward, to point the direction the soul should take, and victuals, and at one time presents, were left with graves to equip souls for their travels. Particularly useful descriptions of Shawnee funerals can be found in Henry Joutel, *Joutel's Journal of La Salle's Last Voyage, 1684–87* (Albany: J. McDonough, 1906), 194; Kinietz and Voegelin, *Shawnese Traditions*, 24–25, 48, 51; "Motshee Linnee," cited above; and Harvey, *History of the Shawnee Indians*, 185–89.

15. Kinietz and Voegelin, *Shawnese Traditions*, 21, 36; Harrington Ms., "Shawnee Indian Notes," 101–2; Alford, *Civilization*, 24–25.

16. *Cincinnati Chronicle and Literary Gazette*, 7 November 1829.

17. Coates, "Narrative of an Embassy to the Western Tribes," 104; Spencer, *Indian Captivity*, 102–7, 111–13; Perrin du Lac, *Travels*, 46; Klinck and Talman, *Journal of Major John Norton*, 174; White, *Lewis Henry Morgan*, 47, 77; Spencer, "Shawnee Indians," 392.

18. Sugden, *Tecumseh*, deals with these movements among the Shawnees, but see also *Missouri Gazette*, 21 March 1812.

19. Kinietz and Voegelin, *Shawnese Traditions*, 16–17; White, *Lewis Henry Morgan*, 45–47.

20. Howe, *Historical Collections of Ohio*, 31.

21. Minutes of a meeting, 10 May 1765, MPCPA, 9:259.

22. Jones, *Journal of Two Visits*, 75–76; *Old Record of the Captivity of Margaret Erskine*, 26; Lewis Mesquerier to Draper, 8 September 1869, Tecumseh papers,

IYY98; John M. Ruddell to Draper, 21 June 1888, Tecumseh Papers, 8YY51; Perrin du Lac, *Travels*, 47; Persinger, *Life of Jacob Persinger*; Kinietz and Voegelin, *Shawnese Traditions*, 26–35; David H. Morris to Benjamin Drake, 25 December 1839, Frontier War Papers 4U98; and Spencer, "Shawnee Indians," 391.

23. General information on Shawnee war ceremonialism and practice is given by Flint, *First White Man of the West*, 127–53, and Kinietz and Voegelin, *Shawnese Traditions*, 17–24, 50, 53–54, 64–65. See also Loskiel, *History of the Mission of the United Brethren*, 145; Jones, *Joural of Two Visits*, 72; Edgar, *Ten Years of Upper Canada*, 344, 347–48; Martin Hardin to Henry Clay, 2 December 1812, Frontier Wars Papers, 7U6; "Neearnemaahkaatar, the Fisherman," in Trowbridge, Ms., "Indian Tales"; and John Johnston to Draper, 13 September 1847, Tecumseh Papers, IIYY31.

24. Lois Mulkearn, ed., *The George Mercer Papers Relating to the Ohio Company of Virginia* (Pittsburgh: University of Pittsburgh Press, 1954), 23; Denny, *Military Journal*, 71–72; and Howe, *Historical Collections of Ohio*, 32.

25. These paragraphs depend on a comparison of Shawnee "captivity" narratives. Those of Daniel Boone (as given by Filson), Margaret Erskine, George Ash, Stephen Ruddell, John Slover, Benjamin Allen, Thomas Ridoubt (Edgar), Charles Johnston, Oliver M. Spencer, and Jacob Persinger are cited above in notes 5, 8, 16, and 22. In addition, see Saunders, *Horrid Cruelty of the Indians*; Ansel Goodman's account in Dann, *Revolution Remembered*, 280–82; narrative of Joseph Jackson, 1844, Boone Papers, 11C62; *True Narrative of . . . Mary Kinnan*; Moore, "Captive of the Shawnee" (another version of the Erskine captivity); and Knowles, "Torture of Captives," 177–79.

26. Minutes of a meeting, 10 May 1765, MPCPA, 9:259; Flint, *First White Man of the West*, 147–48; Butler, "Journal of General Butler," 512–13.

27. Jones, *Journal of Two Visits*, 71, 74; Johnston, *Narrative*, 30–31, 41, 45; Edgar, *Ten Years of Upper Canada*, 355.

28. Joutel, *Joutel's Journal*, 194; Hanna, *Wilderness Trail*, 2:152; Jones, *Journal of Two Visits*, 77–78; Denny, *Military Journal*, 70–71; Beckner, "John D. Shane's Interview with Benjamin Allen," 77; Edgar, *Ten Years of Upper Canada*, 358; Ms. narrative of Jonathan Alder; Spencer, *Indian Captivity*, 54–55, 102–13; Burnet, *Notes on the Early Settlement*, 68–70; Kinietz and Voegelin, *Shawnese Traditions*, 39–40, 49–53; "Autthoakaukau, A Story," Trowbridge, Ms., "Indian Tales"; White, *Lewis Henry Morgan*, 47; Harrington Ms., "Shawnee Indian Notes," 57; and Nettl, "Shawnee Musical Style."

29. These stories, transmitted as oral folktales, enjoyed considerable longevity, although the details changed according to time, circumstance, and narrator. The tale of the grasshopper war (Drake, *Life of Tecumseh*, 15–16) was echoed in a tradition preserved by Spencer "Shawnee Indians," 389, while what seems to have been a variation on "Motshee Linnee, the Bad Man," one of eleven stories collected by Charles C. Trowbridge, was referred to by Gregg, *Commerce of the Prairies*, 386–88. I am indebted to Clifton, *Star Woman and Other Shawnee Tales*, for drawing attention to Trowbridge's important collection.

30. For Shawnee travel, see Beckner, "John D. Shane's Interview with Ben-

jamin Allen," 77; narrative of Joseph Jackson, 1844, Boone Papers, 11C62; Johnston, *Narrative*, 39; Edgar, *Ten Years of Upper Canada*, 378; Kinietz and Voegelin, *Shawnese Traditions*, 47; Harrington Ms., "Shawnee Indian Notes," 42–43; Wilcox, *Ohio Indian Trails*; and Clark, "Shawnee Indian Migration."

31. Sipe, *Indian Chiefs of Pennsylvania*, 268. The components of "Mspeleaweesepe" are "ms" (big), "peleawee" (turkey), and "sepe" (river). Nine contemporary or near contemporary vocabularies of the Shawnee language were used for this study: "Vocabulary of the Shawanese language, taken down by means of a white woman who had been 20 years a prisoner with that nation, by the Revd. John Heckewelder," Indian Language Papers; Jasper Yeates, "A List of Shawnee Words, 1776," Ayer Manuscripts; glossary supplied by the "Grenadier Squaw," 1786, in Denny, *Military Journal*, 277–81; vocabulary from Thomas Ridoubt, 1788, in Edgar, *Ten Years of Upper Canada*, 376–81; a list of words in Long, *Voyages and Travels*, 209; vocabulary in Johnston, "Account," 287–92; Kinietz and Voegelin, *Shawnese Traditions*, 16–17, 52–53, 66–71; a vocabulary of 1854, Galloway, *Old Chillicothe*, 316–19; and the listing given in Schoolcraft, *Information Respecting the History*, 2:471–81.

## 2. Beginnings

1. The Shawnee resettlement of the Ohio is treated by Hanna, *Wilderness Trail*; Downes, *Council Fires*; Voegelin and Tanner, *Indians of Ohio and Indiana Prior to 1795*; and McConnell, *A Country Between*. The number of Ohio Shawnees is given as 905 (return, 1781, Haldimand Papers, 21769:122); 905 with a further 46 among the Iroquois (Britain/Colonial Office Papers, CO 42/49:442); 949 (return of Indians at Swan Creek, 4 December 1794, Claus Papers, 6:291); 810 (Johnston, "Account," 270); and 800 (return of 1825, *Niles' Register* 27 [1824–25]: 364–65).

2. Barnhart, *Henry Hamilton and George Rogers Clark*, 141; Charles A. Stuart to Lyman C. Draper, 17 February 1846, Kentucky Papers, 8CC59; account of Thomas S. Hinde, Hinde Papers, 16Y45–51.

3. Samuel Drake to Anthony Wayne, 30 June 1795, and Thomas Hunt to Wayne, 22 July 1795, Wayne Papers (1); speech of Red Pole, 2 December 1796, Adams Papers, reel 384, pp. 42–43; letter to James McHenry, 27 January 1797, *Hazard's Register of Pennsylvania* 12 (1833): 63; minutes of the treaty of Greenville, 16 June–12 August 1795, ASPIA, 1:581. Musquaconocah was generally translated as Red or Painted Pole, but it may have meant Reed Pool, from "miskeque" (pool). He was termed Reed Pool in the commissary records of Fort Greenville in 1796 (27 February and 13 July 1796, U.S. Army Records, box 1, folders 7, 11).

4. Yeates, "Indian Treaty," 484–85; Barnhart, *Henry Hamilton and George Rogers Clark*, 141; Wallace, *Thirty Thousand Miles with John Heckewelder*, 313; Kappler, *Indian Affairs, Laws and Treaties*, 2:44, 78.

5. Diary of a march to Fort Recovery, June 1794, *Simcoe*, 5:90–94; George Ironside to Alexander McKee, 6 March 1795, Canada/Indian Affairs Papers, 9:8840; instructions to Matthew Elliott, May 1795, Claus Papers, 7:46. The reference is to Whitmore Knaggs, a settler of the lower Maumee River.

6. Kinietz and Voegelin, *Shawnese Traditions*, 26–27; White, *Lewis Henry Morgan*, 45–47. Blue Jacket's paternal grandson, Charles Blue-Jacket (the son of George Blue-Jacket), who was born in 1817, inherited the rabbit clan through the male line (Spencer, "Shawnee Indians," 394). By the mid-nineteenth century clan affiliation among the Shawnees was beginning to change and was no longer necessarily inherited from the father.

7. For an appreciation of pan-tribal movements, see Wallace, "Political Organization"; Spicer, *Short History*; Jennings, *Ambiguous Iroquois Empire*; Dowd, *Spiritual Resistance*; White, *Middle Ground*; and Sugden, *Tecumseh*.

8. James Hamilton to George Clinton, 20 September 1750, MPCPA, 5:464; proceedings at Lancaster, July 1748, and at Philadelphia, 14 November 1753, MPCPA, 5:307, 665; Shawnees to Hamilton, 8 February 1752, MPCPA, 5:569; William Trent journal, 1752, in Hanna, *Wilderness Trail*, 2:297; Corkran, *Creek Frontier*, 118–19. An excellent account of the Ohio Confederacy is given by McConnell, *Country Between*.

9. Speech of Canajachanah, 7 June 1750, MPCPA, 5:438.

10. These conflicts are treated by Sipe, *Indian Wars*; Tootle, "Anglo-Indian Relations"; Jennings, *Empire of Fortune*; Parkman, *Conspiracy of Pontiac*; Peckham, *Pontiac and the Indian Uprising*; and McConnell, "Search for Security." During the Indian uprising of 1763, which followed the French and Indian War, nine forts fell to Indian attack and two withstood siege. See Tanner, *Atlas*, maps 9–10.

11. Moore, "Early Recollections of Nancy Stewart"; John H. Renick interviewed by Lyman C. Draper (1866), Draper Notes, 21S95; notes of Samuel Kercheval, based on interviews in Virginia, 1830s, Draper notes, 31S404; land grant to Nancy Moore, 2 October 1810, Recorder's Office, Logan County, Bellefontaine, Ohio.

12. There is evidence that McKee was himself a mixed-blood, the son of an Irish merchant and a Shawnee woman. He married a Shawnee and wielded great influence with the tribe. "Mr. McKee appears to be a sensible man, and much of the gentleman," wrote a British officer. "His influence with the Shawaneese nation is beyond conception. They solely confide in him" (Arent De Peyster to Frederick Haldimand, 10 March 1780, Haldimand Papers, 21782:327). See also George Croghan to William Johnson, 18 September 1769, JP, 7:182; Coates, "Narrative of an Embassy to the Western Tribes," 105; Indian council, September to October 1792, Canada/Indian Affairs Papers, 8:8250; DCB, 4:499–500; and Hoberg, "Early History of Colonel Alexander McKee" and "Tory in the Old Northwest." For Elliott, see Horsman, *Matthew Elliott*. John Johnston to Draper, 10 July 1848, Tecumseh Papers, 11Y33, stated that Blue Jacket was related to both Elliott and McKee through their Shawnee wives. Because Johnston was a former Indian agent to the Shawnees, his testimony carries weight, but I have found nothing in the correspondence of the two agents to support the claim.

13. DCB, 4:38–40; Britain/Colonial Office Papers, CO 42/316:7.

14. Denny, *Military Journal*, 82–83 (quotation); Charles Blue-Jacket interviewed by Draper (1868), Draper Notes, 23S167; Peter Navarre, Nannette Cald-

well, Joseph Evans, Mrs. Pelage Drouillard, and Capt. William Caldwell, all interviewed by Draper (1863), Draper Notes, 17S135, 17S175, 17S181, 17S185, and 17S212; Jacob Lindley diary, 10 July 1793, *MPHS* 17:607; Denissen, *Genealogy*, 1:32; *Old Record of the Captivity of Margaret Erskine*, 20; William Walker to Draper, 19 October 1870, Frontier Wars Papers, 11U82; and Spencer, *Indian Captivity*, 91. Jim Blue-Jacket was shorter than his younger brother, George, who grew to be tall and thin, but both seem to have been the sons of Miss Baby.

15. Jones, *Journal of Two Visits*, 52–54. A map of the region by St. John de Crèvecoeur, published in Paris in 1787, has Blue Jacket's town on the west bank of the head of Deer Creek (Hanna, *Wilderness Trail*, 2:386). There were then also four Shawnee towns on the Muskingum (Olmstead, *David Zeisberger*, 200–201).

16. Hardman's earlier name was "Bittaamaugh" (Raccoon Caught in a Trap), which indicates that he belonged to the raccoon clan (Yeates, "Indian Treaty," 484–85). He was the son of a former Shawnee head civil chief named Kakowatchiky, who died about 1755 (Schaaf, *Wampum Belts and Peace Trees*, 136). This gives a weak but unique clue to Blue Jacket's birthplace, for Kakowatchiky's band of Shawnees is known to have contained Pekowis. The relationship between Kakowatchiky's son and Blue Jacket might suggest that they originated in the same band and that Blue Jacket was one of Kakowatchiky's Pekowis. If so, Blue Jacket would probably have been born at Kakowatchiky's town at Shawnee Flats, on the north branch of the Susquehanna, below present-day Plymouth, Pennsylvania. The band occupied the site from about 1728 to about 1743 and then relocated to Logstown on the Ohio. Both sites were in western Pennsylvania. For Kakowatchiky, see Sipe, *Indian Chiefs of Pennsylvania*, 102–9, and Wallace, *Indians in Pennsylvania*, 122–23, 174.

17. Jacob Lindley diary, 9 July 1793, *MPHS* 17:606; Joseph Moore diary, 9 July 1793, *MPHS*, 17:649; Joseph Wade interviewed by Draper (1863), Draper Notes, 19S147.

18. Spencer, *Indian Captivity*, 89–93.

## 3. Defending the Dark and Bloody Ground

1. Johnston, "Account," 297–99, errs in saying that "Kentucky" is derived from a Shawnee word. I am indebted to Helen Hornbeck Tanner and William N. Fenton for this clarification.

2. Joseph Jackson (Boone Papers, 11C62) describes the ferry. Born in Virginia in 1755, Jackson was captured by Shawnees in 1778 and remained with them for many years. He was adopted by a woman related to Chief Blackbeard, who married the French trader Louis Lorimier. Jackson's own Shawnee daughter married Cutemwha, a son of Chief Cornstalk. He was interviewed by Lyman Draper in 1844 and committed suicide by hanging himself a short time afterward: report of Jackson, 1 May 1799, Claus Papers, 8:89; John Johnston to Draper, 27 April 1849, Tecumseh Papers, 11YY37. His narrative is a valuable inside account of the wars of the Shawnees, but Jackson was eighty-eight when he gave it and shows some confusion.

3. Useful accounts of colonial expansion are Abernethy, *Western Lands and the American Revolution*; Sosin, *Revolutionary Frontier*; and Rice, *Frontier Kentucky*.

4. Johnson to Hillsborough, 4 April 1774, O'Callaghan, *Documents*, 8:290. Most of the documents used for this chapter can be found in *JP*, vols. 6–12; *MPCPA*, vol. 9; *DAR*, vols. 2–6; Force, *American Archives*, 4th ser., vol. 1; Craig, *Olden Time*, vol. 2; O'Callaghan, *Documents*, vol. 8; Fliegel, compiler, *Index to the Records of the Moravian Missions*; and Thwaites and Kellogg, *Documentary History of Dunmore's War*. For British frontier policy, see Sosin, *Whitehall and the Wilderness* and "British Indian Department"; and Jones, *License for Empire*. Downes, *Council Fires*; Voegelin and Tanner, *Indians of Ohio and Indiana Prior to 1795*, vol. 2; Stevens, "His Majesty's 'Savage' Allies"; White, *Middle Ground*; and McConnell, *Country Between*, are essential to an understanding of the Indian perspective.

5. Deposition of Samuel Wilson, 15 April 1777, *VSP*, 1:282.

6. Proceedings at Fort Pitt, April–May 1768, *MPCPA*, 9:514; Olmstead, *David Zeisberger*, 212–13.

7. John Stuart to Hillsborough, 6 February 1772, *DAR*, 5:33. Documents illustrating Shawnee diplomacy are too numerous to be cited here, but they run as a thread through such sources as *DAR*, vols. 2, 3, 5, 6; *JP*, vols. 7, 8, 12; O'Callaghan, *Documents*, vol. 8; and *MPCPA*, vol. 9.

8. James O'Donnell, "Logan's Oration: A Case Study in Ethnographic Authentication," *Quarterly Journal of Speech* 65 (1979): 150–56. John Logan (whose Indian name was Tachnechdorus, meaning Spreading Out) was a man of outstanding qualities destroyed by the tragedy that overcame his family. He descended into brooding alcoholism. John Heckewelder, who met him, described the "deep melancholy" that had turned his life into "a torment" (Wallace, *Indians in Pennsylvania*, 175).

9. Johnston to Lyman C. Draper, 10 July 1848, Tecumseh Papers, 11YY33.

10. Jacob, *Biographical Sketch of the Life of the Late Captain Michael Cresap*, 71–72; Kercheval, *History of the Valley of Virginia*, 172; Lewis to Samuel Campbell, "A Letter from the Late Colonel Andrew Lewis," *Virginia Historical Register and Literary Advertiser* 1 (1848): 30–33; Samuel Murphey interviewed by Draper (1846), Draper Notes, 3S2.

11. For the medicine bundle, see Loskiel, *History of the Mission of the United Brethren*, 145.

12. Quotations from William Christian to William Preston, 15 October 1774, and W. Ingles to Preston, 14 October 1774, in Thwaites and Kellogg, *Documentary History of Dunmore's War*, 261, 257.

13. Fleming to William Bowyer, October 1774, in Thwaites and Kellogg, *Documentary History of Dunmore's War*, 254; John Stuart, "Memoir of Indian Wars and Other Occurrences," 35–68.

14. Dunmore to the Earl of Dartmouth, 24 December 1774, in Thwaites and Kellogg, *Documentary History of Dunmore's War*, 368.

15. Shawnee speech, 26 June 1775, Haldimand Papers, 21845:483; James Wood's journal, July-August 1775, in Thwaites and Kellogg, *Revolution on the Upper Ohio*,

56–63.

16. Williams, "Journal of Richard Butler," 144–51; William Russell to William Fleming, 12 June 1775, in Thwaites and Kellogg, *Revolution on the Upper Ohio*, 12.

17. Williams, "Journal of Richard Butler," 394–95.

## 4. The Second War for Kentucky

1. Journal, 1775, in Thwaites and Kellogg, *Revolution on the Upper Ohio*, 41; accounts of Alexander McKee, Claus Papers, 1:180; Fliegel, *Index to the Records of the Moravian Missions*, 1044–45; Olmstead, *David Zeisberger*, 239.

2. Volney, *Views of the Soil and Climate*, 380.

3. For primary sources relating to the Revolutionary War I have principally used Davies, *Documents of the American Revolution* (DAR); Haldimand Papers, vols. 21760, 21769, 21782–83, 21842, and 21845; Claus Papers, vols. 1–2; Force, *American Archives*, 4th ser., vols. 5–6, and 5th ser., vols. 2–3; VSP, vols. 2–3; Morgan Papers; Thwaites and Kellogg, *Revolution on the Upper Ohio* and *Frontier Defense*; Kellogg, *Frontier Advance* and *Frontier Retreat*; James, *Clark Papers*; Yeates Papers; and the Daniel Boone (C), George Rogers Clark (J), and Kentucky (CC) papers in the Draper collections. There are numerous valuable secondary works, but particularly useful for the Shawnees are Butterfield, *History of the Girtys*; Bakeless, *Master of the Wilderness*; Downes, *Council Fires*; Talbert, *Benjamin Logan*; Horsman, *Matthew Elliott*; Stevens, "His Majesty's 'Savage' Allies"; Schaaf, *Wampum Belts and Peace Trees*; White, *Middle Ground*; Calloway, *American Revolution in Indian Country*; and Sugden, *Tecumseh*.

4. Williams, "Journal of Richard Butler," 32–33; Cresswell, *Journal*, 114–22; William Wilson, 7 October 1775, Haldimand Papers, 21845:488; Fliegel, *Index to the Records of the Moravian Missions*, 1045; and documents in Thwaites and Kellogg, *Revolution on the Upper Ohio*, 25–127, 155–56, and Force, *American Archives*, 4th ser., 5:815, and 6:541, 542.

5. Schaaf, *Wampum Belts and Peace Trees*, 165–66, 184–96, 195–96 (quotation); typescript of Morgan Letterbook, 1776, following p. 28; deposition of John Montour, 2 October 1776, and other documents in Yeates Papers; Yeates, "Indian Treaty of Fort Pitt"; Fliegel, *Index to the Records of the Moravian Missions*, 93, 1045; Olmstead, *David Zeisberger*, 242.

6. The new locations are described in Voegelin and Tanner, *Indians of Ohio and Indiana Prior to 1795*, 2:237–42, 259–76, and Tanner, *Atlas*, map 16, and revised by Sugden, *Tecumseh*, 30–31. See also Rachel Reno interviewed by Lyman C. Draper, 1863, Draper Notes, 17S81.

7. For the death of Cornstalk, see Matthew Arbuckle to Edward Hand; 6 October, 7 November 1777, Thwaites and Kellogg, *Frontier Defense*, 125, 149; deposition of John Anderson, William Ward, and Richard Thomas, 10 November 1777, Thwaites and Kellogg, *Frontier Defense*, 162; and Stuart, "Memoir of Indian Wars." Attempts to appease the Indians are revealed by documents in Thwaites and Kellogg, *Frontier Defense*, 175, 188, 189, 205, 223, 235, 240, 241, 244, 258. For the Mekoches settling with the Delawares, see Thwaites and Kellogg, *Frontier Defense*,

164; Kellogg, *Frontier Advance*, 142; messages of the Delawares (26 February 1777) and Shawnees (28 February 1777), Morgan Papers; and Olmstead, *David Zeisberger*, 275.

8. Alexander McKee to Matthew Elliott, May 1795, Claus Papers, 7:46.

9. Roll of officers, 5 September 1778, Haldimand Papers, 21782:96; minutes of Indian council at Detroit, 26 April 1781, Haldimand Papers, 21783: 29; Henry Bird, 16 August 1780, Claus Papers, 2:243.

10. Mrs. Ledwell and Joseph Ferris interviewed by Draper, 1863, Draper Notes, 17S200; *Old Record of the Captivity of Margaret Erskine*, 20; Moore, "Captive of the Shawnees," 291.

11. Andrews, "Shaker Mission to the Shawnee Indians," 127; Badger, *Memoir*, 29.

12. Some secondary accounts have Blue Jacket as one of the leaders of the force that captured Boone's party in 1778. The accounts of this, from Boone himself in Filson, *Discovery*, and other sources (*Clark Papers*, 1:41; Thwaites and Kellogg, *Frontier Defense*, 250; Henry Hamilton to Guy Carleton, 26 January–25 April 1778, Haldimand Papers, 21782:29; Stevens, *Louis Lorimier*, 15; Dann, *Revolution Remembered*, 280–82; and the narrative of Joseph Jackson, Boone Papers, 11C62), do not mention Blue Jacket, although he could have been among the eighty Chillicothes and Pekowis present. The statement may, however, have originated in the interview given Draper by Christopher Wood in 1852 (Kenton Papers 8BB27), in which case it is baseless, since Wood clearly confused Blue Jacket with Blackfish.

Blue Jacket has also been linked with the captivity of Simon Kenton, who was taken in September 1778 while running off Indian horses north of the Ohio. According to a son (William Kenton, interviewed by Draper, 1851, Draper Notes, 5S96, 149), Kenton once tried to escape but was intercepted by Blue Jacket and a party of mounted warriors, and although Kenton met Blue Jacket in later years he never liked him. Kenton made no reference to Blue Jacket in the account he gave John H. James in 1832 (Kenton Papers, 5BB100), and I suspect that there is no foundation to the story.

13. I wrote an exploratory sketch of Buckongahelas for *ANB*, 3:867–69, but he merits a more extensive treatment.

14. Few of the Wabash and Illinois Indians had been attending Hamilton's councils. See councils, 14–20 June 1778, 26 January 1779, Haldimand Papers, 21782:45, 55, 181; Barnhart, *Henry Hamilton and George Rogers Clark*, 168–70.

15. McKee to Richard Berenger Lernoult, 25 October 1778, Haldimand Papers, 21760:72; Hamilton to Carleton, 15 January 1778, Haldimand Papers, 21782:22; return, 24 December 1778, Haldimand Papers, 21782:170; Barnhart, *Henry Hamilton and George Rogers Clark*, 104–5, 118–19. I am indebted to Helen Hornbeck Tanner for drawing my attention to Hamilton's references to Blue Jacket. Hamilton's journal, reprinted in Barnhart, is the main source for this expedition, but see also Hamilton to Haldimand, 18–30 December 1778, Haldimand Papers, 21782:157; map of Fort Sackville, 1779, Haldimand Papers, 21782:167; and *Clark Papers*, 1:174.

16. Egushaway is treated by Bauman, "Pontiac's Successor," Horsman (*DCB*), and Sugden (*ANB*).

17. Hamilton journal, 15–16 January 1779, in Barnhart, *Henry Hamilton and George Rogers Clark*, 164–65, and Hamilton to Haldimand, 18–30 December 1778, Haldimand Papers, 21782:157.

18. Kellogg, *Frontier Advance*, 349; Haldimand Papers, 21760:48, 137, 167, and 21782:259, 278.

19. Joseph Jackson (Boone Papers, 11C62) says the party settled above Cape Girardeau (Missouri) on Spanish land grants, but he was nearly ninety when he made the statement and confused. The contemporary record confirms the emigration of a party of Shawnees but implies they were heading south, probably to what is now Alabama (Alexander Cameron to Lord George Germain, 18 July 1780, *DAR*, 18:120). Louis Lorimier settled Shawnees and Delawares in the Cape Girardeau region from 1787: Sugden, *Tecumseh*, 52–53, and my sketch of Lorimier in *ANB*, 13:921–22.

20. Letters relating to the defeat of the convoy under Col. David Rogers are filed in Haldimand Papers, 21760:244, 248, and 21782:287, 289, and in Claus Papers, 2:139. For the Shawnee lobbying of the British and its results, see McKee to De Peyster, and De Peyster to M. Bolton, 6 January, 10 March 1780, Haldimand Papers, 21760:269, 273; Lernoult's speech to the Shawnees, 19 July 1779, Haldimand Papers, 21782:246; speeches at Sandusky, Chillicothe, Pekowi, and Wakatomica, December 1779–January 1780, Haldimand Papers, 21782:302–8; De Peyster to Haldimand, 8 March 1780, Haldimand Papers, 21782:321; De Peyster to McKee, 2 November 1779, Claus Papers, 2:139.

21. The "defection" of the neutral Shawnees may have had something to do with the death of Nimwha; see Mekoches to Delawares, February 1780, in Kellogg, *Frontier Retreat*, 139.

22. Sources for Bird's campaign are De Peyster to McKee, 4 April, 8 May, 22 June 1780, Claus Papers, 2:197, 221, 231; Bird to McKee, 16 August 1780, Claus Papers, 2:243; Haldimand to Lord George Germain, 25 October 1780, *DAR*, 18:208; dispatches in Haldimand Papers, 21760:281, 285, 291, 315, 316, 325, 326, 331, 338; Talbert, *Benjamin Logan*, 105–7.

23. The defeat of William Crawford's militia on the Sandusky on 4–6 June 1782 is dealt with in documents in Haldimand Papers, 21783:153, 157, 169; Butterfield, *Washington-Irvine Correspondence*, 370; *Clark Papers*, 2:71, 76, 79; Cornelius Quick interviewed by Draper (1849), Brady and Wetzel Papers, 10E155; *VSP*, 3:232; and the narrative of John Slover, *Pennsylvania Archives*, 2nd ser. 14:717.

24. Sugden, *Tecumseh*, 35–37; *VSP*, 3:571, 601.

25. Daniel Brodhead to George Rogers Clark, 20 May 1780, *Clark Papers*, 1:419; Valentine Dalton to Clark, 29 October 1782, *Clark Papers*, 2:145; Peter Hare to De Peyster, and McKee to John Johnson, both 15 September 1780, Haldimand Papers, 21760:363, 364; minutes of Detroit councils, 5, 26 April 1781, Haldimand Papers, 21783:18, 29; Stevens, *Louis Lorimier*, 17–18.

26. Speech of Snake, 7 June 1782, in Butterfield, *Washington-Irvine Correspondence*, 369; De Peyster to McKee, 11 June 1782, Claus Papers, 3:123; William

Caldwell to McKee, 4 July 1782, Claus Papers, 3:137; black's statement, 7 August 1782, Irvine Papers, IAA275; Irvine to George Washington, 11 July 1782, *Clark Papers*, 2:76. Irvine remarked that John Slover, who had just escaped from the Shawnees, verified the black's report: "Mr. Slover was present when I examined the Negro. He says he lived in the family with him at the town, and thinks he may be depended on." This indicates that Blue Jacket's family may have tried to adopt Slover. In his own narrative, cited in note 23, Slover refers to "the squaw with whom I lived" and does not mention Blue Jacket.

27. William Christian to Benjamin Harrison, 28 September 1782, *VSP*, 3:331.

28. Andrew Steele to Benjamin Harrison, 12 September 1782, *VSP*, 3:303.


### 5. Trouble Is Coming upon Us Fast

1. For peace negotiations involving the Shawnees, see *Clark Papers*, 2:218; *VSP*, 3:521, 531; Haldimand Papers, 21763:25, 84, 90, 125, 129, 131, 207; and Alexander McKee to Simon Girty, 14 May 1783, Claus Papers, 3:219. Useful studies of British and American policies toward the Indians at the end of the Revolution are Burt, *The United States, Great Britain and British North America*; Horsman, *Matthew Elliott* and *Expansion and American Indian Policy*; Wright, *Britain and the American Frontier*; Calloway, *Crown and Calumet*; and Allen, *His Majesty's Indian Allies*.

2. Minutes of Indian congress, 26 August–8 September 1783, Britain/Colonial Office Papers, CO 42/45:9; McKee to John Johnson, 9 September 1783, Britain/Colonial Office Papers, CO 42/45:17; and Shawnee statements of 5 September 1783 (Haldimand Papers, 21763:248) and 9 August 1793 (Brant journal, Canada/Indian Affairs Papers, 8:8466). Isabel Thompson Kelsay has produced the standard life of Brant, but the earlier biograhies by William Leete Stone (1838) and Marc Jack Smith are well worth consulting.

3. The little-known paper by Wallace, "Political Organization," develops this, among other valuable insights into pan-Indianism.

4. My source for the Shawnees in the South is Joseph to Alexander Martin, 1784, in Clark, *State Records of North Carolina*, 16:924.

5. Anthony Wayne to Henry Knox, 12 February 1795, in Knopf, *Anthony Wayne*, 384; McKee, instructions to Matthew Elliott, May 1795, Claus Papers, 7:46. Blue Jacket's father-in-law, Jacques Baby, who headed the British Indian department at Detroit until 1785, when he was evidently succeeded by McKee, was a continuing contact between the Shawnee chief and the British; see "List of officers," January 1784, Britain/Colonial Office Papers, CO 42/46:105; Henry Hope to Evan Nepean, 31 August 1785, Britain/Colonial Office Papers, CO 42/17:252.

6. *VSP*, 3:536, 537, 548, 558, 565, 575.

7. Horsman, *Expansion and American Indian Policy*, 19. Material on the Fort Stanwix treaty can be found in Kappler, *Indian Affairs*, 2:6; Henry S. Manley, *The Treaty of Fort Stanwix* (Rome NY: Rome Sentinel Co., 1932), and Graymont, *Iroquois in the American Revolution*, chap. 10.

8. Major Snake, Thomas Snake, Captain Johnny, and Chiaxey to McKee, received 11 April 1785, Additional Manuscripts, 24322:98.

9. Wakatomica council, 18 May 1785, Britain/Colonial Office Papers, CO 42/47:370; McKee to John Johnson, 29 May 1785, Britain/Colonial Office Papers, CO 42/47:364. In his reminiscences of the council, given many years later, John Crawford, then a prisoner in Wakatomica, identifies Blue Jacket as the principal speaker, but the contemporary materials are clear that it was Captain Johnny (Kentucky Papers, 12CC159).

10. Daniel Elliott and James Ranken to U.S. commissioners, enclosing Indian speeches, 1785, Draper Notes, 14S195.

11. Speech of Snake, November 1785, Britain/Colonial Office Papers, CO 42/49:21. This paragraph also depends on accounts in Britain/Colonial Office Papers, CO 42/48:121, 162, 164, 184, 211, and CO 42/49:258; *ASPIA*, 1:38; Draper Notes, 12S36, 14S225; Smith, *St. Clair Papers*, 2:632; and Bushnell, "Journey Through the Indian Country Beyond the Ohio," 261–73.

12. The proceedings at Fort Finney are drawn from Richard Butler's journal, October 1785–February 1786, Durrett Manuscripts, and Denny, *Military Journal*. See also Kappler, *Indian Affairs*, 2:16; *Carlisle Gazette and the Western Repository of Knowledge*, 1 March 1786.

13. *Minutes of Debates in Council on the Banks of the Ottawa River*, 9.

14. Speech of Shawnee chiefs, 29 April 1786, Britain/Colonial Office Papers, CO 42/49:349.

15. Denny, *Military Journal*, 80–87; *Carlisle Gazette*, 17 May 1786; Beatty, "Diary," 178.

16. "Instances of Penetration in an Indian," *Western Review and Miscellaneous Magazine* 2 (1820): 168.

17. Denny, *Military Journal*, 82–84; Walter Finney to Clark, April 1786, Clark Papers, 53J30; E. Beatty to John Armstrong, 14 June 1786, Armstrong Papers.

18. Josiah Harmar, 15 June 1788, in Smith, *St. Clair Papers*, 2:44; "Observations upon the Colony of Kentucky," Britain/Colonial Office Papers, CO 42/65:91.

19. *Virginia Gazette or American Advertiser* (Richmond), 17 May 1786; *Carlisle Gazette*, 8, 15 November 1786; Clark to Patrick Henry, May 1786, *VSP*, 4:122; information of Captain Tunis, 6 July 1786, and of Joseph Saunders, 24 July 1786, Harmar Papers, 1W155, 1W185; Joseph Brant to John Butler, 10 September 1786, Britain/Colonial Office Papers, CO 42/49:433; John Hart to John Doughty, 27 April 1786, Armstrong Papers.

20. Jean Marie Phillipe Le Gras to Clark, 22 July 1786, in Kinnaird, *Spain in the Mississippi Valley*, 2:175.

21. Leonard C. Helderman, ed., "Danger on the Wabash: Vincennes Letters of 1786," *Indiana Magazine of History* 34 (1938): 455–67; *MPHS*, 24:29; Smith, *St. Clair Papers*, 2:26; and White, *Middle Ground*, 422–33. Daniel Strother, a black man then in Vincennes and sometimes residing with Le Gras, one of the French settlers who negotiated with the Indians, said in an account he gave when he was about eighty years old, that Blue Jacket and the Crane led the Indians (Strother, interviewed by Lyman C. Draper, 1846, Clark Papers, 8J43). Yet again the account

suggests the dangers of using evidence recalled long after the event, even by genuine eyewitnesses. In fact, the Indians seem to have been Wabash Indians, and the Crane belonged to the peaceful faction of the Sandusky Wyandots. Strother seems to have simply selected famous Indian names.

22. Sugden, *Tecumseh*, 46–47.

23. William North, 7 August 1786, Northwest Territory Collection (IHS).

### 6. The War for Ohio

1. Josiah Collins interviewed by John D. Shane (1840s), Kentucky Papers, 12CC72; Rachel Reno interviewed by Lyman C. Draper (1863), Draper Notes, 17S281.

2. Minutes of Indian congress, 28 November–18 December 1786, Frontier Wars Papers, 23U39; united Indian nations to United States, 18 December 1786, Britain/Colonial Office Papers, CO 42/50:70; documents in Britain/Colonial Office Papers, CO 42/49:433, and CO 42/50:1, 74, and in Claus Papers, 4:131, 149.

3. Lord Dorchester to Lord Sydney, 16 January 1787, 9 June 1788, Britain/Colonial Office Papers, CO 42/50:25, and CO 42/59:116; Sydney to Dorchester, 5 April, 14 September 1787, Britain/Colonial Office Papers, CO 42/50:37, and 42/51:40; Stone, *Life of Joseph Brant*, 2:270.

4. Dorchester to Sydney, 15 July 1789, Britain/Colonial Office Papers, CO 42/65:3; Quaife, "Henry Hay's Journal," 217, 223, 226, 234, 247–49, 255–58; John Armstrong's journal, 17 October 1790, and Josiah Harmar's journal, 17–18 October 1790, in Meek, "General Harmar's Expedition," 82–83, 92; Smith, *St. Clair Papers*, 2:99; *Kentucky Gazette*, 25 August 1787; George Ironside, 15 April 1787, Lasselle Papers (1); and Thornbrough, *Outpost on the Wabash*, 58, 76. Although Hay refers to him as Blackbird, this chief may have been the man usually known as Blackbeard, although Blackbird's town was called Chillicothe, and Blackbeard was, by his own statement, a Mekoche (Blackbeard's speech, February 1807, Shawnee File). The letter John Cleves Symmes wrote to the Shawnee chiefs on 5 June 1789 (Claus Papers, 4:175) establishes that Blackbeard was identical with the Shawnee named Nenessica. Blackbeard had been a leading chief in the Revolutionary War and was present at the siege of Boonesborough in 1778. He led a successful raid on some flatboats on the Ohio in 1788 and remained hostile to the Americans even after the treaty of Greenville in 1795. When he did join the more pacific Shawnees at Wapakoneta, about 1800, he supported the established chiefs, visiting Washington in 1806–7 and opposing Tecumseh and the Prophet. Nevertheless, the British still regarded him as "a very confidential man" and summoned him to Fort Malden in 1808, when they were trying to resuscitate the British-Indian alliance. He had visited the Cherokees in 1794, and the British employed him to carry an alliance belt to them. Then of a great age, he returned from the trip in 1809, worn out by his labors, and apparently died shortly afterward. See narrative of Joseph Jackson, 1844, Boone Papers, 11C62; Edgar, *Ten Years of Upper Canada*, 339–56; council proceedings, June 1797, Canada/Military Papers, C 250:233; Francis Gore to James Craig, 27 July 1808, Canada/Indian

Affairs Papers, 11:9901; and Matthew Elliott to William Claus, 28 June 1809, Canada/Indian Affairs Papers, 11:10040.

5. Levi Todd to Beverley Randolph, 12 May 1788, *VSP* 4:438; Edgar, *Ten Years of Upper Canada*, 366.

6. John Murphy interviewed by Draper (1846), Clark Papers, 8J64. Murphy believed Hubbs had been captured in the raid in which William Christian and Isaac Kelly were fatally wounded in April 1786, but contemporaries attributed that to Wabash tribesmen, not Shawnees (*VSP*, 4:119).

7. For Blue Jacket at Limestone, see Todd to Randolph, 12 May 1788, *VSP*, 4:438; A. Nicholson interviewed by Draper (1858), Draper Notes, 7S33; and John Hanks interviewed by John D. Shane (1840s), Kentucky Papers, 12CC140. Lewis Collins, *Historical Sketches of Kentucky* (Cincinnati: Collins and James, 1848), 431, says that Blue Jacket promised to assist the citizens of Limestone thereafter and shortly redeemed the pledge by getting a local man, Samuel Blackburn, released. Other materials on the exchange are in the Patterson Papers, 1MM162, 2MM6, 2MM7; Harmar Papers, 1W284; Draper Notes, 18S168, 23S167, 23S172; Frontier Wars Papers, 7U9, 7U83, 7U124; Kenton Papers, 9BB7; *VSP*, 4:344; *Kentucky Gazette*, 25 August 1787; Bushnell, "Daniel Boone at Limestone"; Talbert, *Benjamin Logan*, 215–21.

Both captive Shawnee boys had distinguished careers. The elder, Peter Cornstalk, was released in 1789, aged about fifteen. He married a girl who had shared his captivity and became a notable chief and orator. He signed treaties in 1814, 1817, 1825, and 1831 and as the head of a family of seven left Ohio for Kansas in 1832. In 1841 he opposed selling tribal land to the Wyandots. Remembered as a big, good-looking, honest man, he appeared by his Indian name, Wynepuechsika, on the 1814 treaty. His brother Nerupeneshequah also used the name Cornstalk, although the boys do not appear to have been sons of the famous chief of that name; see John Johnston to Draper, 1 December 1850, Tecumseh Papers, 11YY40; return of emigrants, 3 December 1832, Shawnee Papers; Harvey, *History of the Shawnee Indians*, chap. 40; George W. Hill, "The History of the Shawnees," in *History of Defiance Couinty, Ohio* (Chicago, 1883), 33–55; Sugden, *Tecumseh*, 100. The other boy, James Logan (ca. 1776–1812), made a good warrior and died in American service during the War of 1812. See my sketch in *ANB*, 13:837–39.

8. The contemporary report of Todd to Randolph, 12 May 1788, *VSP*, 4:438; John D. Shane's 1840s interviews with William Clinckinbeard, Benjamin Allen, William Sudduth, John Hanks, and Thomas Jones, all eyewitnesses, in Kentucky Papers, 11CC64, 11CC78, 12CC74, 12CC140, and 12CC233; and Christopher Wood, interviewed by Draper (1852), Kenton Papers, 8BB50. Secondhand accounts are filed in Draper Notes, 21S187, 21S227, and 25S247, and in Kenton Papers, 3BB68.

9. John Hanks interviewed by Shane, 1840s, Kentucky Papers, 12CC140; Arthur Campbell to Edmund Randolph, 5 December 1787, *VSP*, 4:363.

10. Joseph Martin to Edmund Randolph, 28 June 1787, *VSP*, 4:302; Alexander McGillivray to Arturo O'Neill, 20 June 1787, in Caughey, *McGillivray of the Creeks*, 153; John F. Hamtramck to Harmar, 13 April 1788, in Thornbrough, *Outpost on the Wabash*, 67; George Ironside, 16 February 1787, Lasselle Papers (1).

11. Brant to Patrick Langan, 20 March 1788, Stone, *Life of Joseph Brant*, 2:275. Detailed accounts of the Iroquois can be found in Wallace, *Death and Rebirth of the Seneca*; Kelsay, *Joseph Brant*; and Fenton, *Great Law and the Longhouse*.

12. St. Clair to Henry Knox, 18 January 1789, in Smith, *St. Clair Papers*, 2:108. See also Smith, *St. Clair Papers*, 2:81, 84, 95, 99, 101, 106, 109, 111; Thornbrough, *Outpost on the Wabash*, 150; Stone, *Life of Joseph Brant*, 2:276, 277; Kappler, *Indian Affairs*, 2:18; Dorchester to Sydney, 11 October 1788, 10 January, 11 April 1789, Britain/Colonial Office Papers, CO 42/61:98, CO 42/63:130, and CO 42/64:161.

13. Relevant accounts are Bond, *Civilization of the Old Northwest*, Horsman, *Frontier in the Formative Years*, and Scamyhorn and Steinle, *Stockades in the Wilderness*.

14. Sugden, *Tecumseh*, 52–57.

15. Joseph Asheton to Harmar, 26 August 1789, in Thornbrough, *Outpost on the Wabash*, 182n.

16. The calls prophets made for such reforms as the rejection of white influences reflected a latent guilt about the loss of land and the erosion of Indian culture and identity. It was felt that the neglect of ceremonies of worship and the desertion of ways of life ordained for the Indians by the Creator were alienating the spirit world on which the tribes depended. Intermittently such fears were stoked to great intensity by unusual disasters such as epidemics, famines, or earthquakes, which betokened the fury of the Creator and other deities.

In recent years historians have tended to assume rather than to question the *continuing* influence of prophetic nativism, largely following the excellent and eloquent study by Dowd, *Spirited Resistance*. Although Indians always sought and relied on spiritual aid and holy men and women were important in all villages, and although cultural conservatism and nostalgia are typical elements of societies undergoing change, prophetic nativism of the type espoused by Neolin and Lalawéthika (Tenskwatawa), with its fanatical repudiation of Euro-American influences, was not *invariably* an important dimension of Indian resistance. Such prophets represented peaks that were difficult to sustain when the crises that spawned them subsided, the associated fears diminished, and the dictates of the reformers grew onerous. Moreover, there were always very powerful countercurrents, not least the hunger for European manufactures. A cautious study of these events is needed. Some Shawnees were certainly influenced by prophetic nativism in the 1760s and early 1770s and in the opening years of the nineteenth century, but there is no evidence that it was a major force in the intervening period. For details of these movements, see Charles Hunter, "The Delaware Nativist Revival of the Mid-Eighteenth Century," *Ethnohistory* 18 (1971): 39–49; Wallace, "New Religions Among the Delaware Indians" and *Death and Rebirth of the Seneca*; Edmunds, *Shawnee Prophet*; William G. McLoughlin, "New Angles of Vision on the Cherokee Ghost Dance Movement of 1811–1812," *American Indian Quarterly* 5 (1979): 317–46; Joel W. Martin, *Sacred Revolt* (Boston: Beacon Press, 1991); and Dowd, *Spirited Resistance*. Studies that attempt to weigh their influence with other developments include McConnell, "Search for Security"; White, *Middle*

*Ground*; and Sugden, *Tecumseh*. Refreshingly independent is Helen C. Rountree, *Pocahontas's People* (Norman: University of Oklahoma Press, 1994), chap. 4.

17. Edgar, *Ten Years of Upper Canada*, 346; Hamtramck to St. Clair, 19 April 1790, and William St. Clair to St. Clair, 16 May 1790, in Smith, *St. Clair Papers*, 2:135, 143.

18. Samuel McDowell to the governor of Virginia, 26 July 1789, VSP, 5:7; Patterson Papers, 2MM9, 2MM58, 2MM92, and 2MM106; Bond, *Correspondence of John Cleves Symmes*, 53–95, 100–106; Charles Cist, ed., *Cincinnati in 1841* (Cincinnati: Cist, 1841), 228–29; Symmes to Blackbeard, Mahwaawa the King, Captain [Black] Snake, Captain Johnny, and Kelawwase Tom, 5 June 1789, Claus Papers, 4:175; Shawnees to Symmes, 6 July, 4 September 1789, Claus Papers, 4:183, 191; Symmes to Shawnees, 19 July 1789, Claus Papers, 4:184; *Kentucky Gazette*, 1 August, 10 October 1789; Dorchester to Sydney, 25 June 1789, Britain/Colonial Office Papers, CO 42/65:57.

19. Alexander McKee to John Johnson, 5 May 1790, Britain/Colonial Office Papers, CO 42/68:215.

## 7. Tomahawks and Tobacco

1. Minutes of a council, 7 September 1789, Frontier Wars Papers, 23U72; Quaife, "Henry Hay's Journal," 244. A year later Miami chiefs paid the Shawnees a backhanded compliment by referring to them as "the perturbators of all nations" (journal of Antoine Gamelin, 1790, ASPIA, 1:93).

2. Coates, "Narrative of an Embassy to the Western Tribes," 118. Students of Captain Johnny should not be misled by the statements in Denny, *Military Journal*, 59–60, and the Shawnee testimony of 26 June 1794 (ASPIA, 1:489) or confound the chief with the younger Captain Johnny (Sugden, *Tecumseh*, 431 n. 19) or the Delaware chief Captain Johnny. Sources that identify our Captain Johnny as Kekewepelethy are John Cleves Symmes to Shawnees, 5 June 1789, Claus Papers, 4:174; U.S. Commissioners to Secretary of War, 21 August 1793, Wayne Papers (1); journal of Jacob Lindley, 29, 31 July 1793, MPHS, 17:618–19; and Wallace, *Thirty Thousand Miles with John Heckewelder*, 315. Black Snake (Captain Snake, Peteasua) is even harder to identify. John Johnston and Lyman Draper (Tecumseh Papers, 11YY30; Kenton Papers, 1BB80) confuse two individuals of the name Snake. Both were Shawnee chiefs, and although some documents differentiate (Olmstead, *David Zeisberger*, 312; Britain/Colonial Office Papers, CO 42/48:49; *Scioto Gazette* [Chillicothe OH], 10 March 1806; Frontier Wars Papers, 5U184; Thornbrough, *Letter-Book of the Indian Agency*, 45), most refer to one or the other without clarification. As far as I can determine, Black Snake the war chief was alive at least until July 1813. He lost his cousin James Logan in the war (Martin Hardin to Henry Clay, 2 December 1812, Frontier Wars Papers, 7U6; Shawnee chiefs to William Henry Harrison, 17 July 1813, *Supporter* [Chillicothe], 4 August 1813). The other Snake was Shemenatoo (Big Snake), evidently a younger man. He signed treaties in 1814, 1815, and 1817 and died in Kansas in the 1830s. His daughter Nenexse (born about 1797) married the noted Mekoche chief Black Hoof (Draper

Notes, 23S165, 23S167, 23S172, 23S180). For my attempts to extricate Captain Johnny and Black Snake from confusing documents, see Thrapp, *Encyclopaedia*, 4:82–83, 481–82, and the sketches in *ANB*, 12:467–68, and 20:332–33.

3. Alexander McKee to Joseph Chew, 11 April 1794, Canada/Military Papers, C247:102.

4. Klinck and Talman, *Journal of Major John Norton*, 187.

5. *DCB*, 6:101.

6. Denissen, *Genealogy*; Lasselle Papers (1); marriage settlement of Jacques Lasselle and Therese Berthelet, 1765, Lasselle Papers (2); *ASPIA*, 1:494; deposition of Antoine Lasselle, 22 January 1794, Wayne Papers (1); Claus Papers, 5:259; Draper Notes, 17S175; George McDougall to William Woodbridge, 26 February 1820, Woodbridge Papers; and George Sharp, 10 December 1790, McKee Papers.

7. Quaife, "Henry Hay's Journal," 226–27, 230–38, 240–41.

8. Registrations of 1 July 1796, 29 March 1801, registers of St. Anne's Catholic Church, Detroit; Nannette Caldwell interviewed by Draper (1863), Draper Notes, 17S175.

9. Letter from Detroit, 4 May 1788, Britain/Colonial Office Papers, CO 42/59:236; Montreal merchants, 28 November 1790, Britain/Colonial Office Papers, CO 42/73:51.

10. Minutes of a council, 7 September 1789, Frontier Wars Papers, 23U172; Quaife, "Henry Hay's Journal," 244; Shawnee letter, April 1790, Claus Papers, 4:213.

11. For the calumet, see White, *Middle Ground*, 20–22.

12. Henry Stuart to John Stuart, 25 August 1776, *DAR*, 12:191; Draper Notes, 13S207; Schaaf, *Wampum Belts and Peace Trees*, 188–89; Sugden, *Tecumseh*, 284.

13. Journal of Joseph Brant, 26 July 1793, Canada/Indian Affairs Papers, 8:8461.

14. Cherokee address, 6 May 1789, Britain/Colonial Office Papers, CO 42/68:296; Lord Dorchester to Lord Grenville, 26 July 1790, Britain/Colonial Office Papers, CO 42/68:279; Anthony Wayne to Timothy Pickering, 8 March 1795, in Knopf, *Anthony Wayne*, 386.

15. White, *Middle Ground*, 495.

16. For the Miamis, see Voegelin et al., *Miami, Wea and Eel River Indians*. Little Turtle has been the subject of several biographies that claim for him a role in events unsupported by or at variance to historical evidence. He is credited, for example, with defeating Augustine Mottin de La Balme's troops in 1780, but as far as I know his first verified appearance in history is the reference in Hay's journal for 19 December 1789 (Quaife, "Henry Hay's Journal," 218–19). See also Walker, "Plowshares and Pruning Hooks," 382.

17. Council at Huron village, 16 August 1790, Frontier Wars Papers, 23U88.

18. For the Shawnee-Cherokee embassy, see minutes of a council, 7 September 1789, Frontier Wars Papers, 23U172; Joseph Brant to Captain M'Donnell, September 1789, in Stone, *Life of Joseph Brant*, 2:284; speech of Red Pole in Glaize council, 30 September–9 October 1792, *Simcoe*, 1:218.

19. Quaife, "Henry Hay's Journal," 244, 255, 257; Shawnee letter, April 1790, Claus Papers, 4:213; John Francis Hamtramck to Josiah Harmar, 2, 3 August

1790, in Thornbrough, *Outpost on the Wabash*, 242; speech of Farmer's Brother, 14 May 1791, *ASPIA*, 1:164 (quotation); affidavit of John Hardin, 14 September 1791, *ASPIA*, 1:34; Blue Jacket and Little Turtle to McKee, 2 August 1790, McKee Papers. Blue Jacket signed this letter with his initials, "BJ"; Little Turtle signed with his emblem of the turtle. The letter was written in French, probably by one of the Lasselles.

20. Speech of Gamelin, 1790, Claus Papers, 4:201; journal of Gamelin, *ASPIA*, 1:93. The quotations relating to Gamelin's mission are drawn from his journal. See also Smith, *St. Clair Papers*, 2:123, 125, 130, 132.

21. Quaife, "Henry Hay's Journal," 259; Smith, *St. Clair Papers*, 2:135; Britain/ Colonial Office Papers, CO 42/68:215, and CO 42/69:203; Jacobs, *Beginning of the U.S. Army*, 48; *VSP*, 5:138; *TPUS*, 2:359.

22. Smith, *St. Clair Papers*, 2:146, 147; Knox to Harmar, 7 June 1790, Harmar Papers, 2w268; Kohn, *Eagle and Sword*, chap. 6.

## 8. We Are Determined to Meet the Enemy

1. The principal American testimony for this campaign was furnished by the Court of Inquiry that sat 15–23 September 1791 and is printed in *ASPMA*, 1:20–36, but additional material can be found in Meek, "General Harmar's Expedition." The paper by Michael S. Warner, "General Josiah Harmar's Campaign Reconsidered," confuses Kekionga and Miamitown but contains a clear reconstruction of the main battle. For this paragraph, see the evidence of Major Ferguson and Ebenezer Denny and the plan of the march, all in *ASPMA*, 1:20, 24, 31; and John Armstrong's journal in Meek, "General Harmar's Expedition," 79–84.

There is no entirely satisfactory history of the Indian war of 1786 to 1795. Kohn, *Eagle and Sword*, is excellent on the American military context, on which subject James R. Jacobs's *Beginning of the U.S. Army* is still worth consulting. Jack Jule Gifford, "Northwest Indian War," and Wiley Sword, *President Washington's Indian War*, are full accounts of the war, with many useful details, but both are stronger on the American than the Indian perspective. Short but safe treatments are Horsman, *Matthew Elliott*, Kelsay, *Joseph Brant*, and White, *Middle Ground*. For the British handling of the crisis, see in addition Burt, *The United States, Great Britain and British North America*; Hatheway, "Neutral Indian Barrier State"; Wright, *Britain and the American Frontier*; and Calloway, *Crown and Calumet*.

2. Arthur St. Clair to the Senecas, 8 September 1790, Britain/Colonial Office Papers, CO 42/72:75; St. Clair letters, Britain/Colonial Office Papers, CO 42/72:77, 85, and CO 42/73:203.

3. American information, 18 September 1790, Britain/Colonial Office Papers, CO 42/69:304; Alexander McKee to Sir John Johnson, 13 June, September 1790, Britain/Colonial Office Papers, CO 42/69:296, 302; John Smith to Francis Le Maistre, 22 September 1790, Britain/Colonial Office Papers, CO 42/69:308; McKee to Smith, 19 September, 13 October 1790, McKee Papers.

4. Thornbrough, *Outpost on the Wabash*, 258–64; McKee to Johnson, 18 October 1790, Britain/Colonial Office Papers, CO 42/73:83.

5. George Sharp to McKee, 9, 17 October 1790, McKee Papers, and Britain/ Colonial Office Papers, CO 42/73:23; letters of McKee and Smith, Britain/Colonial Office Papers, CO 42/73:23, 24; Thornbrough, *Outpost on the Wabash*, 266; evidence of Ferguson, Denny, and Maj. David Zeigler in *ASPMA*, 1:21, 24, 25; Armstrong journal, 13 October 1790, in Meek, "General Harmar's Expedition," 82; Harmar journal, Harmar Papers, 2W335–48.

6. Testimony of Ferguson, Asa Hartshorn, Britt, Denny, and Zeigler in *ASPMA*, 1:21, 23, 24, 26; affidavit of John Hardin, *ASPMA*, 1:34; Armstrong journal in Meek, "General Harmar's Expedition," 82–83; McKee, October 1790, and the statement of Matthew Elliott, 28 October 1790, Britain/Colonial Office Papers, CO 42/73:23, 33.

7. Zeigler and Captain Doyle in *ASPMA*, 1:26; Denny, *Military Journal*, 145; Meek, "General Harmar's Expedition," 84; Smith, 19 October 1790, Britain/ Colonial Office Papers, CO 42/73:24; Harmar to St. Clair, 18 October 1790, Northwest Territory Collection (IHS).

8. Harmar journal, 18 October 1790; Denny, *Military Journal*, 145; Ferguson, Denny, and Armstrong in *ASPMA*, 1:21, 25, 26; Thomas Irwin to Benjamin Drake, October 1840, Frontier Wars Papers, 4U3.

9. Harmar journal, 19 October 1790; evidence of Ferguson, Hartshorn, Denny, Zeigler, Armstrong, Gaines, Heart, and Hardin in *ASPMA*, 1:21, 22, 25 (twice), 27, 28, 29, 34; Denny, *Military Journal*, 145–46; Meek, "General Harmar's Expedition," 83–84; Elliott to McKee, 23 October 1790, Britain/Colonial Office Papers, CO 42/73:29; Klinck and Talman, *Journal of Major John Norton*, 177.

10. See documents filed in Britain/Colonial Office Papers, CO 42/73:25, 29, 31, 33; statement of Blue Jacket, 1 November 1790, Britain/Colonial Office Papers, CO 42/73:37.

11. Harmar to Henry Knox, 6 November 1790, in Thornbrough, *Outpost on the Wabash*, 268n.; Harmar journal, 18 October 1790; Smith, *St. Clair Papers*, 2:188; Denny, *Military Journal*, 146–47; Denny in *ASPMA*, 1:25.

12. Harmar journal, 21 October 1790; Thomas Irwin, interviewed by Lyman C. Draper, 1844, Frontier Wars Papers, 4U1; Ferguson, Strong, Morgan, Hartshorn, Britt, Denny, Zeigler, Captain Asheton, and Hardin in *ASPMA*, 1:21, 22, 23 (twice), 24, 25 (twice), 28, 34; statements of Godfroy and Elliott, Britain/Colonial Office Papers, CO 42/73:31, 33; "Harmar's Expedition"; Denny, *Military Journal*, 147–49; Harmar to St. Clair, 24 October 1790, Northwest Territory Collections (IHS); statement of Charles Wells, Wells Papers.

13. Statements of Godfroy (26 October 1790) and Blue Jacket (1 November 1790), Britain/Colonial Office Papers, CO 42/73:31, 37; evidence of Doyle and Armstrong in *ASPMA*, 1:26, 27; narrative of Joseph Jackson, 1844, Boone Papers, 11C62.

14. Spencer, *Indian Captivity*, 79–80; Hopkins, *Mission to the Indians*, 63–64.

15. Speech of Blue Jacket, 4 November 1790, Britain/Colonial Office Papers, CO 42/73:39; documents in Britain/Colonial Office Papers, CO 42/72:81, 87, and CO 42/73:35, 40, 47, 51.

16. Statement of Blue Jacket, 1 November 1790, Britain/Colonial Office Papers, CO 42/73:37; Thornbrough, *Outpost on the Wabash*, 283.

17. Lord Dorchester to Andrew Gordon and John Smith, 20 January 1791, Britain/Colonial Office Papers, CO 42/73:55; letters of Dorchester in Britain/Colonial Office Papers, CO 42/67:116, and CO 42/73:19, 69; Lord Grenville to Dorchester, 7 March, 16 September 1791, Britain/Colonial Office Papers, CO 42/73:15, and CO 42/83:134; McKee to Johnson, 13 June 1790, Britain/Colonial Office Papers, CO 42/69:296; Stone, *Life of Joseph Brant*, 2:296; Henry Motz to Sir John Johnson, 9 May 1791, McKee Papers.

18. St. Clair to Knox, 1 May 1791, Claus Papers, 4:259; Olmstead, *Blackcoats Among the Delaware*, 85.

19. Delaware speech, 29 November 1790, George Sharp to McKee, 10 December 1790, Antoine Lasselle to McKee, 15 December 1790, and Le Gris and Nay Wois Ser, 9 January 1791, all in McKee Papers.

20. Valuable discussions of Indian methods of warfare are in Mahon, "Anglo-American Methods of Indian Warfare," and Eid, " 'National' War" and " 'A Kind of Running Fight.' "

21. Smith, *St. Clair Papers*, 2:201; letter of Rufus Putnam, 6 January 1791, Buell, *Memoirs of Rufus Putnam*, 247.

22. Jacob Kingsbury to Harmar, 12, 17, 19 January 1791, Harmar Papers, 2W85–90; Thornbrough, *Outpost on the Wabash*, 269, 282; *Kentucky Gazette*, 5 February 1791; Antoine Lasselle to McKee, 15 December 1790, McKee Papers; Wiseman, "Personal Narrative"; the William Wells account published in Beckwith, "Fort Wayne Manuscript," 83, which is almost certainly the source of "credit" used in "Anecdotes of Sundry Conflicts with the Indians," 302–5; and Scamyhorn and Steinle, *Stockades in the Wilderness*, 65–74.

William Wiseman, a twenty-year-old defender of Dunlap's, recalled more than sixty years afterward that during parleys the Americans ascertained that Blue Jacket and Simon and George Girty were among their attackers. William Wells, who does not appear to have been present, said his father-in-law, Little Turtle, was in the expedition. Neither source is unimpeachable, but the expedition consisted largely of Shawnees, Miamis, and Delawares, Moreover, although Blue Jacket and Le Gris issued the orders concerning the traders at Miamitown in December 1790, Le Gris and Nay Wois Ser assumed that authority in the beginning of January, when the warriors were expected back daily. This, with Le Gris's comment that all the warriors had "gone to war," leads me to conclude that Blue Jacket and Little Turtle were in the foray against Dunlap's Station.

23. Journal for March–May 1791, Britain/Colonial Office Papers, CO 42/73:193; McKee to John Smith, 27 April 1791, McKee Papers; *VSP*, 5:282.

## *9. General Blue Jacket and Arthur St. Clair*

1. For Captain Johnny, journal for March–May 1791, Britain/Colonial Office Papers, CO 42/73:193; Alexander McKee to John Smith, 14 April 1791 McKee Papers.

2. Blue Jacket and Little Turtle's purchase of provisions from Francis La-fontaine, Detroit, 1 July 1791, Claus Papers, 4:283. This and the following paragraph depend on Britain/Colonial Office Papers, CO 42/73:143, 149, 199, CO 42/82:361, 363, CO/83: passim, and CO 42/316:13; Claus Papers, 4:281, 285; Stone, *Life of Joseph Brant*, 2:300; and *Simcoe*, 1:55.

3. John Francis Hamtramck to Josiah Harmar, 15 June 1791, in Thornbrough, *Outpost on the Wabash*, 283; McKee to Smith, 18 August 1791, McKee Papers.

4. McKee to Smith, 30 May, 4, 13, 15, 26, 27 June, 18 August 1791, McKee Papers.

5. Anthony Shane, interviewed by Benjamin Drake (November 1821), Tecum-seh Papers, 12YY36–38, has Tecumseh's party encountering a wounded Indian between the Mad and Great Miami Rivers and learning that a force of Americans was advancing. Tecumseh sent one of his warriors ahead to warn the Indians at the Glaize and arrived there himself in August 1791. As I have argued elsewhere (Sugden, *Tecumseh*, 62), this fits with Wilkinson's expedition, which left Fort Washington on 1 August. Shane's information is paralleled, however, in a letter written by Alexander McKee, presumably to Smith at Detroit, on 29 July 1791 (McKee Papers). According to this letter, some Indians, including wounded Indians, had come into the Glaize with reports of an American advance. A force of five hundred cavalry preceded a second party of Americans. They scattered hunting parties in the region of the Shawnees' "old villages" some fifty miles from the Glaize, i.e., those about the Mad River, and were believed to have captured some women and children. The Indians at the Glaize sent "spies" out about 25 July and appealed for the support of the British and other tribesmen. Matthew Elliott went to the Glaize to investigate, returning to McKee's depot on 29 July. Although the Indian scouts had not yet returned, and Indians were collecting on the Maumee quickly, ready to repel an attack, it was being concluded that the American force had probably withdrawn. This, rather than Wilkinson's campaign, may have been the incident involving Tecumseh.

6. For St. Clair's campaign, see St. Clair to Henry Knox, 1, 9, 24 November 1791, 22 January 1792, in Smith, *St. Clair Papers*, 2:249, 262, 269, 277; St. Clair to Major Brown, 12 November 1791, in Smith, *St. Clair Papers*, 2:267; St. Clair to Edmund Butler, 3 March 1792, in Smith, *St. Clair Papers*, 2:280. The general's captured correspondence passed to Alexander McKee and is filed in volume 4 of the Claus Papers. His *Narrative of the Manner in Which the Campaign Against the Indians . . . Was Conducted* (1812) contains his narrative, the two reports of the committee of inquiry into his conduct, the general's "observations" on the evidence before the committee, extracts of testimony given the committee, and other papers. The reports are also printed in *ASPMA*, 1:36, 41, and elsewhere. Other important accounts are by William Darke (Darke to Sarah Darke, 1 November 1791, *MPHS*, 24:331; Darke to John Morrow, 1 November 1791, *MPHS*, 24:333; and Darke to Knox, 9 November 1791, Knox Papers); Sargent, "Winthrop Sargent's Diary"; Denny, *Military Journal*, 164–69; Wilson, *Journal of Captain Daniel Bradley*, 19–35; and Quaife, "Journal of Captain Samuel Newman." See also the statement of Thomas Irwin in "St. Clair's Defeat"; John Van Cleve, ed., "Van

Cleve's Memoranda"; Edmund Butler to St. Clair, 1792, in Smith, *St. Clair Papers*, 2:280; the statement of Charles Wells, Wells Papers; and John Rogers to Henry Lee, 26 November 1791, *VSP*, 5:399.

7. Darke to Knox, 9 November 1791, Knox Papers.

8. Sargent, "Winthrop Sargent's Diary," 250, 255; John Armstrong to St. Clair, 10 November 1791, Armstrong Papers; *Knoxville Gazette*, 12 January 1793.

9. Simon Girty to McKee, 28 October 1791, McKee Papers. Girty gives the most authoritative of several statements of the size of the Indian force. Another participant, George Ash, said that 850 warriors went out but that 50 Kickapoos joined en route (*Cincinnati Chronicle and Literary Gazette*, 7 November 1829), while Joseph Jackson counted 900 men, 600 of them Lakes Indians (Boone Papers, 11C62). See also the speech of the confederated Indians, 16 May 1792, *Simcoe*, 1:157, and Beckwith, "Fort Wayne Manuscript," 84.

10. See chapter 1, note 11. It was also possibly remarks made by Little Turtle and Wells on a visit east in 1801–2 that prompted John Pershouse to write at that time that "Little Turtle is the chief who commanded the Indians when they routed the American army under Genl. Wayne" (Pershouse to his brother, 26 February 1802, Pershouse Papers). He was referring, of course, to St. Clair, not Anthony Wayne.

11. James Wilkinson to Josiah Drake, 12 December 1791, Frontier Wars Papers, 4U166; Absalom Baird to Wayne, 30 July 1792, Frontier Wars Papers, 4U203, 4U209; Sargent (23 April 1792), "Winthrop Sargent's Diary," 272; Alexander Macomb to Henry Knox, 16 February 1792, Knox Papers.

12. *MPHS*, 17:606, 649; Knopf, "Two Journals of the Kentucky Volunteers," 263; Buell, "Fragment from the Diary," 268; George McDougall to William Woodbridge, 26 February 1820, Woodbridge Papers; Wayne to Hamtramck, 25 February 1795, Wayne Papers (1).

13. Delaware message, January 1794, and Anthony Wayne to Alexander Gibson, 26 March 1794, both in Wayne Papers (1); Wayne to James McHenry, 3 October 1796, in Knopf, *Anthony Wayne*, 532 (emphasis added).

14. See note 18, below. Among other assertions to the same effect is that of Thomas Ridoubt, who had Shawnee friends and described Blue Jacket as the one who "commanded the party who afterwards vanquished the American general, St. Clair" (Edgar, *Ten Years of Upper Canada*, 366).

15. John Johnston to Lyman C. Draper, 21 August 1847, Tecumseh Papers, 11YY30.

16. Schoolcraft, *Travels*, 40, 42.

17. Klinck and Talman, *Journal of Major John Norton*, 177–78.

18. Ash's account in the *Cincinnati Chronicle and Literary Gazette* for 7 November 1829 is supported in some details by John Norton (note 17, above) and the narrative of Joseph Jackson, 1844, Boone Papers, 11C62.

19. Sargent, "Winthrop Sargent's Diary," 271–72; Joseph Brant to Joseph Chew, 30 December 1791, *MPHS*, 24:358.

20. Sargent, "Winthrop Sargent's Diary," 258.

21. St. Clair, *Narrative*, 221.

22. Denny, *Military Journal*, 165.

23. Denny, *Military Journal*, 166.

24. For the Wyandot and Mingo charge, see Klinck and Talman, *Journal of Major John Norton*, 178; desposition of William May, 11 October 1792, *ASPIA*, 1:243.

25. Sargent, "Winthrop Sargent's Diary," 261; Denny, *Military Journal*, 167.

26. Sargent, "Winthrop Sargent's Diary," 260, 265, 269; Denny, *Military Journal*, 171; Gifford, "Northwest Indian War," 226–30. See also Gibson to Wayne, 11 May 1794, Wayne Papers (1); *Cincinnati Chronicle and Literary Gazette*, 7 November 1829; Beckwith, "Fort Wayne Manuscript," 84; Sargent, "Winthrop Sargent's Diary," 272; Klinck and Talman, *Journal of Major John Norton*, 178; *MPHS*, 24:335; *TPUS*, 2:380; and the Joseph Jackson narrative (Boone Papers, 11C62), which says that the Indian loss of twenty warriors at Pekowi (1780) exceeded that at St. Clair's defeat.

27. The action on the Little Big Horn in 1876, when 1,500 Sioux and Cheyennes massed on Col. George A. Custer's inferior and divided command, killing 276 men, is not militarily comparable. To find other similar victories by "native" warriors we have to look further afield. Possible examples that come to mind are the Peruvian leader Túpac Amaru's defeat of the Spaniards at Sangarara on 18 November 1780; the destruction of Pedro Acereto's army by Mayas under José Crecencio Poot in Yucatan in 1860; and the Zulu victory over the British at Isandhlwana in Natal in 1879.

## 10. All the Nations Are Now of One Mind

1. *Minutes of Debate in Council*. This pamphlet, published in 1792, purports to report the speeches at a council on the Maumee in November 1791. The editor, who is not named, claims authenticity (p. 3), but although the speeches fairly represent Indian opinion and refer to verifiable incidents, and were probably taken down by British observers, there must remain a question of provenance.

2. Indians to the British, 7 March, 15 April 1792, McKee Papers.

3. Bliss, *Diary of David Zeisberger*, 2:244; Spencer, *Indian Captivity*, 90; Alexander McKee to Sir John Johnson, 28 January 1792, *MPHS*, 24:365; George Ironside to McKee, 6 March 1795, Canada/Indian Affairs Papers, 9:8840.

4. Bliss, *Diary of David Zeisberger*, 2: 244; *ASPIA*, 1:264, 327; Smith, *St. Clair Papers*, 2:302; Winthrop Sargent to Henry Knox, 12 July 1792, with enclosures, Sargent Papers; George Welbank to McKee, 12 April 1791, and McKee to Dragging Canoe and Welbank, Claus Papers, 4:253, 313; Kelsay, *Joseph Brant*, 457.

5. Speech of Shawnees and Delawares, 11 June 1792, *MPHS*, 24:421; Coates, ed., "Narrative of an Embassy to the Western Tribes," 79; Israel Chapin to Knox, 17 July 1792, *ASPIA*, 1:241; Indians to Matthew Elliott, 7 March 1792, McKee Papers.

6. Speech of Red Pole, 2 October 1792, Canada/Indian Affairs Papers, 8:8250; Iroquois report, 16 November 1792, *ASPIA*, 1:323; Indians to the British, 15 April 1792, McKee Papers.

7. Alexander McCormick was born in 1790 and may have misremembered his father's story. His description of Blue Jacket as "a small athletic fellow" does not fit the famous chief, although it might have been appropriate for his son Jim Blue Jacket (McCormick interviewed by Lyman C. Draper, 1863, Draper Notes, 17S203). For the Glaize, see *Simcoe*, 1:157; Knopf, "Two Journals of the Kentucky Volunteers," 263; *ASPIA*, 1:494; Coates, "Narrative of an Embassy to the Western Tribes," 97–98; *MPHS*, 24:365; Voegelin, *Indians of Northwest Ohio*, 235–36; Tanner, "The Glaize in 1792," and her "Coocoochee: Mohawk Medicine Woman," *American Indian Culture and Research Journal* 33 (1979): 23–41; and Spencer, *Indian Captivity*, which contains vivid memories of the Glaize in 1792.

8. These figures are based on Dwight L. Smith, ed., "William Wells and the Indian Council of 1793," 217–26; *ASPIA*, 1:489; *Simcoe*, 2:366; and the deposition of Nicholas Rosencrantz, 23 September 1793, Wayne Papers (1).

9. Stone, *Life of Joseph Brant*, 2:333; Voegelin, *Indians of Northwest Ohio*, 236–37; Spencer, *Indian Captivity*, 97–102; *Kentucky Gazette*, 5 May, 21 July 1792; Knopf, *Anthony Wayne*, 55; Buell, *Memoirs of Rufus Putnam*, 273; *MPHS*, 24:421; Joseph Brant to McKee, 27 March 1792, Claus Papers, 5:3; McKee to Richard England, 24 August 1792, McKee Papers; and Sabathy-Judd, "Diary of the Moravian Indian Mission," 134.

10. Samuel G. Drake, *Biography*, 575; *Philadelphia Independent Gazette*, 29 September 1792; Knopf, *Anthony Wayne*, 27, 34, 44, 55; *Simcoe*, 1:157; Coates, "Narrative of an Embassy to the Western Tribes," 123–25.

11. *Simcoe*, 5:7; Knopf, *Anthony Wayne*, 83; *MPHS*, 24:456; Brant to McKee, 27 March 1792, Claus Papers, 5:3; Sabathy-Judd, "Diary of the Moravian Indian Mission," 29 September 1792; Kelsay, *Joseph Brant*, chap. 22.

12. For Egushaway see chapter 5, note 16, and Sabathy-Judd, "Diary of the Moravian Indian Mission," 8 September, 25 October 1792. The comments of Indians at the Glaize in this and the following paragraph depend on Coates, "Narrative of an Embassy to the Western Tribes," 89, 97–98, 103, 106–7, 114, 123–25.

13. Marschalk, "Mio-qua-coo-a-caw."

14. The minutes of the council, 30 September–9 October 1792, are printed in *Simcoe*, 1:218–31. Seneca versions may be found in the minutes of a council at Buffalo Creek, 13–14 November 1792, *MPHS*, 24:509–16, and *ASPIA*, 1:323–24. For a broadly compatible account, see Coates, "Narrative of an Embassy to the Western Tribes," 86, 106–7, 113–31. See also the journal of William Johnson, 1792, Britain/Colonial Office Papers, CO 42/317:38–44, and the deposition of William May, 11 October 1792, *ASPIA*, 1:243.

15. For the relations between the Senecas and the United States, see the studies by Stone, *Life and Times of Red Jacket*, Wallace, *Death and Rebirth of the Seneca*, and Fenton, *Great Law*.

16. *Simcoe*, 1:230, 283, 295, 301, 363; *MPHS*, 24:509; John Graves Simcoe to Alexander McKee, 23 January 1793, Claus Papers, 5:67; Henry Knox to the Indians, 12 December 1792, Claus Papers, 5:59; Simcoe to Henry Dundas, 23

August 1793, Britain/Colonial Office Papers, CO 42/317:176. See also the valuable paper by Horsman, "British Indian Department."

17. Coates, "Narrative of an Embassy to the Western Tribes," 122; *Cincinnati Chronicle and Literary Gazette*, 7 November 1829; speech of Red Pole, 10 August 1795, *ASPIA*, 1:581. The reference to the mission in the deposition of William May, 11 October 1792 (*ASPIA*, 1:243), appears to be confused. Hamer, "British in Canada," and *ASPIA*, vol. 1, print most of the documents for the Shawnee canvass, but Cotterill, *Southern Indians*, 100–104, gives the only secondary account. See Hamer, "British in Canada," 124, and documents in *ASPIA*, 1:378, 381, 437, 444; and *Knoxville Gazette*, 12 January 1793. Cheeseekau's activities among the Chickamaugas are described in Sugden, *Tecumseh*, chaps. 5–6.

18. For contextual material on the Creeks, see Caughey, *McGillivray of the Creeks*; McDaniel, "Relations Between the Creek Indians, Georgia and the United States"; and Wright, *Creeks and Seminoles*. Broader background is supplied by Cotterill, *Southern Indians*; Whitaker, *Spanish-American Frontier*; Wright, *Anglo-Spanish Rivalry*; and Coker and Watson, *Indian Traders*.

19. For the Shawnees among the Creeks, see *ASPIA*, 1:353, 375–79, 381–84, 387–88, 437; *Knoxville Gazette*, 23 March 1793; and Knopf, *Anthony Wayne*, 248.

20. William Blount to Knox, 23, 28 May 1793, *ASPIA*, 1:454–55; John Watts and Little Turkey to Blount, 23 May 1793, *ASPIA*, 1:457; Little Turkey to Blount, 5 June 1793, *ASPIA*, 1:461; *Knoxville Gazette*, 1 June 1793.

21. McKee to Simcoe, 15 July 1793, and Simcoe to George Hammond, 24 July 1793, *Simcoe*, 5:58, 64. For the resident Shawnee community on the Tallapoosa, see Schoolcraft, *Information Respecting the History*, 5:260.

22. For attempts to recruit Choctaws and Chickasaws, see Cotterill, *Southern Indians*, 95–97, and James Robertson to Wayne, 7 July 1793, Northwest Territory Collection, IHS.

## 11. *Just Rights and an Uncertain War*

1. Instructions to U.S. commissioners, 26 April 1793, *ASPIA*, 1:340; instructions of Timothy Pickering, 4 June 1793, *ASPIA*, 1:346; John Graves Simcoe to George Hammond, 8 September 1793, *Simcoe*, 2:49; Henry Knox to Joseph Brant, 27 June 1792, Claus Papers 5:13; western Indians to the Iroquois, February 1793, Claus Papers, 5:87; Indians to George Washington, Febrary 1793, Claus Papers, 5:93. Relevant studies of the American political and military preparations are Jacobs, *Beginning of the U.S. Army*; Knopf, *Anthony Wayne*; Horsman, *Expansion and American Indian Policy*; Kohn, *Eagle and Sword*; Walsh, "Defeat of Major General Arthur St. Clair"; and Nelson, *Anthony Wayne*.

2. Joseph Brant to Alexander McKee, 17 May 1793, Claus Papers, 5:117; Thomas Duggan to McKee, 30 July 1793, Claus Papers, 5:273; list of Indians drawing provisions, July 1793, Claus Papers, 5:227; McKee to Edward Baker Littlehales, 11 April 1793, *ASPIA*, 1:343; council minutes, 7–9 July 1793, *ASPIA*, 1:349; deposition of Nicholas Rosecrantz, 23 September 1793, and A. Prior to Anthony Wayne, 20 December 1793, Wayne Papers (1); *Simcoe*, 1:383, 5:38; and Smith, "William

Wells," 220, 223, 226. Wells abandoned the Indians in 1792 and began scouting for the Americans. His report, reprinted in Smith's article, is valuable, but there is doubt as to whether Wells was himself at the rapids, as he implies, or received his information from John Kinzie (Indians to McKee, 6 May 1794, *Simcoe*, 2:230). Burt, *The United States, Great Britain and British North America*, Hatheway, "Neutral Indian Barrier State," and Sword, *President Washington's Indian War* are worth consulting on the abortive treaty negotiations of 1793, but the best accounts are Horsman, "British Indian Department" and his *Matthew Elliott*, chap. 4, and Kelsay, *Joseph Brant*, chap. 23.

3. For Indian opinion, see *Simcoe*, 1:383, 5:55; Smith, "William Wells," 220, 222; MPHS, 17:592, 605; diary, 8–11 August 1793, in Lincoln, "Journal of a Treaty Held in 1793," 154–56; Indians to the United States, 2 January 1794, and statement of Delaware envoys, 13 January 1794, Wayne Papers (1); report of Matthew Elliott, 11 February 1794, Canada/Indian Affairs Papers, 8:8576; Brant to McKee, 23 March 1793, Claus Papers, 5:95; and Coates, "Narrative of an Embassy to the Western Tribes," 106.

4. British views can be sampled in Claus Papers, 5:1 (with enclosures), 41, 57, 103, 111, 171; and *Simcoe*, 1:27, 207, 214, 322, 357, 365, 368, 383, 2:4, 40, 49, and 5:25, 28. Burt, *The United States, Great Britain and British North America*, and Wright, *Britain and the American Frontier*, supply an essential context.

5. Simcoe to McKee and John Butler, 22 June 1793, *Simcoe*, 1:365.

6. Alex Clark to McKee, 27 May 1793, Canada/Indian Affairs Papers, 8:8362; chiefs to McKee, 27 May 1793, Canada/Indian Affairs Papers, 8:8365; journal of Brant, 1793, Canada/Indian Affairs Papers, 8:8442; western Indians to Iroquois, 27 February 1793, Claus Papers, 5:87; Brant to Prideaux Selby, 23 March 1793, Claus Papers, 5:95.

7. Benjamin Lincoln, "Journal of a Treaty Held in 1793," recorded the activities of the commissioners.

8. Klinck and Talman, *Journal of Major John Norton*, 187; George Ironside and Ronald McDonald, 3 May 1794, Canada/Indian Affairs Papers, 8:8589.

9. Richard England to McKee, 8, 15 July 1793, Claus Papers, 5:215, 233.

10. Wallace, *Thirty Thousand Miles with John Heckewelder*, 313; letter of John Parrish, 9 July 1793, Wayne Papers (1); diary entries of Jacob Lindley and Joseph Moore, MPHS, 17:606, 649.

11. Thomas Duggan to McKee, 17 July 1793, Claus Papers, 5:259.

12. *Simcoe*, 1:371, 374, 377, 402, and 5:64; Lincoln, "Journal of a Treaty Held in 1793," 129–35; Wallace, *Thirty Thousand Miles with John Heckewelder*, 313; MPHS, 17:605, 615. The journal of Joseph Brant (Canada/Indian Affairs Papers, 8:8442) is essential for these negotiations throughout.

13. Brant to McKee, 4 August 1793, Claus Papers, 4:287; Lincoln, "Journal of a Treaty Held in 1793," 142–43; Brant to Simcoe, 2 September 1793, *Simcoe*, 2:47.

14. *Simcoe*, 5:58, 59, 64; Simcoe to McKee, 23 July 1793, Claus Papers, 5:241; Edward Baker Littlehales to John McGill, 29 July 1793, Canada Papers; MPHS, 17:611; Wallace, *Thirty Thousand Miles with John Heckewelder*, 313–14; Lincoln, "Journal of a Treaty Held in 1793," 169–72; deposition of Nicholas Rosecrantz, 23

September 1793, and details of a council at Buffalo Creek, 8 October 1793, both in Wayne Papers (1); and Smith, "William Wells," 225–26.

15. Lincoln, "Journal of a Treaty Held in 1793," 142–50; Wallace, *Thirty Thousand Miles with John Heckewelder*, 314–18; speech of American commissioners, 31 July 1793, *Simcoe*, 1:405; *MPHS*, 17:618–22; and U.S. commissioners to Henry Knox, 21 August 1793, Wayne Papers (1).

16. McKee to Simcoe, 22 August 1793, *Simcoe*, 2:34; Brant to McKee, 4 August 1793, Claus Papers, 5:285; Smith, "William Wells," 220, 222; Thomas Pasteur to Wayne, 29 October 1793, Wayne Papers (1).

17. Brant's journal, (see note 12); Smith, "William Wells," 222; Simcoe to Lord Dorchester, 10 November 1793, *Simcoe*, 2:101; Lincoln, "Journal of a Treaty Held in 1793," 154–56; and commissioners to Knox, 21 August 1793, Wayne Papers (1).

18. Confederacy to U.S. commissioners, 13 August 1793, *Simcoe*, 2:17; commissioners to Indians and McKee, 14 August 1793, *Simcoe*, 2:21.

19. Commissioners to Indians, 16 August 1793, *Simcoe*, 2:24; Smith, "William Wells," 222–23; deposition of Nicholas Rosecrantz, 23 September 1793, Wayne Papers (1); speech of Brant, 1801, Canada/Military Papers, c254:18.

## 12. The Expedition to Fort Recovery

1. Alexander McKee to Richard England, 26 September, 22 October 1793, McKee Papers; Alexander Gibson to Charles Scott, 17 October 1793, Todd Papers; "Journal of Indian Affairs," 1793, Canada/Military Papers, c247:49; deposition of Nicholas Rosecrantz, 23 September 1793, Wayne Papers (1); Smith, "William Wells," 220, 222–24; Knopf, *Anthony Wayne*, 278; *Kentucky Gazette*, 2 November 1793; and Weld, *Travels Through the States of North America*, 2:225–26.

2. McKee to England, 18 October, 4, 10, 15, 19 November, 2 December 1793, McKee Papers; Klinck and Talman, *Journal of Major John Norton*, 180–81; *MPHS*, 24:627; Abner Prior to Wayne, 20 December 1793, Wayne Papers (1); "Journal of Indian Affairs," 1793, Canada/Military Papers, c247:49. Captain Johnny even had difficulties finding guides to escort George Welbank's delegation of southern Indians home (Claus Papers, 6:7, 13, 25, 113; George Ironside to McKee, 10 May 1794, Canada/Indian Affairs Papers, 8:8348).

3. *Simcoe*, 2:85, 99, 141, 189, 214, and 5:86.

4. Indians to United States (2 January 1794), the statement of the Delaware envoys (13 January 1794), Wayne to the Indians (14 January 1794), Wayne to Gibson (17 January 1794), Wayne to Knox (18 January, 10 March 1794), Wayne to James Wilkinson (14 March 1794), and the deposition of Christopher Miller (1794), are all in Wayne Papers (1). See also Klinck and Talman, *Journal of Major John Norton*, 181; *Simcoe*, 2:138, 139; McKee to England, 21, 28 January 1794, and Matthew Elliott's report, 11 February 1794, all in McKee Papers.

5. Spanish and Indian speeches, 7 May 1794, Canada/Military Papers, c247:141; McKee to Joseph Chew, 8 May 1794, Canada/Military Papers, c247:138.

6. *Simcoe*, 2:149, 154, 184, 211, 220; Thomas Duggan to Joseph Chew, 10 April 1794, Canada/Military Papers, c247:110; Thomas Talbot to Francis Le Maistre,

12 May 1794, Canada/Military Papers, C247:146; McKee to Chew, 8 May 1794, Canada/Military Papers, C247:138.

7. Examination of Antoine Lasselle, 28 August 1794, *ASPIA*, 1:494.

8. Examination of Shawnee prisoners, 26 June 1796, *ASPIA*, 1:489.

9. Spanish and Indian speeches, 7 May 1794, Canada/Military Papers, C247:141; McKee to Chew, 8 May 1794, Canada/Military Papers, C247:138; letters of McKee, 3, 5 May 1794, McKee Papers; examination of two Potawatomis, 7 June 1794, *ASPIA*, 1:489; Sabathy-Judd, "Diary of the Moravian Indian Mission," 223, 225–29.

10. Shawnees, Delawares, and Miamis to McKee, 6 May 1794, Canada/Military Papers, C247:134; information of American prisoner, 6 May 1794, Claus Papers, 6:125; McKee to England, 29 April 1794, McKee Papers; *Simcoe*, 2:305; Knopf, *Anthony Wayne*, 345; and Smith, "From Greene Ville to Fallen Timbers," 277.

11. Thomas Duggan, 24 May 1794, Canada/Military Papers, C247:155; Indian speech, 25 May 1794, Canada/Military Papers, C247:161; McKee to England, 26 May 1794, McKee Papers; Elliott to McKee, 20 June 1794, Claus Papers, 6:181; Klinck and Talman, *Journal of Major John Norton*, 182.

12. McKee to Chew, 2, 8, 9, 10 June 1794, Canada/Military Papers, C247:168–73; message from British and Indians at the Glaize, 9 June 1794, Canada/Military Papers, C247:172.

13. The expedition to Fort Recovery is principally given from the diary of an unidentified British participant, *Simcoe*, 5:90–94. See also Matthew Elliott to McKee, 20 June 1794, Claus Papers, 6:181, and McKee to England, 23 June 1794, McKee Papers.

14. Alder, ms., "History of Jonathan Alder," dictated to his son Henry.

15. Wayne to James O'Hara, 29 June 1794, James O'Hara letterbook, Northwest Territory Collection, IHS; letter of 13 July 1794 in *Kentucky Gazette*, 26 July 1794; Klinck and Talman, *Journal of Major John Norton*, 182.

16. Smith, "From Green Ville to Fallen Timbers," 277, 312; Klinck and Talman, *Journal of Major John Norton*, 182–83.

17. This account of the engagement at Fort Recovery is drawn from Gibson to Wayne, 30 June 1794, Wayne to Gibson, 3 July 1794, and Wayne to Robert Elliott and Eli Williams, 4 July 1794, all in Wayne Papers (1); Wayne to O'Hara, 4 July 1794, James O'Hara letterbook, Northwest Territory Collection, IHS; "Extracts from Winthrop Sargent's Journal, 1793–1795," 277; Buell, "Fragments from the Diary," 110–11; Knopf, "Precise Journal," 300–302; statement of John Vorris, 24–25 July 1794, Canada/Military Papers, C247:200; *Simcoe*, 2:305, 306, 310, 315, 317, and 5:90–94, 96; *ASPIA*, 1:495; Alder, ms., "History of Jonathan Alder"; Klinck and Talman, *Journal of Major John Norton*, 182–83; evidence of a Potawatomi, 23 July 1794, Wayne Papers (1); William Doyle to Charles Langlade, 26 July 1794, *Wisconsin Historical Collections* 18 (1908): 443; Bliss, *Diary of David Zeisberger*, 2:364–65; G. LaMothe to Chew, 19 July 1794, Canada/Indian Affairs Papers, 8:8619; and *Cincinnati Chronicle and Literary Gazette*, 7 November 1829.

18. Gibson to Wayne, 10 July 1794, Wayne Papers (1).

19. *Simcoe*, 2:237, 278, 344; McKee to England, 10 July 1794, McKee Papers;

George Ironside and Ronald McDonald, 3 May 1794, Canada/Indian Affairs Papers, 8:8589.

20. England to Simcoe, 22 July 1794, *Simcoe*, 2:333; McKee to England, 22, 25 July 1794, McKee Papers.

21. Knopf, "Precise Journal," 285; information of Robert Newman, 4 August 1794, *Simcoe*, 2:351.

### 13. The Final Battle

1. McGrane, "William Clark's Journal," 427; deposition of Thomas Stephenson, 14 October 1794, Wayne Papers (1); Bricknell, "Narrative"; Klinck and Talman, *Journal of Major John Norton*, 184–85; *Simcoe*, 2:402, 411; John Naskell to Benjamin Gilman and Griffin Greene, 29 August 1794, Hildreth Papers, vol. 2, Marietta College Collection; and Draper Notes, 17S203.

2. *Simcoe*, 2:227, 344, 357, 360, 362, 365, 366, 374, 376, 411, and 3:12, 13.

3. McKee to England, 17 August 1794, McKee Papers; Wayne to Christopher Miller, 13 August 1794, and Indians to "Brothers Big Knives," 15 August 1794, Wayne Papers (1); and *Simcoe*, 2:271, 387.

4. Bricknell, "Narrative"; *Simcoe*, 2:371.

5. Smith, "From Greene Ville to Fallen Timbers," 309; Schoolcraft, *Travels*, 49–50; reminiscences of H. Brady, 1842, Frontier Wars Papers, 5U126. Brady may also have been the source for McAfee, *History of the Late War in the Western Country*, 8, who stated that Little Turtle and Blue Jacket "disagreed about the manner of opposing Wayne's army. The plan of Blue Jacket was adopted, and eventuated in the total defeat of the Indians, as predicted by the other." Whatever their views about the propriety of the respective battle plans, these sources do not state that Little Turtle was the confederacy's head war chief and resigned his position in favor of Blue Jacket before the battle, as many secondary writers assert. In fact, if anything, they suggest the greater influence of Blue Jacket, whose opinion prevailed.

6. Alder, ms. "History of Jonathan Alder"; *Simcoe*, 3:7, 98; Kinnaird, *Spain in the Mississippi Valley*, 3:385; John Forsyth to Bleakley, 17 September 1794, Wayne Papers (1); Isaac Weld, *Travels Through the States of North America*, 2:210–15; *Cincinnati Chronicle and Literary Gazette*, 7 November 1829; Klinck and Talman, *Journal of Major John Norton*, 184–85; Joseph Evans, interviewed by Lyman C. Draper (1863), Draper Notes, 17S181; John M. Ruddell interviewed by Draper (1868), Draper Notes, 22S41; and accounts by Stephen and John M. Ruddell and Anthony Shane in Tecumseh Papers, 2YY120–32, 8YY43, and 12YY40–42. Antoine Lasselle stands out among "inside" informants in stating that more than one thousand men defended the Indian line (*Simcoe*, 3:13), but this is contradicted by the bulk of the British-Indian testimony and also by Wayne's second in command, who observed that the scale of Indian fire in the battle denoted a small force.

7. In addition to sources already mentioned, the following have been the principal foundations for my account of the battle of Fallen Timbers: Wayne to Henry Knox, 14, 28 August 1794, ASPIA, 1:490, Knopf, *Anthony Wayne*, 351;

Wilkinson to John Brown, 28 August 1794, in Quaife, "General James Wilkinson's Narrative"; the narratives of Nathaniel Hart and William Sudduth, Frontier Wars Papers, 5U93 and 14U114; and the accounts listed in Bowyer, "Daily Journal"; Cooke, "General Wayne's Campaign"; Knopf, "Two Journals of the Kentucky Volunteers"; Shepard, *Journal of James Taylor Underwood*; Smith, "From Greene Ville to Fallen Timbers" and *With Captain Edward Miller*; and Wilson, *Journal of Captain Daniel Bradley*.

8. Thomas Worthington and Duncan McArthur to Thomas Kirker, 22 September 1807, Kenton Papers, 7BB49; MPHS, 40:194, 247; Sugden, *Tecumseh's Last Stand*, 45, 55.

9. For American casualties, Davis, "Casualties," and Gifford, "Northwest Indian War," chap. 10. Indian losses are suggested by Kinnaird, *Spain in the Mississippi Valley*, 3:385; *Simcoe*, 2:395, 413, and 3:7, 98, 147; Forsyth to Bleakley, 17 September 1794, Wayne Papers (1); Knopf, *Anthony Wayne*, 369; and Klinck and Talman, *Journal of Major John Norton*, 184–85. Wilkinson's remarks must always be evaluated in the light of his animosity toward Wayne, but his statement that a diligent American search of the battlefield revealed less than thirty enemy bodies, including those of a few whites, seems to have been true. Among the latter killed was the clerk of the court at Detroit, Charles Smith, who had once lived with the Shawnees (*Simcoe*, 3:29, 46). The complaint of some Ojibwes that "not a single Shawano was in the fight, though they were always instigating the Indians to go to war" (Bliss, *Diary of David Zeisberger*, 2:372) is a manifest falsehood, perhaps motivated by their resentment of the Shawnees since the attack on Fort Recovery. Alexander McKee and condolence ceremonies conducted by Joseph Brant indicate that the Indian losses were suffered by the Wyandots, Shawnees, Ottawas, and Delawares (McKee to Richard England, 21 August 1794, McKee Papers; Brownstown council, October 1794, Britain/Colonial Office Papers, CO/319:127).

10. For grave robbing see Matthew Elliott to McKee, 29 March 1795, Canada/Indian Affairs Papers, 9:8895.

11. *Simcoe*, 3: 23, 73, 119, 156, 169, 197, 200; Thomas Smith to McKee, 19 October 1794, Canada/Indian Affairs Papers, 9:8740; and returns of the Indians at Swan Creek, 15 September, 4 December 1794, Claus Papers, 6:213, 291.

12. Wayne to the Indians, 12 September 1794, Wayne Papers (1); England to Simcoe, 17 September 1794, *Simcoe*, 3:96.

13. Isaac Williams to the Wyandots, 25 September 1794, Tarhe to Wayne, 26 September 1794, and Williams to Wayne, 27 September 1794 (enclosing Confederacy to the Wyandots), all in Wayne Papers (1); Smith to McKee, 14 October 1794, *Simcoe*, 3:128.

14. Smith to McKee, 11, 16 October 1794, *Simcoe*, 5:112, and 3:129. The italics are mine. For the potency of stories of French revivals among the Indians at an earlier period, see Gregory Evans Dowd, "The French King Wakes up in Detroit: 'Pontiac's War' in Rumor and History," *Ethnohistory* 37 (1990): 254–78.

15. Tappon Lasselle's statement, October 1794, ASPIA, 1:526; recollections of John Johnston, 1840s, Jones Collection; deposition of American deserters, 15

September 1794, McKee Papers; note by John Francis Hamtramck, 15 October 1794, Lasselle Papers (2).

16. Documents in *Simcoe*, 3:73, 85, 95, 97, 121, 147; McKee to Joseph Chew, 11 August 1795, Canada/Military Papers, C248:260; Joseph Brant to Chew, 22 October 1794, Canada/Military Papers, C247:281; William Johnson Chew to Chew, 24 October 1794, Canada/Military Papers, C247:283; proceedings at Brownstown, October 1794, Britain/Colonial Office Papers, CO 42/319:127; and several documents in the Wayne Papers (1), including the Wyandot account of the Brownstown council enclosed in Isaac Williams to Wayne, 18 November 1794, the statement of Abraham Williams, 10 November 1794, and Tarhe's account, November 1794.

17. *Simcoe*, 3:145–49 (three of Simcoe's letters to the Duke of Portland), 255, and 5:115, 121.

18. For the Wyandot initiative, see Wayne to Tarhe, 4 November 1794, 1 January 1795, and Isaac Williams to Wayne, 18 November 1794, Wayne Papers (1); *ASPIA*, 1:527, 528, 549; "Substance of Wayne's speech," Canada/Military Papers, C247:336; Adam Brown to Williams, 3 December 1794, Canada/Military Papers, C247:361; Willliams to Brown, 13 November 1794, Britain/Colonial Office Papers, CO 42/319:209; Knopf, *Anthony Wayne*, 361, 369; *Simcoe*, 3:219, 220, and 4:9; Buell, "Fragment from the Diary," 262, 266; and McKee to Richard England, 21 November 1794, McKee Papers.

19. Statement of Tappon Lasselle (*ASPIA*, 1:526) and Antoine Lasselle, 1 November 1794 (*Simcoe*, 3:166); McKee, 18 November 1794, Canada/Military Papers, C247:335; Smith to McKee, 23–24 October 1794, Claus Papers, 6:241; Knopf, *Anthony Wayne*, 358; Antoine to Jacques Lasselle, 31 January 1795, *Simcoe*, 3:281. "Tappon" must have been a nickname for Antoine's only surviving brother, Hyacinth. His other brother, Jacques Sr., had died in August 1791. Jacques Jr., Blue Jacket's son-in-law, was sometimes referred to as "Coco" or "Cuckoo" Lasselle, for which compare *Simcoe*, 3:281, 294, 4:19, and 5:131.

20. Edmund Burke to E. B. Littlehales, 27 May 1795, *Simcoe*, 4:19. The charge that the Lasselles tried to sabotage Blue Jacket's defense at Fallen Timbers is a fabrication.

21. Statement of Paul St. Bernard, 24 January 1795, Canada/Indian Affairs Papers, 9:8827; letters of George Ironside, 10, 14 February 1795, Canada/Indian Affairs Papers, 9:8854, 8857; Antoine Lasselle to John McGregor, 31 January 1795, Canada/Military Papers, C248:118; *Simcoe*, 3:281, 286; statement of Thomas Nelson, 13 February 1795, Claus Papers, 7:33; John Francis Hamtramck to Wayne, 29 December 1794, 15 January 1795, Van Cleve, "Letters of Colonel Hamtramck," 389–90; Knopf, "Surgeon's Mate at Fort Defiance," 64; Buell, "Fragment from the Diary," 266, 268; preliminary peace articles, 21 January 1795, deposition of Antoine Lasselle, 22 January 1795, and license for Lasselle, 28 March 1795, all in Wayne Papers (1); and papers relating to the meeting between Wayne and the Ottawas, Potawatomis, Ojibwes, Miamis, and Sacs, January 1795, Wayne Papers (2).

## 14. We Must Think of War No More

1. Buell, "Fragment from the Diary," 268.

2. Entry of 11 October 1794, Bowyer, "Daily Journal," 355; information given to Shawnees and Mingoes, Claus Papers, 2:153; Joseph Brant to Joseph Chew, 24 February 1795, *MPHS*, 15:395; deposition of Abraham Williams, 10 November 1794, and Thomas Pasteur to Anthony Wayne, 3 November 1794, Wayne Papers (1).

3. Speech of Jean Baptiste Laplante, 30 October 1794, McKee Papers; Lutz, "Methodist Missions," 183.

4. Klinck and Talman, *Journal of Major John Norton*, 187.

5. Antoine to Jacques Lasselle, 31 January 1795, *Simcoe*, 3:281.

6. Jacques to Antoine Lasselle, 20 February 1795, Wayne Papers (2); speeches delivered by Blue Jacket, 8–9 February 1795, Wayne Papers (1).

7. Wayne to Timothy Pickering, 8 March 1795, in Knopf, *Anthony Wayne*, 386. In addition to the sources already cited, for Blue Jacket's mission to Greenville, see *Simcoe*, 3:275, 276, 279; letter from Swan Creek, 3 February 1795, Claus Papers, 7:24; Alexander McKee's instructions to Matthew Elliott, May 1795, Claus Papers, 7:46; Robert Stiell to McKee, 7 February 1795, Claus Papers, 7:28; George Ironside to McKee, 10 February 1795, Canada/Indian Affairs Papers, 9:8843; Ironside to Stiell, 10 February 1795, Canada/Indian Affairs Papers, 9:8854; Wayne's letters to Winthrop Sargent (10 February 1795) and Henry Knox (13 February 1795), Wayne Papers (1), and to William Atlee (22 February 1795), Wayne Papers (2); Wayne to Knox, 12 February 1795, in Knopf, *Anthony Wayne*, 384; Knopf, "Surgeon's Mate at Fort Defiance," 67; and the Greenville commissary notes of 10–11 February 1795 in the Harrison Papers (3). At Fort Defiance four white prisoners of the Indian party were mentioned, but the chief's speeches at Greenville state that the Shawnees had two and the Delawares three.

8. Wayne to James O'Hara, 15 February 1795, Northwest Territory Collection, IHS.

9. Thomas Swaine to Anthony Bartlett, 27 February 1795, Northwest Territory Collection, IHS.

10. Jacques to Antoine Lasselle, 20 February 1795, Wayne Papers (2); speech of Shawnees and Delawares to the British, 1795, Claus Papers, 7:24; Ironside to McKee, 27 February 1795, Canada/Indian Affairs Papers, 9:8877; Knopf, "Surgeon's Mate at Fort Defiance," 72–73.

11. Minutes of the treaty of Greenville, 19 July 1795, *ASPIA*, 1:568.

12. Examination of William McKinney, 30 June 1795, Wayne Papers (1).

13. Ironside to McKee (10, 12 February 1795) and Ironside to Stiell (10 February 1795), Canada/Indian Affairs Papers, 9:8843, 8849, 8854.

14. Wayne to Delawares, 21 March 1795, Wayne Papers (2); letter of John Francis Hamtramck, 27 March 1795, Van Cleve, "Letters of Colonel Hamtramck," 391.

15. Ironside to McKee, 27 February 1795, Canada/Indian Affairs Papers, 9:8877; Elliott to McKee, 29 March 1795, Canada/Indian Affairs Papers, 9:8895; commissary notes issued at Greenville, 21, 27, 29 March 1795, Harrison Papers (2), and

U.S. Army Records, box 1, folder 4; Knopf, "Surgeon's Mate at Fort Defiance," 71–72, 77–79, 84. Among those who came into Fort Defiance was Anthony Shane, "half Indian and the other moiety French," who lived with the Shawnees. Shane spoke English, French, and five Indian languages, and the commandant, Maj. Thomas Hunt, hired him as an interpreter and set him to work on a Shawnee vocabulary (Knopf, "Surgeon's Mate at Fort Defiance," 78).

The first indication of Red Pole's return is contained in a letter George Ironside wrote to McKee on 12 February 1795 (Canada/Indian Affairs Papers, 9:8849), in which Blue Jacket's "brother" was said to be accompanying a courier carrying Antoine Lassalle's letters from Swan Creek to Detroit in Manoka's "cariole." The following August Red Pole remarked in council, "I have just returned from an absence of two years to the southward" (Minutes of treaty of Greenville, 10 August 1795, *ASPIA*, 1:581; *Simcoe*, 4:62).

16. E. B. Littlehales to Francis Le Maistre, 29 March 1795, Canada/Military Papers, c 248:54; Ironside to McKee, 6 March 1795, Canada/Indian Affairs Papers, 9:8840; speech of the Mekoches, and McKee's instructions to Elliott, May 1795, both in Claus Papers, 7:124, 46.

17. Van Cleve, "Letters of Colonel Hamtramck," 390–91; Hamtramck to Wayne, 7 May 1795 (two letters), Wayne Papers (2); Thomas Hunt to Wayne, 2 May 1795, Wayne Papers (1); Jacques to Antoine Lassalle, 20 February 1795, Wayne Papers (2).

18. Hunt to Wayne, 2 May 1795, Wayne Papers (1); Knopf, "Surgeon's Mate at Fort Defiance," 85, 161–63.

19. Hamtramck to Wayne, 7 May 1795, and Wayne to Pickering, 15 May 1795, Wayne Papers (1).

20. Hunt to Wayne, 13 May 1795, and Hamtramck to Wayne, 16, 24, 27 May 1795, Wayne Papers (1); Knopf, "Surgeon's Mate at Fort Defiance," 162, 167.

21. Isaac Williams to Wayne, 7 May 1795, and Wayne to Williams, 31 May 1795, Wayne Papers (2); Wayne to Hamtramck, 16 May 1795, and Hamtramck to Wayne, 16 May 1795, Wayne Papers (1); Knopf, "Surgeon's Mate at Fort Defiance," 162.

22. Knopf, "Surgeon's Mate at Fort Defiance," 162; Hamtramck to Wayne, 16 May 1795, Wayne Papers (1).

23. Minutes of the treaty of Greenville, 1795, *ASPIA*, 1:582; Smith, *St. Clair Papers*, 2:374, 375, 386, 387 (two letters); *VSP*, 8:275, 279; *Kentucky Gazette*, 23 May 1795.

24. Thomas Smith to McKee, 23–24, 28 October 1794, Claus Papers, 6:241, 247; Ironside to McKee, 27 February 1795, Canada/Indian Affairs Papers, 9:8877; Knopf, *Anthony Wayne*, 386; *ASPIA*, 1:582; and Smith, *St. Clair Papers*, 2:387.

25. The above paragraphs depend on Antoine Lasselle to François Navarre, 21 March 1795, Canada/Indian Affairs Papers, 9:8891; letter from Detroit, 25 May 1795, Wayne Papers (1); speeches of the Indians around Detroit, June 1795, Wayne Papers (1); Isaac Williams to Wayne, 10 June 1795, Wayne Papers (2); Knopf, *Anthony Wayne*, 427; and Knopf, "Surgeon's Mate at Fort Defiance," 167–68, 171.

26. Marshalk, "Mio-qua-coo-na-caw," 164–65; commissary notes, 5–21 June 1795, Harrison Papers (3), and U.S. Army Records, box 1, folders 4–5; Elliot, *Poetical and Miscellaneous Works*, 141; minutes of the treaty, *ASPIA*, 1:565, 567; and the diary of David Barrow, 1795. The best discussion of the proceedings is Voegelin and Tanner, *Indians of Ohio and Indiana Prior to 1795*, 2:377–427.

27. For the above paragraphs, see the minutes of the treaty, *ASPIA*, 1:566; John Askin Jr. to Richard England, 19 August 1795, Askin Papers; Knopf, "Surgeon's Mate at Fort Defiance," 170–71, 177; and letters in Wayne Papers (1): Hamtramck to Wayne, 25, 27 June 1795; Wayne to Samuel Drake, 29 June 1795; Drake to Wayne, 30 June 1795 (two letters); and J. Breck to Wayne, 1 July 1795.

28. Blue Jacket's speech is quoted from the treaty minutes, *ASPIA*, 1:568, but two manuscript versions of it are to be found in the Ohio Historical Society, Columbus. They vary slightly from each other and from the printed version. For this and the preceding paragraph, see also Askin to England, 19 August 1795, Askin Papers; William Winston to James Findlay, 19 July 1795, W. Blue to James Taylor, 20 July 1795, and John Bowyer to Findlay, 15 July 1795, all in the Torrence Collection; Hunt to Wayne, 8, 14 July 1795, Wayne Papers (1); Knopf, "Surgeon's Mate at Fort Defiance," 184; and commissary notes issued at Greenville, 18–20 July 1795, Wayne Papers (2), and U.S. Army Records, box 1, folder 6. The commissary note for 19 July 1795, in the U.S. Army Records, authorized the issue of eight pounds of beef and flour and eight gills of whiskey for a Shawnee chief and his wife. This may have been a reference to Blue Jacket, but Captain Reed, a Shawnee leader, was also then at Greenville.

29. Askin to England, 19 August 1795, Askin Papers, contains Blue Jacket's reference to his worries about Red Pole.

30. Minutes of the treaty, *ASPIA*, 1:571, 573.

31. Wayne's additions to the cession were made in the belief that the Harmar line would have left the Indians too close to the white settlements. Pickering tried to moderate Wayne's demands, but his final instructions of 29 June did not reach the general in time. See Wayne to Pickering, 15 May, 2 September 1795, and Pickering to Wayne, 8–14 April, 29 June 1795, Wayne Papers (1).

In addition to tracts mentioned in the text, the additional pieces of land ceded by the Indians outside the general boundary were at the portage between the St. Marys and the Great Miami, at the head of navigation on the Auglaize, at the mouth and the rapids of the Sandusky and the mouths of the Chicago and Illinois Rivers, at Peoria Lake (Illinois), at Vincennes and Ouiatenon on the Wabash, at Fort Massac on the lower Ohio, on the Detroit, and at the straits of Mackinac.

32. Tanner, *Atlas*, 96, 101, and Horsman, *Frontier in the Formative Years*, 50.

33. Minutes of the treaty, *ASPIA*, 1:571; Knopf, "Surgeon's Mate at Fort Defiance," 176–77; Hunt to Wayne, 22 July 1795, Wayne Papers (1).

34. Minutes of the treaty, *ASPIA*, 1:579, 581.

35. Knopf, "Surgeon's Mate at Fort Defiance," 184.

36. Minutes of the treaty, *ASPIA*, 1:579.

## 15. Living with Peace

1. Timothy Pickering to George Washington, 28 September 1795, *TPUS*, 2:537.

2. Anthony to Margaretta Wayne, 12 September 1795, Wayne Papers (1); commissary notes, 2 August–21 September 1795, filed in Harrison Papers (2), U.S. Army Records, box 1, folder 6, Wayne Papers (2), U.S. History Papers, and Northwest Territory Collection, IHS; Smith, *St. Clair Papers*, 2:387; Anthony Shane interviewed by Benjamin Drake (1821), Tecumseh Papers, 12YY42–44; Elliott, *Poetical and Miscellaneous Works*, 145–46. Blue Jacket was at Fort Defiance on 20 and 21 September 1795; see Knopf, "Surgeon's Mate at Fort Defiance," 243.

3. "Recapitulation des . . . Sauvages," Tardiveau Papers; Prideaux Selby to Joseph Chew, 28 October 1795, Canada/Military Papers, C248:393; Alexander Mc-Kee to Chew, 4 September, 24 October 1795, Canada/Military Papers, C248:289, and Canada/Indian Affairs Papers, 9:9036; George Ironside to Selby, 7 July 1796, Claus Papers, 7:247; Elliott to Selby, 23 July 1796, Claus Papers, 7:248; Alexander McKenzie to Elliott, 13 January 1796, Claus Papers, 7:143; *Simcoe*, 3:141–44; John F. Hamtramck to James Wilkinson, 11 July 1796, Wayne Papers (1).

4. Hamtramck to Wayne, 8 October 1795, and Wayne to Hamtramck, 20 November 1795, Wayne Papers (1); Van Cleve, "Letters of Colonel Hamtramck," 393; John Johnston to Lyman C. Draper, 10 July 1848, Tecumseh Papers, 11YY33. "That faithful Shawnee," Nekskorwetor, who assisted Fort Defiance by providing game and running down deserters, also had a house built for him by the United States (Knopf, "Surgeon's Mate at Fort Defiance," 242, 257).

5. *Pittsburgh Gazette*, 5 December 1795; Voegelin and Tanner, *Indians of Ohio and Indiana Prior to 1795*, 2:109, 339; Iseta Kelsey to Draper, 4 March 1863, Kenton Papers, 3BB85.

6. Hamtramck to Wilkinson, 1 April, 11 July 1796, Wayne Papers (1). For Blue Jacket's receipts, see commissary notes, 24 April–19 May 1796, Mitten Collection, folder 1, U.S. Army Records, box 1, folder 10, and the Northwest Territory Collection, IHS. Those of Red Pole and other Shawnees between 4 November 1795 and 13 July 1796 can be found in U.S. Army Records, box 1, folders 4, 6–7, 9–11.

7. Hamtramck to Wayne, 23 October 1795, 22 March 1796, and Hamtramck to Wilkinson, 18 April 1796, Wayne Papers (1); Wilkinson to William Winston, 20 March 1796, Hamtramck to Winston, 15 April 1796 (two letters), and Winston to Hamtramck, 3 May 1796, all in Torrence Collection.

8. Hamtramck to Winston, 11 July 1796, Torrence Collection; letters of Hamtramck, 8 June–17 July 1796, are printed in Van Cleve, "Letters of Colonel Hamtramck," 393–94.

9. Winston to Wayne, 5 September 1796, Wayne Papers (1); Isaac Weld, *Travels Through the States of North America*, 2:170–81, 192–200, 289–92; Ironside to Selby, 18 July 1796, 15 June 1801, Claus Papers, 7:250, and 8:150; returns of Indians at Chenail Ecarté and Harsen's Island, 17, 16 October 1797, Canada/Military Papers, C250:294, 339; Selby to Chew, 14 May 1797, Canada/Military Papers, C250:541; council proceedings, Canada/Military Papers, C250:233. The "British" Shawnees

were dissatisfied with their lot and eventually drifted back to Wapakoneta and other places in Ohio.

10. Wayne to Jonathan Taylor, 14 July 1796, Wayne Papers (2), and the following documents in the Wayne Papers (1): Return of Jonathan Meigs to Wayne, 7 August 1796, Wayne to Meigs, 10 August 1796, John Jebb to Wayne, 14 August 1796, David Strong to Wayne, 29 August 1796, John Wallington to Meigs, 29 August 1796, and William Winston to Wayne, 5 September 1796.

11. Wayne to James McHenry, 3 October 1796, Wayne Papers (1). For this delegation, see also Strong to Wayne, 7, 16 September 1796, and Wayne to John Heth, 3 October 1796, Wayne Papers (1); McHenry to Little Turtle, 10 December 1796, Wilkinson Papers; *Aurora General Advertiser* (Philadelphia), 8 December 1796; Bald, *Detroit's First American Decade*, 64; Thomas McKee to William Claus, 15 August 1800, Claus Papers, 8:117; Twohig, *Journals of the Proceedings of the President*, 347.

12. "Letters to [the] President [of] the United States," reel 384 of the Adams Papers, contains copies of the speeches made by and to the Indian delegation. Those given by Blue Jacket and Red Pole can be found on pp. 42–43, 47–49, 61–62, and 65–66. Washington's reply of 29 November 1796 is printed in Fitzpatrick, *Writings of George Washington*, 35:299, 302n.

13. Letters to McHenry, 27 January, 3 February 1797, *Hazard's Register of Pennsylvania*, 12 (1833): 63.

14. White, *Middle Ground*, 494.

15. Shawnees to Wilkinson, 19 May 1797, Wilkinson Papers.


## 16. Uneasy Retirement

1. John Johnston to Lyman C. Draper, 10 July 1848, Tecumseh Papers, 11YY33; Burnet, *Notes on the Early Settlement of the North-Western Territory*, 68–71.

2. William Caldwell interviewed by Lyman C. Draper (1863), Draper Notes, 17S212; O. Risden, *Map of the Surveyed Part of Michigan* (Albany NY, 1825); J. Farmer and T. Bromme, *Karte von Michigan* (Baltimore, 1834); and ms. map of Flat Rock Wyandot Reservation, Surveyor General's Office, Cincinnati, 1843. I am obliged to Helen Hornbeck Tanner for copies of these maps. Brownstown, named for a headman, consisted of about two hundred houses. North of Blue Jacket's village was another Wyandot town, Maguaga, under Walk-in-the-Water, with about twenty houses. Both Wyandot towns were developing economically, with orchards, fences, and cattle in evidence and a substantial number of hogs (Walker, "Plowshares and Pruning Hooks," 402–3).

3. James Bentley interviewed by Draper (1863), Draper Notes, 17S177. See also interviews in Draper Notes, 17S175 and 17S185.

4. Badger, *Memoir*, 29–30, 102.

5. Records of St. Anne's Catholic Church, Detroit, and of La Assumption Catholic Church, Sandwich; Nannette Caldwell interviewed by Draper (1863), Draper Notes, 17S175. Nannette married Thomas Caldwell, the son of Col. William Caldwell and Susanne Baby, at Sandwich on 4 December 1817. She

prospered and owned forty-five farms in 1836, and she had nine children. She died in 1882. Of the other grandchildren Mary gave Blue Jacket, Jacques (21 October 1802–12 January 1827) was buried on the River Raisin and Susanne (20 May 1804–4 May 1806) in Detroit. Julia had a fuller life. She married Lambert Le Duc in Detroit on 3 September 1822 and had seven children.

6. James Galloway to Benjamin Drake, 12–13 January 1839, Clark Papers, 8J45; Clark, *The Shawnee*, 93.

7. Alexander McKee to Joseph Jackson, 15 January 1799, Claus Papers, 8:71; report of Jackson, 1 May 1799, Claus Papers, 8:89; Thomas McKee to Prideaux Selby, 10 January 1803, Claus Papers, 8:243; Selby to Peter Russell, 18 January 1799, Canada/Indian Affairs Papers, 1:256; Joseph Brant to Russell, 27 January 1799, Canada/Indian Affairs Papers, 1:261; Cruikshank and Hunter, *Correspondence of the Honourable Peter Russell*, 2:262, 278; *Philadelphia Gazette*, 29 June 1799; Captain Edward Miller, 15 May 1799, Frontier Wars Papers, 5U169.

8. Hector McLean to James Green, 19 June 1800, Canada/Military Papers, C253:135; Sir John Johnson to Thomas McKee, 21–22 April 1799, letterbook of George Ironside, Ironside Papers; Cruikshank and Hunter, *Correspondence of the Honourable Peter Russell*, 2:285; Shawnee speech, 2 April 1800, and McKee to William Claus, 8 April 1800, McKee Papers.

9. *Western Spy and Hamilton Gazette*, 27 August 1799; Arthur St. Clair to James McHenry, 14, 21 October 1799, 19 May 1800, Smith, *St. Clair Papers*, 2:464, and St. Clair Papers; McHenry to St. Clair, 30 April 1799, Ayer Manuscripts; St. Clair to the Shawnees, 5 October, Shawnee Letters, Mss. q. 211 RM.

10. Thomas McKee to William Claus, 15 August 1800, Claus Papers, 8:117.

11. Ironside to Claus, 11, 12 June 1801, Canada/Indian Affairs Papers, 26:15367, 15372; Ironside to Selby, 15 June 1801, Claus Papers, 8:150; Gipson, *Moravian Indian Mission on White River*, 108; Stone, *Life of Joseph Brant*, 2:407. A report of Blue Jacket on the Illinois River (Dawson, *Historical Narrative*, 41) seems to have been made by Benjamin Parke in 1802. His report and journal were sent to the secretary of war, but I have been unable to trace them: William Henry Harrison to Henry Dearborn, 27 May, 11 June, 22 July 1802, in Clanin, *Papers of William Henry Harrison*, reel 1:306, 311, 338.

12. Jefferson quotation from Woehrmann, *At the Headwaters of the Maumee*, 85. This volume, with Prucha, *American Indian Policy*, Horsman, *Expansion and American Indian Policy*, and Sheehan, *Seeds of Extinction*, competently surveys Jeffersonian Indian policy.

13. Kappler, *Indian Affairs*, 2:77; MPHS, 40:112–19; TPUS, 10:130. Smith, "Indian Land Cessions," is a clear narrative of this and other land negotiations of the period.

14. Among references to this development are Claus to Green, 24 July 1805, Canada/Indian Affairs Papers, 10:9615; Thomas McKee to Claus, 31 May 1806, Canada/Indian Affairs Papers, 11:37; William Hull to Henry Dearborn, 28 October 1805, U.S. SOW/LR/R 1:0238; MPHS, 23:39; TPUS, 10:57; speech of Sacs and Potawatomis and British reply, Claus Papers, 9:139; statement of John Shaw, 24

June 1810, *Western Sun* [Vincennes], 14 July 1810; and accounts by White, *Middle Ground*, 511–13, and Sugden, *Tecumseh*, 133–34, 155–56, 175–78.

15. Little Turtle of the Miamis, Five Medals of the Potawatomis, and Tarhe of the Wyandots were among the first to respond to American offers to help with development programs. See letter to the Indians, 23 May 1796, and letter of representatives of the Society of Friends, 19 September 1796, Minutes of the Society of Friends Baltimore Yearly Meeting and Other Meetings; Wyandot petitions in Parker Papers; and Parsons, "Civilizing the Indians." For the Shawnee trip, see Dearborn to the Shawnees, 10 February 1802, and Dearborn to William Henry Harrison, 23 February 1802, Shawnee File; Harvey, *History of the Shawnee Indians*, 210; report from Paulson's *American Daily Advertiser*, 30 January 1802, in Frontier Wars Papers, 12U105.

16. Perrin de Lac, *Travels*, 45; *Missouri Gazette*, 14 March 1811; William Clark to James Madison, 10 April 1811, with enclosures, U.S. SOW/LR/IA:0548; Amos Stoddard, *Sketches, Historical and Descriptive, of Louisiana* (Phildelphia: Mathew Carey, 1812), 214–15.

17. Horsman, *Frontier in the Formative Years*, chap. 6; Bond, *Civilization of the Old Northwest*, chap. 11.

18. Diary of Abraham Luckenbach, 1808, Shawnee File; William Kirk to Dearborn, 12 April, 10 December 1808, with enclosures, and 12 February 1809, U.S. SOW/LR/R 25:8114, 8143, 8157; Thornbrough, *Letter Book of the Indian Agency at Fort Wayne*, 33, 37, 46; Klinck and Talman, *Journal of Major John Norton*, 173–75; Minutes of Society of Friends Baltimore Yearly Meeting and Other Meetings, 17 October, 15 November 1811, 5 October 1812; James A. Green, ed., "Journal of Ensign William Schillinger, a Soldier of the War of 1812," *Ohio Archaeological and Historical Publications* 41 (1932): 82; Walker, "Plowshares and Pruning Hooks," 396; and Harvey, *History of the Shawnee Indians*, 138–40.

19. Dawson, *Historical Narrative*, appendix 1.

## 17. Voices from the West

1. Diary entries and documents in Gipson, *Moravian Indian Mission*, 359, 361, 381, 382, 529; Andrews, "Shaker Mission," 122; Wyandots to William Hull, 27 June 1810, U.S. SOW/LR/R 37:3872.

2. Epidemics are charted in Tanner, *Atlas*, 169–74. For the Delaware religious awakening, see Wallace, "New Religions Among the Indians"; Charles Hunter, "The Delaware Nativist Revival of the Mid-Eighteenth Century," *Ethnohistory* 18 (1971): 39–49; Dowd, *Spirited Resistance*; and Olmstead, *David Zeisberger*, chaps. 12–13.

3. Andrews, "Shaker Mission," 123. For Lalawéthika, the Shawnee Prophet, see Edmunds, *Shawnee Prophet*; Dowd, *Spirited Resistance*; and Sugden, *Tecumseh*.

4. Thomas Worthington and Duncan McArthur to Thomas Kirker, September 1807, Kenton Papers, 7BB49.

5. For Shawnees and missionaries, see Olmstead, *David Zeisberger*, 83–85, 212–

13; Kinietz and Voegelin, *Shawnese Traditions*, 8; Joseph B. Herring, *The Enduring Indians of Kansas* (Lawrence: University of Kansas Press, 1990), 4.

6. John Tanner, *A Narrative of the Captivity and Adventures of John Tanner* (New York: G. and C. and H. Carvill, 1830), 155–58; *ASPIA*, 1:100; Journal of the Creek Agency, 1813, U.S. SOW/LR/U 8:3266; Joel W. Martin *Sacred Revolt* (Boston: Beacon Books, 1991), 141–45; account of John Johnston, Tecumseh Papers, 11YY17–18; Kirker to Thomas Jefferson, 8 October 1807, Parker Papers; Gipson, *Moravian Indian Mission*, 392; Sabathy-Judd, "Diary of the Moravian Indian Mission," 903–4; *MPHS*, 40:127; Thomas Forsyth to William Clark, 23 December 1812, in Emma H. Blair, ed. *The Indian Tribes of the Upper Mississippi Valley and Region of the Great Lakes* 2 vols. (Cleveland OH: Arthur H. Clark, 1911), 2:273; and report of John Conner, 18 June 1808, U.S. SOW/LR/R 33:1016.

7. Speech of Yealabaheah, 1816, Cass Papers; William Wells to Henry Dearborn, 20–23 April, 5 June 1808, U.S. SOW/LR/R 33:0923, 0988. These events are fully documented in Sugden, *Tecumseh*, chap. 10.

8. Andrews, "Shaker Mission," 117–18.

9. Sacs and Potawatomis speech at Fort Malden, 28 June 1806, Claus Papers, 9:139; *TPUS*, 10:57; *Western Spy and Hamilton Gazette*, 22 July 1806.

10. Dearborn to William Hull, 28 July 1806, notes that "Your Excellency's letter of the 27th ult. enclosing copies of Blue Jacket's speech and your answer has been duly received" (*TPUS*, 10:65). I have been unable to locate Hull's dispatch and enclosures in the records of the secretary of war.

11. Speech of Blue Jacket, Tecumseh, and Lewis, 11 August 1806, *Virginia Argus* (Richmond), 6 September 1806. François Duchouquet, a French Canadian, was born about 1760 and came to the Indian country as a trader in the 1780s. By 1790 he was in partnership with the Detroit merchant Angus McIntosh. In May of that year the Shawnees took some prisoners on the Ohio, and Duchouquet ransomed some of them to set them at liberty. Some of the prisoners gratefully repaid the trader, but Duchouquet was left £170 out of pocket. In 1802 he successfully petitioned the United States government for the sum, receiving in addition 6 percent interest (*Report from the Committee of Claims on the Petition of Francis Duchouquet*, 19 February 1802, IHS). One of the captives, Charles Johnston, corresponded with his benefactor for thirty years and testified that Duchouquet "ever sustained a fair character for integrity and veracity. He is not an enlightened scholar, but possesses a sound understanding, and is capable of judicious observation" (Johnston, *Narrative*, 100). In the War of 1812 some of Duchouquet's Indian debtors joined the hostiles under Tecumseh, defaulting payment, and his business collapsed. He eked out his last years on a small allowance and occasional employment as interpreter to the Ohio Shawnees. Late in 1831 he accompanied a Shawnee delegation to Washington but fell ill and died at Newman's Hotel, Cumberland, Maryland, on 9 January 1832. He was buried in the local Methodist cemetery. Although he drank heavily, Duchouquet was a quiet, gentle man who enjoyed a good character from nearly all of his associates: speech of Black Hoof, 5 February 1802, Shawnee File; William Kirk to Daniel Drake, 16 September 1807, Tecumseh Papers, 3YY74; John Johnston to

Lyman C. Draper, 29 December 1847, Tecumseh Papers, 11YY32; Harvey, *History of the Shawnee Indians*, 210; and Rayner, *First Century of Piqua, Ohio*, 254–55. The complaint of the Stony Creek Shawnees is the only one I have found against him.

Frederick Fisher had been taken prisoner as a child in Kentucky and raised by the Indians. Since his father died and many of his friends dispersed, Fisher later chose to remain with the Indians as a trader, and his command of English, French, Shawnee, and Ojibwe gave him frequent employment as an interpreter. From 1796 to 1798 he was at Chenail Ecarté in the service of the British Indian Department, but the following year saw him at Wapakoneta, escorting some Shawnee leaders to Montreal. In 1801 he secured a trading license from the governor of Indiana Territory and served the Delaware and Shawnee communities in Ohio and on the White River. He traded with the Prophet's party at Greenville in 1806 and 1807 and, despite their complaints about him, continued to visit their towns. On 25 January 1808 Fisher was appointed an interpreter with the British Indian Department at Amherstburg and died in this post in November 1810. See *Western Spy and Hamilton Gazette*, 30 July 1799; traders' licenses, 12 December 1801, Lasselle Papers (1); Elias Langham to Thomas Kirker, 5 September 1807, Kenton Papers, 7BB45; Indian Department list, Canada/Indian Affairs Papers, 27:15761; and Horsman, *Matthew Elliott*, 139, 146, 168, 185.

The Indian village at Greenville was situated southwest of the confluence of Greenville and Mud Creeks, in an area of oak and walnut. The location was not entirely suitable, for recent archaeological research suggests that the town spread over several square miles and occupied the floodplain of both creeks. What appear to have been the principal Indian cabins (excavations reveal the use of hand-forged nails but not the more elaborate debris associated with white pioneer homes) were on the higher ground and ran southwest to northeast toward the confluence of the streams (Green, DeRegnaucourt, and Hamilton, *Archaeology of Prophetstown*).

12. Shawnees to Dearborn and Jefferson, 12 December 1807, U.S. SOW/LR/R 4:1189; Jefferson to the Shawnees, 19 February 1807, Shawnee File.

13. Black Hoof and Black Snake to Dearborn, spring 1807, U.S. SOW/LR/U 2:0949; Hull to Dearborn, 9 September 1807, *MPHS*, 40:197; Andrews, "Shaker Mission," 124.

14. The Shaker journal is reprinted in Andrews, "Shaker Mission."

15. Moore, "Early Recollections of Nancy Stewart," 327–28, names Nancy's children as Elizabeth, Henry, Margaret, and John and states that none ever married. Presumably some did not reach maturity. John H. Renick, interviewed by Draper in 1866 (Draper Notes, 21S95), remembered that Nancy left three sons and a daughter. Most died of consumption, but the youngest, Joseph, survived. Both witnesses knew Nancy, but Renick seems to have been the more accurate, since a Joseph M. Stewart, presumably Nancy's son, was appointed executor at the time of her death in 1840 (records of Logan County, Ohio).

16. McNemar, *Kentucky Revival*, 130–32; J. P. MacLean, "Shaker Mission to the Shawnee Indians," *Ohio Archaeological and Historical Publications* 11 (1903): 228–29. There are alternatives to the theory that Nancy the interpreter was Nancy Blue-Jacket. A "Big Nancy" was later listed with Tecumseh's band when it was

in Canada (Return of Claims of Indians for losses sustained in the War of 1812 under the statute of 1823, Ironside Papers), but there is no evidence that she spoke English. A more plausible candidate is Nancy, the stepdaughter of Anthony Shane. In 1821 Shane was married to Lamateshe, a relation to Tecumseh. Nine years later Shane was said to have had a son, who had been six months in Richard Mentor Johnson's Chocktaw Academy in Kentucky, and a stepdaughter, Nancy, who was then a widow with one child. This Nancy had been raised among whites. George Vashon wrote, "She speaks English very well, and is a woman of most excellent character, and, I think, much disposed to be pious. I think [her] better qualified for all the various duties of a female interpreter than any other that I know of" (Vashon to Jesse Green, July 1830, in Lutz, "Methodist Missions," 166). *If* this Nancy was the daughter of Lamateshe, and was thus herself related to Tecumseh, she may have been the Nancy mentioned by the Shakers in 1807.

17. Wells to John Gerard, 22 August 1807, Kenton Papers, 7BB44. Sugden, *Tecumseh*, chapter 11, summarizes the progress of the Prophet's religion further afield, but a new primary source has recently been made available (Sabathy-Judd, "Diary of the Moravian Indian Mission," 903–4). According to the Moravian diary of Fairfield, on the River Thames in Upper Canada, prophecy was then (24 February 1807) rife in nearby Muncey Town. "The old stories that the heathens have their own God and a different way to salvation from that of the whites are hot topics once again." Onim ("a great sorcerer") was using a board depicting eighty sins to teach the Indians of Muncey Town the way to Heaven. "According to the new custom, supposedly inspired by God, the Indians greet each other in their homes every morning. This is followed by a general meeting wherein it is taught to abstain from killing, whoring, stealing, etc., because it displeases God." The Indians were to thank the Great Spirit for their fires but to shun whites, who "will suffer eternal misery" in the afterworld. "All contact with white people [is] to be done away with. Pork meat is not to be eaten at all. . . . Every deviation is regarded as a sin." This teaching had considerable impact on Muncey Town. It may have originated among the Delawares and Munsees on the White River, where Beata was preaching, but I feel more likely it reflected the activities of the Shawnee Prophet.

18. Meeting of 15 August 1807, Frontier Wars Papers, 5U186; report of William Ward and Simon Kenton, September 1807, Kenton Papers, 7BB46; Ward to James Findley, 8 September 1807, Torrence Collection. One of the interpreters who accompanied Ward and Kenton was James McPherson, who was known to the Indians as "Squa-la-ka-ka," the Red-Faced Man. McPherson was born in 1760 in Carlisle, Pennsylvania, and enlisted with the Eighth Pennsylvania Regiment in 1776. He was captured by Joseph Brant's warriors at Lochry's Defeat in 1781 and was eventually adopted by the Shawnees, with whom he lived until 1793. He married a white woman who had also been living in the Indian villages. The couple liked Indians and later settled as traders on the Great Miami River. McPherson piloted William Hull's ill-fated expedition to Detroit in 1812 and served as Indian agent at Lewis Town in Ohio until 1830. When the Shawnees and Mingoes of Lewis Town decided to migrate beyond the Mississippi, McPherson

promised to help escort them, but he was prevented from going by the death of his wife on 17 September 1832. Two years later, he said regretfully that it was "the first and last time I ever forfeited my word with an Indian" (petition of James McPherson, 1834). Certainly he was trusted by the Shawnees. One who knew him said, "He was most strictly honest and kept a store in Lewis Town. The Indians had such undoubted confidence in him that no other man could buy their furs but him" (Alder, ms., "History of Jonathan Alder"). According to McPherson's daughter, Tecumseh occasionally visited her father before the War of 1812 (Elizabeth Jacket Workman interviewed by Lyman C. Draper, 1863, Draper Notes, 17S76).

19. Benjamin Whiteman to William C. Schenck, 27 August 1807, "Autograph Letters," *Western Reserve and Northern Ohio Historical Society Tracts* 39 (1877): 18–19; William Ward to James Findley, 29 August, 8 September 1807, and letter of James Findley, 31 August 1807, Torrence Collection; Elias Langham to Thomas Kirker, 5, 6 September 1807, Kenton Papers, 7BB45, 47.

20. Speech of the Trout, 4 May 1807, MPHS, 40:127; Hull to Dearborn, 9 September 1807, MPHS, 40:197.

21. Speech of Blue Jacket, 14 September 1807, in Thomas Worthington and Duncan McArthur to Kirker, 22 September 1807, Kenton Papers, 7BB49.

22. Wells to Kirker, 4 August 1807, and Kirker to the Indians, 19 August 1807, in Kenton Papers, 7BB39, 43; Joseph Foos to Kirker, 10 August 1807, Kirker Papers; *Scioto Gazette*, 10 September 1807.

23. William Creighton to Kirker, 23 August 1807, Williams Papers; Worthington and McArthur to Kirker, 22 September 1807, Kenton Papers, 7BB49.

24. The most important sources for Blue Jacket and Tecumseh in Chillicothe are the *Chillicothe Fredonian*, 25 September 1807, and Thomas Kirker to Thomas Jefferson, 8 October 1807, Parker Papers. Thomas Spottswood Hinde, an uncle of the editor of the *Fredonian*, probably supplied the newspaper with a report. His own reminiscences of the occasion can be found in the Hinde Papers, 16Y45–51, but see also Hinde to Benjamin Drake, 17 July 1840, Tecumseh Papers, 3YY130. The other witness quoted in this paragraph is Charles A. Stuart to Draper, 17 February 1846, Kentucky Papers, 8CC59.

*Conclusion*

1. The most authoritative statement about Blue Jacket's death was made by Capt. William Caldwell, who became a brother-in-law to the chief's granddaughter. Caldwell, who was born in 1784, knew Blue Jacket well and said he died at his town in 1808 (Caldwell, interviewed by Lyman C. Draper, 1863, Draper Notes, 17S212). This is supported by Blue Jacket's disappearance from records after his visit to Chillicothe in 1807; by the failure of the British to consult him in mid-1808, when they earnestly canvassed the Shawnees and organized a conference at Fort Malden, close to the chief's town; and by Jacques Lasselle's attempts to provide for Blue Jacket's son later the same year. Other statements are both vague and unauthoritative. In 1848 John Johnston, the U.S. Indian agent, thought Blue

Jacket had died in his village about 1810 (John Johnston to Draper, 10 July 1848, Tecumseh Papers, 11YY33). A Frenchman who claimed to have seen Blue Jacket in 1809 may have been confusing the chief with one of his sons (Draper Notes, 17S175 and 17S281.

2. Moore, "Early Recollections of Nancy Stewart," 328.

3. Land grants, 2 October 1810, deed book, Logan County, Ohio.

4. That Joseph was alive in 1813 is revealed by John Wingate to William Henry Harrison, 15 June 1813, Harrison Papers (1). For Nancy, see the treaty of 29 September 1817 (Kappler, *Indian Affairs*, 2:145); application of the Stewarts for rights of alienation, including John Johnston's letter of 20 June 1820, and land grant of 13 July 1824, Shawnee Papers.

5. Probate records, 1840, Logan County, Ohio.

6. Nannette Caldwell interviewed by Draper (1863), Draper Notes, 17S175.

7. George McDougall to William Woodbridge, 26 February 1820, Woodbridge Papers; *American State Papers, Class VIII, Public Lands*, 8 vols. (Washington DC: Gale and Seaton, 1832–61), 1:492.

8. McAfee, *Late War in the Western Country*, 8–9; William Claus to Francis Gore, 14 February 1808, and Gore to James Craig, 8 April 1808, Canada/Indian Affairs Papers, 2:809, 843.

9. This is the first recruiting trip Tecumseh is definitely known to have made. Shortly after the collapse of the Sac-Winnebago plot of 1809, Tecumseh went to the Mississippi, while the Prophet visited Governor William Henry Harrison of Indiana Territory in Vincennes. While the Prophet was in the town, Harrison reported that a territorial official, Ambrose Whitlock, had "just returned" from Fort Madison on the Des Moines River. "At a council lately held the Indians in that quarter have acknowledged their designs to have been hostile, but have now with great ceremony buried the tomahawk. Amongst them is a brother of the Prophet's [Tecumseh], who acts as his ambassador. The Prophet says that nine tribes had confederated to make war upon us, and he claims the merit of having prevailed upon them to give up the design" (Harrison to John Johnston, 8 July 1809, Jones Collection; William Clark to William Eustis, 25 June 1809, U.S. SOW/LR/R 20:6275). Apparently Tecumseh invited the Indians on the Mississippi to send people to visit the Prophet on the Wabash. Four Sacs were dispatched to investigate the Prophet. They had not returned by October, but when they did they brought with them an Indian schooled in the Prophet's doctrines (*Missouri Gazette*, 4 October 1809; Mile M. Quaife, ed., *Life of Black Hawk* [1916; reprint, New York: Dover, 1994], 11). It was later that same year, 1809, that Tecumseh intensified his efforts to build a confederacy and transformed its purpose, focusing it much more purposefully on the military and political defense of Indian land. The above revises my account in *Tecumseh*, chap. 13.

10. Harrison's manipulation of the treaty proceedings at Fort Wayne is dealt with in Sugden, *Tecumseh*, chap. 14. For this see also TPUS, 7:670, and Harrison to John Johnston, 8 July 1809, Jones Collection. Harrison's letter to Johnston establishes that it was the latter who prompted the inclusion of the Potawatomis

in the negotiations, even though the lands in question had been held to belong to the Miamis and Weas.

11. Autobiography of William Winans, Winans Papers. I am grateful to Doug E. Clanin for drawing my notice to this source.

12. Too often Tecumseh has been seen as unique or unusual because he planned to unite the tribes against the United States. Even recently, seasoned historian R. David Edmunds contended that Tecumseh's ideas were "foreign" or "alien" to the Indians and offered what was essentially "a white [man's] solution to the Indians' problems" (Edmunds, *Shawnee Prophet*, 187–90, and *Tecumseh and the Quest for Indian Leadership*, 224–25). But this is to repudiate seventy years of Shawnee history. Tecumseh's plans for intertribal unity were not new; they were old. He was not the beginning of a tradition but the end of one. He was reviving a strategy the Shawnees had embraced since the 1740s and some other Indians much longer. In 1812 Tecumseh's industry, eloquence, and luck had managed to restore some credibility to what was, in fact, a very tired idea. For current views of Tecumseh, see John Sugden, "Will the Real Tecumseh Please Stand Up?"

13. Anthony Shane, interviewed by Benjamin Drake (1821), Tecumseh Papers, 12YY56–57, said that the Ohio Shawnee chief Lewis promised to accompany Tecumseh to the South, but eventually Jim Blue-Jacket went in his stead. I take this to have been Jim Blue-Jacket Jr., the grandson, rather than the son, of the great war chief. This younger Jim Blue-Jacket lived among the Ohio Shawnees. He was illiterate, and on 10 July 1812 he and Kelleskessimmo accepted payments of $10 each for traveling five hundred miles distributing speeches on behalf of the American general William Hull and signed with crosses (receipted bill, Detroit, 10 July 1812, War of 1812 Manuscripts). He was also known as Tewaskoota and signed the 1814 treaty of Greenville. At the time of the treaty of the Maumee Rapids in 1817, which he also signed, he was living at Wapakoneta. In 1832 he emigrated to Kansas with a family of four, served the United States against the Seminoles in 1837 and 1838, and died in Kansas in 1848. His wife, Pa-tex-ie, also died in Kansas, in 1852.

14. Matthew Elliott to William Claus, 8–11 August 1812, Canada/Indian Affairs Papers, 28:16397; Indian Department establishment, 15 April 1813, Canada/Indian Affairs Papers, 28:16452; John Allen to Henry Clay and George M. Bibb, 1 December 1812, Frontier Wars Papers, 7U8.

15. Sandy Antal's comment (in *Wampum Denied*, 87) that Tecumseh was "clearly responsible" for the execution of a prisoner after the skirmish at Brownstown on 5 August 1812 is inappropriate. Tecumseh's war party did execute a prisoner in the Brownstown council house, in retaliation for the death of Logan, but Tecumseh was not present. Whether he instigated the affair (as Antal alleges), merely felt unable to interfere with the customary right of the relatives of the dead, or was ignorant of the event is an open question. No account by an eyewitness or by someone party to the incident exists.

16. Shawnee speech, 19 May 1813, enclosed in Wingate to Harrison, 15 June 1813, Harrison Papers (1); Peter Navarre interviewed by Draper (1863 and 1866),

Draper Notes, 17S135, 21S81; Joseph Evans interviewed by Draper (1863), Draper Notes, 17S81; and James Knaggs interviewed by Draper (1863), Draper Notes, 17S134.

17. Shane interviewed by Drake (1821), Tecumseh Papers, 12YY63–68; Shawnee speech, 19 May 1813, enclosed in Wingate to Harrison, 15 June 1813, Harrison Papers (1).

18. Letter to Hyacinth Lasselle, 26 May 1813, Lasselle Papers (1); William Woodbridge to Henry Clay, December 1823, Woodbridge Papers; Registers of St. Anne's Catholic Church, Detroit, 4 November 1802, 17 June 1806. If true, the oft-told story of Tecumseh's defense of Hubert Lacroix, a River Raisin settler, might also be explained by the Blue Jacket connection. According to Timothy Alden, *A Collection of American Epitaphs and Inscriptions*, 5 vols. (New York: S. Marks, 1814), 5:198, Tecumseh demanded the release of Lacroix in 1813, after the British had put him aboard a vessel for removal. He was suspected of aiding the enemy. Henry Procter, commanding the British troops, had to release Lacroix ("the King of the Woods" required it, Procter is said to have written) when Tecumseh threatened to abandon the British-Indian alliance. Alden is not himself an authority, and some of the details of the story sound suspicious. Given Tecumseh's ambitions, he was not in a position to abandon the British, nor does Procter's alleged response seem in character. Legend notwithstanding, the two men enjoyed a good relationship until the late summer of 1813. There may have been some truth in the story, however, despite the cloudy details. Years later Lacroix's daughter supported it, stating that the incident occurred after the fall of Detroit in 1812 and that Tecumseh interceded after being approached by Lacroix's brother-in-law, a Mr. Bou[r]gard (Talcott Wing to Draper, 2 December 1887, 11 September 1888, Tecumseh Papers, 5YY35–36). Lacroix was a captain in the American militia from the River Raisin in 1812 and could have eventually been arrested. Furthermore, he was a friend of the Lasselles and Mary Blue-Jacket and had stood witness to the formal marriage of Jacques and Mary in 1801. He might thus have had a claim on Tecumseh's protection (*MPHS*, 8:625; Registers of St. Anne's Catholic Church, Detroit, 29 March 1801). Though regularly published as authentic, the Lacroix story must be regarded as credible but unproven.

19. For Shortt, see Antal, *Wampum Denied*, 257, 270; casualty returns, Britian/War Office Papers, WO 25/1768; *A List of All the Officers of the Army and Royal Marines* (published annually by the British government), volumes up to 1813. For Sally Blue-Jacket and Thomas Shortt, see return of claims of Indians for losses sustained in the War of 1812 under the statute of 1823, and Joseph Barnett and the Blue Jacket family to George Ironside, 24 January 1844, both in Ironside Papers; William Walker to Draper, 19 October 1870, Frontier Wars Papers, 11U82; Shawnee census, 1857, and Shawnee applications for bounty lands, 14 December 1867, Shawnee Papers. William Walker, born in 1799, was the son of Catherine Walker (1771–1844) and her husband, a Virginian named William Walker.

20. Charles Blue-Jacket interviewed by Draper (1868), Draper Notes, 23S167, and letter of a Wyandot, 16 August 1843, *Cincinnati Gazette*, 21 September 1843. The daughter was probably the Nancy Blue-Jacket known also as Wa-na-see, who

was listed in the 1857 Shawnee census as being forty-five years old, and who died in Kansas in 1876.

21. George's children included Betsy, Kate (died about 1835), Henry (died 1855), George (ca. 1815–67), John (born after 1811), and Charles (1817–97). For George himself, see McDougall to Woodbridge, 26 February 1820, Woodbridge Papers; Charles Blue-Jacket interviewed by Draper (1868) Draper Notes, 23S167; Emmanuel F. Heisler and D. M. Smith, *Atlas Map of Johnson County, Kansas* (Wyandott KS: Heisler, 1874), 71; Spencer, "Shawnee Indians," 398; Rayner, *First Century of Piqua, Ohio*, 251–53; and Joseph Barnett and the Blue Jacket family to George Ironside, 24 January 1844, and return of the claims of Indians for losses sustained in the War of 1812, both in Ironside Papers. Under the British statute of 1823 George was awarded £24.13s.2½d.

22. Harvey, *History of the Shawnee Indians*, 287–88, 309; Spencer, "Shawnee Insians," 398, and "Shawnee Folk-Lore," 319–26; Heisler and Smith, *Atlas Map of Johnson County, Kansas*, 71, 85; Lutz, "Methodist Missions"; Caldwell, *Annals of the Shawnee Methodist Mission*, 16, 100; and Staab, "Blue Jacket Led Shawnees Through Traumatic Period Here."

# Selected Bibliography

## Manuscript Collections

Adams Papers. Massachusetts Historical Society, Boston.

Additional Manuscript 24322. British Library, London.

Alder, Jonathan. "The History of Jonathan Alder." OHS.

Armstrong, John. Papers. IHS.

Askin, John. Papers. BHC.

Ayer, Edward E. Manuscripts. Newberry Library, Chicago.

Barrow, David. Diary. Filson Club, Louisville KY.

Blue Jacket's speech, Greenville, 1795. OHS.

Boone, Daniel. Papers. C series. SHSW/D.

Brady and Wetzel Papers. E series. SHSW/D.

Britain/Colonial Office Papers (CO), cited by class, volume, and page. CO 42/vols. 16–22 (miscellaneous Canadian materials); CO 42/vols. 45–83 (Quebec, 1783–92); CO 42/vols. 316–20 (Upper Canada, 1791–97); CO 5 (Board of Trade). Public Record Office, Kew, England.

Britain/War Office Papers (WO), cited by class, volume, and page. WO 28/10 (Indian Department); WO 25/1768 (casualty returns). Public Record Office, Kew, England.

Brown, Henry. Papers. Cincinnati Historical Society.

Butler, Richard. Journal, 1785–86. University of Chicago Library.

Canada Papers. Chicago Historical Society.

Canada/Indian Affairs Papers (Record group 10), cited by volume and page. Vols. 1–4, 8–11, 26–28. Microfilms C-10996–97, C-10999–11000, C-11007–8. National Archives of Canada, Ottawa.

Canada/Military papers (Record Group 8), cited by volume (C number) and page. Volumes C 247–56. Microfilms C-2848–52. National Archives of Canada, Ottawa.

Cass, Lewis. Papers. Clements Library, University of Michigan, Ann Arbor MI.

Clark, George Rogers. Papers. J series. SHSW/D.

Claus, William. Papers. Vols. 1–9, 14–16. MG19/fl. National Archives of Canada, Ottawa.

Covington, Leonard. Papers. BHC.

Drake, Daniel. Papers. O series. SHSW/D.

Draper, Lyman C. Miscellanies. Q series. SHSW/D.

Draper, Lyman C. Draper Notes. S series. SHSW/D.

Durrett Manuscripts. University of Chicago Library.

Elliot, Robert. Letters. Cincinnati Historical Society.

English, William H. Papers. IHS.

Forsyth, Thomas. Papers. T series. SHSW/D.

Frontier Wars Papers. U series. SHSW/D.

Gano, John Stites. Papers. Cincinnati Historical Society.

Haldimand, Frederick. Papers. Additional manuscripts 21760–63 (Niagara); 21765, 21842, 21845 (Miscellaneous); 21766–68 (Guy Johnson); 21769–72 (Indian affairs); 21775 (John Johnson); 21782–83 (Detroit); 21876 (memorials relating to Indian Department). British Library, London.

Hamilton, James. Papers. Historical Society of Pennsylvania, Philadelphia.

Harmar, Josiah. Papers. W series. SHSW/D.

Harrington, M. R. "Shawnee Indian Notes." Newberry Library, Chicago.

Harrison, William Henry. Papers (1). Library of Congress, Washington DC.

Harrison, William Henry. Papers (2). IHS.

Harrison, William Henry. Papers (3). Eli Lilly Library, Bloomington IN.

Harrison, William Henry. Papers. (4). Cincinnati Historical Society.

Harrison, William Henry. Papers (5). Chicago Historical Society.

Harrison, William Henry. Papers (6). X series. SHSW/D.

Heckewelder, John. Papers. American Philosophical Society, Philadelphia.

Hinde, Thomas S. Papers. Y series. SHSW/D.

Horsfield, Timothy. Papers. American Philosophical Society, Philadelphia.

Indian Languages, papers relating to. American Philosophical Society, Philadelphia.

Indiana Territory Collection. IHS.

Indians Collection. Missouri Historical Society, St. Louis.

Invoices for Indian goods. IHS.

Ironside, George. Papers. BHC.

Irvine, William. Papers. AA series. SHSW/D.

Johnston, John. Papers (1). OHS.

Johnston, John. Papers (2). Cincinnati Historical Society.

Jones, Frank Johnston. Collection. Mss qJ767. Cincinnati Historical Society.

Kenton, Simon. Papers. BB series. SHSW/D.

Kentucky Papers. CC series. SHSW/D.

Kirker, Thomas. Papers. OHS.

Knox, Henry. Papers. Pierpont Morgan Library, New York City.

La Assumption Catholic Church, Sandwich, Ontario. Registers. BHC.

Lasselle papers (1). Indiana State Library, Indianapolis.

Lasselle papers (2). Eli Lilly Library, Bloomington IN.

Logan County, Ohio. Deed book and Probate records, supplied by Louise F. Johnson.

Logan, James. Letterbooks. American Philosophical Society, Philadelphia.

McArthur, Duncan. Papers. OHS.

McKee, Alexander. Papers (Intercepted correspondence, 1789–1814). National Archives of the United States, Washington DC.

McPherson, James. Petition. Eli Lilly Library, Bloomington IN.

Marietta College Collection. OHS.

Mitten, Arthur. Collection. IHS.

Morgan, George. Papers. Carnegie Library of Pittsburgh.

Morgan, George. Letterbook, 1776. Pennsylvania State Archives, Harrisburg.

Northwest Territory Collection. OHS.

Northwest Territory Collection. IHS.

Parker, Daniel. Papers. Mss.466 Historical Society of Pennsylvania, Philadelphia.

Patterson, Robert. Papers. MM series. SHSW/D.

Pershouse, John. Papers. Historical Society of Pennsylvania, Philadelphia.

Preston Family Papers (Joyes Collection). Filson Club, Louisville KY.

Prince, William. Folder. IHS.

St. Anne's Catholic Church, Detroit. Registers. BHC.

St. Clair, Arthur. Papers. OHS.

Sargent, Winthrop. Papers. OHS.

Shawnee File. Great Lakes–Ohio Valley Ethnohistory Archive transcripts. Glenn A. Black Laboratory of Archaeology, Indiana University, Bloomington IN.

Shawnee letters, 1799. Mss. q 211, 258 RM. Cincinnati Historical Society.

Shawnee Papers, including censuses and applications for bounty lands, supplied by Louise F. Johnson and Marylen M. Williams.

Society of Friends. Minutes of Baltimore Yearly Meeting and Other Meetings. OHS.

Tardiveau, Barthelemi. Papers. Chicago Historical Society.

Tecumseh Papers. YY series. SHSW/D.

Tennessee Papers. XX series. SHSW/D.

Tiffin, Edward. Papers. OHS.

Todd, Robert. Papers. Eli Lilly Library, Bloomington IN.

Torrence, Aaron. Collection. Cincinnati Historical Society.

Trowbridge, Charles C. "Indian Tales." State Historical Society of Wisconsin, Madison.

United States of American/Letters Received by the Secretary of War, Registered series (Record Group 107), cited by reel and frame. Microfilm M221. National Archives of the United States, Washington DC.

United States of America/Letters Received by the Secretary of War,
Unregistered series (Record Group 107), cited by reel and frame. Microfilm
M222. National Archives of the United States, Washington DC.

United States of America/Letters Received by the Secretary of War Relating to
Indian Affairs (Record Group 75), cited by frame. Microfilm M271. National
Archives of the United States, Washington DC.

U.S. Army Records. OHS.

U.S. History Manuscripts. Eli Lilly Library, Bloomington IN.

Voegelin, Erminie Wheeler. Papers. Newberry Library, Chicago.

War of 1812 Manuscripts. Eli Lilly Library, Bloomington IN.

Wayne, Anthony. Papers (1), filed in date order. Mss.699. Historical Society of
Pennsylvania, Philadelphia.

Wayne, Anthony. Papers (2). Chicago Historical Society.

Wells, William. Papers. Chicago Historical Society.

Wilkinson, James. Papers. Chicago Historical Society.

Williams, Samuel. Papers. Eli Lilly Library, Bloomington IN.

Winans, William. Papers. Millsaps-Wilson Library, Millsap College, Jackson MS.

Woodbridge, William. Papers. BHC.

Worthington, Thomas. Papers. OHS.

Yeates, Jasper. Papers. Historical Society of Pennsylvania, Philadelphia.


## Principal Newspapers

*Aurora General Advertiser* (Philadelphia)
*Carlisle* (PA) *Gazette*
*Centinel of the North-West Territory* (Cincinnati)
*Kentucky Gazette* (Lexington)
*Knoxville* (TN) *Gazette*
*Missouri Gazette* (St. Louis)
*Niles' Register* (Baltimore)
*Palladium* (Frankfort KY)
*Philadelphia Gazette*
*Scioto Gazette* (Chillicothe OH)
*Virginia Gazette or American Advertiser* (Richmond)
*Western Spy and Hamilton Gazette* (Cincinnati)
*Western Sun* (Vincennes)


## Books, Articles, and Dissertations

Abernethy, Thomas Perkins. *Western Lands and the American Revolution.* 1937.
Reprint, New York: Russell and Russell, 1959.

Alden, John Richard. *John Stuart and the Southern Colonial Frontier.* 1944.
Reprint, New York: Gordian, 1966.

Alford, Thomas Wildcat. *Civilization and the Story of the Absentee Shawnees, As
Told to Florence Drake.* Norman: University of Oklahoma Press, 1936.

Allen, Robert S. *His Majesty's Indian Allies: British Indian Policy in the Defense of Canada, 1774–1815*. Toronto: Dundurn, 1992.

*American National Biography*. Edited by John A. Garraty and Mark C. Carnes, 24 vols. New York: Oxford University Press, 1999.

*American State Papers, Indian Affairs*. 2 vols. Washington DC: Gales and Seaton, 1832–34.

*American State Papers, Military Affairs*. 7 vols. Washington DC: Gales and Seaton, 1832–61.

Andrews, Edward Deming, ed. "The Shaker Mission to the Shawnee Indians." *Winterthur Portfolio* 7 (1972): 113–28.

"Anecdotes of Sundry Conflicts with the Indians." *Western Review and Miscellaneous Magazine* 1 (1819): 302–5.

Anson, Bert. "The Fur Traders of Northern Indiana." Ph.D. diss., Indiana University, 1953.

———. *The Miami Indians*. Norman: University of Oklahoma Press, 1971.

Antal, Sandy. *A Wampum Denied: Procter's War of 1812*. Ottawa: Carleton University Press, 1997.

Badger, Joseph. *A Memoir of Rev. Joseph Badger*. Hudson OH: Sawyer, Ingersoll and Co., 1851.

Bakeless, John. *Background to Glory*. Philadelphia: J. B. Lippincott, 1957.

———. *Master of the Wilderness, Daniel Boone*. New York: William Morrow, 1939.

Bald, F. Clever. *Detroit's First American Decade*. Ann Arbor: University of Michigan Press, 1948.

Barnhart, John D., ed. *Henry Hamilton and George Rogers Clark in the American Revolution*. Crawfordsville IN: R. E. Banta, 1951.

Bauman, Robert F. "Pontiac's Successor, the Ottawa Au-goosh-away." *Northwest Ohio Quarterly* 26 (1954): 8–38.

Beatty, Erkuries. "Diary of Major Erkuries Beatty." *Magazine of American History with Notes and Queries* 1 (1877): 175–79, 235–43, 309–15, 380–84, 432–38.

Beckner, Lucien. *Eskippakithiki, the Last Shawnee Indian Town in Kentucky*. Louisville: Filson Club, 1932.

———, ed. "John D. Shane's Interview with Benjamin Allen, Clark County." *Filson Club History Quarterly* 5 (1931): 63–98.

Beckwith, Hiram W., ed. "The Fort Wayne Manuscript." *Fergus Historical Series* 26 (1883): 63–95.

Belue, Ted Franklin. "Did Daniel Boone Kill Pompey, the Black Shawnee, at the 1778 Siege of Boonesborough?" *Filson Club History Quarterly* 67 (1993): 5–22.

Bennett, John. *Blue Jacket, War Chief of the Shawnees*. Chillicothe OH: Fromm Printing Co., 1943.

Berthrong, Donald J. *Indians of Northern Indiana and Southwestern Michigan*. New York: Garland, 1974.

Bliss, Eugene F., ed. *Diary of David Zeisberger*, 2 vols. Cincinnati: Robert Clarke, 1885.

Bond, Beverley W. *The Civilization of the Old Northwest*. New York: Macmillan, 1934.

———, ed. *The Correspondence of John Cleves Symmes*. New York: Macmillan, 1926.

Bowyer, John. "Daily Journal of Wayne's Campaign, July 28–November 2, 1794." *American Pioneer* 1 (1842): 315–22, 351–57.

Brice, Wallace A. *History of Fort Wayne*. Fort Wayne IN: D. W. Jones and Sons. 1868.

Brickell, John. "Narrative of John Brickell's Captivity among the Delaware Indians." *American Pioneer* 1 (1842): 43–56.

Brown, John P. *Old Frontiers*. Kingsport TN: Southern Publishers, 1938.

Buell, John Hutchinson. "A Fragment from the Diary of Major John Hutchinson Buell, U.S.A." *Journal of the Military Service Institution of the United States* 40 (1907): 102–13, 260–68.

Buell, Rowena, ed. *The Memoirs of Rufus Putnam*. Boston: Houghton Mifflin, 1903.

Burnet, Jacob. *Notes on the Early Settlement of the North-Western Territory*. Cincinnati: Derby, Bradley, 1847.

Burt, A. L. *The United States, Great Britain and British North America*. 1940. Reprint, New York: Russell and Russell, 1961.

Bushnell, David I. "Daniel Boone at Limestone, 1786–1787." *Virginia Magazine of History and Biography* 25 (1917): 1–11.

———, ed. "A Journey Through the Indian Country Beyond the Ohio, 1785." *Mississippi Valley Historical Review* 2 (1915): 261–73.

Butler, Richard. "Journal of General Butler." In *The Olden Time,* edited by Neville B. Craig, 2 vols. Pittsburgh: Dumars, 1846–48. 2:433–64, 481–531.

Butterfield, Consul W. *History of the Girtys*. Cincinnati: Robert Clarke, 1890.

———, ed. *Washington-Irvine Correspondence*. Madison WI: David Atwood, 1882.

Caldwell, Martha B. *Annals of the Shawnee Methodist Mission and Indian Manual Labor School*. Topeka: Kansas State Historical Society, 1939.

Callendar, Charles. *Social Organization of the Central Algonkian Indians*. Milwaukee: Public Museum Publications in Anthropology, 1962.

Calloway, Colin G. *The American Revolution in Indian Country*. New York: Cambridge University Press, 1995.

———. "Beyond the Vortex of Violence: Indian-White Relations in the Ohio Country, 1783–1815." *Northwest Ohio Quarterly* 64 (1992): 16–26.

———. *Crown and Calumet: British-Indian Relations, 1783–1815*. Norman: University of Oklahoma Press, 1987.

———. " 'We Have Always Been the Frontier': The American Revolution in Shawnee Country." *American Indian Quarterly* 16 (1992): 39–52.

Carter, Clarence E., and John Porter Bloom, eds. *The Territorial Papers of the United States,* 28 vols. Washington DC: Government Printing Office, 1934–75.

Carter, Harvey Lewis. *The Life and Times of Little Turtle*. Urbana: University of Illinois Press, 1987.

Caughey, John Walton, ed. *McGillivray of the Creeks*. Norman: University of Oklahoma Press, 1938.

Clanin, Douglas E., et al., ed. *The Papers of William Henry Harrison, 1800–1815*, 10 reels and printed guide. Indianapolis: Indiana Historical Society, 1999.

Clark, Jerry Eugene. *The Shawnee*. Lexington: University Press of Kentucky, 1977.

———. "Shawnee Indian Migration." Ph.D. diss., University of Kentucky, 1974.

Clark, Walter, ed. *The State Records of North Carolina*, 16 vols. Goldsboro and Winston NC: Nash Brothers, M. I. and J. C. Stewart, 1895–1905.

Clifton, James A. *Star Woman and Other Shawnee Tales*. Lanham MD: University Press of America, 1984.

———, ed. *Being and Becoming Indian: Biographical Studies of North American Frontiers*. Chicago: Dorsey Press, 1989.

Coates, B. H., ed. "A Narrative of an Embassy to the Western Tribes, from the Original Manuscript of Hendrick Aupaumut." *Memoir of the Historical Society of Pennsylvania* 2 (1827): 61–131.

Coker, William S. and Thomas D. Watson. *Indian Traders of the Southeastern Spanish Borderlands*. Gainesville: University Press of Florida, 1985.

Cooke, John. "General Wayne's Campaign in 1794 and 1795: Captain John Cooke's Journal." *American Historical Record* 2 (1873): 311–16, 339–45.

Corkran, David H. *The Creek Frontier, 1540–1783*. Norman: University of Oklahoma Press, 1967.

Cotterill, Robert S. *The Southern Indians*. Norman: University of Oklahoma Press, 1954.

Craig, Neville B., ed. *The Olden Time*, 2 vols. Pittsburgh: Dumars, 1846–48.

Cresswell, Nicholas. *The Journal of Nicholas Cresswell*. London: Jonathan Cape, 1925.

Cruikshank, Ernest A., ed. *The Correspondence of Lieutenant-Governor John Graves Simcoe*, 5 vols. Toronto: Ontario Historical Society, 1923–31.

Cruikshank, Ernest A., and A. F. Hunter, eds. *The Correspondence of the Honourable Peter Russell*, 3 vols. Toronto: Ontario Historical Society, 1932–36.

Dann, John C., ed. *The Revolution Remembered*. Chicago: University of Chicago Press, 1980.

Darlington, William M., ed. *Christopher Gist's Journals*. Pittsburgh: J. R. Weldin, 1893.

Davies, Kenneth G., ed. *Documents of the American Revolution*, 19 vols. Shannon: Irish University Press, 1972–78.

Davis, W. B. "Casualties of the Battle of Fallen Timbers." *Ohio Archaeological and Historical Society Publications* 41 (1932): 527–30.

Dawson, Moses. *Historical Narrative of the Civil and Military Services of Major-General William Henry Harrison*. Cincinnati: Cincinnati Advertiser, 1824.

Denissen, Christian. *Genealogy of the French Families of the Detroit River Region, 1702–1936*, 2 vols. Detroit: Detroit Society for Genealogical Research, 1987.

Denny, Ebenezer. *Military Journal of Major Ebenezer Denny*. Philadelphia: J. B. Lippincott, 1859.

*Dictionary of Canadian Biography,* vols. 3–7. Toronto: University of Toronto Press, 1974–88.

Dowd, Gregory Evans. *A Spirited Resistance: The North American Indian Struggle for Unity, 1745–1815*. Baltimore: Johns Hopkins Press, 1991.

Downes, Randolph C. *Council Fires on the Upper Ohio: A Narrative of Indian Affairs in the Upper Ohio Valley Until 1795*. Pittsburgh: University of Pittsburgh Press, 1940.

Drake, Benjamin. *Life of Tecumseh and of His Brother the Prophet*. 1841. Reprint, Cincinnati: Anderson, Gates and Wright, 1856.

Drake, Samuel G. *Biography and History of the Indians of North America*. 1832. Reprint, Boston: Antiquarian Institute, 1837.

Edgar, Matilda, ed. *Ten Years of Upper Canada in Peace and War*. Toronto: William Briggs, 1890.

Edmunds, R. David. *The Potawatomis, Keepers of the Fire*. Norman: University of Oklahoma Press, 1978.

———. *The Shawnee Prophet*. Lincoln: University of Nebraska Press, 1983.

———. *Tecumseh and the Quest for Indian Leadership*. Boston: Little, Brown, 1984.

Eid, Leroy V. "'A Kind of Running Fight': Indian Battlefield Tactics in the Late Eighteenth Century." *Western Pennsylvania Historical Magazine* 71 (1988): 147–71.

———. "'National' War Among Indians of Northeastern North America." *Canadian Review of American Studies* 16 (1985): 125–54.

Elliot, James. *The Poetical and Miscellaneous Works of James Elliot*. Greenfield MA: T. Dickman, 1798.

Esarey, Logan, ed. *Messages and Letters of William Henry Harrison*, 2 vols. Indianapolis: Indiana Historical Commission, 1922.

Fenton, William N. *The Great Law and the Longhouse: A Political History of the Iroquois Confederacy*. Norman: University of Oklahoma Press, 1998.

Filson, John. *The Discovery, Settlement and Present State of Kentucke*. 1784. Reprint, New York: Corinth, 1962.

Fitzpatrick, John C., ed. *The Writings of George Washington,* 39 vols. Washington DC: Government Printing Office, 1931–44.

Flick, A. C., et al., eds. *The Papers of Sir William Johnson*, 13 vols. Albany: The University of the State of New York, 1921–62.

Fliegel, Carl J., comp. *Index to the Records of the Moravian Missions Among the Indians of North America*. New Haven: Research Publications, 1970.

Flint, Timothy. *The First White Man of the West*. 1847. Reprint, Cincinnati: J. Applegate, 1851.

Force, Peter, ed. *American Archives*, 4th and 5th series, 9 vols. Washington DC: M. St. Clair Clarke and Peter Force, 1837–53.

Galloway, William Albert. *Old Chillicothe*. Xenia OH: Buckeye Press, 1934.

Gifford, Jack Jule. "The Northwest Indian War, 1784–1795." Ph.D. diss., University of California, 1964.

Gipson, Lawrence Henry. *The British Empire Before the American Revolution, 1748–1776*, 14 vols. New York: Knopf, 1958–68.

———, ed. *The Moravian Indian Mission on White River*. Indianapolis: Indiana Historical Bureau, 1938.

Goltz, Herbert C. W. "Tecumseh, the Prophet, and the Rise of the Northwestern Indian Confederacy." Ph.D. diss., University of Western Ontario, 1973.

Goodman, Alfred T., ed. *Journal of William Trent from Logstown to Pickawillany*. Cincinnati: Robert Clarke, 1871.

Graymont, Barbara. *The Iroquois in the American Revolution*. Syracuse: Syracuse University Press, 1972.

Green, Richard, Tony DeRegnaucourt, and Larry Hamilton. *Archaeology of Prophetstown, Greene Ville, Ohio, 1805–1808*. Arcanum OH: Historic Archaeological Research, 1994.

Gregg, Josiah. *Commerce of the Prairies*. 1844. Reprint, Norman: University of Oklahoma Press, 1954.

Griswold, Bert J. *The Pictorial History of Fort Wayne*, 2 vols. Chicago: Robert O. Law, 1917.

Hadlock, Wendel S. "Warfare Among the Northeastern Woodland Indians." *American Anthropologist* 45 (1947): 204–21.

Hamer, Philip M., ed. "The British in Canada and the Southern Indians." *East Tennessee Historical Society Publications* 2 (1930): 107–34.

Hanna, Charles A. *The Wilderness Trail*, 2 vols. New York: G. P. Putnam's Sons, 1911.

"Harmar's Expedition." *Western Review and Miscellaneous Magazine* 2 (1820): 179–82.

Harvey, Henry. *History of the Shawnee Indians*. Cincinnati: E. Morgan and Sons, 1855.

Hatheway, G. G. "The Neutral Indian Barrier State." Ph.D. diss., University of Minnesota, 1957.

Hazard, Samuel, ed. *Minutes of the Provincial Council of Pennsylvania*, 10 vols. Harrisburg PA: T. Fenn, 1851–52.

Hazard, Samuel, et al., eds. *Pennsylvania Archives*, 138 vols. Philadelphia and Harrisburg, 1852–1949.

Heckewelder, John. *History, Manners and Customs of the Indians Nations Who Once Inhabited Pennsylvania and the Neighbouring States*. 1819. Reprint, NewYork: Arno Press, 1971.

———. *A Narrative of the Mission of the United Brethren Among the Delaware and Mohegan Indians*. 1820. Reprint, Cleveland OH: Burrows Brothers, 1907.

Hill, Leonard U. *John Johnston and the Indians of the Three Miamis*. Columbus OH: Stoneman Press, 1957.

*History of Logan County and Ohio*. Chicago: O. L. Baskin, 1880.

*History of Ross and Highland Counties, Ohio*. Cleveland OH: W. W. Williams, 1880.

Hoberg, Walter R. "Early History of Colonel Alexander McKee." *Pennsylvania Magazine of History and Biography* 58 (1934): 26–36.

———. "A Tory in the Old Northwest." *Pennsylvania Magazine of History and Biography* 59 (1935): 32–41.

Hodge, Frederick W., ed. *Handbook of American Indians North of Mexico*, 2 vols. Washington DC: Bureau of American Ethnology, 1907–10.

Hopkins, Gerard T. *A Mission to the Indians*. Philadelphia: T. Ellwood Zell, 1862.

Horsman, Reginald. "The British Indian Department and the Abortive Treaty of Lower Sandusky, 1793." *Ohio Historical Quarterly* 70 (1961): 189–213.

———. *Expansion and American Indian Policy, 1783–1812*. East Lansing: Michigan State University Press, 1967.

———. *The Frontier in the Formative Years, 1783–1815*. New York: Holt, Rinehart and Winston, 1971.

———. *Matthew Elliott, British Indian Agent*. Detroit: Wayne State University Press, 1964.

Houck, Louis, ed. *The Spanish Regime in Missouri*, 2 vols. Chicago: R. R. Donnelley and Sons, 1909.

Howard, James H. *Shawnee!* Athens: Ohio University Press, 1982.

Howe, Henry, ed. *Historical Collections of Ohio*. 1847. Reprint, Cincinnati: Robert Clarke, 1869.

Hutton, Paul A. "William Wells, Frontier Scout and Indian Agent." *Indiana Magazine of History* 74 (1978): 183–222.

Indian Claims Commission. *Indians of Ohio, Indiana, Illinois, Southern Michigan, and Southern Wisconsin*, 3 vols. New York: Garland, 1974.

"Instance of Penetration in an Indian." *Western Review and Miscellaneous Magazine* 2 (1820): 168.

Jacob, John J. *A Biographical Sketch of the Life of the Late Captain Michael Cresap*. 1826. Reprint, Cincinnati: W. Dodge, 1866.

Jacobs, James Ripley. *The Beginning of the U.S. Army, 1783–1812*. 1947. Reprint, Port Washington NY: Kennikat Press, 1972.

Jacobs, Wilbur R. *Dispossessing the American Indian*. New York: Charles Scribner, 1972.

———. *Wilderness Politics and Indian Gifts*. 1950. Reprint, Lincoln: University of Nebraska Press, 1967.

Jakle, J. A. "The American Bison and the Human Occupation of the Ohio Valley." *Proceedings of the American Philosophical Society* 112 (1968): 299–305.

James, James Alton. *Life of George Rogers Clark*. Chicago: University of Chicago Press, 1928.

———, ed. *George Rogers Clark Papers*, 2 vols. Springfield IL: Illinois State Historical Library, 1912–26.

Jennings, Francis. *The Ambiguous Iroquois Empire*. New York: Norton, 1984.

———. *Empire of Fortune*. New York: Norton, 1988.

Johnson, Frederick, ed. *Man in Northeastern North America*. 1946. Reprint, New York: AMS, 1980.

Johnson, Louise Franklin. *Six Men Named Van Swearingen and Their Fathers*. Round Rock TX: L. F. Johnson, 1992.

———. "Testing Popular Lore: Marmaduke Swearingen a.k.a. Chief Blue Jacket." *National Genealogical Society Quarterly* 82 (1994): 165–78.

Johnston, Charles. *A Narrative of the Incidents Attending the Capture, Detention and Ransom of Charles Johnston*. New York: J. and J. Harper, 1827.

Johnston, Charles M., ed. *Valley of the Six Nations*. Toronto: University of Toronto Press, 1964.

Johnston, John. "Account of the Present State of Indian Tribes Inhabiting Ohio." *Archaeologia Americana* 1 (1820): 269–99.

Jones, David. *A Journal of Two Visits Made to Some Nations of Indians on the West Side of the River Ohio in the Years 1772 and 1773*. Burlington NJ: Isaac Collins, 1774.

Jones, Dorothy V. *License for Empire*. Chicago: University of Chicago Press, 1983.

Kappler, Charles J., ed. *Indian Affairs, Laws and Treaties*, 4 vols. Washington DC: Government Printing Office, 1904–29.

Kellogg, Louise Phelps, ed. *Frontier Advance on the Upper Ohio, 1778–1779*. Madison: State Historical Society of Wisconsin, 1916.

———. *Frontier Retreat on the Upper Ohio, 1779–1781*. Madison: State Historical Society of Wisconsin, 1917.

Kelsay, Isabel Thompson. *Joseph Brant, 1743–1807, Man of Two Worlds*. Syracuse: Syracuse University Press, 1984.

Kent, Donald H., and Sylvester K. Stevens, eds. *The Papers of Colonel Henry Bouquet*, 17 vols. Harrisburg: Pennsylvania Historical Commission, 1940–43.

Kercheval, Samuel. *History of the Valley of Virginia*. Winchester: Samuel H. Davis, 1833.

Kinietz, W. Vernon, and Erminie Wheeler Voegelin, eds. *Shawnese Traditions*. Ann Arbor: University of Michigan Press, 1939.

Kinnaird, Lawrence, ed. *Spain in the Mississippi Valley, 1765–1794*, 3 vols. Washington DC: American Historical Association, 1946–49.

Klinck, Carl F. and James T. Talman, eds. *The Journal of Major John Norton, 1816*. Toronto: University of Toronto Press, 1970.

Knopf, Richard C., ed. *Anthony Wayne: A Name in Arms*. 1960. Reprint, Westport CT: Greenwood Press, 1975.

———. *Campaign into the Wilderness*, 5 vols. Columbus OH: Anthony Wayne Parkway Board/Ohio State Museum, 1955.

———. "A Precise Journal of General Wayne's Last Campaign." *American Antiquarian Society* 64 (1954): 273–302.

———. "A Surgeon's Mate at Fort Defiance: The Journal of Joseph Gardner Andrews for the Year 1795." *Ohio Historical Quarterly* 66 (1957): 57–86, 159–86, 238–68.

———. "Two Journals of the Kentucky Volunteers, 1793 and 1794." *Filson Club History Quarterly* 27 (1953): 247–81.

Knowles, Nathaniel. "The Torture of Captives by the Indians of Eastern North America." *Proceedings of the American Philosophical Society* 82 (1940): 151–225.

Kohn, Richard H. *Eagle and Sword.* New York: Free Press, 1975.

Lewis, Andrew. "A Letter from the Late Colonel Andrew Lewis." *Virginia Historical Register and Literary Advertiser* 1 (1848): 30–33.

Lewis, Virgil A. *History of the Battle of Point Pleasant.* Charleston: Tribune Printing Co., 1909.

Lincoln, Benjamin. "Journal of a Treaty Held in 1793, with the Indian Tribes Northwest of the Ohio, by Commissioners of the United States." *Collections of the Massachusetts Historical Society* 5 (1836): 109–76.

Long, John. *Voyages and Travels of an Indian Interpreter and Trader.* London: J. Long, 1791.

Loskiel, George Henry. *History of the Mission of the United Brethren.* London: Brethren's Society for the Furtherance of the Gospel, 1794.

Lossing, Benson J. *The Pictorial Field-Book of the War of 1812.* 1868. Reprint, New York, Harper and Brothers, 1896.

Lutz, J. J. "The Methodist Missions." *Kansas Historical Collections* 9 (1905–6): 160–235.

McAfee, Robert Breckinridge. *History of the Late War in the Western Country.* Lexington KY: Worsley and Smith, 1816.

McConnell, Michael N. *A Country Between: The Upper Ohio Valley and Its Peoples, 1724–1774.* Lincoln: University of Nebraska Press, 1992.

———. "The Search for Security." Ph.D. diss., College of William and Mary, 1983.

McCoy, Isaac. *History of the Baptist Indian Missions.* New York: H. and S. Raynor, 1840.

McDaniel, Mary Jane. "Relations between the Creek Indians, Georgia and the United States, 1783–1797." Ph.D. diss., Mississippi State University, 1971.

McDowell, J. L., ed. *Documents Relating to Indian Affairs, 1750–1765,* 2 vols. Chapel Hill: University of North Carolina Press, 1958–70.

McGrane, R. C., ed. "William Clark's Journal of General Wayne's Campaign." *Mississippi Valley Historical Review* 1 (1914): 418–44.

McKenney, Thomas L. and James Hall. *The Indian Tribes of North America,* 3 vols. Philadelphia: Biddle, Greenough and Clark, 1836–44.

McNemar, Richard. *The Kentucky Revival.* 1808. Reprint, New York: E. O. Jenkins, 1846.

Mahon, John K. "Anglo-American Methods of Indian Warfare, 1676–1794." *Mississippi Valley Historical Review* 45 (1958): 254–75.

Marschalk, Andrew. "Mio-quo-coo-na-caw." *Hazard's Register of Pennsylvania* 12 (1833): 164–65.

Martin, Calvin. *Keepers of the Game.* Berkeley: University of California Press, 1978.

Meek, Basil, ed. "General Harmar's Expedition." *Ohio Archaeological and Historical Society Publications* 20 (1911): 74–108.

*Michigan Pioneer and Historical Society Historical Collections*, 40 vols. Lansing: George, Thorp, Godfrey, Smith, et al., 1877–1929.

*Minutes of Debate in Council on the Banks of the Ottawa River . . . November 1791*. Philadelphia: William Young, 1792.

Mohr, Walter H. *Federal Indian Relations, 1774–1788*. Philadelphia: University of Pennsylvania Press, 1933.

Moore, John H., ed. "A Captive of the Shawnees, 1779–1784." *West Virginia History* 23 (1962): 287–96.

Moore, S. M. "Early Recollections of Nancy Stewart." In Joshua Antrim, *The History of Champaign and Logan Counties*, pp. 327–28. Bellefontaine OH: Press Printing Co., 1872.

Moorehead, Warren K. "The Indian Tribes of Ohio." *Ohio Archaeological and Historical Quarterly* 7 (1898): 1–110.

Nelson, Paul David. *Anthony Wayne, Soldier of the Early Republic*. Bloomington: Indiana University Press, 1985.

Nettl, Bruno. "The Shawnee Musical Style." *Southwestern Journal of Anthropology* 9 (1953): 277–85.

O'Callaghan, Edmund Bailey, ed. *Documents Relating to the Colonial History of the State of New York*, 15 vols. Albany: Weed, Parsons, 1853–87.

O'Donnell, James H. *The Southern Indians in the American Revolution*. Knoxville: University of Tennessee Press, 1973.

*Old Record of the Captivity of Margaret Erskine*. Baltimore: Lord Baltimore Press, 1912.

Olmstead, Earl P. *Blackcoats Among the Delaware*. Kent OH: Kent State University Press, 1991.

———. *David Zeisberger: A Life Among the Indians*. Kent OH: Kent State University Press, 1997.

Palmer, William P., et al., eds. *Calendar of Virginia State Papers and Other Manuscripts*, 11 vols. Richmond: Virginia State Library, 1875–93.

Parkman, Francis. *The Conspiracy of Pontiac*. 1851. Reprint, New York: Crowell-Collier, 1962.

Parsons, Joseph. A. "Civilizing the Indians of the Old Northwest, 1800–1810." *Indiana Magazine of History* 56 (1960): 195–216.

Peckham, Howard H. "Josiah Harmar and His Indian Expedition." *Ohio Archaeological and Historical Quarterly* 55 (1946): 227–41.

———. *Pontiac and the Indian Uprising*. 1947. Reprint, Chicago: University of Chicago Press, 1961.

Perrin du Lac, F. M. *Travels Through the Two Louisianas*. London: R. Phillips, 1807.

Persinger, Joseph. *The Life of Jacob Persinger*. Sturgeon MO: 1861.

Prucha, Francis Paul. *American Indian Policy in the Formative Years*. Cambridge MA: Harvard University Press, 1962.

———. *The Sword of the Republic*. Bloomington: Indiana University Press, 1977.

Quaife, Milo M., ed. "General James Wilkinson's Narrative of the Fallen Timbers Campaign." *Mississippi Valley Historical Review* 16 (1929): 81–90.

———. "Henry Hay's Journal from Detroit to the Mississippi River." *Proceedings of the State Historical Society of Wisconsin* 62 (1915): 208–61.

———. *The John Askin Papers*, 2 vols. Detroit: Detroit Library Commission, 1928–31.

———. "The Journal of Captain Samuel Newman." *Wisconsin Magazine of History* 2 (1918–19): 40–73.

———. *The Siege of Detroit in 1763*. Chicago: R. R. Donnelley and Sons, 1958.

Rafert, Stewart. *The Miami Indians*. Indianapolis: Indiana Historical Society, 1996.

Rayner, John A., ed. *The First Century of Piqua, Ohio*. Piqua: Magee Brothers, 1916.

Rice, Otis K. *Frontier Kentucky*. Lexington: University Press of Kentucky, 1975.

Royce, Charles C. *Indian Land Cessions in the United States*. Washington DC: Bureau of American Ethnology, 1899.

Sabathy-Judd, Gerlinde, trans. and ed. "The Diary of the Moravian Indian Mission of Fairfield, Upper Canada, 1792–1813." Ph.D. diss., University of Western Ontario, 1998.

St. Clair, Arthur. *A Narrative of the Manner in Which the Campaign Against the Indians . . . Was Conducted Under the Command of Major General St. Clair*. Philadelphia: Jane Aitken, 1812.

"St. Clair's Defeat." *Ohio Archaeological and Historical Society Publications* 10 (1901–2): 378–80.

Sargent, Winthrop. "Winthrop Sargent's Diary While with General St. Clair's Expedition Against the Indians." *Ohio Archaeological and Historical Society Publications* 33 (1924): 237–73.

Saunders, Charles. *The Horrid Cruelty of the Indians*. Birmingham, England: T. Warren, 1963.

Saunders, William L., ed. *The Colonial Records of North Carolina*, 10 vols. Raleigh: P. M. Hale, 1886–90.

Scamyhorn, Richard, and John Steinle. *Stockades in the Wilderness*. Dayton OH: Landfall Press, 1986.

Schaaf, Gregory. *Wampum Belts and Peace Trees*. Golden CO: Fulcrum, 1990.

Schermerhorn, John F. "Report Respecting the Indians Inhabiting the Western Posts of the United States." *Collections of the Massachusetts Historical Society* 2, ser. 2 (1814): 1–45.

Schoolcraft, Henry Rowe. *Travels in the Central Portions of the Mississippi Valley*. New York: Collins and Hannay, 1825.

———, ed. *Information Respecting the History, Condition and Prospects of the Indian Tribes of the United States*, 6 vols. Philadelphia: Lippincott, Granbow, 1853–60.

Schutz, Noel William. "The Study of Shawnee Myth in an Ethnographic and Ethnohistorical Perspective." Ph.D. diss., Indiana University, 1975.

Schweinitz, Edmund de. *The Life and Times of David Zeisberger.* Philadelphia: J. B. Lippincott, 1870.

Scribner, Robert L., ed. *Revolutionary Virginia*, 7 vols. Charlottesville: University Press of Virginia, 1973–82.

Sheehan, Bernard W. *Seeds of Extinction.* Chapel Hill: University of North Carolina Press, 1973.

Shepard, Lee, ed. *Journal of James Taylor Underwood.* Cincinnati: Society of Colonial Wars in the State of Ohio, 1945.

Siberell, Lloyd Emerson. *Tecumseh.* Chillicothe OH: Ross County Historical Society, 1944.

Sipe, Chester Hale. *The Indian Chiefs of Pennsylvania.* Butler PA: Ziegler, 1927.

———. *The Indian Wars of Pennsylvania.* Harrisburg PA: Telegraph Press, 1929.

Smith, Dwight L. "Indian Land Cessions in the Old Northwest, 1795–1809." Ph.D. diss., Indiana University, 1949.

———. "A North American Neutral Indian Zone: Persistence of a British Idea." *Northwest Ohio Quarterly* 61 (1989): 46–63.

———. "Shawnee Captivity Ethnography." *Ethnohistory* 2 (1955): 29–41.

———, ed. "From Greene Ville to Fallen Timbers: A Journal of the Wayne Campaign, July 28–September 14, 1794." *Indiana Historical Society Publications* 16 (1952): 237–326.

———. "William Wells and the Indian Council of 1793." *Indiana Magazine of History* 56 (1960): 217–26.

———. *With Captain Edward Miller in the Wayne Campaign of 1794.* Ann Arbor MI: William L. Clements Library, 1965.

Smith, Marc Jack. "Joseph Brant, Mohawk Statesman." Ph.D. diss., University of Wisconsin, 1946.

Smith, William Henry, ed. *The St. Clair Papers*, 2 vols. 1881. Reprint, Freeport NY: Books for Libraries Press, 1970.

Sosin, Jack M. "The British Indian Department and Dunmore's War." *Virginia Magazine of History and Biography* 74 (1966): 34–50.

———. *The Revolutionary Frontier, 1763–1783.* New York: Holt, Rinehart and Winston, 1971.

———. *Whitehall and the Wilderness.* Lincoln: University of Nebraska Press, 1961.

Spencer, Joab. "Shawnee Folk-Lore." *Journal of American Folk-Lore* 22 (1909): 319–26.

———. "The Shawnee Indians: Their Customs, Traditions and Folklore." *Transactions of the Kansas State Historical Society* 10 (1907–8): 382–401.

Spencer, Oliver M. *The Indian Captivity of O. M. Spencer.* 1834. Reprint, Chicago: R. R. Donnelley and Sons, 1917.

Spicer, Edward H. *A Short History of the Indians of the United States.* New York: Van Nostrand Reinhold, 1969.

Staab, Rodney. "Blue Jacket Led Shawnees Through Traumatic Period Here." *Kansas City Journal Herald*, 11 June 1986.

Stevens, Paul Lawrence. "His Majesty's 'Savage' Allies" Ph.D. diss., State University of New York, 1984.

———, ed. *Louis Lorimier in the American Revolution, 1777–1782*. Naperville IL: Center for French Colonial Studies, 1998.

Stone, William Leete. *The Life and Times of Red Jacket, or Sa-go-ye-wat-ha*. 1841. Reprint, St. Clair Shores MI: Scholarly Press, 1970.

———. *Life of Joseph Brant-Thayendanegea*, 2 vols. 1838. Reprint, St. Clair Shores MI: Scholarly Press, 1970.

Stuart, John. "Memoir of Indian Wars and Other Occurrences." *Collections of the Virginia Historical and Philosophical Society* 1 (1833): 35–68.

Sugden, John. "Early Pan-Indianism: Tecumseh's Tour of the Indian Country, 1811–1812." *American Indian Quarterly* 10 (1986): 273–304.

———. *The Shawnee in Tecumseh's Time*. Nortorf, Germany: Abhandlungen der Völkerkundlichen Arbeitsgemeinschaft, heft 66, 1990.

———. "The Southern Indians in the War of 1812: The Closing Phase." *Florida Historical Quarterly* 61 (1982): 273–312.

———. *Tecumseh, A Life*. New York: Henry Holt, 1998.

———. *Tecumseh's Last Stand*. Norman: University of Oklahoma Press, 1985.

———. "Tecumseh's Travels Revisited." *Indiana Magazine of History* (forthcoming).

———. "Will the Real Tecumseh Please Stand Up? New Footsteps on an Old Indian Trail." Paper presented at the Indiana Historical Society, July 1999.

Swanton, John R. *The Indians of the Southeastern United States*. Washington DC: Bureau of American Ethnology, 1946.

Sword, Wiley. *President Washington's Indian War*. Norman: University of Oklahoma Press, 1985.

Talbert, Charles Gano. *Benjamin Logan, Kentucky Frontiersman*. Lexington: University of Kentucky Press, 1962.

Tanner, Helen Hornbeck. "Cherokees in the Ohio Country." *Journal of Cherokee Studies* 3 (1978): 94–102.

———. "The Glaize in 1792: A Composite Indian Community." *Ethnohistory* 25 (1978): 15–39.

———, ed. *Atlas of Great Lakes Indian History*. Norman: University of Oklahoma Press, 1987.

Thomson, Charles. *An Enquiry into the Causes of the Alienation of the Delaware and Shawanese Indians*. London: J. Wilkie, 1759.

Thornbrough, Gayle, ed. *Letter Book of the Indian Agency at Fort Wayne, 1809–1815*. Indianapolis: Indiana Historical Society, 1961.

———. *Outpost on the Wabash, 1787–1791*. Indianapolis: Indiana Historical Society, 1957.

Thrapp, Dan L. *Encyclopaedia of Frontier Biography*, 4 vols. Glendale CA: Arthur H. Clark, 1988–94.

Thwaites, Reuben Gold, and Louise Phelps Kellogg, eds. *Documentary History of Dunmore's War, 1774*. Madison: State Historical Society of Wisconsin, 1905.

———. *Frontier Defense on the Upper Ohio, 1777–1778*. Madison: State Historical Society of Wisconsin, 1912.

———. *The Revoution on the Upper Ohio, 1775–1777*. Madison: State Historical Society of Wisconsin, 1908.

Tootle, James. R. "Anglo-Indian Relations in the Northern Theater of the French and Indian War, 1748–1761." Ph.D. diss., Ohio State University, 1972.

Trigger, Bruce, ed. *Handbook of North American Indians: Northeast*. Washington DC: Smithsonian Institution, 1978.

*True Narrative of the Sufferings of Mary Kinnan*. Elizabethtown: Shepard Killock, 1975.

Twohig, Dorothy, ed. *The Journal of the Proceedings of the President, 1793–1797*. Charlottesville: University Press of Virginia, 1981.

Van Cleve, John W., ed. "Letters of Colonel Hamtramck." *American Pioneer* 2 (1843): 388–94.

———. "Van Cleve's Memoranda." *American Pioneer* 2 (1843): 148–53.

Voegelin, Charles F. *Shawnee Stems and the Jacob P. Dunn Miami Dictionary*, 4 vols. Indianapolis: Indiana Historical Society, 1938–40.

Voegelin, Erminie Wheeler. *Indians of Northwest Ohio*. New York: Garland, 1974.

———. "Mortuary Customs of the Shawnee and Other Eastern Tribes." *Indiana Historical Society Prehistory Research Series* 2 (1944): 225–444.

———. "The Place of Agriculture in the Subsistence Economy of the Shawnee." *Papers of the Michigan Academy of Science, Arts and Letters* 26 (1940): 513–20.

———. "Some Possible Sixteenth- and Seventeenth-Century Locations of the Shawnee." *Proceedings of the Indiana Academy of Science* 48 (1939): 13–18.

Voegelin, Erminie Wheeler, and David B. Stout. *Indians of Illinois and Northwestern Indiana*. New York: Garland, 1974.

Voegelin, Erminie Wheeler, and Helen Hornbeck Tanner. *Indians of Northern Ohio and Southeastern Michigan*. New York: Garland, 1974.

———. *Indians of Ohio and Indiana Prior to 1795*, 2 vols. New York: Garland, 1974.

Voegelin, Erminie Wheeler, et al. *Miami, Wea and Eel River Indians of Southern Indiana*. New York: Garland, 1974.

Volney, Constantin F. *A View of the Soil and Climate of the United States of America*. Philadelphia: J. Conrad, 1804.

Wainwright, Nicholas B. *George Croghan, Wilderness Diplomat*. Chapel Hill: University of North Carolina Press, 1959.

Walker, Joseph E., ed. "Plowshares and Pruning Hooks for the Miamis and Potawatomis: The Journal of Gerard T. Hopkins, 1804." *Ohio History* 88 (1979): 361–407.

Wallace, A. F. C. *The Death and Rebirth of the Seneca*. New York: Knopf, 1973.

———. "New Religions Among the Delaware Indians, 1600–1900." *Southwestern Journal of Anthropology* 12 (1956): 1–21.

———. "Political Organization and Land Tenure Among the Northeastern Indians, 1600–1830." *Southwestern Journal of Anthropology* 13 (1957): 301–21.

Wallace, Paul A. W. *Indians in Pennsylvania*. Harrisburg: Pennsylvania Historical and Museum Commission, 1961.

———, ed. *Thirty Thousand Miles with John Heckewelder.* Pittsburgh: University of Pittsburgh Press, 1958.

Walsh, W. P. "The Defeat of Major General Arthur St. Clair, 1791: A Study of the Nation's Response, 1791–1793." Ph.D. diss., Loyola University, 1977.

Warner, Michael S. "General Josiah Harmar's Campaign Reconsidered: How the Americans Lost the Battle of Kekionga." *Indiana Magazine of History* 83 (1987): 43–64.

Weld, Isaac. *Travels Through the States of North America and the Provinces of Upper and Lower Canada*, 2 vols. London: John Stockdale, 1799.

Wells, William. "Indian History." *Western Review and Miscellaneous Magazine* 2 (1820): 201–4.

Weslager, C. A. *The Delaware Indians: A History.* New Brunswick NJ: Rutgers University Press, 1972.

Whitaker, Arthur Preston. *The Spanish-American Frontier, 1783–1795.* 1927. Reprint, Lincoln: University of Nebraska Press, 1969.

White, Leslie A., ed. *Lewis Henry Morgan: The Indian Journals, 1859–62.* Ann Arbor: University of Michigan Press, 1959.

White, Richard. *The Middle Ground: Indians, Empires and Republics in the Great Lakes Region, 1650–1850.* New York: Cambridge University Press, 1991.

Wilcox, Frank N. *Ohio Indian Trails.* 1933. Reprint, Kent OH: Kent State University Press, 1970.

Wilkinson, James. *Memoirs of My Own Times*, 3 vols. Philadelphia: Abraham Small, 1816.

Williams, Edward G., ed. "The Journal of Richard Butler, 1775." *Western Pennsylvania Historical Magazine* 46 (1953): 381–95, 47 (1964): 31–46, 141–56.

Wilson, Frazer E., ed. *Journal of Captain Daniel Bradley.* Greenville OH: F. H. Jobes and Son, 1935.

Wiseman, William. "Personal Narrative of William Wiseman." *Cist's Weekly Advertiser* (Cincinnati), 13, 20, and 27 December 1850, 3 January 1851.

Witthoft, John, and William A. Hunter. "The Seventeenth-Century Origins of the Shawnee." *Ethnohistory* 2 (1955): 42–57.

Woehrmann, Paul. *At the Headwaters of the Maumee.* Indianapolis: Indiana Historical Society, 1971.

Wright, J. Leitch Jr. *Anglo-Spanish Rivalry in North America.* Athens: University of Georgia Press, 1971.

———. *Britain and the American Frontier, 1783–1815.* Athens: University of Georgia Press, 1975.

———. *Creeks and Seminoles.* Lincoln: University of Nebraska Press, 1986.

Yeates, Jasper. "The Indian Treaty at Fort Pitt in 1776." *Pennsylvania Magazine of History and Biography* 5 (1881): 484–85.

# Index

Blue Jacket: legend of him being white, 1–4; birthdate of, 25–26; birthplace of, 275 n.16; and family of origin, 26, 188–89, 219; other names of, 27; as probably a Pekowi, 26–27; clan of, 27, 274 n.6; as a warrior, xi, 5–6, 30, 33, 43, 68, 86–87, 89–90, 100–106, 110–11, 117–27; appearance of, 33–34, 82, 148, 189, 219, 251; mixes with white traders and agents, 31–32, 53–54, 80, 90–91, 113, 146–49, 210–11; and facility in dual Indian-white world, 34–35, 54, 218–19, 241, 262–64; marriages of, 3–4, 31–32, 254–56; children of, 3–4, 31–32, 34, 254; grandchildren of, 2, 258, 260–63, 305–6 n.5, 309 n.15, 313 n.13, 314–15 n.20, 315 n.21; as trader and farmer, 33, 54, 63, 80, 146, 171, 218, 230; chieftainship of, 32, 33, 68, 83, 162, 196, 207–8, 212–13, 215–17; towns of, 32–33, 52, 65, 75, 77, 130–31, 170–71, 218; houses of, 34, 54, 219; and drunkenness, 48–49, 82, 134, 148, 219; and prisoners, kindness to, 21, 31, 54, 63, 76–77, 80; and religion, 16, 122; vanity of, 33–34, 76, 129, 189, 192, 208; in battle of Point Pleasant, 41–43; visits Gnadenhütten and Pittsburgh (1775–76), 48–49, 51–52; removes to Mad River, 52; splits with Shawnee peace party, 53–55; with Henry Hamilton on Vincennes expedition (1778), 55–58; probably with Henry Bird's expedition (1780), 61; scouts the Ohio (1782), 63; at Fort Finney (1786), 72–73; raids into Kentucky and Tennessee by, 76, 81–83; moves to Miamitown, 79–80, 90; and Isaac Freeman mission, 86–87; as pan-Indian diplomat, xi, 5, 88–97, 114, 129–30, 135, 138, 141, 159, 191–203, 223–25; and Antoine Gamelin mission, 96–97; war aims and strategies of, 88–89, 91–97, 132–38, 140–41, 156–57, 160, 164–65, 168; defeats Josiah Harmar's army (1790), 100–106; repulsed at Dunlap's Station (1791), 110–11, 289 n.22; defeats Arthur St. Clair's army (1791), 117–27, 291 n.14; visits western and northern tribes (1792, 1794, 1801, 1802), 130, 159, 224–25; and proposed trips to Montreal and England, 89–90, 146–49; and expedition to Fort Recovery (1794), 160–68; defeated at Fallen Timbers, 172–80, 298 n.5; breaks with the British, 147–48, 173, 179, 180, 181, 182, 184–86, 190, 192, 194–96, 214; visits U.S. posts to negotiate (1795), 182, 185, 188–94, 196–98, 201–2; creates peace party among the Indians, 191–203, 209; acknowledges loss of Ohio, 192–93; at treaty of Greenville, 202–7; establishes base at Fort Wayne, 209–12, 218; assists Americans after the peace, 209–12, 223–24; persuades U.S. to supply Indians, 210, 217; visits Philadelphia, 213–16; falls from influence, 217–18; at Wapakoneta, 218; moves to Detroit River, 218–20; and proposed Shawnee relocation (1799), 222–23; and story of silver mine, 220–21; and treaty of Fort Industry (1805), 227; supports Tecumseh and the Prophet, 239–53, 257–58; visits Detroit and Chillicothe, 239, 240, 246–47, 251–53; dispenses treaty annuities, 210, 212–13, 223, 240, 246; visits Wyandots, 247, 250; advocates neutrality in dispute between Britain and U.S. (1807), 247–48, 250–53; at Greenville council (1807), 248–51; death of, 254, 311–12 n.1; relations with the British, 27, 68, 89–90, 96–97,

Brodhead, Daniel, 62–63

Brown, Adam (Wyandot), 2

Brownstown (Wyandot town), 77, 91, 183–85, 199, 218–19, 222, 225, 250, 258, 305 n.2

Brownstown, battle of , 258

Buckongahelas (Delaware), xi, 33, 51, 55, 69, 74, 79, 93, 110, 122, 131, 133, 135, 137, 151–52, 162–64, 168, 170, 173, 181, 185, 187, 195–97, 201, 203, 208, 214, 225, 233

Buell, John Hutchinson, 188–89

Buffalo (Shawnee), 212

Buffalo Creek, (near Niagara), 94, 222, 225

Butler (Shawnee), 115, 237

Butler, Richard, 13, 70–71, 115, 121, 123–24

Cahokia, 56

Caldwell, Capt. William, 218

Caldwell, Col. William, 60, 63–64, 90, 173–74, 179

Campbell, Robert Mis, 177

Campbell, William, 173, 180

Canada, 27–28, 66–67, 80, 91, 107–8, 139, 144–46, 158, 173, 183, 221, 229, 258

Canawya (Shawnee), 146, 149

Cape Girardeau, 230

Captain Johnny, (also known as Kekewepelethy and Great Hawk; Shawnee), 50–51, 69–72, 79, 81, 87–88, 113–14, 130–31, 133–35, 146, 150–53, 157–58, 161, 170, 181, 191, 198–99, 209–10, 212–13, 238, 285 n.2

Captain Reed (Shawnee), 206, 209

Carleton, Sir Guy. *See* Dorchester, Lord

Carondelet, Hector, Baron de, 139, 141

Cass, Lewis, 238

Cawechile (Shawnee), 51, 69

Chattahoochee River, 139

Chaukalowaik (Shawnee), 237

Cheeseekau (also known as Shawnee Warrior; brother of Tecumseh), 85, 115, 139

Chenail Ecarté, 209, 212

Chenussio (Seneca town), 40

Cherokee Indians, 10, 36, 38–40, 45, 59–60, 83, 92, 140, 151, 158, 162, 224–25, 282 n.4; in Ohio, 62, 65–66, 69–70, 72–74, 81, 85, 87, 92–94, 98, 111, 113, 117, 131–34, 153, 181, 190, 199–200, 203; Chickamauga Cherokees, 67, 85, 92, 115, 129, 139–41, 215

*Chesapeake* crisis (1807), 245

Chickasaw Indians, 39, 59–60, 83, 116–17, 141, 158, 161, 163, 165, 215, 225

Chillicothe (Great Miami River; also known as Standing Stone; Shawnee town), 63

Chillicothe (Little Miami River; Shawnee town), 52, 55, 59, 62

Chillicothe (Maumee River; Shawnee town), 80, 101–3

Chillicothe (Scioto River; Shawnee town), 13, 32

Chillicothe (St. Marys River; Shawnee town), 69, 72

Chillicothe (OH), 239, 246, 248–53

Choctaw Indians, 39, 60, 83, 141, 158, 163, 215

Cincinnati, ix, 97, 218

Clark, George Rogers, 62–63, 70–73, 75, 143, 151, 204

Claus, William, 256

Cochenawaga (Seven Nations of Canada), 136

Colbert, George, 115, 215

Connecticut, ix, 227

Connecticut Land Company, 227

Connolly, John, 40

Conoy Indians, 113, 134, 153

Coocoochee (Mohawk prophetess), 131

Coonaniskey (Cherokee), 199

Cornstalk (Shawnee), 34, 40–46, 48–53, 59, 72, 75, 236

Cornstalk, Peter (Shawnee), 81, 86, 283 n.7
Coshocton (Delaware town), 52
Covington, Leonard, 177
Creek Indians, 10, 29, 39, 55, 59–60, 66–67, 83, 93, 129, 134, 139–41, 151, 153, 158, 209, 215, 257
Creighton, William, 248–49
Cresap, Michael, 41
Crooked Nose's Town (Shawnee town), 13, 32
Crow, John, 81
Cumberland Gap, 73
Cumberland River, 9, 139–40, 270 n.4
Cutemwha (also known as the Wolf and Piaseka; Shawnee), 45, 80–81, 237, 275 n.2
Cuyahoga Association, 214
Cuyahoga River, 100, 204, 227

Dakota Indians, 227
Darke, William, 121, 124, 126–27
Darrow, David, 242
Deer, the (Miami), 93
Deer Creek OH, 32
Delaware Indians, 6, 10, 23, 25, 28, 30, 38, 40, 41, 46, 48, 51, 52, 53, 55, 60, 62, 63, 66, 67, 68–69, 70, 74, 77, 79–80, 84, 85, 93–94, 95–96, 100, 102–3, 108–9, 110, 113, 117, 120, 122, 130, 131–35, 137, 144, 150, 152–53, 157–58, 160, 162, 164, 173–74, 181, 185, 187, 188, 190, 191–92, 195–97, 204–6, 227, 229, 233–36, 239, 270 n.7, 310 n.17
Denny, Ebenezer, 126–27
De Peyster, Arent Schuyler, 60
Detroit, 32, 51, 53–55, 60, 62, 69, 80, 86, 90, 91, 96, 100, 128–29, 145, 146–49, 152, 160, 168, 169, 185–86, 194, 198–99, 201–3, 213–14, 220, 236, 239, 246–47. *See also* Fort Detroit
Detroit River, 51, 77, 129, 151
diseases, 14–15, 17, 30–31, 85, 233–34
Dolsen, Matthew, 148

Dorchester, Lord (Sir Guy Carleton), 108, 114, 128, 158–59, 184, 197
Dragging Canoe (Cherokee), 38, 93, 129
Drake, Samuel, 201
Drinnon's Lick (KY), 76
Duchouquet, Francois, 162, 240, 308 n.11
Duggan, Thomas, 148
Dunlap's Station, attack on, 110–11, 289 n.22
Dunmore, Earl of (John Murray), 40–42, 45–46

Eel River, 114
Eel River Indians, 90, 93, 114, 200, 204–6, 214
Egushaway (Ottawa), 56–57, 71, 94, 128, 132–33, 150, 157, 160, 162, 168, 173, 180, 187, 195, 198–203, 208, 214
Elkhart River, 100
Elkhorn Creek, 45
Elk River, 114
Elliott, Matthew, 31, 58, 91, 102, 105, 148, 151–52, 161, 212, 219, 290 n.5
England, Richard, 146–48, 169, 173–75
Erie Indians, 37
Erskine (nee Paulee), Margaret, 21, 54
Eskippakithiki (Shawnee town), 36

Fallen Timbers (near the Auglaize River), 161–64, 172
Fallen Timbers (Maumee River), 172; battle of, 172–80
Farmer's Brother (Seneca), 94–95, 136
Filson, John, 36
Finley, John, 37
Finney, Walter, 73
Fisher, Frederick, 240, 249, 309 n.11
Five Medals (Potawatomi), 186
Fleming, William, 43, 45
Flemingsburg (KY), 83
Flint River, 139
Flying Crows (Iroquois), 51
Fontaine, James, 104

Greenville Creek, 242
Grenadier Squaw (Shawnee), 34
Grey Eye's Town, 161
Grosse Ile, 212, 218, 260, 261
Guyasota (Seneca), 89

Haldimand, Frederick, 66
Hall, Horatio, 103–4
Hamilton, Henry, 26, 51, 53–58, 60, 80, 107, 133
Hamtramck, John Francis, 177, 182, 193, 195, 197–98, 201, 209–11
Handsome Lake (Seneca), 234
Hardin, John, 101–3
Hardman (Shawnee), 9, 33, 39–40, 46, 49–50, 52–53, 59, 68, 236, 275 n.16
Harmar, Josiah, 73, 97–106, 115
Harrison, William Henry, 6, 227, 257, 312 n.10
Harrodsburg, 45
Heckewelder, John, 148, 152, 276 n.8
Helm, Leonard, 57–58
Henderson, Richard, 37–38, 45
Henry, Moses, 13
Heth, John, 214, 215
High-Headed Jim (Creek), 241
Hillsborough, Earl of, 37–38
Hinde, Thomas S., 251, 253
Hiwassee River, 92
Hocking River, 42, 84, 253
Hopoithle Mico (also known as Tame King; Creek), 140
Hughes, Thomas E., 219, 243
Hull, William, 227, 239, 240, 246
Hunt, Thomas, 196–97, 206–7, 223–24
Huron River, 132, 261

Illinois River, 9, 29, 39, 56, 60, 129, 130, 144, 200, 225, 241
Illinois Territory (later state), 35, 227
Indiana Territory, 6, 35, 186, 190, 204, 226, 227, 231, 233–34, 257, 258
Indians: and Anglo-French colonial

rivalry, 27–30; authority and government among, 11, 89, 120; and British aid, 74, 79, 89–91, 106–8, 113–14, 128–29, 138–41, 144–46, 151, 158–61, 168–69, 179–81, 183–84, 228; calumet, use of, 21, 69, 87, 91–92, 114, 129, 130, 135, 152, 157, 158; and captives, 2, 57–58, 110–11; and Christianity, 233, 236; and "civilization" program, 137, 214–15, 226–27, 229, 257; and crime on the frontier, 38, 215; and diseases, 233–34; dish with one spoon, use of, 92, 228; divisions among, 28–29, 68–70, 84, 88–89, 141, 149–55, 164–68, 181–85, 225; economies of, 100–101, 228–29; fighting abilities and tactics of, 57–58, 61, 102–3, 105–6, 109–10, 117–23, 141–42, 156–57, 161–67, 172–80; and fur trade, 29, 30, 34, 91, 169, 170, 228–29; and intertribal protocol, 10, 135, 203, 206; land problems of, ix, 30, 36–38, 45–46, 65–72, 77, 79, 83, 139, 151–52, 154, 203–5, 215, 226–29; land tenure among, 37, 67, 93–94, 200, 205–6, 228, 257; languages of, 89; and liquor, 95, 129, 157, 161, 162; and pan-tribalism, 4–5, 11, 28–29, 39–40, 55, 60, 66–72, 74, 77, 79, 83–84, 88–89, 91–98, 100, 102–3, 108–9, 113–14, 128–30, 132–41, 143–55, 157–68, 172–200, 209, 221–22, 224–25, 227–28, 241, 256–58, 282 n.4, 312 n.9, 313 n.12; and Pontiac's rebellion (1763), 30–31; population of, 35, 132; poverty among, 228–29; presents to, 30, 66, 100, 113, 215–16; religion and religious movements among, 30, 38, 85, 105, 109, 176, 233–34, 284 n.16, 310 n.17; removal of, 261–262; in Revolutionary War, 49–66, 106–7; and tomahawks as emblems, 92, 114, 155; and treaty annuities,

Nannette; Blue Jacket's granddaughter), 91, 220, 305–6 n.5

Lasselle, Antoine, 80, 90, 103, 131, 147, 149, 159, 169, 173, 175, 179, 180, 182, 185, 186, 191, 194, 195, 196, 201

Lasselle, Francois, 90, 262

Lasselle, Hyacinth, 90

Lasselle, Hyacinth (also known as Tappon), 90, 182, 185, 300 n.19

Lasselle, Jacques, 80, 90, 300 n.19

Lasselle, Jacques (also known as Coco; Blue Jacket's son-in-law), 4, 90–91, 131, 147–49, 159, 169, 173, 179, 185, 191, 194, 196, 198, 199, 200, 201, 220, 256, 259–60, 261–62, 300 n, 19, 314 n.18

Lasselle, Jacques (Blue Jacket's grandson), 220

Lasselle, Julia (Blue Jacket's granddaughter), 220

Lasselle, Susanne (Blue Jacket's granddaughter), 220

Lathensica (Shawnee), 81

Lawoughgua (Shawnee), 18

Leatherlips (Wyandot), 190

Lee, Robert, 188, 193

Le Gris (Miami), 56, 57, 80, 90, 93–94, 95–97, 101, 109, 187, 191, 195, 201

Lewis, Andrew, 41–44

Lewis, Charles, 43

Lewis, "Colonel" (Shawnee), 229, 238, 240

Lewis, Howell, 177

Licking River, 45, 55, 59, 61, 63–64, 81

Limestone (Maysville), 81, 82, 111

Lincoln, Benjamin, 143, 149–55

Lindley, Jacob, 147–48

Little Miami River, ix, 52, 55, 59–60, 65, 84, 85, 97, 99, 220

Little Otter (Ottawa), 156–57, 160, 161–62, 173, 180, 195, 199

Little Tennessee River, 92

Little Turkey (Cherokee), 92–93, 140

Little Turtle (Miami), 4–6, 33, 93, 95, 100, 101, 103, 105, 106, 109–10, 113,

118–21, 122, 124, 131, 162, 169, 170, 173, 175, 185, 186, 187, 191, 197, 201, 205, 209, 214, 215, 217, 286 n.16, 289 n.22, 298 n.5

Logan, Benjamin, 74–76, 79, 80, 81

Logan, James (Shawnee), 81, 283 n.7, 285 n.2

Logan, John (Shawnee), 240, 258, 313 n.15

Logan, John (also known as Tachnechdorus; Mingo), 40, 276 n.8

Logstown (Shawnee town), 25, 28, 29, 31, 39, 275 n.16

Longhouse (Wyandot), 234

Long Shanks (Shawnee), 206

Lorimier, Louis, 85, 95, 275 n.2, 279 n.19

Lower Sandusky (Wyandot town), 66–67, 138, 143, 146, 147, 150

Lower Shawnee Town, 25

Lowry, John, 157

Ludlow's Station, 116

Mackachack (Mad River; Shawnee town), 52, 68, 70, 74–75

Mad Dog of Tuckabatchee (Creek), 140

Mad River, 52, 59, 63, 74, 93, 115, 239, 245, 248, 253

Maguaga (Wyandot town), 218, 305 n.31

Mahican Indians, 133, 134, 153

Main Poc (Potawatomi), 241

Marietta, ix, 84, 110, 144

Marschalk, Andrew, 134, 211–12

Martin's Station, 61–62

Mascouten Indians, 39

Mashipinashiwish (also known as Bad Bird; Ojibwe), 186, 205, 214

Massie, Nathaniel, 198

Maumee River, 25, 62, 79–80, 95, 99, 100, 102–4, 108, 113–14, 115, 130–32, 137, 146, 150–55, 157, 159–62, 169–81,

Maumee River (*cont.*)
197–98, 210, 212, 219. *See also* Glaize, the; Swan Creek

McArthur, Duncan, 249–51

McClellan's Station, 45

McCormick, John, 131, 172, 293 n.7

McDougall, George, 201, 262

McGary, Hugh, 75

McGillivray, Alexander (Creek), 139, 140

McGregor, John, 186

McHenry, James, 215, 216

McKee, Alexander, 13, 31, 48, 53, 56, 60–61, 63, 69, 87, 91, 97, 100, 106–8, 113, 114, 131, 134–35, 138, 143, 144, 145, 147–48, 150, 152–53, 155, 159, 160, 161, 169, 173, 176, 184–85, 194, 196, 209, 219, 224, 274 n.12

McKee, Thomas, 155, 194–95, 224

McMahon, William, 165–66

McMullen, James, 103

McNemar, Richard, 241

McPherson, James, 310–11 n.18

McQueen, Peter (Creek), 241

Menominee Indians, 245, 250

Miami Indians, 4–6, 39, 56, 60, 63, 67, 70, 74, 77, 79–80, 90, 93–94, 95–97, 110, 113, 114, 117, 122, 130, 132, 133, 134–35, 144, 153, 157–58, 162, 164, 168, 169, 173, 181, 186, 191–92, 195, 196, 197, 200, 203, 204–6, 214, 223, 257. *See also* Little Turtle; Miamitown

Miami Land Company, 84–85, 86, 110

Miamitown, 80, 90, 93, 95–97, 100–5, 108, 113, 114, 115, 117, 121, 130, 137, 180, 196

Michigan, 35, 132, 144, 159, 186, 227, 238, 246, 258, 260, 261

Miller, Christopher, 174, 214

Mingo Indians, 28; of the Ohio, 10, 28, 29–30, 40, 41, 46, 50, 51, 55, 58, 59, 61, 63, 65, 69, 70, 72, 73, 75, 77, 79, 80, 81, 85, 87, 92, 93, 111, 113, 117, 120, 122, 124, 131, 132, 133, 134, 153,
162, 164, 173, 199, 200, 203, 205, 206, 212, 230, 233; of the Sandusky, 99–100, 184, 186, 227, 233

missionaries, 7, 32–33, 34; Moravians, 34, 39, 48, 67, 93, 129, 148, 236; Presbyterians, 54, 219–20; Society of Friends, 147–48, 229, 236, 237

Mississauga Indians, 153, 183

Mississippi River, 17, 25, 60, 65, 95, 103, 129–30, 158, 221, 222, 223, 226, 227–28, 239, 241, 256

Missouri, 17, 85, 95, 134, 160, 224, 227

Mobile River, 83

Mohawk Indians, 66, 92, 106, 131

Mohawk River, 37

Moluntha (Shawnee), 68–72, 74–75, 81

Monongahela River, 30, 37, 73, 127, 188

Montreal, 32, 91, 132, 146, 147, 220

Moore, Joseph (son of Blue Jacket), 3, 31, 254, 255, 312 n.4

Moore, Margaret (wife of Blue Jacket), 3–4, 31, 243, 254, 255

Morgan, George, 51

Muccatiwasaw (also known as Black Chief; Ojibwe), 214

Munsee Indians, 132, 134, 153, 160, 161, 181, 227

Muskingum River, 25, 33, 38, 40, 72, 73, 84, 97, 113, 133, 144, 145, 150, 153, 155, 157, 188, 275 n.15

Musquaconocah. *See* Red Pole

Nanticoke Indians, 113, 131, 132, 134, 153, 181

Nehinissica (Shawnee), 69

Nekskorwetor (Shawnee), 195, 197, 198, 206

Neolin (Delaware), 284 n.16

New Madrid, 17, 230

New York (colony, later state), 9, 25, 37, 60, 64, 68, 83, 134, 139, 141, 145, 157

Niagara, 70, 94, 146, 149, 151

Nianimsica (Shawnee), 69, 81, 188, 192, 197, 206

Nihipeewa (Shawnee), 69

Nimwha (Shawnee), 48, 50, 51

North Bend, 86, 87

North Carolina, 37, 45

Northwest Territory, 79, 217, 223

Norton, John, 89, 102, 120

Ockillissa Chopka (Creek), 140

Ohio, ix–x, 9, 52, 65, 66, 67, 68, 69, 71, 73, 79, 84–85, 97, 107, 109–10, 144, 145, 149, 154, 157, 192, 200, 204, 205, 206, 224, 227, 230–31, 233, 238–40, 242, 243–44, 245, 248, 251–52, 258, 262. *See also* Shawnee Indians

Ohio Company, 45, 84, 110

Ohio River, ix–x, 9, 10, 12, 14, 24, 25–26, 27–28, 30, 36, 37–38, 40, 41, 42, 44, 45, 46, 53, 58, 59–60, 63–64, 66, 68, 73, 81, 85, 87, 97–98, 111, 138, 145, 149–54. *See also* Shawnee Indians

Ojibwe Indians, 39, 51, 56, 59, 60, 63, 66, 68, 70, 74, 77, 84, 85, 94, 105, 113, 117, 118, 120, 122, 130, 132, 133, 134, 143–44, 150, 152, 153, 155, 157, 158, 159–68, 172, 173, 186, 191, 192, 195, 199, 201, 202, 203, 204, 205, 206, 209, 214, 216, 225, 227, 245, 250

Old Shade (Shawnee), 216

Old Tassell (Cherokee), 92

Oleantangy River, 50

Omissas (Ojibwe), 202

Onanguisous (Potawatomi), 186

Onim (Munsee), 310 n.17

Osage Indians, 228

Ottawa Indians, 6, 28, 39, 51, 56, 59, 60, 63, 66, 68, 70, 74, 77, 84, 85, 94, 103, 105, 108, 113, 117, 120, 122, 128, 130, 132, 133, 134, 144, 150, 152, 153, 156–57, 158, 159–68, 172, 173, 180, 181, 182, 186, 187, 191, 195, 198, 199–200, 201–2, 203, 204, 205, 206, 211, 225, 227, 238, 245, 250. *See also* Egushaway

Pacanne (Miami), 56, 80, 93, 186

Paint Creek, 74, 198

Panther, the (Shawnee; 1795 ref.), 195

Panther (Shawnee; 1807 ref.), 251

Parrish, John, 148

Parsons, Samuel, 70–71

Paumthe (Shawnee), 229

Pawotgue (Shawnee), 195

Paxinosa (Shawnee), 24, 236

Peihetalmena (Delaware), 195

Pekowi (Great Miami River; Shawnee town), 62

Pekowi (Mad River; Shawnee town), 52, 59, 60, 62; reestablished, 69, 75

Pekowi (Scioto River; Shawnee town), 32

Pemenacawah (Shawnee), 81

Pemenewa (Shawnee), 217

Pennsylvania, 9, 10, 12, 14, 18, 23, 24, 25, 30, 37, 40, 51, 68, 83, 99, 105, 145

Pesekwassicsica (Shawnee), 195

Philadelphia, 133, 136, 212, 229

Piankeshaw Indians, 29, 39, 74, 93, 130, 168, 200, 205, 206, 214

Pickering, Timothy, 143, 149–55, 193, 204, 208, 303 n.31

Piomingo (Chickasaw), 116, 215

Pipe (Delaware), 51

Pittsburgh, 40, 49–52, 59, 62, 73, 115, 214, 215

Pontiac (Ottawa), 89, 274 n.10

Portland, Duke of, 184

Potawatomi Indians, 39, 51, 56, 59, 60, 63, 66, 70, 74, 84, 94, 110, 113, 117, 120, 122, 130, 133, 134, 144, 150, 152, 153, 157, 158, 160, 161, 162, 164, 167–68, 172, 173, 182, 186, 187, 190, 191, 195, 200, 204, 205, 206, 214, 225, 227, 239, 240, 245, 246, 250, 312 n.10

Presque Isle, 214

Price, William, 176, 177

Procter, Henry, 259, 261, 314 n.18
Puckeshinwau (Shawnee), 41
Pucksekaw (also known as Jumper; Shawnee), 198, 209

Quebec, 108, 114, 143, 158, 173
Quilawa (Shawnee), 216

Randolph, Beverley, 143, 149–55
Reaume, Charles, 54
Reaume, Susanne, 32, 90, 174
Red-Faced Fellow (Shawnee), 196
Red Jacket (Seneca), 135–36
Red Pole (probable half-brother of Blue Jacket), 26–27, 69–72, 73, 88, 130, 134–41, 151, 195, 199, 201, 202, 203, 206–7, 210, 211, 212, 213, 215, 216–17, 273 n.3
Richard, Gabriel, 260
Richardville, Jean Baptiste (Miami), 186
Ridoubt, Thomas, 21
River Raisin area (MI), 190, 220, 259–60
Roche de Bout, 62, 132, 156, 159, 160, 161, 162, 168, 172, 174
Roundhead (Wyandot), 162, 238, 250–51
Ruddell, Isaac, 61, 81
Ruddell, Stephen, 18, 173, 249, 251, 252
Ruddell's Station (KY), 59, 61–62

Sac Indians, 84, 103, 134, 144, 186, 191, 225, 227, 228, 238, 245, 250, 256, 312 n.9
Saginaw Bay, 162, 163
Sandusky River, 50, 51, 62, 68, 70, 99, 100, 102, 108–9, 132, 173, 180, 181–82, 184, 190–91
Sargent, Winthrop, 116, 123, 126, 127, 193, 217
Savannah River, 7, 9, 270 n.4
Sayenqueraghta (Seneca), 70
Scattameck (Delaware), 38, 85
Schoenbrunn (Moravian Delaware town), 48

Schoolcraft, Henry Rowe, 120, 175
Scioto River, 13, 25, 31, 32–33, 41, 43, 50, 52, 84, 92, 190, 199, 205, 238, 253
Scott, Charles, 114, 115, 177
Seagrove, James, 139–40
Selby, Prideaux, 152
Seneca Indians, 84, 94, 133–38, 144, 234. *See also* Iroquois Confederacy
Seven Nations of Canada, 88, 134, 136, 143, 152, 153, 157, 196
Shakers, 54, 234, 242, 246
Shane, Anthony, 302 n.15, 310 n.16
Shane, Nancy, 310 n.16
Shawnee Flats, 275 n.16
Shawnee Indians, 7; and Anglo-French colonial rivalry, 12, 27–30; appearance of, 12, 13, 20, 33–34, 43, 82, 234, 254–55; authority and chieftainship among, 9–10, 16, 19, 20, 21–22, 26, 27, 33, 40, 42, 67–68, 86–87, 207, 213, 215; and the British, 1213, 29, 30, 51, 53–64, 72, 79, 86, 87, 88–90, 96–97, 106–8, 138, 139, 144–46, 160–61, 209, 212, 222, 256; and burials, 15, 19, 23, 271 n.14; in Canada, 212; ceremonies of, 11, 15–17, 19–20, 21–22, 23; child-rearing and education among, 15, 17–19, 22, 27; Chillicothe division of, 8, 15, 46, 50, 52, 62, 72, 181, 230, 269 n.4, 278 n.12; and and Christianity, influence of, 7, 16, 34, 39, 236, 243; and "civilization" plan, 229–31, 235–38; clans of, 14, 17–18, 27, 274 n.6, 275 n.16; conservatism among, 22, 34, 231, 235–38, 262; dances, music, and games of, 11, 17, 20, 21, 22–23, 137, 155; demeanor of, 13, 22; and dependence on whites, 12–14; diseases among, 13, 14, 17, 231–32, 233–34; divisions and divisional responsibilities of, 8–9, 14, 26–27, 53, 213, 237, 269 n.4; and Dunmore's War (1774), 40–45; economy of, 11–12, 13, 14, 16, 22, 34,

Tey-yagh-taw (Wyandot), 205

Thames River, 132, 141, 143, 153, 160

Three Fires. *See* Ojibwe Indians; Ottawa Indians; Potawatomi Indians

Tiffin, Edward, 239, 240, 248

Todd, Robert, 176

traders, x, 12–13, 28, 31–32, 34, 39, 50, 66, 80, 90–91, 100, 107, 109, 130–31, 146–49, 161, 169, 173, 174, 184, 185, 186, 190–91, 195, 196, 202, 207, 211, 218, 226, 228–29

Transylvania Company, 45

treaties, Indian: Camp Charlotte (1774), 45, 46; Fort Finney (1786), 69–72, 77, 84; Fort Harmar (1789), 79, 84–85, 86, 95, 97, 132–33, 143, 185, 204, 205; Fort Industry (1805), 227; Fort McIntosh (1785), 68–69, 77, 84; Fort Stanwix (1768), x, 37–38, 44, 65, 66–67, 138; Fort Stanwix (1784), 68, 70, 77, 84; Fort Wayne (1803), 227; Fort Wayne (1809), 257, 312–13 n.10; Greenville (1795), 5, 200–207, 215–16, 222, 303 n.31; Maumee Rapids (1817), 262

treaties, international: Jay's Treaty (1794), 184–85, 195, 209, 211; Paris (1783), 65, 158–59

Trotter, Robert, 101, 102

Trout (Ottawa), 246–47, 249

Tuckabatchee (Creek town), 83, 140

Turtle Island, 159, 168

Tuscarawas River, 48, 52, 59, 204

United States: army of, x, 73, 97, 99, 102, 104, 113, 115, 116, 142, 176–77; and Britain, receive the West from, 65–66, 152; and Britain, relations with, x, 65–66, 145, 158–59, 184–85, 195, 209, 211, 245; and "civilization" plan for the Indians, 137, 214, 226–27, 229, 257; constitution of, x, 142; convention of 1800, 223; expansion of, ix–x, 59, 64, 73, 79,

84–85, 97–98, 139, 142–43, 145, 205, 222, 226, 230–31, 245; and France, relations with, 59, 60, 158; Indian policies of, 49, 51–52, 66, 68, 70–71, 79, 98, 114, 133, 136–37, 142, 214–16, 229; and Indians, expeditions against, 98–106, 114, 115–27, 170–80; and Indians, negotiations with, 79, 84–85, 86, 95–97, 114, 133, 135–38, 142–55, 157, 185–86, 190–93, 200–207, 303 n.31; and Indian trade, 60, 226, 228–29; and Jay's Treaty (1794), 184–85, 195, 209, 211–12; land claims by, ix, 65–66, 68–72, 79, 98, 136–38, 142–43, 151–52, 204–207, 226–27, 257; militia of, x, 64, 99, 101, 102, 103, 104, 113, 115, 116, 123, 142; and Northwest Ordinance, ix, 79; population of, ix, 34–35, 59, 64, 226; and Revolutionary War, 49–64; secessionism in, 98, 145; and Spain, relations with, 59, 60, 158; and War of 1812, 258–61

Vermont, 145

Vincennes, 56–58, 60, 74, 93, 95, 96, 109, 257

Virginia, ix, 30, 31, 37, 40, 41–46, 48–50, 51, 55, 59, 60, 68, 75, 84, 198–99, 219

Volney, Constantin, 6

Wabash River, 25, 39, 55, 56, 58, 60, 67, 74, 79, 85, 90, 93, 95, 100, 114, 115, 121, 144, 168, 205, 223, 256, 257

Wabekahkahto (also known as White Bark; Shawnee), 54

Wainway (Shawnee), 216

Wakatomica (Mad River; Shawnee town), 52, 56, 60, 62, 69, 75, 181

Wakatomica (Muskingum River; Shawnee town), 33

Walhonding River, 55

Walker, Catherine, 260–61, 314 n.19

# In the American Indian Lives series